D1563888

The Author's Due

The Author's Due

Printing and the Prehistory of Copyright

Joseph Loewenstein

The University of Chicago Press
Chicago and London

Joseph Loewenstein is professor of English at Washington University. He is the author of *Responsive Readings: Versions of Echo in Pastoral, Epic, and the Jonsonian Masque* and *Jonson and Possessive Authorship.*

The University of Chicago Press, Chicago 60637
The University of Chicago Press, Ltd., London
© 2002 by The University of Chicago Press
All rights reserved. Published 2002
Printed in the United States of America

11 10 09 08 07 06 05 04 03 02   1 2 3 4 5
ISBN: 0–226-49040–8 (cloth)

Library of Congress Cataloging-in-Publication Data

Loewenstein, Joseph, 1952–
    The author's due : printing and the prehistory of copyright / Joseph Loewenstein.
        p.   cm.
Includes bibliographical references and index.
    ISBN 0-226-49040-8 (alk. paper)
    1. Book industries and trade—England—History.   2. Printing—England—History.
3. Book industries and trade—Law and legislation—England—History.   4. Printing
industry—Law and legislation—England—History.   5. Copyright—England—History.
6. Intellectual property—England—History.   7. Authorship—History.   8. English
literature—Early modern, 1500–1700—History and criticism.   I. Title.
Z325 .L84 2002
070.5'0942—dc21   2002000552

♾ The paper used in this publication meets the minimum requirements of the American
National Standard for Information Sciences—Permanence of Paper for Printed Library
Materials, ANSI Z39. 48–1992.

To my teachers

Contents

Acknowledgments

This book is a by-product of research supported by the Graduate School of Arts and Sciences at Washington University, the American Council of Learned Societies, the National Endowment for the Humanities (which sponsored a fellowship at the National Humanities Center), and the Exxon Education Foundation (in sponsorship of a fellowship at the Newberry Library). But the time spent reading not only at the Newberry Library and the National Humanities Center but also at the British Library and the Warburg Institute was perhaps less valuable than the conversations fostered in all those institutions, particularly those with Albert Ascoli, Leonard Barkan, and Mary Beth Rose (at the Newberry); Jonathan Dollimore, Alan Sinfield, Dan Gunn, Roy Weintraub, and Marcia Homiak (at the National Humanities Center); Joe Trapp, Jill Kraye, and Michael Baxandall (at the Warburg Institute).

I am grateful for occasions to present early versions of portions of this book to The English Institute; to the English Departments at Brown University, the University of Alabama (where I enjoyed the special intellectual hospitality of David Miller), and the University of California at Irvine; and to the participants at Martha Woodmansee and Peter Jaszi's seminal 1991 conference on intellectual property at Case Western Reserve (where discussions with Mark Rose, Margreta de Grazia, and Jeff Masten proved especially helpful) and to Erica Sheen and Lorna Hutson's conference on early modern law and literature at Cambridge University. Valuable as these occasions were, presentations at one's home institution put a scholar's work under more strenuous pressure, so I'm especially grateful to Washington University, where colleagues in the intellectual property group of the Economics Department, in the History Department, in my own English Department, and in the early modern dissertation seminar have offered warm audiences and vigorous challenges. I should single out Steven Zwicker, Derek Hirst, George Pepe, Wayne Fields, and Mary Bly: they asked the hardest questions. Several students have helped me with this book, and their questions were challenging, too: Theresa Everline, Lisa Pon, and Christiane Auston in the early stages; and, later, crucially, Kevin J. Kalish and Chris D'Addario.

I wonder if it's not the case that the longer the book, the more unfinished it feels. It becomes a report on continuing meditations and, best, ongoing conversations. (In my own case, the most important ongoing conversations are with Richard Halpern, Jon Haynes, Rosemary Kegl, Chris Kendrick, and, above all, Lynne Tatlock.) And since I am endlessly grateful to Paul Schwaber, Ted Tayler, Bart Giamatti, John Hollander, Margie Ferguson, and Naomi Lebowitz for schooling me in habits of inquiry that sustain conversation, I've dedicated this book to them.

I

The Regulated Crisis of New Media

CHAPTER ONE

AN INTRODUCTION TO
BIBLIOGRAPHICAL POLITICS

I conceive you trade in knowledge, and here [at the Royal Ex-
change] is no place to traffick for it; neither in the book of rates
is there any imposition upon such commodities: so that you have no
great businesse either here or at the Custome-house. Come let us
goe into the fields.

Gabriel Plattes, Macaria

$\mathbf{W}$hat is the history of authorship, of invention, of mental making?

From the Old Law to the New Bibliography

"The term Literary Property, he in a manner laughed at"
Observed of Sir John Dalrymple, arguing for
the appellants in *Donaldson v. Becket* (1774)

In 1909, the Berne Convention of 1886 providing for international copyright protection was revised in Berlin.[1] In order to retain its place in an even
barely rationalized international marketplace in intellectual property, Britain
acceded to the revision—the British capitulation was confirmed in the Copyright Act of 1911—and English copyright law was thus radically transformed.[2]
The Berlin revision fixed the period of copyright protection at the term of the
author's life and fifty years after her death, thus obviating the regulatory difficulties that arise in legal systems in which the term of copyright is figured

from the date of publication. This was a subtle assault on English ways, since it brought to an end the persistent debate within British law on the appropriate term of copyright, making the author, once and for all, the sole measure of protection.

Profuse and incommensurable international laws were not the only stimuli to simplification. The pressure to simplify was felt from within as well as from without. Thus the unsigned article on "Copyright" in the eleventh edition of the *Encyclopedia Brittanica* (1910–11) records with obvious perplexity the then current state of legal affairs:

> To sum up the position of artistic copyright in 1909, we find five
> British acts, three dealing with engraving, one with sculpture, and
> one with painting, drawing and photography, and between them
> very little relation. We have three terms of duration of copyright—
> 28 years for engraving, 14 for sculpture, with a second 14 if the
> artist be alive at the end of the first, life and 7 years for painting,
> drawing or photography. There are two different relations of the
> artist to his copyright. The sculptor's right to sell his work and
> retain his copyright has never been questioned so long as he signs
> and dates it. The painter's copyright is made to depend upon the
> signing of a document by the purchaser of his work. The engraver
> and the sculptor are not required to register; but the author's
> name, and the date of putting forth or publishing, must appear
> on his work. The painter cannot protect his copyright without
> registration, but this registration as it is now required is merely a
> pitfall for the unwary. Designed to give the public information as
> to the ownership and duration of copyrights, the uncertainty of its
> operation results in the prevention of information on these very
> points.[3]

The issue of what is here called "registration" points to the most obviously revolutionary aspect of the Copyright Act, the etiology of copyright now legally mandated in Berlin. According to the new principles articulated there, an author's rights arose from the act of creation itself. This may seem unexceptionable, but in fact it entails a dismissal of very old institutional arrangements in Britain. Up until the Copyright Act of 1911, all suits for infringement of copyright depended upon the procedure mentioned above, registration, which dates from the sixteenth century. In order to secure a printed work from unfair competition, a printer—acting as author's agent as jurisprudential tradition would have it—would record his claim on the work in the Stationers' Register at the printers' guildhall, and this registration constituted the foundation of all claims of copyright.[4] Thus the law, the political structure, of literary property had long been organized around procedures essentially industrial. The Copyright Act of 1911, in accordance with the Berlin agreement, broke with this tradition and reorganized the legal foundations of copyright simply by canceling the necessity of registration.

Thus reconstructed, copyright law functions to protect authorial creativity, to provide a statutory hedge against industrial concerns around an author's somewhat mysterious, if not mystified, creative act; the new law enables a bracketing, a willed forgetting, of the marketplace.[5] The forgetfulness is part of a general simplification, for the 1911 act consolidated all the various forms of copyright within a single text and framed those rights in such a way that the complex realities of the publishing industry become, in effect, ancillary to copyright law.[6] The *Encyclopedia Brittanica* reviews the changes with composed relief: "The sensible basis on which the new bill was framed, and the authority it represented, commended it."

With relief, and with sober caution: "commended it, in spite of many controversial points."[7] Radical and simple as it was, the act of 1911 still had the feel of the Provisional. And no wonder: during the preceding two decades the marketplace for intellectual property had been an unruly one, partly because of new forms of unfair competition, partly because of pressure on the patent system, but largely because of new developments in what we now call "the media."[8] The proliferation of phonographic recording (Edison's phonograph dates from 1877; the Path and Gramophone phonograph factories began production in 1893; Victor initiated its Red Seal issues in 1902) and the development of the pianola provoked a rethinking of the landscape of intellectual property similar to the rethinking that had attended upon the invention of photography.[9] Such new apparatuses for sound reproduction blurred already contested boundaries between musical text and musical performance, and between artisanal and mechanical production. The legal difficulties presented by the new technology were thrown into relief by a 1908 case brought in America: the plaintiff, a music publisher, alleged infringement of musical copyright when two songs were transcribed on piano rolls.[10] This was plainly a small matter compared to the more fully consequential problem of phonographic reproduction, which led to the articulation of mechanical rights, the so-called neighboring rights proximate to the monopoly in recording. In 1910, the parliamentary committee that was charged with digesting the Berlin revisions in order to draft the 1911 legislation recognized that the new medium of "publication" could not easily be subsumed within existing legal structures. The committee therefore recommended the formation of the Mechanical

Copyright Licences Company to protect composers' rights in mechanical reproduction. The Copyright Act of 1911 provided for compulsory licensing
of mechanical reproduction and then conferred copyright on the producers
of the licensed recordings. This was obviously not a simplification, but it did
secure, if only temporarily, a remarkable comprehensiveness in the face of
burgeoning disseminative technology.

Most important, the Berlin revisions forced Britain to respond to new
technology in Parliament and not in the courts, by statutory intervention in
the law and not by interpretive extension of it. The displacement of common
law by statute is, of course, characteristic of legal developments since the
mid-nineteenth century, a key feature of the rise of parliamentary democracy.
This displacement, which reverses a key shift in the late seventeenth-century
history of copyright, effects a partial erasure of the past from the code of law;
it secures an enfeebling of memory. The past was variously subsiding, for
as the Parliamentary Committee on Copyright was assimilating the Berne
Convention, W. A. Copinger, the greatest English authority on copyright law,
was dying. The Copyright Act of 1911, by making an antiquarian curiosity of
the Stationers' Register, quite literally closed a book on the history of literary
culture.

On the other hand, the antiquarians were particularly curious during
these years. The Bibliographical Society, which Copinger had founded in
1892, was rolling up its sleeves, reopening the Stationers' Register.[11] The
Bibliographical Society was on a campaign against selective memory. In 1903,
with Sidney Lee's 1902 facsimile of the First Folio under review, W. W. Greg
pronounced not only on Lee's ignorance of the regulation of the Tudor and
Stuart book trade, but on the historiographical amateurishness of virtually all
professed literary historians; as if Copinger were setting his historiographical agenda, Greg remarks, "With regard to the old copyright regulations, it
should be frankly confessed that we know very little about them."[12] Greg's
mentor and student, A. W. Pollard, rose to the challenge of this review in
his *Shakespeare Folios and Quartos* (1909) by attempting to specify the various property rights variously haunting Renaissance dramatic manuscripts,
performances, and printed texts. Together, Greg and Pollard made it their
larger project to clarify the history of copyright, of stationer's registration,
of printing, and of publishing, even as that history was being wiped from
the practice of the law.[13] To sum up the conjunctural paradox: in 1909, the
Berlin revision of the Berne Convention represented literary culture, for the
purposes of law, as a vacuous space with author and a book-buying public
at its poles, and with the book as a thin material line of communication between them; in 1909, *Shakespeare Folios and Quartos* represented literary

culture as a space thick with books, with scribes and printers, guildhalls and printshops and bookstalls, proclamations and regulations, actors and acting companies, booksellers and book buyers, a crowded historical field within which one might hope to discern conventions and recurrences and so bring into focus the historically specific lineaments of author and literary work. Legislator and bibliographer offer us two starkly different representations of literary culture, but both, I think, respond to the same conceptual-regulatory crisis, the revolution in reproductive technologies.

"Ad Imprimendum Solum"

Pollard's historical representation was thick but imperfect, and he soon recognized as much. The received wisdom in bibliography was rapidly changing: though the traditions of Shakespeare scholarship continued to provide the organizing questions, these years saw an exceptional ferment in research into all aspects of the Renaissance literary marketplace.[14] So it was no wonder that Pollard felt that he must undertake his historical account of Shakespearean book culture again, and only a few years after the appearance of *Shakespeare Folios and Quartos,* in the Sandars Lectures of November 1915.[15] The opening of these lectures dates them: "Legal writers on English copyright have not shown much interest in the steps by which the conception of literary property was gradually built up, nor are any data easily accessible for comparing the course of its development in England and foreign countries."[16] Pollard's words derive from the era of the Berlin Convention and of the British Copyright Act, the era of the law's forgetting and of bibliographic anamnesis.

Pollard approaches the history of the text as a problem in the history of regulation, as I mean to do. Hence the title of his first lecture, "The Regulation of the Book Trade in the Sixteenth Century." Now, by "regulation" one may mean many things, but Pollard tended to surprisingly narrow constructions. This tendency provoked a bibliographical debate, the pertinence of which endures, and not simply because it remains unresolved merely as a matter of historical interpretation.

The debate concerns the meaning of a proclamation of King Henry VIII dated 16 November 1538. The proclamation begins by announcing the need for censorship, for an essentially and—as I shall be obliged to put it again and again in these pages—*narrowly* or *crudely* ideological regulation. Here are Pollard's citations and discussion (such early typographical conventions as the use of *i* for *j* and *u* for *v* and vice versa, or the use of long *s* and double

V, are normalized to accord with modern practice, as they will be throughout this book; abbreviations will also be silently expanded):

> "The Kynges moste royall majestie beinge enfourmed, that sondry contentious and sinyster opinyon[s], have by wronge teachynge and naughtye printed bokes, encreaced and growen within this his realme of Englande," forbids the importation, sale, or publication, "without his majesties speciall licence," of any English books printed abroad, and then proceeds:
>
>> Item that no persone or persons in this realme, shall from hensforth print any boke in the englyshe tonge, onles upon examination made by some of his gracis privie counsayle, or other suche as his highnes shall appoynte, they shall have lycence so to do, and yet so havynge, not to put these wordes *Cum privilegio regali,* without addyng *ad imprimendum solum,* and that the hole copie, or els at the least theffect of his licence and privilege be therwith printed, and playnely declared and expressed in the Englyshe tonge underneth them.
>
> Here we have the first of several enactments which forbade the printing of any book in English except after it had been examined by *some* (which implies two or more) of the Privy Council, "or other suche as his highnes shall appoynte." Incidentally we may note that while a distinction appears to be drawn between a licence and a privilege, the one word "privilegium" seems to be used as a Latin equivalent for both. Every book, as I understand the proclamation, required a licence; but this licence was not to be paraded by the use of the words "Cum privilegio regali," without these words being limited and restricted by the addition "ad imprimendum solum." These must therefore be construed "only for printing," i.e. not for protection, unless this was expressly stated, in which case the "licence" was raised to the higher rank of a "privilege." The words "ad imprimendum solum" have been generally interpreted as equivalent to "for sole, or exclusive printing." Whether or not they can legitimately bear this meaning in Tudor Latin is perhaps doubtful. It seems quite clear from this Proclamation that this is not the meaning they were originally to bear.[17]

To cite Pollard at length, as I have done, is to preserve a bibliographic tradition. In 1919, E. M. Albright initiated the tradition with almost the identical citation followed by the acerbic comment, "I cannot agree with Mr. Pollard in his innovation."[18] Albright's analysis provoked a response in *The Library* from Pollard, and he later revised his original argument for the second edition of *Shakespeare's Fight with the Pirates,* but the matter did not rest there—in 1954, Greg made his own settled intervention in the dispute.

I shall takes sides in this debate in a subsequent chapter, but at this point, I wish only to point out the historiographical issues at stake in the argument that Pollard initiated. Pollard argued that Henry was concerned only with the ideological control of books. Books were to be submitted to the Privy Council for approval; the sign that such approval had been secured was the phrase *"Cum privilegio regali."* Moreover, said Pollard, Henry wished to limit the significance of the sign of that approval. The royal *privilegium* was, first of all, significantly mediated and therefore susceptible to summary withdrawal in case, for example, the king wished to correct an instance of imprudent permissiveness on the part of his delegated censors. And second, even the approval signified by the words "cum privilegio regali" was straitened as a license *for printing only*—that is, it was not to be understood as an endorsement of the book.

Albright argued that Pollard had made nonsense of the context of the passage: the proclamation, she said, was quite clearly concerned with censorship alone. She quotes the manuscript version, "they shall have lycence so to do, and yet so havyng nott to put thes words cum privilegio regali wt owght addyng ad imprimendum solum," and asserts that Henry added the key words "to provide against a deceptive garbling of the royal privilege to make it seem to be a larger protection of a work than a mere protection of exclusive printing rights, such as, for example, a protection against recall and suppression."[19] Now this may not seem a grave difference from Pollard's construction; indeed, Pollard claimed that "Miss Albright is only forcing an open door."[20] Both were arguing that Henry was concerned primarily with censorship. But where Pollard argues that the phrase "ad imprimendum solum" is a limitation on the Privy Council approval, a limitation coming *from within* the new censorship system, Albright suggests that the phrase limits the degree to which a different regulatory mechanism, a mechanism controlling competition within the nascent book trade, may interfere with the new censorship system *from without*.[21]

Pollard amassed, in the course of his career, some very thick descriptions of early English book culture, but he had a passion for the simple explanation. "When I wrote my *Shakespeare Folios and Quartos,* I wrote as a bibliographer and a lover of logical economy impatient of hypotheses disproportionately large compared with the facts they were framed to explain."[22] Pollard's representation of the 1538 Proclamation reveals just such a zeal for simplicity, and in this case, the love of "logical economy" led him to present an argument in which the confusing interference of an emergent *market* economy was set aside. At one crucial historiographic moment Pollard describes a book culture that is nearly as attenuated as that of the Copyright Act of 1911. The Crown and its agents concern themselves exclusively with ideological control of the press. This simulacrum of book culture casts a long, stark shadow.

Situating the Penal: Lea or Heckscher?

> "Writing has become linked to sacrifice, even to the sacrifice of life."
>
> > Michel Foucault, "What Is an Author?"

Insofar as we are sensationalists by nature, insofar as we are McCarthyites of the imagination, we make our approach to the dual subject of politics and literature through a desolate terrain; insofar as we possess a sensationalist disposition, we seek the quintessential creative act in the gulag and understand the One True State as a tyranny. Given such dispositions, we will find the most significant context of authorship, the site of its truest history, within the regime of censorship. No recent evocation of such a history has been as influential as that of Michel Foucault.[23]

I refer to his essay "What Is an Author?" (1979, based on a lecture given in 1969). The essay is an extended meditation on the relationship between texts and the "author-function" that modern culture attributes to those texts. Turning, at the end of the essay, to the " 'ideological' status of the author," Foucault asks,

> How can one reduce the great peril, the great danger with which
> fiction threatens our world? The answer is: One can reduce it
> with the author. The author allows a limitation of the cancerous
> and dangerous proliferation of significations within a world where
> one is thrifty not only with one's resources and riches, but also
> with one's discourses and their significations. The author is the
> principle of thrift in the proliferation of meaning.[24]

Here authorship has a nearly diacritical status. It is an index by which writing becomes particular, local. Note the notion of discursive *threat*—a constant in Foucault's own writing: this account of literary culture is infused with a thematics of violence. This violence appears elsewhere in the essay, in his account of pre-Enlightenment discourse, but it is resituated: the "dangerous proliferation of significations" calls forth a punitive answer.

> Discourses are objects of appropriation. The form of ownership from which they spring is of a rather particular type, one that has been codified for many years. We should note that, historically, this type of ownership has always been subsequent to what might be called penal appropriation. Texts, books, and discourses really began to have authors (other than mythical, "sacralized" and "sacralizing" figures) to the extent that authors became subject to punishment, that is, to the extent that discourses could be transgressive.

This moment of beginning is not so easy to place, partly because of the difficulty of figuring out how a proportion—"to the extent that"—can enable us to fix a "real" beginning. One may surmise that this is a myth about a human prehistory. As he goes on, Foucault's etiology of the author retains a primitivist character:

> In our culture (and doubtless in many others), discourse was not originally a product, a thing, a kind of goods; it was essentially an act—an act placed in the bipolar field of the sacred and the profane, the licit and the illicit, the religious and the blasphemous.[25]

Though this does seem to refer primarily to an ancient era of anonymity—the discursive culture of which eludes our knowledge—its reference is perhaps not so exclusive. "To the extent that" the anonymous persisted, by so much may we presume a postponement of the beginnings of Foucauldian authorship. That is, this primitivist myth evokes not only ancient anonymity but its early modern afterlife, not only a prehistoric and bloody priesthood but the Inquisition. The proposition is simply that penal appropriation is prior to all other forms of appropriation. "Historically, it [i.e., the discursive act] was a gesture fraught with risks before becoming goods caught up in a circuit of ownership."[26] The author emerges from the gulag; writing depends on censorship.

Foucault's account is valuable in many ways: the essay makes extremely useful assessments of the cultural function of authorship—in discriminating "fields" of writing, in articulating a public sphere, and in endowing the various grammatical "persons" with richly differentiated rhetorical characters and efficacies within scribal culture. I *press* Foucault's historiographic thesis because it raises the same question that haunts our constructions of Henry VIII's proclamation. Again the commercial is tested against what must be styled narrowly ideological claims. ("Narrowly," because the provenance of ideology is much contested; some would argue—I would argue this way myself—that commerce itself has ideological functions.)[27] That this problem should present itself in otherwise profoundly different attempts to produce a history of discourse deserves our attention. Is penal appropriation inevitably prior to the commercial appropriation of discourse? More generally, to what extent does the penal determine the emergence of modern discourse?

Foucault's essay begins, "The coming into being of the notion of 'author' constitutes the privileged moment of *individualization* in the history of ideas, knowledge, literature, philosophy, and the sciences" (141). Characteristically, Foucault traces the origins of a crucial feature of modern bourgeois culture, the ostensibly autonomous creative artist, to innovations in public practice— in this case, to the development of censorship. That is, an individualism is discovered to be a back-formation, an effect, of an institutionalization.[28] In Foucault's work, the individual-effect might be seen as bipolar: thus, in the model Foucauldian case, the Police "normalizes" the Criminal and, thence, the law-abiding Citizen; in the related case at hand, the Censor normalizes the heretical Author and, thence, the orthodox Author. In fact, Foucault tends to represent these individual-effects as single: the police normalizes the citizen (or, perhaps, the legal subject as the possessor of rights beyond mere property rights); the censor normalizes the author. The excess here, the degree to which the social being of the citizen seems to exceed a supposed constitutive moment in the jurisdiction of the police, or to which the various potencies of authorship exceed the fine violence of the censor, betrays, I think, an inadequacy, or at least a reticence, in Foucauldian historiography.[29] The notion that individualisms are back-formations of institutionalizations is a useful etiological model, yet we need more institutional divinities in this myth of origins. The Author is a censorship-effect, and also a book-effect, a press-effect, a market-effect.

Milan Kundera once observed that "the struggle of man against power is the struggle of memory against forgetting."[30] My purpose here is to suggest that the quickening of memory may yield more than a tyrant and a gulag, a censor and a heretic; and although a quickened memory *regularly* yields tyrant, censor, gulag, and heretic it does not *necessarily* do so. We might also remember how diffuse has been the struggle of women and men against the harrowing constraints of nature and of human culture; we might also remember, as Foucault in his last years so cunningly recalled, how mobile and various power has been. It comes to this: shall we regard the history of literary culture as an appendix to Henry C. Lea's *History of the Inquisition,* or to Eli Heckscher's *Mercantilism?* Might not these histories be coordinated?

Remembering the Stationers

Mr. Attorney General *Thurlow* opened as counsel for the
appellants. . . . He was very diffusive upon grants, charters,
licences, and patents from the crown, both to corporate bodies
and individuals, tracing them far back.[31]

There have been many struggles to remember the emergence of early modern authorship, but none was more consequential than the particular struggle of *Donaldson v. Beckett.*[32] Thomas Becket, together with several partners, had purchased the copyright in Thomson's *Seasons* from the estate of Andrew Millar, the original publisher, in 1769; in 1772, Becket alleged that Alexander Donaldson had printed and sold thousands of copies of the book and received a perpetual injunction against Donaldson in Chancery. Donaldson appealed to the House of Lords on the grounds that the Statute of Anne (8 Anne, c.19) enacted in 1710 had provided for a statutory copyright (two fourteen-year terms) that had lapsed in 1757.[33] The question at stake was whether a *common law* copyright subsisted, as it were, beneath and beyond the statutory copyright. Beckett and his partners had paid £505 at Millar's estate auction in 1769; had they bought anything? The Lords tried to remember: the counsel for the appellants "was very diffusive upon grants, charters, licences, and patents from the crown, both to corporate bodies and individuals, tracing them far back" as I shall do; "he particularly adverted to the statute of the 8th of queen Anne," as we must.[34]

Copyright litigation in the eighteenth century had the task of construing the Statute of Anne, known to most legal and literary historians—though the knowledge is often quite approximate—as the first English copyright law. It is fair to say that the statute is significantly misrepresented by such definitive decisions as *Donaldson v. Becket.* That is, the case law that interprets it transforms the Statute of Anne into a clarification of the nature of common law authorial copyright. In fact, the Statute of Anne was promulgated to clarify the traditional stationer's copyright that had evolved from sixteenth-century guild regulations. Stationer's copyright, to be discussed in detail in the next chapter, is a limited industrial monopoly, conferred by the guild on its members. The Statute of Anne was providing for a clear, statutory rendering of a traditional form of trade regulation. At the center of its concerns were the manufacturers of books, not the original producers of manuscripts.

Since 1557, the London Stationers' Company had a monopoly, sanctioned by the Crown, in all English printing. That monopoly was sustained through much of the seventeenth century in a sequence of Licensing Acts devised to preserve systematic state censorship, but in 1694 the monopoly was allowed to lapse. For the next few years, petitions from London's printers and publishers were steadily ignored or dismissed by Commons; the opposition in Commons seems to have been primarily antimonopolist in character.[35] The stationers persisted in their petitions, bringing in bills at first for the renewal of licensing and then (in 1706 and again in 1709), somewhat more directly, "for the securing Property." They tried, however, to confer a veneer of altruism on their proposal by casting their own appeal for security as an appeal on behalf of authors: they petitioned, that is, "to bring in a Bill for the securing Property in such Books, as have been, or shall be, purchased from, or reserved to, the Authors thereof."[36] The central provisions of the bill passed in 1710 were that "the *Author* of any Book or Books and his *Assignee or Assigns*, shall have the sole Liberty of printing and reprinting such Book or Books for the Term of fourteen Years" from the date of first publication (section 1), that success in claims against infringement depended upon "registration" (section 2), and "That after the Expiration of the said Term of fourteen Years, the sole Right of printing or disposing of Copies shall return to the *Authors* thereof, if they are then living, for another Term of fourteen Years" (section 11).[37]

Thus, despite the bias inherent in his position as counsel for the appellant in *Donaldson v. Becket* sixty-five years later, Thurlow's assessment of the Statute of Anne is quite plausible. According to the reporter for Cobbitt's *Parliamentary History,* Thurlow

> dwelt much upon the sense of the word "property," defining it philosophically, and in the separate lights of being corporeal and spiritual; the term Literary Property, he in a manner laughed at, as signifying nothing but what was of too abstruse and chimerical a nature to be defined. The booksellers, he observed, (exemplifying his observations by several cases) had not, till lately, ever concerned themselves about authors, but had generally confined the substance of their prayers to the legislature, to the security of their own property; nor would they probably have, of late years, introduced the authors as parties in their claims to the common law right of exclusively multiplying copies, had not they found it necessary to give a colourable face to their monopoly.

His laughter was particularly polemical. By mocking the very idea of literary property, Thurlow prepares his audience for the key allegation in his case, which comes when

> He particularly adverted to the statute of the 8th of queen Anne, maintaining that it was not merely an accumulative act declaratory of common law, and giving additional penalties, but that it was a new law to give learned men a property they had not before, and that it was an incontrovertible proof that there previously existed no common law right, as contended for by the respondents.[38]

To say that Thurlow's laughter is polemical does not, however, master or mute it. A sharp mixture of learning and banter may be characteristic of a good deal of parliamentary oratory, perhaps particularly so at this period, but the humor ladled out during these proceedings seems slightly nervous.[39] It betrays even Cobbett's reporter to strained irony: having summarized the speeches of the second speaker for the apellants—"Such are the substance of the most of sir John Dalrymple's arguments"—the reporter observes with uneasy superiority, "sir John spoke for two hours and a half, and seemed to exhaust, in this one speech, all the knowledge, metaphysical, legal, chemical and political, he possesses."[40] This volubility obviously seemed both slightly comic and somehow exposed. The book trade had forced a public reckoning with the social construction of property per se; memory, wit, ingenuity, together with "all the knowledge, metaphysical, legal, chemical and," above all, "political" were marshaled. According to one modern historian of the law, by the time the Lords reached a decision on the Question of Literary Property, "Property had suffered its first major defeat."[41] Small wonder the laughter in Lords had been nervous and miscellaneous.

These debates jitter with laughter because they are haunted by the specter of incorporeal property, the uncanny daemonism of thought. The respondents defend authorial rights by characterizing the Whig appellants as obsessed with real property: the first speaker for the respondents points out that "the interpretation they [the counsel for the appellants] had put upon the word 'property' was, that it implied something corporeal, tangible, and material."[42] English property law had, historically, taken real property as its central object; the respondents argued that literary property, here functioning as the quintessential incorporeal property, constituted a commanding challenge to that centrality. And though this challenge makes much of the archaism of a jurisprudence centered on real property, it was by no means itself a new argument. In one of the key interpretive tests of the Statute of Anne, *Millar v. Taylor* (1769), Judge Aston had spoken firmly for the Mansfield court on behalf of a modernization of property:

> The written definitions of property, which have been taken notice
> of at the bar, are, in my opinion, very inadequate to the objects
> of property at this day. . . . Distinct properties, says Pufendorf,
> were not settled at the same time, nor by one single act, but
> by successive degrees; nor in all places alike: but property was
> gradually introduced, according as either the condition of things,
> the number and genius of men required; or as it appeared
> requisite to the common peace.

Real property is no longer the model for all property, according to Aston. Not just Pufendorf but Hume and Adam Smith voice themselves here as Aston insists:

> The rules attending property must keep pace with its increase and
> improvement, and must be adapted to every case. A distinguish-
> able existence in the thing claimed as property; an actual value in
> that thing to the true owner; are its essentials; and not less evident
> in the present case,

—*Millar v. Taylor* was also a dispute over property in Thompson's *The Seasons*—

> than in the immediate object of those definitions.
>   And there is a material difference in favour of this sort
> of property, from that gained by occupancy; which before was
> common, and not yours; but was to be rendered so by some act of
> your own. For, this is originally the author's: and, therefore, unless
> clearly rendered common by his own act and full consent, it ought
> still to remain his.[43]

This is the tradition in which the argument for the respondents in *Donald-son v. Becket* is situated. But *their* defense, the defense before the House of Lords, is framed as a deep conservatism. Instead of urging a conception of property that can "keep pace with its increase and improvement," they urge on behalf of incorporeal property those rights articulated by Roman law on behalf of real property: the *"jus utendi, fruendi, disponendi."*[44] Again the backward squint of *Donaldson v. Becket.*

The respondents' defense of incorporeal property is by no means the most radical aspect of the arguments in *Donaldson v. Becket*. The case was found for the appellants, and theirs is the truly revolutionary position. Three questions were originally put before the judges in the case:

> Whether, at common law, an author of any book or literary compo-
> sition, had the sole right of first printing and publishing . . . ?

> If the author had such right originally, did the law take it away
> upon his printing or publishing such book or literary composi-
> tion . . . ?

> If such action would have lain at common law, is it taken away
> by the statute of 8th Anne: and is an author by the said statute,
> precluded from every remedy except on the foundation of the said
> statute . . . ?

Lord Camden, attempting to secure a full defeat of the principles estab-lished by the Tory Mansfield court in *Millar v. Taylor*, proposed two addi-tional questions that reflect upon and refine the first three: whether an au-thor had an exclusive and perpetual copyright at common law and whether that right was in any way altered by the Statute of Anne.[45] A firm major-ity of the judges were persuaded that an author did possess a common law copyright.[46] Yet it was the third and fifth questions that proved telling. By a vote of six to five, the Statute of Anne was found to be the preeminent source of authorial protection: even if it were granted that an author had property rights at common law in his or her published work, the Statute of Anne was found to have taken away those common law rights once and for all.[47] The vote would surely have split had Lord Mansfield given his opin-ion, but he did not attend the debates: his opinion had already been given in *Millar v. Taylor* and it would have been a breach of etiquette for him to advise the House since he was himself a member. Thus the decision was de-cidedly weak, but it was decisive nonetheless. What had prevailed was an artificial property, created by statute in abridgment of a common law prop-erty. By a narrow margin, the idea of "natural" property was checked by an idea of property as artificial, as the product of deliberate social will. Near the conclusion of Dalrymple's successful arguments, "sir John contended, that a decision in favour of the appellants would benefit authors, promote trade, and increase the revenue."[48] These arguments in favor of social good stand opposed to conceptions of rights based on the primacy, the presocial precedence, of property. Hence it is that "property suffered its first major defeat."[49]

Six to five with a nonvoting twelfth vote that without question would have aligned itself with the minority: *Donaldson v. Becket* comes as close to a split decision as a case can come. And although the decision stood, the uncertainty of its assessment of the status of intellectual property has persisted. I think it is fair to say we do not yet "know" what an idea is, by which I mean that we have developed wildly inconsistent social practices with respect to ideas. We act as if they are owned by the thinker (cautioning students and ourselves against plagiarism), as if the idea were simply the vaporous image of the thinker ("pure Foucault" and "vintage Spielberg"), or as if the thinker were a transmitter, a middleman to the Muse, and deserved some compensation for transportation expenses (as when a choreographer becomes the greatest exponent of American modern dance or when someone becomes the spokesperson for an entire generation). "What property can a man have in ideas? whilst he keeps them to himself they are his own, when he publishes them they are his no longer. If I take water from the ocean it is mine, if I pour it back it is mine no longer."[50] This is Dalrymple, working to undermine the notion of common law authorial property, but the insecurity invoked here weakens our embrace of virtually all univocal representations of ideation.

Yet for all the persistent uncertainty, it is also the case that changing social, political, and economic practices govern such representations, so that there *is* an intellectual and cultural history of intellectual property that separates our confusions from those in the House of Lords in 1774. Anyone who doubts this has only to consider how Baron Eyre, one of the judges in *Donaldson v. Becket,* speaks of property in ideas, for his is an opinion virtually unthinkable little more than two centuries after it was delivered: "He observed . . . that the thinking faculty was a gift with which all men were endowed: that ideas produced by the occupation of a thinking faculty common to all, should likewise be held in common, and no more be deemed subject to exclusive appropriation than any other of the common gifts of nature."[51] Eyre's position has a long history: the thrust of Augustine's arguments in the second half of the *De Doctrina* is that truth belongs to God and is not *proper to* any particular cultures or *auctores.* Such thinking, and later derivatives, like Eyre's, oriented to the common weal, have been substantially denigrated in the regime of late capitalism. We have "advanced" beyond this—by which I mean that our attitudes and practices concerning intellectual property have simply shifted, but those practices are still confused. We still feel the claims of Eyre's argument: when we discover that "Happy Birthday to You" will remain under copyright until 2010 most of us experience some slight tremor of disorientation.[52] We still don't know, don't feel that we know, what an idea is.

Lord Camden's Skepticism

The response in the House of Lords to confusion over the nature of intellectual property in 1774 is a quest for original clarity. With the place of property itself within the structure of English law under interrogation, the backward glance of *Donaldson v. Becket* is even more profoundly polemical than most historical representations. We have seen how the respondents seek to confirm and secure the continuity of real and incorporeal property, whereas the appellants seek to trivialize or demonize incorporeal property. Thus the appellants present an account of bibliographic history in which authors have been forever without property rights. Dalrymple describes the charter granted to the Stationers' Company in 1557 as "a charter enacting a body of licensers, sued for on a principle of interest, and granted by the crown on a principle of policy."[53] The book trade is thus described as part of a mercantilist economy— an important contribution to the historiography of book culture, and one to which I shall give sustained consideration; Dalrymple insists that the book trade is sectored off from the rest of the economy, not by an extrapolitical aesthetic prestige but by a densely political royal calculus. "That books were published during all this time by privilege, or patent was a notorious fact": this is Whig historiography at its most cunning, for it prepares us for a history of book culture in which a barrier that cannot be breached is erected between manuscript propagation, the sphere of private authorial action, and the circulation of books, the sphere of public social contract.[54] Dalrymple takes us on through the Civil Wars:

> The commonwealth-men abused the king and ministry for edicts
> laying restraints upon the press; and yet no sooner had they
> obtained the reins of government, than they caused ordinances
> to be issued prohibiting a book to be published that had not
> undergone state revision. But, though the press was ever an object
> both to legal and usurping princes, yet in no regulations respecting
> it was a common law right in books noticed in the most distant
> manner; yet had such right existed, we surely must have heard of
> it, particularly as some of the British princes were authors.[55]

Continuing his historical survey, Dalrymple takes up the Statute of Anne, which, as he represents it, provides for communications between the authorial sphere and that of social consumption:

> The word "vest" was adopted in the title, and the word "secured" was inserted in the body of the Act. This he thought was a distinction of greatest propriety, for the Act was framed to give an author or his assignees a property in that which he had not before. . . . It serves for an universal patent, and supercedes the necessity of an author's applying for particular ones. It passed in the reign of a Tory prince, under the influence of a Tory ministry; yet the statute is defensible.[56]

The respondents' historiography contests this opposition between the patent, a piece of social engineering, and the common law right, a given of primitivist individualism.[57] Solicitor General Wedderburn thus counters that "licenses in general . . . proved not that common law right did not inherently exist, but were the universal fetters of the press at the times in which authors were obliged to obtain them."[58] This history depicts a sixteenth- and seventeenth-century Dark Ages in which the common law had been eclipsed, and in which an idea of authorial property was somehow "there" in the culture and unrecognized by the interpretive grid of law.

The contest between these rival histories was unresolved, for the Statute of Anne ultimately obviated the claims in eighteenth-century intellectual property disputes not only of common law but of the past itself. The appellants contrived that the retrospection of *Donaldson v. Becket* should never attain to the customary retrospection of law. Justice Perrot, declaring his allegiance to the Camden camp, claimed to be confounded by the historiographic proceedings: "As to the Stationers Company, surely we were not to look for the common law among them."[59] In their attempt to limit the authority of common law within the then-modern world of social regulation, the appellants successfully argued that the common law "covered" the English past inadequately. Since common law was inadequate to the past, it could not, they implied, be held adequate to the present. This is a powerful strategy. The inaccesibility of the past—an inaccessibility perhaps augmented by mystification—grounds the novelties (here, the statutory novelties) of the present.[60] Brilliant litigation; troubling historiography.

Still, it would be a mistake to dismiss the histories mustered in *Donaldson v. Becket,* for, however polemical, they constitute a formidable challenge to the historian. All who spoke in the case inquired into the existence of common law copyright during the first two centuries of printing; all sought evidence of actual property in the economic and legal behavior of authors and printers. Though the decision in the case "defeated" property, the proceedings yielded a communal concession that property—all property—is a social institution, not one of the visibilia of the created universe. If the institution of corporeal property conduced to the illusion of primeval, extrasocial property, the challenge of incorporeal property was, precisely, the exposure of that illusion. And this is, after all, as much a problem for historiography as for law. The critical historian can learn from the disillusioned lawyer that he or she must not ask "What is a property?" and "Who owns it?" but rather "What practices articulate the social relations of property?" and "How are cultural arrangements manifest?" They must wonder "What are the physics of ideas?"

To begin a history of intellectual property with a history of the law of intellectual property has been to beg these questions for a time. For this merely initial moment, I have treated the *law* of intellectual property here as if it were a significant index of *cultural experience* of intellectual property. Of course the arguments in *Donaldson v. Becket* suggest that at any given cultural moment the institutions regulating intellectual property may conflict; they suggest, that is, that rival reifications of the cultural status of intellectual property may coexist—hence Wedderburn's response that the existence of licenses can provide no evidence for a common law right and were simply "fetters" imposed on authors by a particular economic conjuncture. Wedderburn proposes that the law itself may have lacked self-consistency. Moreover—and it is a principle of historiography central to *Donaldson v. Becket*—the *legal* history of intellectual property may entail a significantly different narrative than the commercial history of intellectual property. Here is Lord Camden, narrowly skeptical:

> The arguments to be maintained on the side of the Respondents,
> were founded on patents, privileges, Star-chamber decrees, and
> the bye laws of the Stationers' Company; all of them the effects of
> the grossest tyranny and usurpation; the very last places in which I
> should have dreamt of finding the least trace of the common law
> of this kingdom.[61]

Lord Camden's skepticism has guided my own historiographic project. The interpretive fit of common law, patents, privileges, Star Chamber decrees, and the bylaws of the Stationers' Company to the sense of the proprietary in the intellectual life of the past is inevitably imperfect; each regulatory structure has limited representational power. Nor may they be assembled, like parts of a puzzle or pieces of a mosaic, into an image of a cultural whole, for they overlap and gap, corroborate and conflict, lag and anticipate. The House of Lords was forced to make a decision; my purpose is to reproduce not the image of literary property but the imagery of literary property, the political economy of the book as it is traced in law, in commerce, in the behavior of writers and booksellers, and in the rhetoric of books themselves.

What follows may be taken as a contribution to the history of book culture. McLuhan, Ong, Eisenstein, Anderson, and Johns have given us very powerful arguments about how European printing contributed to major, indeed revolutionary, changes in European life.[62] Eisenstein's work has been especially provocative for my own: following the lead of Steinberg, Febvre, and Martin, she has examined the book trade—the production, marketing, and regulation of books—as a way of exhorting us to consider the *institutional* formations and disruptions implied (but to some extent concealed) by the genial term "book culture."[63] Febvre, Martin, Eisenstein, and de Certeau have reminded cultural historians that the "print revolution" was something more than an invasion of daily life by printed books: paper production flourished, new inks were developed, new markets emerged and trade routes were adjusted, State and Church provided for systematic censorship, literacy rates rose. On such practical transformations rest more abstract ones: the idea of the book, the notion of a readership, the purposes of writing—all were transformed. My primary purpose in what follows is to begin to describe those abstract transformations in terms of the practical transformations that produced them. As I wrote this book, I was trying to find out what book *culture* has to do with the book *trade*.

The changes in industrial organization characteristic of early modern economic practice can be seen with particular clarity in the early history of the book trade: it is exemplary. In fact, the book trade led some of those transformations: it *was* exemplary. That is, the book trade is both a significant instance and a significant agent in the transition from feudalism to capitalism. In effect, then, an account of the late Renaissance reader is significantly an account of the early capitalist consumer; the history of printing is a history of early capitalist industry; the book is quintessentially a modern commodity and the author in some ways quite an unexceptional laborer. Therefore, the intellectual, political, and commercial competitions that produce modern intellectual property as we know it are vividly engaged in struggles central to the construction of postfeudal reality.

Let me describe the purposes of this inquiry in another way. For a decade and a half critics of Renaissance art and literature have been accustomed to speak at once of the pressure of history (or "culture" or "power") on texts and the reciprocal pressure of texts on history, yet, more often than not, criticism has (perhaps inevitably) continued to favor the study of literature as a product, and not as a producer, of history. The instrumentality of literature still remains more asserted than described. At best, Jauss, Marotti, Chartier, Halasz, and Moretti have led an inquiry into the sociology of literary culture, while Jauss, Davis, Moretti, and Radway have written brilliantly of the consumption of books, the intricate social feedback that keeps book culture in a specifically historical motion.[64] These scholars have produced superb studies of the agency of books, but this hardly exhausts the historical study of agency in book culture. The agency of authors themselves has a history, a history the importance of which has only been sharpened by a half-century of critiques of subjectivity.[65]

In my attempt to account for the author, I have been able to rely on a century of brilliant scholarship. Edward Arber, A. W. Pollard, W. W. Greg, E. K. Chambers, and their scholarly heirs assembled and carefully pondered the annals of Renaissance English book culture. They undertook their historiography of the book in hopes of securing a foundation of historical fact to aid in the methodical reconstruction of "ideal" Renaissance texts, particularly the texts of Shakespeare. This goal has been subjected to stringent and usually convincing criticism of late, and I shall have more to say of this critique in what follows; fortunately, a good deal of the historical scholarship of the "New Bibliography" has remained largely unimpugned.[66] A good thing: the work of a Greg or a Pollard deserves the renewed attention of contemporary cultural historians that it has begun to receive. Although there are good reasons to relinquish the bibliographic dreams of the New Bibliography and to reject the vestigial bardolatry that permeated their enterprise, there are no good reasons to forget their achievements. I have attempted to compile from their researches, and from those of their heirs, a new "introduction to bibliography," one that places earlier bibliographic scholarship in service of an enlarged understanding of both literacy and creativity. Not the mystery of Shakespearean creativity, but an institutional history of such authorships as Shakespeare's or Jonson's, Harington's or Wither's, may be the fruit. In the penultimate chapter of this book, Milton will be discovered in the courtroom.

The chapters that follow are, then, historical investigations of the institutions that interpellate English authorship. Chapter 2 takes up a labor dispute within the Stationers' Company arising in the late 1570s. (I begin here because the episode is a watershed in the history of English intellectual property; the reader seeking an account of earlier stages of English book production will find it in chapters 3 and 4.) Though this industrial dispute seems to arise relatively early in the history of English printing, it is the result of the actual belatedness of the guild system, of conflicts between archaic and progressive ideologies of craft production. My local aim is to show how an industrial dispute within the book trade led to a heightening of the value of manuscripts, and so promoted the eventual reconception of the printable manuscript as a commercial property; my larger purpose is to adumbrate a larger thesis, which is that the modern individualist intellectual rises from the decaying corpse of the craft guild. In chapter 3, I examine the interplay of economic policy and ideological control in the early European book trade, a reexamination of the questions raised by the New Bibliographers, the questions on which Foucault less meticulously pronounced.

In a related study, *Jonson and Possessive Authorship*, I describe how the new valuation of manuscript copy redounded to the advantage of authors.[67] Earlier literary historians have attempted sociological explanations for the sudden rise of authorial self-promotion around the middle of the reign of Elizabeth I. My purpose in the study of Jonson and his contemporaries is to situate this "author-campaign" within the quickening (and mutually interfering) economies of book trade and theater and so to offer a close-grained and localized account of the experience of discursive production at what I take to be a key phase in the institutional development of authorship.[68] It is the possibility of authorial participation in these early economies that transforms the rhetoric of authorial self-presentation and accelerates the decay of literary patronage. But because a purely institutional and economic account of the origins of commercial authorship would necessarily be partial, one chapter in *Jonson and Possessive Authorship* recalls an antique instance of intellectual possessiveness, the development of a discourse of plagiarism, and examines its revival in and around the work of Ben Jonson: my goal there is to examine the crucial ways in which economic conditions interact with a renaissance, a very specific revival, in intellectual culture. Since my study of possessive authorship is designed to complement, test, and inflect the argument that unfolds in these pages, I have summarized it in a short interchapter in the middle of this book.

Having situated the regulation of English printing within early European mercantilist practices in chapter 3, chapters 4 and 5 go on to investigate the relationship between the growth of English monopolies and the rise of intellectual property. They take up some early instances in which authors seek and secure privileges modeled on the printing patent and they trace the swift growth of antimonopolistic polemic in the late Tudor period. It thus prepares for an examination of the interaction between commercial and ideological control in the regulation of the early English press, an examination that recurs to the penal thematics of Foucault's historiography of authorship. In chapter 6, ideological regulation now takes its place among the other regulatory determinants of authorship and intellectual property. In this chapter it is at last appropriate to ask how economic and physical violence contributes to the making of authors and the reification of intellectual work. Chapter 7 pursues the interaction of economic and ideological regulation from the Restoration to the passage of the Statute of Anne and fastens on the various ways that the figure of Milton governs this interplay. The shimmering, vagrant rhetoric of authorial prerogative in the late seventeenth century once more raises the problem of our confusion before the notion of intellectual property. I close with a meditation on the problem of authorship as it was provoked at the turn of the last century, of how historical scholarship intervened in a technological and legal turmoil that anticipates that of our own moment.

This book concerns itself with a revolution in the idea of property. It is not, however, concerned with an instantaneous transformation: there are long revolutions and short ones. Indeed, some revolutions, some crucial historical transformations, partake of various temporalities. The print revolution, the Reformation, the Copernican revolution—each may be described as a sudden transformation of ways of thinking and doing or as a slow modification of traditional structures of behavior. And sometimes temporalities conflict, conflict so fully that the responsible cultural historian may be forced into what seem paradoxical descriptions—as, for example, that Jonson is at once the most progressive and the most reactionary of English playwrights, at once a feudal client and a capitalist literary practitioner; or, to take another example, that modern notions of authorial property significantly "originate" in late fifteenth-century Venice, in 1774, in first-century Rome, or "within the late-Renaissance book trade." These descriptions seem to me to be useful and true, by which I mean true enough to merit sustained exposition. I say this in full cognizance of the poststructuralist critique of the humanist quest for origins. That *post*structuralist critique, prefigured in the systemic, antidevelopmental *structuralist* theory of culture, has been overextended: the salutary assault on preemptive origins, on such representations of origins as may be used to ground value, has modulated into a politically (and intellectually) enfeebling assault on sequence, cause, change, and explanation. My "quest for origins" is no more and no less than an inquiry into sequence, cause, and change within literary culture, and it yields multiple origins; my narrative traces an uneven development and a revolution.

This is an institutional history, but it is also an inward one. I was reminded of that inwardness by a postcard from a former student, Mei-Mei Wu, which began, "I have a recurring nightmare . . ." I should say that two years ago, when I received this postcard, I could hardly imagine a psyche cursed with such nuanced nightmares, yet this dream was proof and reminder that the political unconscious is an institution riven by uneven development. Ms. Wu had taken classes with me during her undergraduate years, but what compelled her to tell her dreams was a paper I'd read at her graduate institution, on the trope of the book-as-person in Jonson and Milton. The paper seems to have spoken not so much to the intrinsic eeriness of personification as to the excitements of regulation. Hence her "recurring nightmare": "Every descriptive word in the English language has been registered as a trademark and cannot be used by anyone else and every merely descriptive term has acquired a secondary meaning as a trademark; so I decide to use ordinary words [I chuckled over the happy semiotic confidence that such words lie ready-to-hand, and puzzled over the proximity of that confidence to regulatory paranoia], but to convey different meanings, and find that they have all been registered as arbitrary trademarks. In desperation, I make up new words from the letters in the alphabet, but find that they too have already been registered, as coined or fanciful marks. Then I awake and remember the fair use defense and fall peacefully back to sleep." No one has dreams like *that*, I thought, but I later learned that Roger L'Estrange, sometime surveyor of the Restoration press, had very particularly anticipated those dreams. The difficulty of possessing the forms of thought has a history, but as the following chapters will illustrate it is a history punctuated by ingenious recurrence.

CHAPTER TWO

THE REFORMATION OF THE PRESS:
PATENT, COPYRIGHT, PIRACY

The pessimists, of whom Mr. Lee has made himself the champion,
seem to me to have piracy on the brain.

A. W. Pollard, *Shakespeare Folios and Quartos*

Irregularities

Transgression is one of the historian's most useful data, for the pointed figure of the scandalized is often our index of the norm. To begin with an imputed infringement of intellectual property, then, is to begin to see what the structure of that property once was, what territory might be said—by some interested party or parties—to have been protected. Begin with a scoundrel, John Wolfe.[1]

He makes his last appearance in the historical record when the government suppressed John Hayward's *Life and Raigne of King Henry IIII*, a work that Wolfe published at the beginning of 1599.[2] There is nothing inflammatory or otherwise remarkable about the book, yet an accumulation of circumstances combined to make it appear seditious. At Wolfe's suggestion, Hayward's book had been dedicated to Essex, who, knowing that the queen looked with suspicion on the story of Bolingbroke's glamorous rebellion, asked to have the book called in and the dedication removed; a year later, as the campaign of Essex's enemies got firmly underway, both author and publisher were haled into court. Six months after that, Essex had taken up the stance of a Bolingbroke in earnest: as is well-known, his treasons cost him his life; they earned Hayward, incidentally, a permanent confinement in the Tower. Even the official licenser who had vetted Hayward's book was prosecuted, but Wolfe somehow got off unscathed.

Wolfe departs from the historical record, then, having neatly evaded the jurisdiction of the censorious. But what brings him solidly into the historical record are jurisdictions of quite another sort. Some preliminary generalizations concerning those other jurisdictions are in order.

For convenience we can say that, besides the market forces shaping the book trade, there were three important institutions for regulating the Elizabethan press.[3] One was statutory and censorious, the required royal licensing that constrained the printing of books. There may have been some sort of licensing system in the second decade of the century, but Henrician licensing as we know it seems to have developed out of the ecclesiastical proscription of particular books during the mid-1520s.[4] A more supple means of ideological control was formally inaugurated by Henry VIII in 1530 in a proclamation that provided for a licensing system; in 1538 (in the proclamation so much pored over by Pollard, Albright, Reed, and Greg) the responsibility for such licensing was transferred from diocesan ordinaries to "his gracis privie counsayle, or other suche as his highnes shall appoynte."[5] Licensing is the subject of repeated royal proclamations from this time forth, and the system was subject to various modifications in procedural detail, some of which will be discussed in greater depth later. At this point, it will be sufficient to note that Tudor censorship constrains both Haywards *and* Wolfes, authors and stationers—with stationers including publishers, printers, and booksellers. It is perhaps as common to see a stationer suffering for the publication of seditious or heretical works as to see authors so suffering: that Wolfe got off scot-free after the scandal over Hayward's *Henry IIII* is quite unusual.[6] Indeed, the language of those Tudor royal proclamations and Star Chamber rulings that promulgate licensing is aimed specifically at the book trade and not at authors (or at readers), whose activities were not constrained by *special* forms of legislation.

Licensing, originating outside the printing industry, was complemented by an internal institution, "entrance," the institution from which modern copyright is the direct descendant.[7] In order to control competitive pressures within the printing industry, the Stationers' Company developed a system whereby individual members could secure an exclusive right to market a given text—to print it or to have it printed, to distribute the printed text, to sell it or to have it sold. A guild member submitted a manuscript, the so-called copy, to the guild leadership and paid a registration fee; upon his doing so, the text was usually "licensed to him" or "entered to his copy" in the company register.[8] It was not always so registered: from the somewhat casual nature of the convention of actual registration ensued a number of disputes concerning what procedure was necessary and sufficient to secure copy; of this, more in the next chapter. One can say securely, however, that a stationer's exclusive right to market a manuscript was not originally seen as the sort of personal property right that we associate with modern copyright; it was a privilege conferred by the guild on one of its members, part of an imperfect but not ineffective system by which the guild sought to preserve internal order.[9] Licensing served the Crown as a mechanism of ideological control, safeguarding England from sedition or heresy; entry served the guild as a mechanism of economic control, safeguarding the stationers from internal hostility and profit-shrinking competition.[10]

But the Crown had more particular interests than those of ideological control, and the guild had broader concerns than those of mere internal stability and prosperity. That it was normal company policy to enter only copies that had been approved by a reputable licensing authority is implied by occasional entries in the Stationers' Register indicating the exceptional and grudging registration: copies "tollerated unto" their owners and those to be printed "at the peril" of the registrant.[11] The draft ordinances drawn up for the company in 1559 (but probably never approved), for example, suggest that the company intended to conduct, or to continue conducting, its own blanket scrutiny of all manuscripts to be printed.[12] The guild eventually assumed some of the responsibility for licensing, so that by the seventies entrance can usually be assumed to entail license.[13] More important than guild participation in censorious regulation, though, is the fact that the Crown frequently involved itself intimately in the regulation of competition. It did so by granting printing patents to favored stationers, following an older model of privileged printing, originating in Venice, which had long flourished on the continent: the patent constitutes the third of the major English regulatory institutions.[14] English printing privileges were remarkably broad grants, and very lucrative ones, whereby certain stationers gained control of whole classes of publication: Tottel, for example, held a patent for the printing of all law books; Byrd and Tallis had the patent for all printing of music.[15]

Naturally, such royal interventions could not but disturb the guild's own attempts at self-regulation, the institution of registration. Registration developed after many of the more lucrative of Tudor patents had been granted: there is reason to believe that any earlier forms of company regulation of printing rights do not long antedate the surviving records, which date from 1554.[16] It is probably fair to say that entrance was an institution doomed at its inception, however long and well it served the guild. The Elizabethan rights of copy could not accrue coherence, just as the fragile internal stability of a self-regulated guild economy could not endure, under the disruptive pressure exerted by royal privileges. It could be argued that the tension between the two systems is largely responsible for the evolution of copyright as we know it, for under the pressure of privilege entrance had to strengthen itself, and the dream of a regulated economy could only be realized when the entrance system received extrinsic political support. At first this meant burgeoning power for the guild, as the stationers sought and received legal support for their internal decisions. But eventually legal regulation overshadowed that of the guild; hence, the development of copyright may be keyed both to the steady growth of the Stationers' regulatory power into the first decade of the seventeenth century *and* to an equally steady decline of that power in the course of the next century. These adjustments *in* the power of the press and *over* it were influenced more than a little by the career of John Wolfe.[17] Indeed, the significance of that career extends quite as far as the Statute of Anne of 1710, and beyond: in his arguments in *Donaldson v. Beckett,* Sir John Dalrymple recalls the essential cultural transformation originating during the Wolfe era thus: "When the members of the Stationers Company however quarrelled (as it was natural to suppose they would) amongst themselves, then each talked of some favourite book as his property."[18]

Wolfe's professional life began in 1562, when he was apprenticed to John Day, one of the wealthiest and most privileged printers in London. Day was offering himself as something of a Protestant hero during the period of Wolfe's apprenticeship, for he was then engaged in the huge project of printing Foxe's *Book of Martyrs*—though one contemporary suggested that Day encouraged Foxe's prolixity in hopes of turning a larger profit on the venture.[19] Day was nothing if not prudent. During the reign of Edward VI, he had secured one of the most profitable of royal patents, the right to exclusive printing and sale of the *A.B.C. with the Little Catechism.*[20] Besides the Bible, there were few more important books printed in England: this text initiates at once both literacy and private orthodoxy, and most literate householders would have wanted a copy.[21] In 1557, Day was made city printer; with the accession of Elizabeth, he acquired a further royal patent in the metrical Psalter, a work that he could job out for production at twopence half-penny a copy and then sell for sixpence. Wolfe was working for Day while the master was thus exploiting this patent, but he seems not to have served out his apprenticeship.

He went to Italy instead, probably for several years, spending at least enough time in Florence to find work and training in Italian printing methods.[22] Before his return to permanent residence in London, Wolfe may have gone to Frankfurt. One suspects as much because, by the late 1580s, a substantial part of Wolfe's output was being marketed at the Frankfurt Book Fair, and being marketed in ways unconventional enough to suggest intimate acquaintance with the shadier side of international literary marketing.[23]

During the seventies and eighties the Frankfurt Fair was Catholic Europe's chief source for prohibited books; a thriving smuggling industry brought Indexed titles into Venice, and in the years between 1584 and 1589, we find Wolfe printing and sending to Frankfurt Aretino's *Ragionamenti* and *Quattro Comedie*, Caro's pornographic *Commento . . . sopra la prima ficata del padre Siceo*, and a full range of works by Machiavelli—*Il Prencipe*, the *Discorsi*, the *Arte della Guerra*, the *Historie*, and *L'Asino d'Oro*.[24] All these are Indexed works and all of them went to Frankfurt with false imprints, attributed to fictitious printers working in Rome or Palermo.[25] The false imprints suggest a characteristic style. After the defeat of the Armada, Burghley—who, incidentally, owned Wolfe's Aretinos and did not need his Machiavellis, having acquired most of Machiavelli's works in manuscript long before Wolfe had thought to print them—forged some letters ostensibly from an English Catholic lamenting the Spanish defeat and attributing that defeat to the failures of Spanish espionage. The English, according to these letters, are a much more potent military force than Catholic Europe had suspected, while the English queen commands, they say, the unshakable loyalty of her Catholic subjects. Wolfe printed Italian translations of these forgeries for continental distribution, again with false imprints.[26]

"Wolfe, leave your Machevillian devices, and conceit of your forreine wit, which you have gained by gadding from countrey to countrey," Christopher Barker, upper warden of the Stationers' Company, sputtered in 1582; yet his exasperation long antedates Wolfe's practical engagement with Machiavelli.[27] Barker's annoyance had nothing to do with Wolfe's machinations within the international book trade; indeed, Wolfe didn't begin his career as an international Machiavel until a fascinating domestic career in that role had nearly run its course. In the late seventies, when Wolfe returned from his time on the continent, he found incipient tensions among the Stationers. Early in the autumn of 1577, Burghley had received a petition from thirty-five freemen of the company, complaining that "the privilidges latelie granted by her Majestie under her highnes greate seale of England . . . Conserninge the arte of printing of bookes hath and will be the overthrowe of the Printers and Stacioners within this Cittie being in nomber .175. Besides their wyves Children Apprentizes and families."[28] The petition complained that privileged books were being shoddily printed and sold at exorbitant prices, that privileges were being granted to nonstationers—hardly an unusual procedure, since such royal favors were frequently granted without respect to the particular industrial skills or mercantile practices of the recipient—and that some of the grants were being horribly abused by extension, as in the case of William Byrd, who claimed, by virtue of his patent in all music books, a monopoly in the printing of ruled paper. John Day's monopoly of the *A.B.C.* with the Catechism was one of those singled out: "these bookes," it was protested, "weare the onelie releif of the poorest sort of that Companie."[29] It may indeed be the case that the renewal of Day's patent in this book on 26 August of that year was the immediate provocation for the petition.

These complaints came steadily during the next few years. By late in the summer of 1582, the younger workers in the book trade had several times formally complained that the commissioners appointed by the Privy Council to investigate their grievances had refused to listen to their side of the case. But some of the more disgruntled of London's printers had given up on civil procedures. Earlier in the year John Day entered a complaint before Star Chamber against Roger Ward and William Holmes for infringing his patent in the *A.B.C.* and Catechism: Ward had been printing forged copies of the book (10,000 copies, he later claimed) and Holmes had been selling them. This was not the first occasion of infringement of a printing patent. In the 1560s the Court of High Commission had commanded that the wardens of the Stationers' Company take action to stop what seems to have been an isolated infringement of William Seres's patent on the two key private devotional texts, the Primer and the Psalter. But Ward's forgeries were not so isolated, nor was he first of the many pirates who soon entered the field.

By no means the first: the reason that, on 14 May 1582, Christopher Barker called Wolfe a Machiavel was that Wolfe had been pirating a whole variety of patented books, and had been at it for a while. In the summer of 1581, he had been bound over by the Privy Council not to print any more copies of Francis Flower's patented *Grammar.* Though Barker prepared his official report on the 1582 meeting almost a year after the fact, the document betrays a fresh and complicated exasperation, an exasperation that has at least three plausible explanations. First of all, though Barker was one of the Stationers' wardens, his jurisdiction over Wolfe was uncertain. Never having completed his apprenticeship to Day, Wolfe was not officially a stationer; he *had* secured those rights of citizenship that belonged to all freemen of the London guilds but he had done so by having himself made free—by patrimony, and not by apprenticeship—of the Fishmongers. So Barker was feeling the particular frustration of impotent authority. But he was also suffering the frustrations of the thwarted monopolist, for the bulk of Wolfe's piracies, which may have begun as early as the summer of 1580, were some of Barker's own patented titles.

There is very little justice in Barker's indignation, which probably explains its intensity. Having himself been one of the signatories of the 1577 petition against privileges, Barker had secured the post of queen's printer only a few weeks later, which meant that he could monopolize the printing of royal proclamations as well as two of the most lucrative books in England, the Book of Common Prayer and the Bible, to say nothing of Erasmus's *Paraphrases*, itself no mean source of income. He was a made man. Barker reported that shortly after Wolfe's return from the continent Wolfe had himself tried to acquire such a guaranteed income, suing the Privy Council for patents of his own, but the privileges sought were apparently so greedily broad that they were refused.[30] This story, which may be simply an imputation of guilty authority, is fairly difficult to credit, since Wolfe soon gained a considerable following among the less powerful members of the book trade, largely for the vigor of his polemics against the very idea of privilege. Wolfe was certainly capable of such hypocrisy—hypocrisy of a degree that only Barker could top—but one doubts whether Wolfe could have acquired the following that he did had he really made a recent suit for a privilege of his own. Such damaging facts have a way of leaking out among dissidents.

At any rate, there was a third reason for Barker to be exasperated. He claims to have had a *first* encounter with Wolfe a year earlier, in the spring of 1581, at which he had tried to pacify the unruly young man. He had offered Wolfe commissions worth eighty pounds to print works from Barker's own patent in exchange for a promise that Wolfe would change guilds, transferring his freedom from the Fishmongers to the Stationers—already we find Barker hankering to strengthen his jurisdiction. Wolfe had accepted the printing commissions but then failed to make good on his promise to change his guild membership. Not only that: when his commission ran out in 1582, he continued to print from Barker's patent, and from the patents of three or four other wealthy stationers, underselling the privileged stationers in provincial markets.[31] In his report, Barker added a false allegation to his list of Wolfe's abuses, namely that Wolfe's work on Barker's commission "was so untruely and evilly done, that it was not onely to *Barkars* great hinderance, but an exceeding discredit to all his owne labours."[32] Wolfe was a very skilled printer, and a meticulous pirate—hence his later success in Frankfurt at passing his own books off as Italian imprints. But the accusation of faulty workmanship turns out to be a significant one; I shall return to this issue shortly.

By the time they met in May 1582, Barker must have realized that he was not dealing with just a single refractory printer. Day's complaint against Ward and Holmes went into Star Chamber at about this time; by midsummer the company's journeymen commenced formal protests against privilege, low wages, and lack of work. Wolfe was jailed during this period (the charge is uncertain) and was released in October, at which moment he is said to have had four confederates; by the following spring reports refer to a band of ten leading conspirators and a large body of followers.[33] The trade was by now overtly polarized.

There had already been deliberate government action to control the unrest. Wolfe had been released on the authority of Thomas Norton, the last significant figure in these events. Sometime during the summer, the Privy Council had appointed Norton, together with Dr. John Hammond, to conduct an inquiry into unrest within the book trade. Almost immediately, the journeymen of the company began to protest this commission. A petition to the mayor, who still preserved considerable legislative power over the London guilds, led to the appointment of a separate board of inquiry drawn from the City Board of Aldermen. Wolfe seems to have capitalized on the legitimacy that official recognition conferred on his insurgency; he was now the leader of a large body of aggrieved tradesmen. According to one of the infringed patentees, Wolfe was "assocyating hym self with" this body of poor but law-abiding stationers "and incensynge them [so that] they chaunged their myndes and ever synce . . . have laboured and yett do laboure to overthrowe all . . . priviledges."[34] Wolfe is, significantly, the last signatory of a petition drawn up shortly after his release from prison, in which he and twenty-one other stationers lodged a complaint against Norton, whom they claimed "is altogether hired agaynst us, for that he sayth, he hath authority to imprison us, except we will enter into unreasonable bondes, being coloured with an outward shew of good meaninge, as neither law nor Justice would permitte."[35]

They had some right to question Norton's impartiality. Recall that Day's patent included the Little Catechism: it had been Englished in 1577 by Norton himself. By this time, in fact, Day held patents on all the official catechisms save that in the Book of Common Prayer, and for each Norton had been the translator. Day also had the patent on the metrical psalter; again, Norton had provided several of the translations. Moreover, as standing counsel to the stationers Norton was paid a fee by the wardens to provide them with legal advice, so he could hardly be expected to respond fairly to complaints against the controlling figures in the company. Small wonder that in these circumstances Wolfe had so little trouble radicalizing the poorer members of the guild.

Norton and Hammond spent more than a year gathering information. That they failed to produce an impartial assessment can hardly be doubted, for the records they compiled are top-heavy with testimony from the patentees. Unfortunately, this makes it difficult to assess the extent of the unrest, for the patentees adopted the most alarmist vocabulary they could muster. William Seres alleged that the very principle of monopoly grant was under attack:

> they pretend that in good Justice yt standeth with the best pollicye
> of this realme that the printinge of all good and laufull bookes be
> at libertye for every man to prynt without grauntinge or allowinge
> of any priviledge by the prynce to the contrary And in dede
> they . . . derogate the princes awthoritye aswell for grauntinge . . .
> of all lycences for the transportacon of clothe wolle beare and
> suche like.[36]

He goes on to point out that many of the dissidents—not the least of all, John Wolfe—were not even Stationers, putting them in violation of the extraordinary terms of the company's 1557 charter, which denied the right of any non-stationer to print, and restricted *all* English printing, excepting that done at the universities, to London. These two allegations against the rebels, that they sought to undermine both royal prerogative in the granting of monopolies and the company's exclusive control of the ranks of English bookmen, are so often repeated in the documentary record that it is difficult to believe that the rebels themselves had *not* enunciated them. But the Crown of the assembled reports is the one to which I have referred so frequently, the wardens' supplication to the Privy Council, submitted in the spring of 1583. In it Barker aims to expose the full villainy of Wolfe's actions and opinions. Thus Wolfe is accused of personal greed, lining his pockets with money ostensibly collected to fund his campaign, of making personal threats, of inciting to riot, even of promising to make the poor rich. Yet as Barker's notes slip into indirect discourse or quotation, Wolfe emerges as a plausible figure—a man of casual insolence whose savvy ambition led him somewhat fortuitously to a moment of stubborn principle, a practical radical. Here are some particularly revealing passages from the report:

> *Wolfe* and some of his confederats affirmed openly in the
> Stationers hall, that "it was lawfull for all men to print all lawfull
> bookes what commandement soever her Majestie gave to the
> contrary."

> *Wolfe* hath oftentimes delivered most disloyall and unreverent
> speaches of her majesties governement, not once giving her
> highnesse any honorable name or title, as "She is deceaved,"

> "she shall know she is deceaved," Also "she is blindly lead, she is
> deceaved."

> [When] *Barker* sent for the said *Wolfe* and demanded of him
> why he printyed the Copies belonging to his office: he answered,
> "Because I will live."

and finally

> *Wolfe* being admonished that he being but one so meane a man
> should not presume to contrarie her Highnesse governmente:
> "Tush," said he, "*Luther* was but one man, and reformed all the
> world for religion, and I am that one man, that must and will
> reforme the government in this trade."[37]

Barker must have included the last assertion thinking that its very extravagance was somehow damning, though how he could miss the peculiar *dignity* of the claim is a mystery.[38] But perhaps the most striking mystery that
the documentary record, however full, does not dispel is what to make of
Wolfe himself during this period. One does not know, for example, whether
to take the comparison to Luther as the flamboyant improvisation of a mere
opportunist, or as a densely serious remark, the expression of a man whose
opportunism is momentarily in abeyance and who is fully caught up in the
ideological situation of those for whom he speaks.

Though he had been released from jail in October, Wolfe was back in
prison before Barker submitted his report. He tempered his words, again got
himself released, and went back to illicit printing. His home was then duly
raided—the Stationers' records note payment of the sheriff's expenses—and
his stock confiscated. Perhaps he *had* been lining his pockets: he owned five
presses by now, giving him a physical plant that could, in fact, rival Barker's
and surpass Day's. The raid would seem to have broken his will, for in less
than two months, he agreed to transfer his freedom to the Stationers. But his
resilient cunning should not be doubted, for the Aretino and Machiavelli editions began to appear within the year, and, in even less time, he had printed
some more copies of the metrical psalter. Day arranged for another raid on
Wolfe's presses and the story now trails off into farce, for Wolfe immediately
brought a complaint against Day before Star Chamber for property damages. He naturally lost the case, but not without gaining an opportunity for
impugning the propriety of Day's marketing practices and the quality of his
presswork.

Meanwhile, just before an enlarged commission of inquiry finished its work, the patentees made gestures sufficiently conciliatory to justify a bland report. The Privy Council was reassured that the company was about to redress all grievances, so their only substantive action on behalf of the insurgents was to recommend that in the future the Crown should refrain from making *broad* grants of privilege.[39] The patentees, meanwhile, took the occasion to eliminate the overlaps between their privileges, and then donated, for a short term, some of the least lucrative privileged books to the general use of the company.[40] But the most important result of the inquiry was that the company consolidated its own regulatory control over English printing.[41] The unrest was ascribed to the disproportionate number of presses and pressmen; both were to be restricted in the future. The number of apprentices was to be limited, and a minimum apprenticeship of seven years was to be rigorously enforced. Price regulations, never very firmly adhered to, were reaffirmed. This begins a trend that continued into the 1590s, by which time there was a limit on the number and output of letter founders, a prohibition on books left standing in type, and limits on the number of impressions to be taken from a single setting of type.[42] Printer, type founder, bookseller, apprentice— all were to be under substantial bonds to adhere to state law and company regulations.

At Stationers' Hall these restrictive rigors were masked at first. Most of the dissidents seem to have calmed down by the middle of 1584, perhaps demoralized by Wolfe's apparent capitulation, and perhaps genuinely pacified by the donation of selected patents to their general use. The leaders, meanwhile, were busily lobbying, first in Parliament, and then in the Privy Council, for new regulatory powers.[43] Sporadic piracies were still occurring, and the Stationers' Court of Assistants wanted more efficient means of retaliation. Their success came with the Star Chamber decree of 26 June 1586.[44] It restricted the number of presses and of printers, it strengthened the mechanisms of censorship, and, most important, it extended the company wardens' rights of search, seizure, and arrest in any suspected infringement of state or company regulation of the book trade.[45] Suddenly the company beadle became an active and important figure. That the Stationers' Court of Assistants could esteem experience and exploit talent is proved by the fact that in 1587 they nearly doubled the salary for the post and appointed John Wolfe.[46] The story of the revolt against privilege may be left off here.

But the *implications* of the episode shoot off in what I take to be three significant trajectories. First there is the arc of Wolfe's subsequent career as a professional stationer. In a few years he began to curtail his activities as a printer per se; by 1594, he'd all but given it up. After the mid-eighties he becomes more and more the publisher, which is as much a tribute to his business sense as is his decision to begin surreptitiously publishing selected titles from the Roman Church's Index of prohibited books.[47] The latter part of the century saw an increasing specialization within the book trade, and Wolfe's career enacts just this development in miniature.[48] Price inflation simply spurred the proliferation of markets and the increased capitalization of the trade, and capitalization, together with the restriction on the number of presses allowed to operate in London, meant decreased power for the industrial side of the book trade—a shift in power from producer to trader variously recapitulated throughout the European guild system.[49] It was with the most powerful, the most fully capitalized sector of the book trade that Wolfe allied himself, and not with those disenfranchised workers whom the patentees sought to pacify by donation of discrete copies from their patents. No longer identifying his interests with those of the least powerful, we find him instead *policing* the company, securing the rights of capital, rights that he had now arrogated to himself.[50]

This brings us to the second trajectory to be traced out from the incidence of piracy. The unrest of these years brought about a new regulatory drive within the book trade. The Star Chamber ruling of 1586 secures the support of the state as never before for the internal arrangements of the company. Where the early Tudors had concerned themselves with the suppression of seditious and schismatic works, and had simply extended archaic forms of patronage by granting printing patents, late Elizabethan policy secured those patents, increased the emphasis on licensing, and then transferred the power to license, in practice, to the leadership of the Stationers, while conferring increased rights of self-regulation upon the company. The extent to which that internal authority developed can be illustrated by a 1616 suit in Chancery discussed at length by C. J. Sisson.[51] The suit concerned disputed rights to Rider's Latin *Dictionary* and several of the defendants were members of the Stationers' Court of Assistants; because the judge felt himself to be insufficiently skilled in the matter, he sought—and followed—expert advice. He turned for that advice to the only group experienced in such matters, in effect reconvening the Court of Assistants within his own court, so that we have a jury not of peers, but of colleagues.[52]

From the late eighties we find more formality in the entry of copies, as the spirit of regulation pervaded the company.[53] Indeed, we can detect a somewhat more serious attitude to entry. Though it was *never* the case that all books printed were first entered—copies that were unlikely to sustain censorious scrutiny, or copies the rights in which were hardly worth the trouble or expense of registering frequently did not find their way into the Stationers'

Register—still, after 1586 there was considerably *less* negligence. Indeed, in the year after the Star Chamber decree of 1586, the Record contains an unprecedented 340 entries.[54] Wolfe went on a binge, registering books he had printed years earlier. Here, then, is the major institutional effect of the revolt against the printing patent: the rights conferred by entry were consolidated, while the risks of failing to register also increased. The status of guild membership was also bolstered: restrictions on alien printing, and on printing and publishing by nonstationers, were suddenly much more rigorously enforced. At the same time we find the alliance of guild interests with those of the Crown growing stronger, a trend that George Unwin finds among many other Elizabethan guilds, often mediated by a steadily strengthened municipal jurisdiction over guild affairs.[55]

These are matters of economic and political history. What might the cultural historian, the literary scholar, make of these events? The third trajectory can hardly be so well-defined a curve; it will be sketched in the chapters that follow. I think that this was a moment when political economy had specific and important effects on the very idea of the literary work.[56]

In 1643, Parliament passed a Licensing Act, the first regulation of the press that implies the idea that a literary work must have something like a common law *owner* and not simply a stationer whose economic rights might need defense.[57] Printing of even regularly entered copies was prohibited if the entry was made for "any particular member . . . [of the Stationers' Company] without the license and consent of the Owner or Owners."[58] Now the 1643 act hardly recognizes authorial rights in ways that a modern author could endorse. But it does articulate an issue that had become particularly vexed in the course of the preceding six or seven decades, the matter of what kind of economic rights a reproducible manuscript might entail. On rare occasions in the course of these decades, not only competing printers but authors, inventors, and artists would attempt to claim such economic rights either by influencing the dissemination of their writings or designs or by protesting their inability to influence such dissemination. These efforts are, I take it, practical meditations on—and reconceptions of—intellectual production, the work of art, and authorship. Walter Ong and Elizabeth Eisenstein have implied that such meditations are provoked by the general influence of a shift to print culture, the sudden efflorescence of cheap, durable words.[59] I should like to strengthen this implication by insisting on the local contexts that mediate and specify that highly generalized influence. I am saying, that is, that particular legal and economic arrangements, and particular discursive conventions—some relatively autonomous from a set of particular technological developments—contributed to just such assertions about what kind of thing creative endeavor brought forth, who controlled it, who deserved credit for it.[60] To take a well-known case—though, as we shall see, there are more revealing cases that should be better known—Jonson's vociferously proprietary attitude with regard to his printed texts, his *Workes*, was conditioned by recent contests within the book trade concerning the regulation of literary property, contests that had occasionally thrown off authorial protections, like regulatory sparks.[61] For example, although the rights of registration grew in strength during the late 1580s, those rights were also interestingly limited by an order of 1588 stipulating that any member of the company could reprint any book that had been out of print for six months, *provided that the author did not refuse permission*.[62] Jonsonian authorship is in some ways a by-product of John Wolfe's reformation.

The suite of practices and affects that we call authorship, always internally incoherent, was thrown into a rich flux in the late sixteenth century. In an episode that anticipates many of the paratextual fictions of *Don Quixote*, two Elizabethan authors who had begun their careers as printers, Henry Chettle and Anthony Munday, struggled to assert and assess the proprieties of publication when Munday's translation of the second part of *Gerileon of England* was published in 1592. The first part of Maisonneufve's chivalric romance had appeared in an English translation in 1578, and it would seem that Munday was the then-unidentified translator. Certainly that is what is implied by Chettle's letter to Munday published with the second part, a letter that disparages as interlopers both another translator and the book-binder who had set *him* on to translate the second part before Munday had completed "his own" translating project. Chettle casts aspersions on everyone involved in that "improper" edition—of which no exemplar survives: "I marvell who the divell is his Printer: and but that I am assured, it cannot bee done but by some mans helpe of that profession, I should hardly be perswaded, that anie professor of so excellent a Science would bee so impudent, to print such odious and lascivious ribauldrie, as *Watkins Ale, The Carmans Whistle,* and sundrie such other" news sheets as this hack's (A_4^v). These titles are presumably listed to identify the author, or the printer, or both, an unspecific specification of the agents of literary bad taste. Various exclusivities are alleged by this letter; some loose sense of violated property is assumed. We are to concede that Maisonneufve's book is somehow rightfully Munday's in English, but the impulse to violate that uncertain right is diffuse, generally associated with the unscrupulousness of stationers, but also taking in the unoriginal unscrupulousness of Munday's rival translator. The personal claims on discourse are fragile—Chettle's letter to A.M. is attributed to "T.N.," a compositor's error, one supposes, that substitutes the initials of Thomas Nashe for those of his friend, Chettle—but a culture of claiming is quickening: Chettle took pains, in *Kind-Hartes Dreame* (1592), to insist that the letter was *his*.[63]

Wolfe ushered in a tradition, if not an age, of sometimes piratical claiming. One of his early co-conspirators, Roger Ward, went on to have a prolific and dismal career as a pirate, shuttling in and out of jail for printing not only Day's *A.B.C.* and metrical *Psalter*, but Seres's *Primer*, and Flower's *Grammar*, until for his penultimate infringement, in 1588, he was arrested by beadle John Wolfe. But it wasn't just hardened criminals like Ward, or radical-Puritan sympathizers like Waldegrave, who engaged in piracy. By 1585, some of the most respected of London's stationers were involved. When John Day died, his son, Richard, was forced into a frenzy of litigation because a number of printers, including the impeccable Ponsonby, began to print works on Day's patent.[64] Now the Day privilege had been granted "to John Daye and Richard Daye, and to the longer liver of them for terme of their lives, and to the assigns of them, and either of them," but many of the defendants in Day's suit claimed to be unaware that both father and son had been recipients of the royal grant. It is dimly possible that the details of this grant had never been fully publicized or that popular memory of these details had failed within the Stationers' Company.[65] After his father's death, Richard Day had assigned rights in the *A.B.C.* to five of the erstwhile insurgents, no doubt as an act of trade pacification; a third and more likely explanation for the infringements, therefore, is that Ponsonby and others, well aware of the younger Day's rights but peeved at the conciliatory treatment of the rabble-rousers, went after books on Day's patent motivated by outraged virtue. At any rate, whether the "assigns" specified in the grant could maintain rights after the death of both Days might have been the focal issue in the case, but Richard Day's complaint, which he brought before Star Chamber, seems to have been turned back to the Stationers' Court of Assistants for review, and the legal issues remained unclarified. The repeated challenges to Day's patent suggest that many stationers failed (again perhaps conveniently) to remark any resemblance between rights in privileged works and heritable rights in personal property, but in effect two conceptions of rights with respect to printing were beginning to compete. The infringing printers held to an idea that the right to print even patented works was fundamentally a right conferred by the guild—conventional, revocable, provisional, practical; Day was defending the idea that the Crown had conferred something very like common law ownership, something above trade regulation. Suddenly a new pressure was exerted on the status of texts: as the stationers went about their increasingly stringent self-regulation, they were stirring up issues concerning the propriety and indeed the phenomenology of literary works. Yet to focus too narrowly on the literary aspect of this cultural ferment would be to miss the momentousness of the piracies of the eighties. As we shall see, Wolfe and his co-conspirators turn out to be the advance guard of a broad-based English movement against monopolistic competition.

The three transformations traceable to the piracies of the early eighties—accelerated stratification of the book trade, a concomitant rejuvenation of internal industrial regulation, and new forms of proprietary instability (provoked by and provoking the regulatory drive)—mark a watershed in English book culture, but it will be useful to articulate the limits of this transformation as precisely as possible. Another transgression, another index: for a sense of what norms of property—we could call them "proprieties"—prevail in the aftermath of Wolfe's reformation, consider the following record of the Stationers' Court of Assistants.

> Whereas the wardens on monday the 17 day of october 1586.
> vpon serche of Roger wardes house dyd fynd there in printinge a
> book in verse intytled Englandes albion beinge in english and not
> aucthorised to be printed / which he had ben forbidden to prynte
> /.aswell by the Lord archbishop of Canterburye as also by the
> Wardens at his own house. / Item they found there in printinge
> the grammar in octavo belonginge to the privilege of Mr ff fflower
> Item certen formes readie sett of the catechismes belonging
> to Richard dayes privilege. and of the prymmers belonginge to
> William Seres priviledge by her majesties patentes. Item Psalter
> calender ready sett. and certen other formes redy sett of other
> mens copies.[66]

The account is useful as an index of proprieties, first of all because it represents Ward's as a crime against the *state*—a violation of specifically *royal* privileges for printing of such crucial ideological agents as grammar, catechism, and primer, a flouting of Star Chamber rulings, a transgression of licensing laws. Within a regicentric historiography this record could serve as evidence that the Stationers' Court was now functioning directly as a servant of royal interests. To be sure, Ward's criminality is not described as a violation of patents; his offense in printing William Warner's *Albion's England* is specified as violating the proscription of the archbishop of Canterbury. But this specification is hardly as straightforward as the language of the company records makes it seem, for there is nothing particularly seditious about *Albion's England*. In fact, the Stationers' Register records the archbishop's approval of the text in an entry made three weeks after Ward's arrest.[67] What is represented as a violation of censorship regulations would seem, then, actually to be a flouting of newly stiffened conventions of entrance. The licensing regulations have been invoked to legitimize a regulation of competition internal to the industry. The Star Chamber ruling of 1586 and the older licensing laws were functioning less as ideological mechanisms than as industrial ones, though the language of offense against church or state clearly provides a more serviceable rhetoric. Because the stationers trafficked in words it was particularly easy for them to represent economic insubordination, industrial irregularity, as ideological crime, and it is precisely this ease of access to a rhetoric of transgression that explains the curiously anomalous history of the stationers under Elizabeth: though other London guilds saw their powers of self-determination eroded in the course of her reign, the power of the London stationers grew.

It would be imprudent, however, to suppose that a firm boundary can be drawn between ideological and industrial irregularity. Ward had a dismal career during the next decade, a career of clandestine production and arrest. Sometimes the stationers pursued him on their own authority; sometimes on behalf of the archbishop of Canterbury. In a sense this is fitting: in 1590 he is arrested both for pirating patented books and for printing Puritan literature. His career presses the figurative limits of Wolfe's metaphor, for Ward is at once Reforming and reforming the trade. For Ward, for Archbishop Whitgift, and perhaps for many of London's stationers, the distinction between economic sharp practice and schism may well have been blurred in ways that the cultural historian would wish to respect.

I have been arguing that literary property is preeminently an industrial matter, but one might object that Ward's piracies—be they the patent infringements of 1582 or the more *various* infringements of 1586—do not produce any defenses of author's rights. That is, one might object that, though I am speaking of matters industrial, I may not in fact be speaking of matters literary. Here the record of Ward's arrest in 1586 is again particularly revealing. The Crown did not grant patents in works like *Albion's England*. Unlike most of the privileged books—catechisms, calendars, prayerbooks, and primers—*Albion's England* is what we would describe as a creative work. Those privileged books that had been the objects of the earliest piracies had no authors, had dead authors, or were born of activity so thinly creative, so "nonfictive," as it were, as to leave the rights of authors mooted. But the vocabulary of creativity or authorship, by which we might designate a special status for a work like *Albion's England,* makes no appearance even in the record of Ward's arrest; the stationers do not accuse Ward of violating authorial property. Not genre, nor subject matter, nor authorship are marked here. For the stationers, *Albion's England* is distinguished primarily as the sort of commodity that, because of its probably fugitive appeal, should have been *entered*. It is hardly surprising that the rhetoric of the stationers should maintain a focus on conventions of production and trade organization: printers attacking early piracies tend to focus public arguments on the supposed poor quality of the piracy, as if the only injury done was to the reader and to the reputation of the printer; piracy damages a market in durable goods.[68] But the peculiar nature of the stationers' monopolies extended the field of their attention, kept their eyes focused on Crown and Cross. For this reason, the language of industrial regulation is seldom carried on exclusively in a trade argot. But the rhetorical extension of the regulatory debates is not extended in all conceivable directions: the vocabulary of authorial proprieties had little utility within the book trade of the 1580s. At this juncture, stationer's copyright and royal privilege constitute the crucial modalities of literary property; the Star Chamber ruling of 1586 helped to stiffen entrance by analogy with privilege, yet the two sorts of property remain distinct, and they are also insulated from anything yet resembling modern proprietary authorship. As assaults on the patent modulate into transgressions of stationer's copyright, modern notions of literary property begin to surface within industrial disputes: the assent of the author becomes one of the anchors of disputed entrance. Author's rights will thus appear as back-formations within the development of industrial copyright.

The Egos in the Arcadia

> *Sir John.* Why? every man, that writes in verse is not a *Poet*; you have of the Wits, that write verses, and yet are no *Poets*: they are *Poets* that live by it.
>
> *Dauphine.* Why? would you not live by your verses, sir JOHN?
>
> *Clerimont.* No 'twere pittie he should. A knight live by his verses? he did not make 'hem to that ende, I hope.
>
> *Dauphine.* And yet the noble SIDNEY lives by his, and the noble family not asham'd.
>
> Jonson, *Epicoene,* II.iii.109–18

Ponsonby, whose career registers the various stresses on literary property, the confused regulatory culture of books during the reign of Elizabeth, can carry us across this volatile moment and so bear us closer to that discourse of authorial property we have been seeking. The son-in-law of Francis Coldock (who, like Barker, had been a warden of the Stationers' Company during the crackdown on Wolfe and his confederates), Ponsonby had firm ties to the company establishment, yet in the aftermath of Wolfe's reformation, he had himself challenged—perhaps one should say "investigated"—the scope of royal privileges by printing and marketing five thousand unauthorized copies of the *A.B.C.*[69] The infringement must have come in the middle of 1585; in February of the following year, Ponsonby advanced a hedged critique of royal interference in the market in his reply to Richard Day's bill of complaint. There is no documentary record of the disposition in Day's case against Ponsonby, but the Star Chamber decree of June 1586 surely indicated that a wholesale transformation of property relations within the book trade, the sort of transformation anticipated in Ponsonby's "investigative" infringement and self-defense, was not soon to come. It must have become clear to everyone in the Stationers' Company that industrial property was *not* dissolving and that the English book trade was to remain committed to monopolistic competition, an unfree market, for the foreseeable future. One might expect a printer seeking advantage within this highly regulated market to make an appeal to the royal prerogative, but Ponsonby chose a different course.

Here is Fulke Greville's account; he is writing to Walsingham:

> This day one ponsonby a booke bynder in poles church yard,
> came to me, and told me that ther was one in hand to print,
> Sir philip sydneys old arcadia asking me yf it were done, with
> yor honors consent or any other of his frends, I told him to my
> knowledge no, then he advised me to give warning of it, ether to
> the archebishope or doctor Cosen, who have as he says a copy of it
> to peruse to that end.[70]

Ponsonby, it seems, was informing Greville that one of the several manuscripts of the *Old Arcadia* then in circulation had been submitted for licensing by some unnamed stationer. He must have known of Greville's interest in the manuscript, may even have known that Greville had a revised version of the *Arcadia* in his possession. Moreover, Ponsonby may have had his eye on Sidney and other members of the Leicester circle for several years, for as early as 1582 Ponsonby's press output shows some signs of affiliation with the cautious religious tolerances of the Leicester circle.[71] Insofar as the unrest of the preceding years had created at least a rhetorical continuity between the projects of trade reform and religious reformation, it is possible to find in the careful antimonopolism of Ponsonby's legal defense in 1586 an idiom consistent with that of the books he published. As a moderate ecclesiastical and industrial reformer he had done much to promote himself to the patronage of the Dudleys and Sidneys.

Of course, the 1586 address to Greville illuminates some firmer pragmatisms. There in Paul's churchyard Ponsonby explained just how Greville (or Walsingham, who was Sidney's executor) could put a stop to an unwanted publication, by a direct intervention with the licensers. The *Old Arcadia* is, of course, no more objectionable on political or religious grounds than was *Albion's England.* Ponsonby proposes the mechanisms of censorship as simply the most practicable means of controlling the dissemination of texts, of shaping the literary marketplace. He has read the terms of the Star Chamber decree and knows its decorums.

It was a successful power play; the unnamed stationer lost control of his manuscript of the *Old Arcadia* and, in 1588, Ponsonby entered Greville's *New Arcadia* to his copy in the Stationers' Register. By thus coordinating the apparatus of ideological control—licensing—with the apparatus of internal guild regulation—stationer's copyright—Greville secured to himself some of the powers of a modern literary executor and Ponsonby became unofficial stationer to the Sidney circle.[72] The compact between Greville and Ponsonby effects significant cultural modifications, for Ponsonby thus develops a new form of clientage for himself and Greville develops a distinctly modern aristocratic publicity, a form of printed magnificence, on behalf of the noble Sidney. And by means of this complementary ingenuity, Ponsonby and Greville become the Sidney industry.

This collaboration merits somewhat more lingering attention, for the effort to control vulgar access to Sidney's words underwrites a central concern *of* those words. That texts can usefully valorize social eminence is, of course, an old topos in defenses of poetry: Achilles needs Homer. In England, the example of Wyatt and Surrey initiates the possibility that "Achilles" and "Homer" can be joined in a single person; they open the possibility of noble self-commemoration. Thus, despite the commonplace strictures on vulgar dissemination, the courtly makers extended the sphere of aristocratic grandeur, appending writing to more traditional forms of display, textualizing magnificence. Sidney himself bears witness to the importance of this cultural development in the deep pun on "title" in the ninth sentence of the *Defence of Poesie:*

> I will give you a nearer example of myself, who (I know not by
> what mischance) in these my not old years and idlest times having
> slipped into the title of a poet.[73]

This is quite finely calibrated. It metes out its assent to literary effort and to publicity. It acknowledges and seems to laugh away the indecorous supposition that literary distinction might be comparable to social distinction. It regulates literary reputation, the degree to which reputation may be supposed literary. This regulation, achieved within the restricted sphere of manuscript circulation (where *The Defence of Poesie* remained until 1595), is a matter of choosing the right words; things were perhaps not so simple within the larger, more *unaccustomed* sphere of print culture. Yet just such a regulation is what Ponsonby offered to Greville on behalf of the dead Sidney—a means of regulating the posthumous display of a textualized aristocracy: "I desyre only care to be had of his honor who I fear hathe Caried the honor of thes latter ages w[i]th him," wrote Greville to Walsingham.[74] The relatively new conditions of publicity—the development of a competitive market in printed books with all that this entailed for an aristocracy whose cultural heritage was massively committed to perfecting its own visibility—produced in Greville and Ponsonby a remarkable complementarity of interest.

It was an important moment. Although Greville expressed disdain for the "common errors of mercenary printing" in his letter to Walsingham, he was plainly impressed with the stationer's power to stabilize texts and regulate their circulation. Ponsonby was effectively offering him control of Sidney's literary reputation and, thereby, a unique means of preserving the favor and protection of the Herberts.[75] (Thus experienced, Greville would later take decisive control over other aspects of Sidney's personal legacy.) For his part, Greville, supported by Walsingham, enabled Ponsonby to wrest rights in a valuable copy from another stationer. Walsingham need not have invoked principle when he contacted the licensers about stopping the publication of a 1586 *Arcadia;* indeed it is hard to imagine what principle might have been invoked. Since no convention had yet been established to enable authors to restrain publication during their lives, their friends or heirs could hardly hope to restrain posthumous publication. But just such restraints began to hedge the work of the Sidney circle. In 1592, for example, the Herberts managed to curb the unauthorized publication of *Astrophil and Stella;* in 1595, Ponsonby secured the cancellation of Henry Olney's entrance of Olney's copy of the *Defense.*[76] Copyright had originated as a means of regulating competition within the Stationers' Company, but the interest of people as powerful as the Herberts, and the aura in which they managed to enshrine Sidney's texts—an aura not yet proper to the author-in-print, but proper rather to the aristocrat and to his public traces—helped Ponsonby imagine a copyright detached from its industrial origins and reconceived as a piece of heritable intellectual property, like old John Day's patent in the *A.B.C.* Of the various events, agents, circumstances, and forces conjoined in determining modern intellectual property, the coincidence of Sidney's death and of the promulgation of the Star Chamber decree in the summer of 1586 is surely among the more important.

The identification of particular authors with particular publishers is, of course, a staple of contemporary literary culture, in which a publishing house has a product line within which authors are made to function as brand names. Print is the enabling condition of this sort of literary identity. The various literary *cursus* transmitted by manuscript culture to early modern Europe, the conventions that unite several literary products behind a single *auctoritas,* receive powerful reinforcement by print culture, for individual works *look* a great deal like one another under the homogenizing influence of typography.[77] When the identity, the singularity, of an author like Sidney is given the visual support of a printer's house style across a range of distinct authorial products, the nature of the literary cursus is massively transformed. Ponsonby did not use the same printer for all of his Sidney texts—he assigned them variously, to John Windet, Thomas Creed, and Richard Field: his Sidney is nothing like, say, the Vintage—Random House Faulkner. But Field's 1598 printing of the *Arcadia,* together with the *Defense, Certain Sonnets, Astrophel and Stella,* and *The Lady of May* in a single volume, produced for Ponsonby during his last term as warden of the Stationers, completes the monumental consolidation both of Sidney's work as a single oeuvre, and of Ponsonby's commercial control of that oeuvre: bibliography underwrites the unity of the writing. This consolidation of the authorship *in* a typographically and commercially unified object—one of the distinguishing features of what is sometimes called, not too carefully, the commodification of authorship—is not, of course, the singular achievement of Ponsonby. When, in the 1580s, Wolfe made himself Alberico and Scipio Gentili's regular publisher and printer, he was not only cultivating a particular and distinguishing "line" of books, he was conferring on both brothers typographic and commercial identities peculiarly public and peculiarly stabilizing. Even this is not entirely an innovation. Printers had long cultivated stable relationships with particular scholars, employing them as editors or press correctors—one thinks of Aldus's relations with Erasmus, or Wolfe's relations with Petruccio Ubaldini, his proofreader for Italian books and the author of several histories issued by Wolfe in Italian— and although it is a small step from resident editor to house author in terms of the organization of a working print shop, this small step helped produce one of the most important of modern transformations in the sociology of authorship.

That "poet" is made a "title" by the combined agencies of Sidney, Ponsonby, and Greville is an important step toward making an "owner" of an
"author" (giving him or her a title *in* a work), but this latter development,
however uneven, was still very far from complete. English authors had not
yet grappled their own economic interests onto the internally stressed book
trade. M. A. Shaaber once supposed that signs of such a relocation of interest might be found in the Stationers' Register as early as the 1590s: he
sought evidence of authors functioning as publishers, inserting themselves
into the established structures of the Stationers' Company to exert a controlling influence on the marketing of their works.[78] He had little success.
He accumulated a list of only nine instances in which authors would seem
to have taken over as publishers of their own works—books designated by
their imprints as having been printed "by" a stationer "for" an author.[79] Four
of these books, three of them published in the next century, are works that
register the abiding friction between royal patent and stationer's copyright (a
problem to be taken up in chapter 4): Arthur Golding's translation of *An epit-
ome of Froissart* (1608), printed for his son, Peter; George Wither's *Hymnes
and songs of the Church* (1623); Philip Rosseter's *Book of ayres* (1601), "to be
solde at his house" according to the imprint; and Peter Bales's *The writing
schoole-master* (1590). In the first two of these instances, the authors had
direct royal patents; they had found cooperative stationers—Wither, as will
be seen, with some difficulty—who would print and distribute their books.
Rosseter's and Bales's books are another matter. Rosseter's book would have
infringed Thomas Morley's music patent had it not been printed, according
to the imprint, "by the assent of T. Morley." It would seem that Rosseter
or Short, the printer who had registered the copy, had made some special
accommodation with Morley, who had succeeded to Byrd and Tallis's music
patent. Indeed, it may well be that the device of printing the book "privately"
was Short's way of getting around the patent: the imprint seems to indicate,
however disingenuously, that the book is not *really* a commercial production.
This is roughly the explanation offered by Kirschbaum for the marketing of
Bales's book: "perhaps, the stationer's fear of selling a book that might be regarded as the infringement of a privilege accounts for the book's being sold by
the author."[80] *The writing schoole-master* is hardly a monument to authorial
property: it was entered to Thomas Orwin, with an unusual array of qualifications and authorizations, in December 1590, five months after Timothy
Bright secured the patent in all works on shorthand. The unusual marketing
arrangements seem to represent an attempt to evade, or to accommodate,
Bright's privilege. The author is an instrumental convenience in regulatory
struggles being carried on within the book trade.

Other books on Shaaber's list infringe no patents. The imprints of both John Speidell's *Geometricall extraction* (1616) and the same author's *New logarithmes* (1619) indicate that the books could be purchased only at the author's house—a small intrusion on a traditional province of English stationers, though not uncommon on the continent where tutors often sold textbooks to supplement their incomes.[81] Even in England, bookselling was not, after all, as strictly controlled as other stationers' functions: many of London's booksellers—and bookbinders—were members of the Drapers' or Haberdashers' Company. John Taylor's *Pennyles pilgrimage* (1618) seems to represent a more substantial invasion of stationers' prerogatives than do Speidell's math books, having been "printed . . . at the charges of the Author" (A₂). Three books in four years—a small cluster of books, barely enough to warrant generalizations about major transformations in the commercial status of authors. Still, they constitute evidence that the book trade was adaptable, susceptible to improvised commercial arrangements, despite the effective persistence of the stationers' corporate monopoly. Before we can discern the changing status of authors within a developing book trade, the range and motives of the stationers' adaptations in the aftermath of John Wolfe's reformation need further assessment.

Such assessment might begin with the remaining books on Shaaber's list, Jacques le Moyne's *Clef des champs* and Petruccio Ubaldini's *Discourse concerninge the Spanishe fleete.* Ubaldini, Wolfe's proofreader for Italian books, had no part in the sales of the *Discourse* and the book was entered to Wolfe in 1590, so it represents no particular development of authorial property. What was unusual in the case is that the book was to be sold by Augustin Ryther, not himself a stationer, who had engraved the plates for the *Discourse.* Le Moyne was also an engraver; and his book of illustrations, *La clef des champs,* was not only printed "for" him, according to the imprint, it was registered to him. The entrance was doubly unusual: Le Moyne was not a stationer, and the entrance in 1587 lagged publication by a year. Again, it is difficult to assess such arrangements with a practitioner of an "adjacent" craft. It may be that the stationers were extending a courtesy to Le Moyne—in 1558–59, we can find a book similarly registered to the draper John Wight. It may be that practitioners of adjacent trades, aware of the highly developed protectionism of the stationers, were willing to pay the company a fee for the "market insurance" of registration, a bargain really. Or it may be that Le Moyne had had to admit to having committed some form of infringement of stationers' rights and to forfeit the cost of registration as a token of submission to their authority.[82] At any rate, there is no reason to suppose anything like a flap ensued over *La clef des champs*, the entrance of which, like the arrangement with Ryther for the sales of the *Discourse concerninge the Spanishe fleete* or the arrangements to print for such authors as Speidell or Taylor, attests to the stationers willingness to accommodate their "suppliers" as long as such accommodations did not seriously challenge the stationers' individual and corporate dominance of the market in books.

What is important about the entrance to Le Moyne is that it suggests that stationer's copyright sheds in this instance its "internal" character, loses its status as expression of the stationers' corporate identity, and becomes—like John Day's privilege—transferable, itself a commodity. This is momentous. It is also not so isolated an instance as it would seem. For there were other markets, other adjacent professions that exerted transforming pressures on the stationers' mechanisms of self-regulation. Those adjacencies and transformations will be taken up in the next chapters.

CHAPTER THREE

MONOPOLIES COMMERCIAL AND DOCTRINAL

Copyright and censorship have really nothing whatever to do with
one another

R. B. McKerrow, *An Introduction to
Bibliography for Literary Students*

In an important essay on the English book trade in the eighteenth century,
John Feather describes the political context in which the Statute of Anne
was promulgated. In my introduction, I suggested that parliamentary resistance to the steady appeals of the booksellers for renewal of licensing was
primarily an expression of antimonopolistic sentiment; Feather points out
other reasons for refusing the booksellers. He argues that the continuation
of licensing began to constitute a threat to the increasing power of the Commons. "Political quarrels inevitably took a printed form; there was no other
medium through which the parties could address their ultimate master, the
electorate."

> The problem was whether everything . . . could be freely dis-
> cussed, and, if not, where the boundary lines were to be drawn;
> these boundaries would have to be delimited by the courts, since
> there was no other statute law on the subject or any realistic
> hope of new legislation. In other words, although the book and
> newspaper trades had to take risks, so too did the government for
> fear that its opponents would be acquitted if they were brought to
> trial.[1]

The passage of the Statute of Anne in 1710, which winnows ideological surveillance from the regulation of intellectual property, was, then, a gamble. Parliament risks freedom of speech—specifically, each parliamentary faction risks the eloquence of its opponents—in order to preserve the independence of a public sphere (a sphere that was increasingly the specific domain of parliamentary authority) from judicial scrutiny.[2] Authorial property—which signals, above all, the growing power of the electorate—emerges when Parliament suddenly finds it expedient to curtail the crude ideological surveillance of licensing. It is worth noting at what distance this account stands from Foucault's narrative. For Foucault authorship is constituted, first, by the mechanisms of penal appropriation. But the Statute of Anne tells another story: it reconstitutes authorship—albeit a very particular proprietary *form* of authorship—as part of an abridgment of penal appropriation.

This politic consecration of the public domain as the sphere of free speech not only secured the sway of Parliament, it also had the limited polemical effect of making Parliament look good. (The *championship* of free speech is arguably always the champion's power play.) In *Donaldson v. Becket,* the Whig case for the appellants insists on the image of a past blighted by the censor. Again, John Dalrymple:

> Sir John then stated the history of the institution of the Stationers
> Company. He said, it was instituted in the reign of Philip and
> Mary, princes who ruled with a despotic sway; that they, like every
> other despotic prince, wished to crush the liberty of the press;
> the booksellers, however, acquiesced in the Act, because such of
> them as were members of the Stationers Company were benefited
> by it.[3]

The pallor of "acquiesced" should be noted, for it betrays the tints of Dalrymple's description. Though no protests are recorded, one can fairly assume with what dismay unincorporated booksellers, in the suburbs or outside London, would have contemplated the terms of the 1557 Stationers' charter:

> That no person within the realm of England or its dominions shall
> practice or exercise, himself, through his agents, servants, or any
> others, the art or mystery of printing of any book or any other
> thing for sale or commerce within this realm of England or its do-
> minions, unless that person be, at the time of the aforementioned
> printing, a member of the community of the aforementioned art
> or mystery of Stationery in the aforementioned city [of London].[4]

Surely this was a triumph for the ninety-seven London stationers thus chartered. But the achievement of a London monopoly is mentioned no-where in the various retrospectives of *Donaldson v. Becket.* Dalrymple's formulation is unspecific; its purpose is to conjure the vague image of an exploitative inner circle colluding with a sinister monarchy: "the charter granted to that company was a charter enacting a body of licensers, sued for on a principle of interest, and granted by the Crown on a principle of policy."[5] It is worth noting that Dalrymple slightly shifts his ground here. Here the booksellers "sue" and the Crown grants; earlier he had asserted that the booksellers had acquiesced in the crushing designs of "princes who ruled with a despotic sway." Either representation suited the ends of the case for Donaldson; the accuracy of neither was challenged in the course of the trial. But surely these representations deserve the interroga-tion of anyone interested in the history of cultural production and dissem-ination, and the place of will in that history. We turn now to the relation between the monarch and the monopolist, between ideological and com-mercial regulation.

Censorship and the Stationers' Charter

In chapter 2, I mentioned that three regulatory mechanisms impinged on the activities of stationers once they were incorporated: license, patents, and registration. (Of course, there is a fourth, just mentioned—the charter of the Stationers' Company itself, which restricts the book trade to London to be-gin with, making possible the smooth functioning of licensing and the com-mercial efficiency of the registration system.) When Henry VIII instituted licensing in 1530, he was adding a flexible system of ideological regulation to the less agile one of the previous decade. The anti-Lutheran censorship of the mid-1520s had singled out particular books for confiscation and burning, but even a skeptical reading of Foxe's *Acts and Monuments* indicates that, for all its persistent violence, the campaign against heretical publishing had only limited success.[6] Moreover, as Henry's own position with respect to ec-clesiastical polity began to shift, it became clear that simple "indexing," the proscription of particular books, would be an insufficiently agile regulatory device. Although he issued a proclamation in the early spring of 1529 pro-hibiting the import, sale, or possession of some fifteen books, he quickly saw the need for systematic and preemptive scrutiny of all books prior to print-ing; so in 1530 Henry issued yet another proclamation, this time providing for a diocesan licensing system.[7] That system was further elaborated in the

1538 proclamation, the interpretation of which so exercised both Pollard and Albright.

Neither Pollard nor Albright contested the importance of the controls instituted in the 1530s: from this time forth, print was to be distinguished among the several linguistic domains as the most fully subject to political surveillance. The 1538 requirement "that no person or persons in this realm, shall from henceforth print any book in the English tongue, unless upon examination made by some of his Grace's Privy Council, or other such as his highness shall appoint, they shall have license so to do" institutes a new analogy: the regularities of the printed word, the fixities, recurrences, and precise replications of print become symbolically continuous with the plenary surveillance to which early modern state authority tends.[8] Henry inaugurates the era of textual and ideological corrigenda. This is not to say that the press may be taken simply as an agent of royal power; there was always an opposition press (though it was never so vociferous as during the reign of Mary Tudor).[9] Nor is it to suggest that censorship was new to England: it may be traced to the campaigns of Richard II and Henry IV against the Lollard heresy.[10] When Lollardry closed in on London in the early sixteenth century, text proscription was revived. But it is worth noting how Tudor censorship eventually adjusted the nature of ideological regulation. Earlier proscriptions had named authors and titles that were to be neither sold nor possessed: that is, it had designated author and book in order to constrain readers and booksellers. The licensing of the 1530s and after turns the focus of censorship onto the press, which becomes the central site of criminality. This is a significant novelty: the first Tudor censorship statute thus responds not only to the ideological crisis of Protestantism, but also to the specific technological challenge of the press, which had extended and thereby effectively transformed the provenance of heresy, which could now be efficiently spread among nonproximate populations. (Sixteenth-century heresy, after all, *constitutes* groups, whereas earlier English heresy had spread for the most part within groups already constituted.) But, having transformed the sociology of ideological challenge, the press also provided for a transformation of ideological control. The name of the heretical author had appeared on the list of banned books, but the author was too slippery for much Tudor regulation; what licensing seeks to control— what even the ecclesiastical censors of the 1520s seek to control—is the market in printed heresy.[11] Indeed the proscriptions in the proclamations of both 1526 and 1529 are organized by title; the names of authors are included only occasionally and they serve a nearly diacritical function.[12] In part this is a response to anonymous publication (itself considerably facilitated by the technology of the press): one can only securely index heretical books by title. The press changes the cultural situation of heresy, which is now as much *in books* as it was once in the souls or mouths of heretics: thus the reduced emphasis on both the reader and the author within Tudor ideological regulation and the inscription—the impression, rather—of the license upon the title page of the printed book. Licensing is specifically, and quite consequentially, a *press* censorship.

The specification may be illustrated from the 1538 proclamation. The prologue to the proclamation broods on the difficulty of fixing the "regulatory object": in a long absolute construction, the king is described as

> esteeming . . . that by occasion of sundry printed books in the
> English tongue that be brought from outward parts, and by
> such like books as have been printed within this his realm, set
> forth with privilege, containing annotations and additions in the
> margins, prologues, and calendars, imagined and invented as well
> by the makers, devisers, and printers of the same books, as by
> sundry strange persons called Anabaptists and Sacramentaries,
> which be lately come into this realm, where some of them do
> remain privily unknown, and by some his highness' subjects,
> using some superstitious speeches and rash words of erroneous
> matters, and fanatical opinions, both in their preachings and
> familiar communications, whereby divers and many of his loving
> simple subjects have been induced and encouraged, arrogantly
> and superstitiously, to argue . . . to the reproach and vituperation
> of this said whole realm and church.[13]

Where is offense located? There is the offense *of* texts: the importation of (heretical) books in English; the printing of "privileged" books rendered heterodox by the addition of heretical marginalia or prefatory material.[14] The offense of texts shades off toward the offense of those persons who offend by *means* of texts—the makers and devisers of such perverting extratexts; the printers of these adulterated texts. The offense of those agents of writing in turn blurs into that of those who offend by word of mouth—immigrant heretics (whom the terms of proclamations make partly responsible for the adulterated texts, but whose agency seems to extend beyond the realm of the printed word) and voluble native heretics. The list makes clear how unstable was the field to be regulated. There is, in fact, no absolutely central object, no axial text or verbal agent: at best, there is a "privileged" book, passably orthodox in its manuscript form, but transformed by the imprint of the press into something insinuating and dangerous. Still, the regulatory process imposes a new order on the discourse, for it not only polices the discursive field, it imposes upon it an official *style*. Returning to a familiar portion of the proclamation, we can see how regulation constitutes the printed book as its object, and specifies the structure of authority imprinted on the very page itself:

> Item, that no person or persons in this realm shall from hence-
> forth print any book in the English tongue, unless upon examina-
> tion made by some of his grace's Privy Council, or other such as
> his highness shall appoint, they shall have license so to do; and yet
> so having, not to put these words *cum privilegio regali,* without
> adding *ad imprimendum solum,* and that the whole copy, or else
> at the least the effect of his license and privilege be therewith
> printed, and plainly declared and expressed in the English tongue
> underneath them; nor from henceforth shall print or bring into
> this his realm any books of divine Scripture in the English tongue
> with any annotations in the margin, or any prologue or additions in
> the calendar or table, except the same be first viewed, examined,
> and allowed by the King's highness or such of his majesty's council,
> or other, as it shall please his grace to assign thereto, but only the
> plain sentence and text, with a table or repertory instructing the
> reader to find readily the chapters contained in the said book,
> and the effects thereof;[15] nor shall henceforth print any book of
> translations in the English tongue unless the plain name of the
> translator thereof be contained in the said book; or else that the
> printer will answer for the same as for his own privy deed and act,
> and otherwise to make the translator, the printer, and the setter
> forth of the same, to suffer punishment, and make fine at the
> King's will and pleasure.[16]

The recurrent emphasis on "plainness"—the plain declaration of license, the plain presentation of Scripture, the plain name of the translator—expresses the royal will to administer the discursive field. Plainness aims systematically to distribute responsibilities among printer, licenser, and translator, and *also* to distinguish text from gloss. On the title page, then, the conjunction of advertising and license, commerce and control, is henceforth "plainly declared and expressed."

On the other hand, censorship organized around author and reader, as opposed to this press-centered licensing, was occasionally reasserted during the next decades, as the early Tudor monarchy sought every possible means of controlling political dissent and of suppressing whatever registered as heresy at any given moment.[17] One of Henry VIII's last proclamations (8 July 1546) combines licensing and indexing, press censorship and policing of readers. It forbids possession of the New Testament in English as well as books by Tyndale, Wycliff, Coverdale, and eight others; it further forbids the possession of books "containing matter contrary to the King's majesty's book called *A Necessary Doctrine and Erudition for any Christian Man*"; it requires royal license for all import of books (this restates the terms of the 1538 proclamation) and mayoral scrutiny of all native imprints; and it stipulates "that from henceforth no printer do print any manner of English book, ballad, or play, but he put in his name to the same, with the name of the author and the day of the print."[18]

Edwardian censorship was a somewhat different matter. After a brief experiment with a relatively free press under Somerset's protectorate, the Crown reasserted its prerogative: though nothing so inflexible as a simple proscription of particular texts or authors would serve Somerset's more earnestly Reforming purposes, in 1549 we find him trying to establish a press censorship by restoring Henry's licensing system.[19] It is an indication of the difficulties of implementing such a system—and not only an indication of Mary's characteristic style of rule—that a month after her accession she herself undertook the responsibility for licensing all printing and all dramatic performances in 1553.[20] Two years after that, she turned back to the crude specificities of proscription; in the summer of 1558, she proclaimed the death penalty for possession of seditious or heretical books.[21]

This regulatory history provides one of the crucial contexts for the incorporation of the Stationers' Company by charter in 1557. The original charter was destroyed in the Fire of London and the copy made in 1684 includes interpolations designed to strengthen the rights of registration, but there is no reason to doubt the fidelity of the transcription to the original terms of the opening.[22] The charter describes incorporation, first, as a response to sedition and heresy:

> The king and queen to all to whom etc. greeting. Know ye that
> we, considering and manifestly perceiving that certain seditious
> and heretical books rhymes and treatises are daily published and
> printed by divers scandalous malicious schismatical and heretical
> persons, not only moving our subjects and lieges to sedition and
> disobedience against us, our crown and dignity, but also to renew
> and move very great and detestable heresies against the faith and
> sound catholic doctrine of Holy Mother Church, and wishing

> to provide a suitable remedy in this behalf, of our special grace
> and from our certain knowledge and mere motion we wil, give
> and grant [here follows a list of the stationers of London] they
> from hence forth may be in fact, deed, and name one body by
> themselves for ever, and one perpetual community incorporated.[23]

The charter articulates the legal status of the company, provides for its gover-
nance, and then goes on to endow the company with some extremely valuable
powers. The incorporation charter grants the company a perpetual monopoly
on printing and commerce in books throughout the realm and confers wide
police powers on the company master and wardens: they may search the
premises of any printer, binder, or bookseller in the kingdom for unlawfully
printed books; they may confiscate and burn any such books; and they may
imprison for three months without bail anyone who may attempt to hinder
them in their exercise of these rights of search and seizure.[24] By "deputizing"
the master and wardens, Mary created in the company an ideological police;
by localizing the book trade, she kept police headquarters where she could
easily keep tabs on it.

Of course, the terms of the charter were a boon to the members of the
company: the creation of a London monopoly was an immeasurable economic advantage. Indeed, several aspects of the charter seem to have very
little to do with ideological surveillance. For example, the master and wardens of the company may confiscate not only heretical and seditious books,
but also books printed or sold by non-members; not just those who print
heresy but also those who infringe on the company monopoly are subject to
imprisonment and fines. This is indeed extraordinary: the charter of the City
of London conferred the right to practice any trade whatsoever on its citizens;
the stationers' charter abridged that right. Other companies aspired fully to
monopolize given trades, but few acquired extensive powers to enforce such
monopolies. It might be argued that these rights were offered as compensation to the stationers for their assistance in royal ideological surveillance, but
this would be to prejudge a more fundamental question, since it presumes
that the charter was offered to the stationers by the Crown, not sued for by
the stationers themselves.

This was Greg's presumption—"The Charter of the Stationers' Company
is now commonly regarded as in the main a master-stroke of Elizabethan
politics"—and it was A. W. Pollard's as well:

> Henceforth the Crown could control the whole printing trade.
> Henceforth every printer was known and under strict regulation,

and a body of expert detectives [Barkers, Wolfes] was enlisted
in the Government service, able to make a shrewd guess as to
whence the type in which any pamphlet or bill was printed had
been obtained, and with their own personal interest in helping to
suppress any illicit work.[25]

This historiography of the book trade draws energy from what might be
called the Cult of the Bloody Mary, receiving perhaps its strongest statement
in Sir John Dalrymple's case for the appellants in *Donaldson v. Becket*: "the
booksellers acquiesced in the Act, because such of them as were members
of the Stationers Company were benefitted by it."[26] But an earlier polemical
historian, Christopher Barker, who had every reason to exaggerate the influence of royal will on the affairs of the Stationers' Company and to downplay
the venality of its members, offered a different glimpse of the incorporation
in his 1582 retrospective: "In the tyme of Q. Marie the Company procured a
Charter for the establishing of a corporation; in the which the Queene gyveth
aucthoritie to all Stacioners, and none other, to print all laufull bookes."[27]
Graham Pollard made the most persuasive case for the stationers' initiative
in securing corporate status. If the charter was imposed on the Stationers'
Company from above, he remarks, "it was the first and last City Company to
be so favoured."[28] Many of the largest London companies had obtained their
charters in the late fifteenth century; customarily the process of incorporation by royal charter was an expensive one and, as Pollard rightly asserted, the
process was always instigated by the company.[29] But if one can speak with no
security of Crown initiative in the incorporation of the Stationers, neither can
one properly speak of the monopoly of English printing by an incorporated
guild located in London as the product of a momentary and serendipitous
complement of tradesmen's economic motives and a monarch's ideological
agenda. A variety of significant historical dispositions shape this instance. In
order fully to explain the regulation of intellectual property and production
we need to speak of more than the invention of printing, the spread of Protestantism, and the consequent pressure toward ideological policing; we need
also to attend to the rise of corporations, the growth of urban government,
and the flourishing of mercantilist thought within European polities.

The pattern of English royal endorsement of localized monopolies is old
enough to have become part of the inner logic of kingly power. As early as
the twelfth century, towns all over Europe strove to secure compulsory or
"staple" trading within their confines by merchants passing through the area;
to this end they appealed for the sanction of royal or aristocratic authority.[30]
Markets and fairs had a tendency to spring up at crossroads in the border

areas *between* town jurisdictions—and the royal licensing of such rural markets both marked and guaranteed the steady permeation of the English countryside by centralized royal authority—but despite the proliferation of rural
markets one of the constants of early modern economic development on into
the seventeenth century is urban effort to restrain rural commerce.[31] Municipal appeals for royal support in this early urbanization of the economy
establish a special alliance of town and Crown, an alliance particularly powerful in England.[32] In most aspects, the late medieval English monarchy was
stronger than continental analogues, so a tradition of royal authority over the
economy is not surprising.[33] But it is important to recognize the relationship,
the mutuality that secures the simultaneous consolidation of royal economic
jurisdiction and the rationalization of local economies. By the logic of late
medieval economic development, innovations in royal administration and in
urban economic regulation collude.

Commercial markets expanded in the thirteenth century; the subsequent
growth of urban oligarchies led to a legislative explosion in the late fourteenth
century, when towns all over Europe began to extend their own political
authority. Older urban economic policies—local quality control and regulation of alien trading—developed a newly restrictive character at this time.[34]
The Malthusian pressures of famine and plague in the fourteenth century
provided an overwhelming and decisive contribution to this regulatory tendency.[35] The crude economic effects of these pressures were a sudden collapse of internal markets, currency instability, and dislocations of agricultural
production (most particularly the beginnings of the enormously consequential shift from food production to sheep grazing); the political effect was to
augment the demands for economic regulation and to increase the authority
of the Crown to make such interventions.[36] The king began to grant national
monopolies in particular manufactures to individual towns during this period;
in the next century, bold protection of the wool trade provoked requests from
other industries for similar protections.[37] Thus there is no novelty whatsoever
in the Tudor formulation of its royal prerogative in 19 Henry VII, c. 7: "No
masters, wardens and fellowships of crafts or misteries nor any of them, nor
any rulers of gilds and fraternities [shall] take upon them to make any acts
or ordinances, nor to execute any acts or ordinances by them afore made, in
diminution of the prerogative of the King, nor of other, against the common
profit of the realm." Although this sort of nationalized protectionism is a distinguishing feature of the Tudor regime, the principles behind it had long
been in place.[38]

This history of centralization was crucially shaped by the craft guilds that
emerged in late thirteenth-century England—perhaps modeled on the guilds

established somewhat earlier in London—and proliferated during the fourteenth century.[39] The Crown quickly endorsed the atomization of economic
association *by trade*: from the reign of Edward III, the craft guild becomes
both the chief instrument and the chief object of economic regulation, and it
is instrumental specifically to the Crown. The statute of 1363 requiring that
"artificers and men of mysteries shall each choose his own mystery before the
next Candlemas, and having so chosen it, he shall henceforth use no other"
may have been a merely local intervention—a response to an appeal to block
the powerful association of the seemingly heterogeneous pepperers, spicers,
and canvas dealers as the grocers' company—but it indicates the focus of royal
power on and in the new guilds.[40] In many cases the craft guilds became the
fundamental structure of local political organization, as some civic constitutions were deliberately reorganized to accommodate them. Economic competition between town and country, once manifest in the efforts of towns to
regulate rural commerce, now showed itself in the effort of urban craft guilds
to control rural production, and the London guilds were especially successful
in securing royal support for these efforts.[41] Thus "as early as the 14th century, the powers of a number of London companies were extended more or
less completely over the whole country."[42] This "urbanization of regulation"
continued and eventually extended beyond the industrial sector to include
the commercial sector.[43]

Two fourteenth-century tendencies, then—the royal control increasingly
exerted through the local guild structure, and the growing pattern of regulation favoring the urban economy—and a third, somewhat later, pattern—that
of allowing London preeminence among urban economies—became normative during the sixteenth century.[44] Thus, however consequential were the
effects of the incorporation of the Stationers, those effects were by no means
unprecedented. Indeed, because of the power of London and the privilege
of her citizens, the Stationers' charter is not, in and of itself, *quite* so consequential as it may seem, for the London stationers already possessed a considerable advantage over the provincial booksellers. Because English printing
transformed a bespoke trade into a wholesale trade, it doubly favored those
stationers based in London—first, because wholesaling is capital intensive
and London was the greatest center of merchant capital in England; second,
because, as Graham Pollard pointed out, London citizenship carried with it
an exemption from tolls throughout the kingdom, a particular advantage for
London mechants as trading volume increased.[45] Thus, owing both to the nature of the new industrial process and to the privileges already arrogated to
the London trade, many of the privileges conferred on the London stationers
by their charter were already effectively in place many years earlier.

One may now ask how the economic motives of the stationers and the force of royal regulatory habit complement the ideological themes of the preamble to the Stationers' charter. Pollard supposes that the charter was based closely on the company's *petition* for a charter: the company accounts record an outlay of eighteen shillings "for ii tymes wrytinge of our boke before yt was sygned be the kynge and the quenes majestie highnes."[46] He supposes that the company must have represented its appeal for monopoly privileges as a disinterested offer of service to the Crown, perhaps hoping that by taking this tack they could reduce the customary costs of securing the charter. This seems plausible enough. It must be added nonetheless that to admit this argument would not necessarily be to reverse Greg's description of the incorporation, to propose it as a masterstroke of *company* politics. The claim of disinterest is Tudor public-discourse-as-usual: the misrecognition of subjugation as service, or of the economic as the affective, calls for no strenuous demystification. The Crown stood to gain immediate revenue, a corporate source of future revenues, and possibly an organization capable of securing a measure of ideological control; the company won its monopoly (at least in principle) and possibly acquired some power to enforce that monopoly. In the short run the incorporation gave the Crown a means, and the company a right, to mount an assault against the thriving trade in Protestant books being smuggled in from the continent. As they do in the passage of, say, the Licensing Acts of the 1640s, the ideological and the economic embrace; it remains uncertain who initiated the embrace.

As we shall see, this would be a lasting romance within English print culture; it needs to be said here that it was already an old one. Not only can we free the incorporation of the stationers from confinement within a history of censorship; even the Henrician licensing statutes may be given an alternative historiography. The charter is only a culmination of a history of attentive industrial adjustments to ecclesiastical and royal impositions.

To begin with the obvious: Printing unsettled an established book trade. A single organized guild of manuscript book producers had existed in England since perhaps 1422 or even earlier, and guilds for writers of court-hand, writers of text-hand, and illuminators had existed severally or in various combinations since at least the middle of the fourteenth century.[47] The shift toward wholesaling forced a relatively stable trade into a commercial reorganization: one way in which print reconstituted literary consumption was by reconstituting the marketplace in books.[48] This reconstitution can be discerned on the very title pages of books. Not unprecedented within manuscript culture, but institutionalized within print culture, the title page advertises: it proposes the ready-made book, instigating a literary transaction that begins with purchase. The manuscript book comes into being at the demand of the purchaser; the printed book anticipates an uncertain desire, which it must quicken. Printer, bookseller, and eventually author must become the producers of desire. But printing not only transformed commercial relations within book culture (and their affects); it transformed the relations of production within the industry. As has already been mentioned, the book trade became suddenly quite capital intensive: although the new craft promised to lower the price of individual books, it brought significant new production costs— and the capitalist uneasiness that attends thereon. Plant was expensive, the costs of producing and maintaining sizable stocks of books were new and substantial, and information costs were high—as they always are in an expanding market.[49] But what must have been the greatest node of unease among the early stationers of London is the simple fact that printing was not an indigenous craft. Caxton was an Englishman, but almost all the other early printers in England were "strangers."[50]

The attitude to strangers—craftsmen from abroad, in the technical parlance of City government (as opposed to "foreigners," craftsmen coming up from the country)—was mixed. The Crown recognized the need for the development of *new* industries and was therefore moved to encourage recruitment of immigrant expertise. But the entrenched craft organizations worked steadily for exclusive labor legislation of many sorts—one of the constants of Tudor economic regulation is the attempt to restrict entry into the labor force, even in the face of growing unemployment—and the restriction of alien production and trade was a particular goal.[51] Craft hostility to immigrant labor burst out in 1517 in the riots of the Evil Mayday; this popular violence was answered in the course of the next few years by statutes designed to restrain alien economic activity.[52]

When alien printers had first come to London, they had simply set up in the suburbs and liberties, outside the jurisdiction of the London company. For two centuries the suburbs had swelled with rural craftsmen coming up from the counties, with those natives of the city who could not afford to set up shop within the city, and with the alien craftsmen who paved the way for their printer brethren—so that by the turn of the sixteenth century much of London's manufacturing was going on in the areas outside of municipal jurisdiction.[53] Printers had been under less pressure to locate in the suburbs than were most strangers, for although hostility to immigrant labor crystallized as law in a parliamentary act of 1484, that act specifically excepted any alien engaged in text-writing, illuminating, printing, binding, or bookselling.[54] Nonetheless, as the printers prospered, they drifted into the city proper: by the end of the first decade of the sixteenth century, most of them had moved into the city. Perhaps they moved in order to acquire the privileges of membership in the Stationers' Company (though no records survive of any of these men being made free of the company); perhaps they had achieved sufficient acceptance among the other members of the trade to enjoy the logistical convenience of a city location. No doubt the stationers of London realized that it was going to be cheaper in the long run to work with skilled resident immigrants than to compete with printers in Antwerp or in Paris whose output dominated the early English market in printed books. We do not know whether alien printers and booksellers suffered from the Evil Mayday, but there is no reason to think that they did. What seems to have happened is that the first generation of printers managed to integrate themselves into the community of native tradesmen during the first two decades of the century, at which point the trade apparently closed ranks somewhat against new immigrant labor. To be sure, the twenties saw a remarkable triumph for the London stationers: at a time when provincial presses were proliferating on the continent, English provincial printing virtually died out.[55]

At any rate, whatever privileges alien printers and booksellers had originally enjoyed began to evaporate in the following decades. Anti-alien legislation of 1523 and 1529 does not perpetuate the exemptions of the act of 1484; and in 1534 a new act, directed specifically at the book trade, firmly rescinded the earlier exemption.[56] Aliens were no longer permitted to retail books printed abroad. Such economic intervention is clearly coordinated with government efforts to suppress heresy, which was being disseminated largely in books imported from the continent; to this extent the 1534 act is part of the legislative campaign of which Henry's Act of Supremacy is the center.[57] But in fact the 1534 Act for Printers and Binders of Books is likely to have been proposed by the stationers themselves. Certainly it is framed as a defense not of English piety but of English craft, a craft no longer dependent on foreign expertise: "many of this Realme being the Kynges naturall subjectes have geven theyme so dylygently to lerne and exercyse the seid craft of pryntyng that at this day there be within the Realme a greatt nombre conyng and expert in the seid science or craft of prynting as abyll to exercyse the seid craft in all poynts as any Stranger in any other Realme."[58] It would be wrong to represent this as a mere smokescreen for blunt ideological motives, for the act not only bars aliens from retailing imported books; it also proscribes the importation of books already bound, a restriction that is merely commercial in character.[59] Because the interests of the book trade were inextricably involved with those of church and state, the Act for Printers and Binders of Books fails to mark any distinction between ideological and economic policing.

This is not to say that the accord of these two aspects of policing was either complete or permanent.[60] Certainly doctrinal regulation and restraint of imports are not *necessarily* complementary. Late in 1534 the Convocation of Canterbury mandated the publication of an authorized English Bible, but no English printer was capable of such production: the Coverdale Bible, the first authorized English Bible, was printed in Cologne. In subsequent years, the Matthew Bible was printed in Antwerp, while the Great Bible was begun in Paris and completed, notoriously, in London only by relocating Regnault's plant, lock, stock, and barrel, in London. The history of Bible publishing suggests that the 1534 act instituted the most stringent possible restrictions consistent with the interests of a book trade determined to preserve its own stability. The booksellers preserved the right to import, but the restriction of imports to unbound sheets protected the London binders; the printers maintained a high level of monopoly control, with alien production a readily available option in instances where demand far exceeded supply.[61] Thus the act perfectly served the needs of an industry that was still adjusting to the difficulties of wholesale commerce in an uncertain market and that was indisposed to hazard rapid expansions of production.

That the accord of Crown and company provided for in the 1534 act was not permanent may be surmised from the failure of the stationers' first attempt to secure a charter, in March 1542. Significantly, they made their appeal to the Canterbury Convocation, proposing the book trade, presumably, specifically as an ideological apparatus. After more than fifteen years of assisting church and Crown in the restraint of heresy, the stationers were seeking official recognition of their services and perks. The Convocation referred the draft charter to the king, who denied it his endorsement; Cyprian Blagden supposes that in this instance the stationers had sought more than the king was willing to grant.[62] Shortly after the Convocation, Henry drafted a proclamation including a list of proscribed authors, reasserting licensing requirements (particularly for imported books), and—in a momentary reversal of an earlier position—insisting that it was the content of books that was being regulated and that licensers should not "be curious to mark who bringeth forth such books."[63] The proclamation entertains the possibility of shifting the center of censorship away from the book trade proper, thereby removing the fulcrum by which the stationers had gained their political leverage. But it is a *draft* proclamation; the industrial fulcrum remained.

Piracy and Privilege

The restraint on imports, the control of alien labor, the achievement of control over virtually all provincial markets—these do not exhaust the regulatory triumphs of the London book trade. Of perhaps slightly less importance to the history of the English book trade, but of overwhelming consequence for the evolution of intellectual property, was the birth of the printing privilege during this period.

Royal and ecclesiastical patronage was not always extended to the entire book trade; the context of "involved interest" benefited several printers and booksellers individually. In 1485, the Savoyard Peter Actor was created Stationer to the King and given unlimited right to import books and manuscripts, free of customs levies. The responsibilities and privileges of the office thus created are uncertain, but both grow steadily more clear and more broad during the reigns of Henry VIII and Edward VI.[64] The king's printer seems not to have been much called upon by his monarch until Pynson received the office, probably late in 1508; from 1509 until his death in 1530, Pynson regularly printed royal proclamations.[65] His successor was Thomas Berthelet, who received his office by patent and who, for his services as printer of virtually all royal proclamations, received a stipend of £4 a year.[66] Berthelet was to have had life tenure, but he seems, in fact, to have been deprived of his office: Richard Grafton, who in 1545 had become official printer to the Prince of Wales, assumed the title of king's printer upon Edward's accession. This time, the office was granted with a monopoly in addition to the salary: henceforth he was to have all printing of statute books.[67] The grant of an industrial monopoly is hardly surprising here, for by 1547 royal patronage of the stationers had taken the monopoly grant as its characteristic form. The monopoly in statute books was not even Grafton's first: together with his associate, Edward Whitchurch, Grafton had received monopolies—also by letters patent—in the printing of Latin and English primers (1535) and of church service books (1544). This particular form of patronage—the individualization of trade monopoly—is, precisely, the threshold of capitalist intellectual property. England crossed that threshold early in 1517.

But the approach to that threshold may be discerned in a particular sharpening of competition between Wynkyn de Worde and Pynson at the end of the first decade of the century. In 1509 both men printed translations of Sebastian Brandt's *Ship of Fools*—Pynson printing Alexander Barclay's verse, de Worde printing Henry Watson's prose. That de Worde's venture was somewhat aggressive may be inferred from a sentence in Watson's humble preface: "Consyderynge . . . that the prose is more famylyer unto every man than the rhyme. I HENRY WATSON, indygne and symple of understondynge, have reduced this present boke into our maternall tongue of Englyshe, out of Frensh, at the request of my worshypfull mayster wynkyn de worde, through the entycement & exhortacyon of the excellent pryncessw Margarete, Countesse of Rychemonde and Derby, and Grandame unto our moost naturell soverayne lorde kynge Henry the .viii." This is de Worde as much as Watson speaking. Not only is prose pitted against verse, de Worde's patron is pitted against Pynson's: de Worde had been styling himself printer to the Queen Mother for several years, and Watson's preface reasserts the connection as a means of countering Pynson's recent elevation to the post of king's printer. De Worde and Pynson began conspicuously to shadow each other, chiefly by each printing books that the other had first issued. This had become something of a habit with de Worde: in 1497–98, and several times thereafter, he reprinted Caxton's *Chronicle and Description of England* (1480). This is hardly a raid on Caxton's market share, for Caxton had been dead for five or so years when de Worde began to reprint the book.[68] But Pynson was very much alive when, in 1496, de Worde reprinted his *Dives et Pauper* of 1493. This seems not to have compromised Pynson's business very considerably, but it is hard to imagine that de Worde's Latin-English dictionary, *Ortus Vocabulorum* (1500), did not crowd Pynson's English-Latin *Promptorius Puerorum* of the previous year at least a bit. This sort of close mutual imitation of output is characteristic of industrial production in immature markets and, of course, it is difficult to assess the degree to which this kind of activity actually cut into either printer's market share—we know far too little about either demand or output at this stage in the history of English printing. Certainly no lasting animosity resulted, for the two men seem to have shared an edition of the *Royal Book* (STC 21430) in 1508. Yet once Pynson became king's printer he began to print books that must have been crucial to de Worde's business: in 1509 he printed de Worde's *Ortus Vocabulorum,* which de Worde had reissued in 1508; and in December 1510 he brought out the *Chronicle and Description* that de Worde had taken over from Caxton. It seems plausible to speak of this as genuinely competitive, for de Worde responded immediately, reprinting the *Promptorius Puerorum* (as the *Promptuarium Paruulorum*) within a month's time. Thereafter, this quiet jostling within the market continues sporadically until 1517, when de Worde printed the *Ship of Fools;* in the following year, a sermon by Richard Pace appeared with the following colophon:

> Impressa Londini anno verbi incarnati M.D.XVIII. idibus
> Novembris per Richardum Pynson regium impressorem cum
> privilegio ab rege indulto ne quis hanc orationem intra biennium
> in regno Angliae imprimat aut alibi impressam et importatam in
> eodem regno Angliae vendat.[69]

Cum privilegio: the authority of the Crown over the ground of English commerce, an authority that had slowly swelled over three centuries, was brought to bear on a very specific commodity.

The inspiration for Pynson's request of the Crown seems to have been a similar grant conferred, most likely, early in 1517: the colophon to Thomas Linacre's *Progymnasmata* advertises that work as "empryntyd . . . by John Rastell with the privylege of our most suverayn lord kyng henry the .VIII. grauntyd to the compyler therof. that noo man inthys hys realme sell none but such as the same compyler makyth pryntyd for the space of ii. yeere."[70] This may well be the earliest English grant of authorial rights of copy. *May* be: the language of the colophon is intriguingly ambiguous. In an early chapter of his *Early Tudor Drama,* A. W. Reed construes "the compyler" as a reference to Rastell; he takes it as a reference to Linacre in a later one.[71] I suppose the colophon to have referred to Rastell, for in the next few years, many such privileges were granted to stationers and very few to writers. But the matter need not be adjudicated. That a context sufficiently competitive to provoke suit for protection of the rights of copy is at least as important as a determination of the subject of protection. The Rastell/Linacre colophon reacts to the fact that, in the immediately preceding years, Pynson and de Worde had both been producing school grammars: Rastell—or Linacre—seems to have sought the royal protection to secure the *Progymnasmata* from the kind of competition that de Worde and Pynson were inflicting on each other. Royal authority, vested in the will of "the compyler," now takes up the work of regulating competition within the book trade.

This regulatory tactic was not unprecedented; on the other hand, neither was it native. Rastell—and Pynson in the following year—were borrowing techniques that had developed in the far more competitive Mediterranean printing markets. It seems hardly coincidental that the first English printing privilege in an individual book protects a work written by England's first teacher of Greek, physician to Henry VIII, a man who had come to Padua for medical training in 1496; who had befriended—to focus more precisely on Linacre's pivotal status—the Venetian printer, Aldus Manutius; who had translated Proclus into Latin for Aldus in 1499, and who, in the same year, had assisted with the Aldine edition of Aristotle in Greek. Linacre could have helped England across the threshold of capitalist intellectual property in 1517 precisely because he knew a good deal about the printing of Greek in Venice at the end of the previous century.

The Venetian connection is crucial, and not only because Venice was the printing capital of Europe by the end of the fifteenth century.[72] A highly developed municipal trade protectionism had flourished there; more particularly, because competition within the Venetian book trade had long been heated, a number of experiments at regulating that competition had already been undertaken there.[73] Indeed, state regulation of the Venetian press was precisely as old as the Venetian press itself. When John of Speyer brought printing to Venice in the 1460s, his first printing efforts (editions of Cicero's *Epistolae ad Familiares* and of Pliny's *Historia Naturalis*) so impressed the members of the Venetian Collegio that on September 18, 1469, they decreed, in response to his request, "for the next five years, let no one but Master John himself, however willing and capable, dare to engage in the said art of printing books within the noble city of Venice or its territories."[74] Note that the value of this decree was not merely economic, in any narrow sense, for it may well have been equally important as a sign of municipal favor and interest; the privilege confers *symbolic* singularity by means of the token of industrial monopoly, thus inviting both cultural patronage and industrial capital.[75] The latent economic value of the monopoly became obvious soon enough, for John of Speyer died in 1470, and—no doubt to the dismay of his brother and partner, Wendelin—his monopoly lapsed. By 1473 there were 134 presses operating in Venice.

The dynamics of the ensuing competition deserve comment: a few decades later, early English printing will reproduce them. One of the most prolific Venetian printers of the seventies, Nicholas Jensen, appropriated one of John of Speyer's original titles, the *Historia Naturalis,* which he printed in 1472. Jensen's choice is characteristic: one effect of the capital pressures on the new industry seems to have been a remarkable conservatism in the choice of titles, as would be seen later in the competitions between de Worde and Pynson.[76] Risking considerable competitive erosion of the marketplace for the security of concentrating in areas of proven demand, early printers frequently went out of business pursuing a fairly inelastic market for traditional manuscript titles rather than diversifying production. In 1473, output from Venetian presses dropped to 25 titles, after outputs of 63 titles for 1471 and 71 for 1472.[77] Since the obsessively conservative early Venetian press operated in a highly competitive local economy, one in which guild and state provided pockets of various industrial and trade protections, it is easy to see how the effects of market constriction might manifest themselves as much in an appetite for market monopoly as in a pressure for diversification of production.

The Collegio's next grant of a printing privilege, made on 1 September 1486, suggests how very mixed their intervention—how uncertain their relation to the new medium—could be:

> The Conciliar lords have considered and resolved that the
> aforementioned work [the *Rerum Venetarum Libri XXXIII*] of
> Marcantonio Sabellicus be given to a diligent printer to print and
> publish at his own expense as befits so fine a history, one that
> deserves to be immortal, and that no one else be allowed to have

the work printed either in Venice or her dominions under penalty
of the displeasure of the most serene Lord and the Council of
Fifty.[78]

Several historians have identified this as the first grant of authorial copyright,
yet the terms of the decree are not so simple.[79] It is the future printer who
will gain exclusive rights to print the work; for the author, the decree simply
secures publication. Venetian printers had not cultivated a market for works
of contemporary historiography—and they were loathe to take risks—so the
Collegio was making an extraordinary gesture of patronage on behalf of the
glory of the republic.[80] (In making these grants the Venetian patriciate had
found a new form of patronage, a new way of rewarding a cultural expertise that was distinctly Venetian. Note that, by constraining competition, it
transfers the costs of cultural patronage to the purchasers of books.) Their
intervention is confusing in that it encourages the printer to risk a venture
outside the usually narrow focus of early Venetian print production, and at
the same time safeguards him from competitive pressures that one would expect to inhibit only a more conventional project. The Collegio was clumsily
attempting both to stimulate demand and to regulate supply.

We are still far from modern copyright. Though the Collegio was praising the historian, it was protecting the printer: protection gravitates to the
manufacturer of a widely marketable object, not to the author. Six years later,
the Collegio shifted its support when it granted a privilege to Pierfrancesco
Tommai da Ravenna for his *Foenix*, a treatise on the art of memory.[81] This
privilege, dated 3 January 1492, stipulates that the work may be printed only
by a printer chosen by the author. In a gesture of explanation that marks
the slight uncertainty of the cultural moment, the grant invokes that legal
principle fundamental to the development of that particular conception of
copyright as an author's right (rather than as a social policy) *"ne alieni colli-
gant fructus laborum et vigiliarum suarum"* that the privilege was meant to
protect in this case.[82] The next printing privilege, granted three weeks later
to Joannes Dominicus Nigro, is similarly grounded—*"ne fructum laborum et
impensarum suarum alii opere et impensae expertes percipiant"*—but here
the Collegio was not rewarding authorship: Nigro was granted ten years' exclusive right to print two manuscripts that he had merely acquired.[83] So the
modern principle of intellectual or creative labor was only beginning to be
objectified by Venetian legislation.[84]

Although the grants of the nineties do not decisively establish a convention of authorial economic rights, they do record the emergence of new forms
of competition within book culture, for as the number of presses began once

more to increase, new irregularities seem to have cropped up. Two applications for printing privileges from March 1496 describe the practice, possibly widespread, of disaffected printshop workers absconding from their employers with the proofs from uncompleted editions, the proofs of which they sold to unscrupulous rival printers; the Collegio's privileges are now being sought as a response to forms of competition represented and, no doubt, increasingly experienced as industrial abuses.[85] Regulation slowly began to resolve nebulous competitive tensions into a constellation of rights. Nothing registers this transformation so uncannily as the events surrounding the publication, in Lyons, of a pocket edition of Virgil's *Opera*. Published in 1501, Balthazar de Gabiano's Virgil is a beautiful little book—this owing largely to its having been set in an elegant new typeface—and quite cheaply produced. These are perhaps equivocal virtues, since they are not exactly the fruits of de Gabiano's labor: his Virgil is almost an exact copy of that which had issued from the Aldine press a year earlier—the first book printed in italics.[86]

So in 1502 Aldus appealed to the authority of the republic. The Senate, not the Collegio, awarded him a privilege on the grounds of what he had done for scholarship, what labors he had been put to in the editorial and mechanical production of books, and *"necnon quantum impenderit impendatque in ipsa admodum et digna sua provincia"*—not least, how much money he had and would spend in his enterprise.[87] It was a grant for ten years' exclusive printing of works in Greek and of Latin works in italic (*"quos vulgo cursivos et cancellarios dicunt"*) characters.[88] This was not Aldus's first typographic monopoly: in 1496, he had received a twenty-year grant of exclusive rights to whatever he should choose to print in Greek and a monopoly in his own particular method of printing in Greek.[89] Two years later Nicola Vlasto and Gabriele Braccio da Brasichella each petitioned for, and received, exclusive rights in their own distinct methods of Greek typography. Braccio also received specific monopoly rights in four works (including Aesop's *Fables*), yet after bringing out two of them in a Greek cursive font remarkably similar, both in typeface and font design, to the Aldine Greek, he disappears from the historical record, and his business associates soon move from Venice to Milan.[90] But Aldus was remarkably well-connected by this time, and he seems to have been able to make the terms of his privilege stick; indeed, in 1499 he printed, in a collection of Greek letter-writers, some epistles of Phalaris included in Braccio's privilege, as if to crow over his triumph.[91] When Thomas Linacre joined the ranks of scholars engaged by Aldus between 1495 and 1498 to prepare a new Greek edition of Aristotle, he was joining in one of the most advanced philological projects of the Quattrocento; yet what was truly revolutionary about the Greek projects of the Aldine press was the unprece-

dented amount of protection that had been sought and secured on their behalf. Linacre is celebrated for having brought Greek studies to England, but
he bore more cultural capital than a language and a pedagogy; his cargo may
have included a regulatory mechanism, the revolutionary novelty of books
published *cum privilegio.*

This does not exhaust the importance of Linacre's Venetian connection. Aldus's small success at routing such competitors in Greek printing as
Gabriele Braccio no doubt inspired his most aggressive step, a 1501 application to the Collegio for a monopoly in his delicate new italic typeface. The
Collegio granted his suit in March and he inaugurated the typeface in the
following month.[92] The terms of this privilege stipulated that for ten years no
Venetian could print in italics nor could works printed abroad be imported
for sale. This latter proscription on infringing imports, a particularly intriguing one, was not new in 1501, for from the beginnings of the upsurge in
the granting of privileges in 1492, the monopolist was protected from both
unauthorized printing within the Venetian dominions and from unauthorized
sales of imported rival editions.[93] The scanty records of enforcement make
it impossible to determine why grants were made in such terms; that is,
one cannot be certain whether foreign competition had already become a
commercial problem, and so provoked these terms, or (as seems more likely)
whether the terms had been introduced into grants of printing monopolies by
analogy with commercial regulations long established within older industries.
At any rate, we can be sure that foreign competition was a real problem by
the *end* of 1501, by which time Baldassare de Gabiano, acting on behalf of
a Venetian publishing syndicate, the Compagnia d'Yvry, had reproduced the
Aldine Virgil in Lyons.

Shortly after the Lyons forgeries began to appear, Aldus's typefounder,
Francesco da Bologna, left Venice, probably lured away by Gershom Soncino of Fano. With his monopoly thus doubly at risk, Aldus went back to the
Venetian authorities in 1502, this time to the Senate and to the doge, for
confirmation of his privilege in italic typeface together with a slightly ridiculous extension of that privilege to include a monopoly on all Greek printing.[94]
The extension is surely a specific response to the loss of Francesco's services,
for Soncino claimed in 1503 that his new typefounder had designed and cut
all of Aldus's types, including the ingenious Greek fonts.[95] Aldus also made
an extraordinary appeal to the pope at this time, asking for an international
extension of the Venetian grants. His request was granted.[96] Though the papal decree vaguely detailed the works protected, it precisely and significantly
extended the geographical range of the protection: there was to be no printing of "counterfeits" within all of Italy (and there were special penalties for

counterfeiting within Rome and the papal states) and no importing of such counterfeits from outside of Italy. (The subsequent bull of Julius II extends the area of the primary prohibition, on printing, to all of Christendom.) That Aldus sought to reinforce his original privileges by appealing to these supplementary authorities is significant, for it suggests anxiety about the actual force inhering in the Collegio's original decree, an uncertainty about potential enforcement that manifests itself in an attempt to shore up legal expression.

Despite Aldus's efforts and what would seem the formidable protections he assembled, the "piracies" kept coming. In Fano, Soncino reproduced, with Francesco's help, the new italic typeface; in Lyons, the Aldine editions—of Virgil, Horace, Juvenal and Persius, Martial, Lucan, Terence, Propertius, Catullus and Tibullus—were hastily reproduced.[97] At the same time that he was petitioning the pope for "international" protection, Aldus sought other forms of economic self-defense. On 16 March 1503, he published a *Monitum* against the printers of Lyons identifying the manifold defects of the Lyonnaise editions: their textual errors, bad paper, and slovenly printing; their *Grandiusculae . . . deformes,* absence of ligatures (the Aldine italic had at least sixty-five), and—resourceful chauvinism—the unpleasantly "gallic" quality of the Lyonnaise typeface.[98] Aldus intended to equip the consumer to detect the imitations by their flaws, but the international book-buying public showed no particular loyalty to the Aldine productions. In his attempt to mobilize a consumerist connoisseurship, Aldus succeeded primarily in proof-reading for his competitors—in subsequent editions, the Lyonnaise printers emended the errors noted in the *Monitum.* Still, he was again pioneering in the attempt to shape the market for the printed word.

We have here a Janus-moment in the history of the book. Scorning the absence of ligatures in the Lyonnaise counterfeits, Aldus defends an aesthetic of nostalgia, for the ligature expresses an effort to disguise the reductive mechanism of the press, to reproduce the synthetic freedoms of scribal handicraft. But for all this "media nostalgia," Aldus's italic enterprise has a remarkably progressive tendency, anticipating a controlled international economy, *property* rights in industrial processes, and a transpolitical economic collective (the "Italy" and the sphere of "humane letters" designated in the papal decrees) that is benefited by individual ingenuity and that ought to reward it.

Aldus's desperate ingenuity was very quickly copied or, at least, parallelled by other, equally influential masters of iteration. Vasari tells the tale of Marcantonio Raimondi's first encounter, in Venice, with the woodcuts of Dürer.[99] Full of admiration and commercial cunning, he purchased a number of the woodcuts and began engraving copies, reproducing even Dürer's famous monogram. When word of the piracy reached Germany, Dürer was so enraged that he rushed to Venice, complained to the signoria, who prohibited not the reproductions but the appropriation of the monogram. Vasari's story is inaccurate in many details but it is true that Marcantonio made engraved reproductions of Dürer's woodcuts and monogram, and that Dürer sought a state ban on such appropriation. In the colophon to the *Life of the Virgin*, produced in book format in 1511, Dürer warns the "envious thieves of the work and invention of others" away from his works: "we have received a privilege from the famous emperor of Rome, Maximilian, that no one shall dare to print these works in spurious forms, nor sell such prints within the boundaries of the empire."[100] Dürer has been forced to Aldus's gambit, a gambit that now serves the reproductive *inventor*, and so contributes to the progress toward proprietary origination within a culture of iterative industries. More might be said: the enlistment of state protection on behalf of exclusive iterative rights inflects the nature of state power. The monopolizing of commercial regulation becomes a defining characteristic of the Modern state: at this key moment, the state flaunts its economic power by contributing to the erection of monopolies in the production of copies, asserting itself as patron of the iterative.

Dürer was not the only figure to reproduce the Aldine gambit. To recur to the English case, Rastell seems to have imported the mechanism of the Venetian printing privilege—and not only that.[101] His 1517 edition of Linacre's *Progymnasmata* also Englishes the burgeoning sense of propriety/property registered in Aldus's campaign against his competitors. Not only the *privilegium* but also the *Monitum* has its counterpart in the *Progymnasmata*; if the privilege recorded on the colophon protects against competition from such publishers of school texts as de Worde and Pynson, a poem prefatory to Linacre's text protects against more proximate challenges to Rastell's enterprise:

> *William Lyly on Linacre's Grammatical Exercises Reclaimed from*
> *Plagiarism*
> The Page which not long since had lay concealed
> And caked with the thick muck of a false name
> Is now washed clean, and "Linacre" revealed,
> And its true author thus restored to fame.[102]

The *Progymnasmata* had already appeared in another edition—a flawed edition, according to Lyly's poem, though in the absence of a surviving text the truth of the charge cannot be assessed. These verses may simply be another strategy for protecting Rastell's investment: from the *Monitum* forward, impugning the workmanship of a competitor was a recurrent tactic in competition within the book trade.[103] So both front and end matter, prefatory warning and conclusive privilege, mark, and strive to control, the incidence of new competitive pressures.

These pressures condition the emphasis on the *authority* of the privileged edition. The syntax of the genitives that crowd into Lyly's verse—*authoris perscribens nomina veri / Linacri*—is difficult to construe: poised between genitives of apposition and of possession, they might be called genitives of competition. The nominal excess here, the transformation of the authorizing *nomen* into the insistent and redundant plural, *nomina,* originates in the commercial necessity of product differentiation. The colophon may be vague in its designation of the "compyler" who received the royal privilege, but Lyly's poem is lavish in its namings. The poem discovers, instigates a specifically modern authorship, a name flaunted as an instrument of monopolistic competition.

It is worthwhile contemplating the long-term effects of what I have been calling the Italian connection. First, English printing privileges seem to have been modeled on Venetian ones, perhaps particularly from Aldus's privileges and thus, insofar as authorial copyright evolves from the printing privilege, one might say that the modern proprietary author is a distant descendent of a *typeface*. But this effect, on the history of authorship, does not exhaust the influence of the Aldine privilege, which has also left its mark on the history of emphasis. Consider the subsequent function of the italic letter, which we steadily use to interrupt the merely written and to provide for the sharp bursting of the highly valent, of meaning *in propria persona.* The italic is that which we continue to use to make the weariness of impression give way to inscription, to designate the truly *authentic.*[104] Having failed to assert his control in Lyons, Aldus extended his influence to London, for there the italic remained the typeface of privilege, as the type of quotation, of accuracy, obtrusion, assertion. In the rhetoric of the English page, the italic is the master-trope. To print in italics is to fracture the English body type, and to assert a human claim on the written; what begins as an assertion of dominion becomes, slowly, an assertion of more highly authored words: even at this early juncture, *authoris perscribens nomina veri.*

Secularizing, Individualizing

It may be useful to consider one other early italicization. Aldus's 1503 *Monitum* makes no mention of the 1503 edition of Catullus, Propertius, and Tibullus printed in Florence by the powerful printing and bookselling firm of the Giunti. Except for its inclusion of a new dedication and a brief biography of each of the three poets, that edition copies the typeface and layout of Aldus's edition exactly, crediting him with having recently emended the texts, and falsely claiming its own texts to be the product of substantial local revision by one "Bendictus." It may be that the *Monitum* was produced before Aldus found out about this Florentine publication, but he probably learned of it shortly; indeed the Giunti had a bookselling establishment in Venice itself (and since 1499, this branch had involved itself in a certain amount of printing in its own right) and may have attempted to market its own rival to the Aldine original on local Venetian turf. Martin Lowry has pieced together a convincing hypothesis that the major lawsuit in which Aldus was engaged in the latter half of 1507 was with the Giunti, by which time they had printed an italic Horace copied from Aldus, but with the order of the *Satires* and *Epistles* reversed, as well as a Petrarch, a Virgil, and an edition of Bembo's *Asolani,* again all modeled on Aldus.'[105] Certainly in 1514, the Giunti would appeal to Leo X for a repeal of his recent grant to Aldus of a printing privilege modeled on that of Alexander VI, on the grounds that the Giunti had been the first to print in italics. The pattern of the challenge is revealing. After imitating the broadly invasive tactics of the Lyons pirates, the Giunti seem to have specified their attack. After 1505, they continued to print in italics, but they seemed to have stopped printing books obviously based on Aldine editions. This suggests the commercially sound resolution to respect privileges in individual titles, but to contest claims to broader monopolies.

The individual printed book, the *work*, thus sustains a specifically commercial reification. That is, the social being of the book is adjusted such that it can serve as a means of commercial regulation, of keeping the peace within a trade. (Here is another crucial sense in which the Venetian privilege anticipates English stationer's copyright.) We can see important signs of that adjustment as early as the 1490s, when new provisions begin to appear in Venetian privileges. Horatio Brown cites a grant "to Alessandro Calcedanio in the year 1493, which closes thus, *declarato, quod haec gratia intelligatur casu quo opera ipsa sint nova* (that is, new to the press) *et aliquis alius jam non caeperit illa imprimere, vel sibi promissum fuerit.*"[106] This proviso became commonplace within a few years. It is by no means the case that priority of publication always secured monopoly rights in subsequent editions, or that the specific efficacy of the privilege was superseded, but for a book to *have been printed* made it a potential bar to subsequent monopolies. The privilege had transformed the market into a heterogeneous economic space; this new provision, which sought to stabilize activity within that space, actually served further to complicate its topography. *To have been printed* changed the specific social potency of a text.

The proviso constitutes an attempt to limit the market power of the privilege: the privilege is thus deployed as a means of constituting a particular market situation, not of canceling a prior situation—such cancellation became, effectively, an abuse. The emphatically prospective nature of the privilege was soon exploited in new ways. By the second decade of the sixteenth century, some printers were using privileges to block publications by others. As a result, local production fell off so drastically, and so many printers emigrated, that the Senate came to feel that the market in books had finally become an obstacle course. Their solution was to promulgate a law, in 1517, repealing all existing privileges and stipulating that, in the future, privileges were to be awarded *"solum pro libris et operibus novis, numquam antea impressis et non pro aliis."*[107] A new value, hence a new valence: it was now to the new work that the charge of commercial exclusivity was attributed. The modern book—that is, the work that newly enters the market in books—moves through that market with a municipal honor guard. Put it another way: the early modern author—or the assiduous Renaissance textual scholar—can provide the early modern printer with copy potentially more valuable than other sorts of copy; small wonder that Erasmus felt himself to be particularly at home in the clattering "festination" of Aldus's printshop. Put it yet another way: textual innovation, textual creativity is privileged.

Venetian developments anticipate English ones, though Venetian state practice was a good deal more interventionist than that of England. The challenge of the Giunti, attempts to confine printing monopolies to privileges in individual works, contests over what constitute the legitimate objects of privilege—all these anticipate Wolfe's "reformation." As we shall see, application for privilege without intent immediately to print anticipates the staying registrations of late sixteenth-century England. These developments, differently paced within each European book culture, gently conduce to the valorization of the "original," modern literary act.

This is not to say that the proto-copyright of the early printing privilege clearly and simply anticipates that copyright discriminated in *Donaldson v. Beckett,* a copyright that takes its origins in the unique and splendid act of creative writing. What presents itself to hindsight as confusion—Lyly's insistent *authoris nomina* diffused by the colophon's compyler, a term so difficult to construe—is the murky sign that proprietary authorship was not quite necessary to Tudor regulation. The colophon that announces Rastell's next privilege—in *The Abbreviation of the Statutes* (1519)—is similarly vague with respect to originative inscription: the privileged object is "translatyd out of

French . . . by John Rastell, and, imprinted by the same John the XXV day of October." No particular agency—authorship, translatordom, printerhood—need be singled out for "the pryvylege of our soverein lord grauntyd to the sayd John."

For several years, only Rastell and Pynson printed and sold books in England *cum privilegio*. A. W. Reed noticed many years ago that around 1519–20 the colophons of their books cease specifying "this seid work" or "haec"; instead they employ the formula *cum privilegio a rege indulto*. He concludes that the colophon is simply a reminder to the members of the book trade that these two printers had been the recipients of general privileges, that they were no longer soliciting particular grants of privilege in individual printing ventures.[108] This situation changed quite suddenly in the middle of the decade, when books produced by eighteen or so other printers begin to appear, the colophons of which represent each book as the object of a particular grant of privilege. Competition had persisted, particularly in that imitative form to which printing was so perfectly adapted: Robert Redman printed so many books first printed by Pynson, books covered by Pynson's general privilege (for whatever that was worth), that Pynson suggested, in the preface to his 1525 edition of Littleton's *Tenures,* that Redman's name ought to be Rudeman. But the proliferation of individual privileges during these years may be attributable to more than the desire to control competition. These are the years of the crackdown on the traffic in Lutheran books, and it is possible that the stationers sought privileges as, in Reed's words, "a mark of respectability."[109] Certainly, a Bill of Complaint submitted to Cromwell in 1534 by a group of Lutherans in Essex claims that this was an arguable construction of the privilege. Having been attacked by a local parish official for reading from an English primer, they counter that there can surely be no harm in "usynge to reade pryvyledgede bookes" and they submit that the king "puts forthwith Certyne bookes printed and openly sold with his ryght royal privyledge sett unto the same to the intente truly (as we do take it) that no man shoulde feare but rather be encoragede to occupye them."[110]

At the beginning of this chapter I pointed out how frequently royal and industrial motives were aligned, how richly coordinated censorious licensing and monopolistic privilege indeed were; yet this confounding of privilege and license by the heretics of Essex may look like an interpretation from convenience, for they had good reasons for wishing royal privilege tantamount to royal license. The circumstances that surround the publication of the Great Bible in 1538–39 suggest that by that time such convenient confusion was widespread. After the embarrassing royal authorization of the Matthew Bible, a composite based primarily on Tyndale's translation (Foxe gloats "that there was Printed upon the same booke, one lyne in red letters with these wordes: *Set forth with the kings most gracious licence"*), Grafton and Whitchurch went to Paris early in 1538 to begin production of the Great Bible.[111] Their plan for this new English Bible was to have Coverdale tone down the reforming diction of Tyndale's translation and to scour their text of the Tyndale glosses that had made the Matthew Bible so assertively Protestant; they set about their work confident that they were doing the royal will.[112] So they were shocked when the king proclaimed, on 16 November 1538—and I hope to be forgiven a last repetition of the reference—that

> no person or persons in this realm shall from henceforth print any
> book in the English tongue, unless upon examination made by
> some of his grace's Privy Council, or other such as his highness
> shall appoint, they shall have license so to do; and yet having so,
> not to put these words *cum privilegio regali,* without adding *ad im-
> primendum solum,* and that the whole copy, or else at the least the
> effect of his license and privilege be therewith printed, and plainly
> declared and expressed in the English tongue underneath them.

The analysis of the regulatory construction of book culture can be substantially enriched if we consider how *Grafton* read this proclamation. He wrote to Cromwell two weeks after the proclamation; he is urgent and ingratiating:

> Of the which bookes [the Great Bible] now beynge fyneshed, I
> have here sent your lordship the fyrst (and so have I also sent unto
> my lorde of Cantorbury another and almoost to every christen
> bysshop that is in the realme, My lorde of harfforde also hath
> sent to Mr. Rychard Cromwell one of the same) thewhich I moost
> humbly desyer your lordship to accept, havyng respecte rather
> unto my harte, then to the gifte; for it is not so well done as my
> harte wolde wysshe it to be: I have also added, as your lordship
> maye perceave, these wordes, Cum gracia et privilegio Regis.
> And the day before this present came there a post named Nycolas
> which brought your lordshipes letters to my lorde of harrforde,
> with thewhich was bounde a certen inhibicion for pryntynge of
> bookes, and for a addynge of these wordes Cum privilegio.

Grafton believed, perhaps correctly, that Cromwell had sent the text of the proclamation as a very specific warning: hence, "inhibicion" for "proclamation"—

> Then assone as my lorde of harfforde had receaved yt, he sent
> ymedyatlye for Mr. Coverdale and me, readynge thesame thynge

unto us, in thewhich is expressed, that we shulde adde these
wordes (ad imprimendum solum) which wordes we never heard
of before. Nether do we take it that those wordes shuld be added
in the pryntynge of the scripture (if yt be truly translated) for then
shuld yt be a great occasyon to the enemyes to saye that yt is not
the kynges acte or mynde to set yt forth, but only lycence the
prynters to sell soche as is put forth.[113]

Like the Essex reformers, Grafton claims to have long assumed that the royal
privilege entailed royal approval, even endorsement. If the institution of the
privilege was ever exclusively an industrial matter, Grafton either does not
know it or affects not to know it. The most stirring effect of the 1538 proclamation lay in its insistence on a relatively novel splitting of ideological from
economic regulation. However the proclamation was specifying privilege—
whether for *sole* printing (as Albright would have it) or only *with respect to*
printing (according to Pollard)—it was declaring, above all, that business was
just business. Hence Grafton's shock: given the ideological anxieties of the
moment (suddenly far more volatile than market concerns), monopoly rights
were insufficient compensation for the attenuation of business thus implied.
A history of monopolies had been interrupted and superseded by a more
egregious history of censorship.

It is now possible to adjudicate the dispute between Albright and Pollard. The 1538 proclamation adjusts two regulatory institutions already in
place. It is remarkable in that it secures *royal* responsibility for licensing;
less remarkably, it accommodates the common, but by no means pervasive,
practice of publication *cum privilegio* so that it will not interfere with what
Henry hoped would be an efficient and comprehensive system for subjecting print to ideological scrutiny. So Pollard is quite correct about the tendency of the restriction, *ad imprimendum solum:* it serves to abridge the
protections of the privilege, which had been extended either in practice
or in the imaginations of those readers and printers who, since the mid-
twenties, might have felt that the print culture they were making was a dangerous one. Albright, insisting that the *privilegium* is permitted to flaunt a
monopoly, points us to the ancestry of the privilege, its roots in trade protectionism. She also indicates the revolutionary character of the privilege,
both its function in individualizing economic powers that had long been
corporate, proper to guilds and to town oligarchies, and in strengthening
monarchy as a specifically economic agency. Finally, Albright directs our
attention toward the eventual fate of the privilege, which was to be sublimated as copyright, as creativity, as the ghostly immanence of authors in
their works.

◈

INTERCHAPTER: POSSESSIVE AUTHORSHIP

The balance of this book narrates the campaign for property in invention and in literary works—the campaign and the opposition. There is a literary history internal to that campaign, the development of the proprietary sentiment in such authors as Shakespeare and Jonson, crucial nodes of an encompassing economy in which intellectual possessiveness was coalescing. I offer an extended account of that literary history in *Jonson and Possessive Authorship,* but it seems appropriate to summarize that account here, since literary practice does more than reflect a general history of possessiveness. In many ways it served as an engine of that history.

Most of the other authors taken up in *Jonson and Possessive Authorship* are playwrights. This is hardly coincidental, for at the very end of Elizabeth's reign, theatrical activity in London slipped into a competitive and mutually stimulating relationship with the book trade. To some slight extent, playwrights were caught between the two media. Those few authors who came to think of themselves primarily (though, probably, never exclusively) as playwrights—Shakespeare, say, and Heywood, Webster, Brome, and a few others—would have felt primary allegiance to the acting companies for whom they wrote; but most dramatic poets engaged in nondramatic writing as well, seeking the notice of influential patrons and, occasionally, the novel "patronage" of stationers, who would reward their efforts by paying cash for manuscripts, or by providing an author with printed copies—for presentation or, sometimes, for sale. The historiographic importance of playwrights should therefore be obvious: they participated in several different markets, each at a different stage of development, each shaped by different structures of regulation and constraint. Jonson has historical importance for these and several other reasons: because of his truculent jealousy and extraordinary ambition, because he wrote in a variety of genres for *especially* disparate audiences, because of the large range of both his social connections and his interests (which included a fascination with commerce and technology). He is a test case for developments narrated in these pages. His social and literary interests, the themes of his career, are observable in the behavior and writing of a number of his contemporaries, stationers, nondramatic writers, politicians, designers, entrepreneurs, and inventors: the practical problem of attribution in collaborative creative activities, the problematic ontology of the occasional or mutable work of art, the emergence of plagiarism in an imitative culture and in industries essentially mass productive, the tension between private property and collective ownership, the friction between related industries at different stages of organizational development and capitalization. His creative arousals, his furies and ambitions are intelligible as a personal node in the history of intellectual property articulated in these pages.

By the end of the sixteenth century, literary activity was widely felt to have been unsettled by commercialization. As Robert Dallington put it in the letter that prefaces his travel guide, *The View of France* (1604), "The Marte is open for writing & this towne at this time more ful of such Novelties then ever was Franckfort, thogh more for the Printers gaine, then the Authors credit, or Benefit of us the Readers." Although he is registering a diffuse disorder in literary sociology, his letter was motivated by a particular grievance. He complains that he wrote the book for the private use of a particular patron, but that a stationer—John Baylie, though Dallington does not name him—had gotten his hands on the book, entered it, and had it printed. Dallington writes that he was powerless to inhibit this publication and that when Baylie undertook a second edition—a reissue, really, with nothing new but a title page and Dallington's letter—he, Dallington, was too dispirited by lack of control to exert himself to correct the book.[1] The letter testifies to conspicuously alienated literary labor. The alienation is of a sort characteristic of work within an economy undergoing rapid, even revolutionary change, like that of an agricultural laborer in a countryside being converted from arable to pasture: Dallington tells us of writing for a patron, but the product of that labor has been forcibly redeployed in a print market.

A similar process seems to have unfolded for playwrights, and with a vengeance. Many late Elizabethan playwrights, perhaps most, had developed their literary skills in anticipation of careers in the clergy, at the bar, or in private or courtly service. Some began writing plays as a glamorous supplement or prelude to these careers; some, frustrated in other professional ambitions, had been gently forced to playwrighting as part of a composite, improvised career of literary production; still others came to it via equally unanticipated work as actors. Few would have hoped early in life to make careers as playwrights or actor-playwrights; most, therefore, would have felt *some* sense of disorientation as they witnessed their own literary abilities, cultivated for one or another intended economic future, taken up by another industry. Jonson reflects this disorientation with particular charm in the prologues to several of his plays, by variously mocking the Poet who characteristically hovers backstage, a fish out of water in a milieu of agile practicality: the actors plan licentious mischief now that the meddling Poet has subsided into a drunken stupor behind the scenes; the Poet, with clumsy incomprehension, attempts to establish a contract with the audience to regulate its behavior. Such wit expresses the uneasiness with which writers assented to the redeployment of their capacities, the assent always apparently tinged with a mild version of Dallington's unhappy experience.

There is counter-evidence, however. Some playwrights—Shakespeare most famously—seem to have *embraced* the stage as "Marte." When plays by Heywood or Marston go into print, they protest that the scripts were written for performance, not print. These protests might be explained away, as the extension of an older nicety, the commonplace (and probably sometimes sincere) disavowal of interest in circulating written texts outside the sphere of a coterie. But when Heywood sounds this note, Dallington's note, he discloses more than commonplace concerns: "It hath beene no custome in mee of all other men (curteous Readers) to commit my plaies to the presse, for though some have used a double sale of their labours, first to the Stage, and after to the presse, for my owne parte I heere proclaime my selfe ever faithful in the first, and never guiltie of the last."[2] Heywood is often a particularly interesting witness to the economic situation of authors, representing writing not as genteel leisure but as productive labor. Even more telling in this historical context is his sense of being caught between rival markets, of being tempted to a sharp practice that pits commerce in one medium against commerce in another. Like Marston, Heywood expresses loyalty to the stage in reaction to temptations from the press.

If the stage and the press were indeed rival disseminative markets, then Heywood's loyalty would not be difficult to explain. As a leading member of the Queen's Men, his interests were closely allied with those of the company, and if press publication would hurt their fortunes, it would hurt his. But were the two markets indeed rivals? The answer cannot be simple and would not have *been* simple for Heywood and his contemporaries. Like modern novelizations of films and film versions of novels, the two forms are both complementary *and* mutually derogating, the one form stimulating interest and, occasionally, exposing inadequacies in the other. Moreover, each medium was apparently capable of exciting (economically and intellectually) irrational partisanship. Within the framework of this general situation of complement and derogation, we can make sense of particular details of literary and theatrical culture—of complaints by authors that their plays were being printed without their consent; of similar complaints by actors of the fact (difficult to explain) that popular plays were being entered to individual stationers, but being withheld (for periods of varying length) from publication; of a stationer's exultant boast at having wrested *Troilus and Cressida* from the control of an acting company in order to print it.

There is plenty of evidence that the two media were *felt* to be rivals. At various points in his career, Jonson was vocal and interesting concerning the rivalry. Though a play like *The Staple of News* (1626) fiercely criticizes certain aspects of the book trade, Jonson can frequently be shown to have used print as a means of denigrating performance. In the printed texts of his plays, he criticizes audiences and actors, restores passages cut from performance (and makes note of the restoration), revises passages that have elicited unfortunate responses, arranges for typographic emphases untethered from performance features, provides elaborate glosses designed to associate scripts with a bookish and scholarly tradition impertinent to the theater, and so forth. In the texts of his printed masques and elsewhere, he takes occasion to theorize this practice by claiming the philosophical preeminence of poetry over stagecraft. There is, moreover, an individualizing drive to Jonson's practice and polemics: although printed books are collaborative products, the press is favored insofar as it affords him greater control over the form in which his work is circulated and consumed than does the heterogeneous sphere of performance. For Jonson, then, the theater is to the press as public to private, as commons to private property.[3]

The theater was itself unquestionably rivalrous. Acting companies seem to have occasionally attempted to regulate the flow of plays to the press— a defense against industrial outsiders analogous to that frequently sought by the members of traditional guilds—and they also attempted to regulate competition within their industry, working out arrangements to inhibit direct competition between companies. Stuart acting companies even sought to monopolize subject matter and to bind playwrights into exclusive contracts. But because there was no players' guild, competition in the theatrical community was irregular and improvisatory. That community developed a culture of aesthetic *fashion*, in which successful companies repeated their own successes and copied others'; and then, having been copied, stigmatized the imitation and strove nervously for more striking innovation, thus establishing a rhythm of intense artistic coalescences followed by rapid reconfigurations.[4] Competition affected the form and manner of dramatic output itself: it is manifest, obviously, in parody, but, more subtly, in intensely agonistic plotting.

Operating in an urban economy in which commerce was frequently shaped by monopoly, the business of the theater was hardly a sphere of competitive freedom. Days and sites of playing were limited, as was the number of companies allowed to perform in London and its environs: this enabled theater owners and company shareholders to monopolize performers, actors, and audiences, and focused the competition for those resources. (It also es-

pecially sharpened the difference between sharers in theatrical enterprises—
Henslowes, Burbages, and Shakespeares—and those who did piece work—
Jonsons, Greenes, and Chettles.) Monopoly inflated ticket prices; it should
have constrained theatrical wages, and no doubt it did so, though the prices
paid for plays rose between, say, the beginning of Shakespeare's career and
the end of Jonson's. This was due to a variety of important inflationary forces,
of which, naturally, the dynamic of a fashion culture was the most powerful.
There is manifold evidence for increased appreciation of authors' contributions to the theater: lengthening scripts; a decline in improvisational performances, at least in the venues with highest ticket prices; plenty of theatrical
satire focusing on authors.

The press itself provides a good deal of the evidence for the rise of an
author's theater, the essential datum in this case being the rapid growth in
the publishing of dramatic texts. In the early stages of dramatic publishing, a
script seems to have derived its interest from the fact of professional performance: title pages of Elizabethan plays characteristically identify the acting
company that has performed the play, or the venue of performance. But in
the mid-1590s, playwrights' names begin to appear on title pages. The Shakespeare quartos are no exception to this pattern. Several early Shakespearean
plays appeared in print associated only with the names of the earls of Derby,
Sussex, or Hunsdon, patrons of the acting companies that had performed
them—and this despite the fact that earlier editions of his nondramatic poems had named him on their title pages; his name does not appear on the title
page of a play until 1598, when Andrew Wise brought out a second quarto
of *Richard II*.[5] For Shakespeare, then, the end of the century marks an attributive takeoff: in the next few years, plays and poems are regularly and, by
modern standards, quite indiscriminately attributed to him. That the name
of the dramatic author was taken up as an inducement to book sales corrob-
orates other evidence for the increase in authorial prestige.

Title pages often thicken the gloss of authorship by advertising authorial
press correction, revision, or augmentation—a renewal of authorial attention,
this time specified to print. (A lighter version of this device is to emphasize
special fidelity to an authorial original.) Sometimes this device seems to have
served stationers—not well, usually—as a device for infringing another stationer's copyright, or of devaluing an infringement; sometimes it supports
the stationer's effort to present the printed text as superior to the transitory
stage tie-in. Whether or not authors actually did renew their attention, the
fact that stationers steadily claimed such renewal as a special source of value
instructed authors that they might think more seriously of the durable *commercial* aspect of the connection between themselves and their work: the

advertisement of revision per se advances toward the telos of what we now call moral rights, the right to shield one's creative work from derogation, even after a sale of copyright.

Increased authorial prestige in a competitive environment: how else is this to be registered in a history of intellectual property? Simply put, it undermined the durable institution of literary imitation. To an extent, all aesthetic practice is deeply imitative, more committed to replicating other aesthetic objects than to mimesis, but in highly competitive environments, in which a culture of severe connoisseurship can flourish, imitation is vulnerable to remapping as overproduction. The young Shakespeare, egregiously ambitious, at least in the eyes of at least one elder man of letters, was accused of tastelessness, self-promotion, and what we have come to call plagiarism. "Have come to call": the word, a Latin derivative, seems to have had no currency in English before the late sixteenth century, at which point Joseph Hall introduced the term in a book of nondramatic satires and, notably, Ben Jonson began using it in satiric drama, in which barely disguised representations of certain fellow playwrights level the charge at each other.[6]

That Jonson exercised his possessiveness in practice as well as in theory may be traced in the ways he prepared texts for the various quartos of his plays and masques, for the famous 1616 folio edition of his *Workes*, and for the second folio of 1640.[7] If the historical importance of the 1616 folio has sometimes been slightly exaggerated, the recalibration of that importance is more than a little revealing. To recall that the Jonson folio is anticipated by Samuel Daniel's 1601 *Works* is to place the Jonson volume in the context of author-centered publishing. To qualify the received belief that Jonson attended carefully to all the typographic aspects of the book, and to many of the industrial negotiations necessary to its production, entails a recognition of the compositorial attention that Jonson had *earlier* brought to the production of certain of his quartos, and an acknowledgment of the persistent industrial control of the business aspect of publishing, including the securing of copyrights. Indeed, reconstructing the industrial negotiations that led, in the course of many years, to the issue of the second, much larger Jonson folio—a disheveled and inelegant book—enables us to get a fairly clear sense of the standing of an important author on the eve of the Civil War; more specifically, it enables us to gauge the state of authorial property at that juncture. That the first folio was a success has long been recognized: the subsequent production of folio collections of Shakespeare, Marston, Lyly, and, somewhat later, Beaumont and Fletcher is evidence that such collections of dramatic literature seemed viable commodities, but we could gauge as much and more by observing the copyright negotiations that take place in the aftermath of the

1616 Jonson edition. A sequence of stationers traded rights in Jonson's later plays, poems, and masques until, in 1639, two emerged, John Benson and Andrew Crooke, each controlling substantial portions of the corpus.[8] They must have been anticipating either a proprietary showdown or a collaborative production, but their positions were radically compromised in 1640 when a third stationer, Thomas Walkley, laid claim to some texts, not by virtue of registration (or transferred registration), but rather of authorial intention. Jonson had made Sir Kenelm Digby a kind of literary executor, and Digby had passed the texts he possessed to this third stationer. Most of Digby's texts had never been published or registered, but a few overlapped one of the other stationer's holdings. A Chancery case followed but its issue is unrecorded. Still, the fact that, in 1640, stationer's copyright could sustain serious authorial challenge, and that that challenge should have been prosecuted in Chancery, rather than within the narrow jurisdiction of the Stationers' Court of Assistants, is more than a little revealing. It points us down the road to the future, a future of shrinking autonomy for the Stationers' Company and of slowly accumulating authorial prerogatives.

As will be shown in the following chapters, these events of the 1630s and '40s were not unprecedented: George Wither had volubly asserted authorial rights over stationers in the early 1620s; even earlier, Jonson had begun to encroach on the stationers' prerogatives. The conflict over the second Jonson folio tells us that Wither's assertion had resounded into practicability. Indeed, the dull practicalities of this conflict give us a precise sense of the industrial background against which we may most clearly discern the figurative work of *Areopagitica*. Elizabethan, Jacobean, and Caroline authorial practice, and particularly the practice of playwrights, powerfully conditions the slow revolution in the political theory and industrial construction of intellectual property to which the following chapters attend.

II

FROM PROTECTIONISM TO PROPERTY

CHAPTER FOUR

INGENUITY AND THE MERCANTILE MUSE:
AUTHORSHIP AND
THE HISTORY OF THE PATENT

"He then read an observation cited by Grotius as having been made
by Paulus, a Roman lawyer, who declared, that one mode of acquir-
ing property was invention, and that from the nature of things, he
who made a matter was the owner of it."

Observed of Solicitor General Wedderburn
in the case of *Donaldson v. Becket*

Past attempts to situate literary activity in the economic history of early
modern England have proceeded by searching for literary, and particularly
dramatic, representations of the social and political disturbances produced
by price inflation, the fiscal crisis of the Tudor state, and the transformation of the agrarian economy. L. C. Knights, who provided the great model
for this critical enterprise, naturally concentrated his attention on Jonson's
plays.[1] Jonson's attack on the vanity of economic innovation was relentless,
sustained throughout his career as a dramatist, yet his attack on "projecting"
is concentrated in *The Devil Is an Ass* and *The Staple of News*. The second
of these plays specifically addresses the commodification of language, but
the first, with its hectic attack on projecting, elicited from Unwin the admir-
ing remark that "a study of the leading characters in *The Devil Is an Ass* . . .
would be by far the best introduction to the economic history of the period."[2]
That Jonson rallied himself to his most specific attack on monopolistic competition in this play of 1616 may at least partly explain Unwin's enthusiasm.
The conceptual advance of this play is to correlate the psychology of whim
and compulsion—the rendering of which had been Jonson's specialty since

the earliest comedies—with the yeasty commercial mania of projection and monopoly: coney-catcher and eccentric coney, sharper and humorous gull had never suited each other as do Meer-craft and Fitzdottrell.

Knights has some very fine pages on *The Devil Is an Ass,* linking the play generally to the Jacobean boom in monopolies and specifically to Cockayne's cloth-finishing scheme, which was undertaken in 1614 with the protection of a Crown grant and which collapsed in 1616, to the complete disruption of the cloth trade.[3] Though Knights will eventually reduce the play to a generalized indictment of greed, he begins his discussion by remarking on the emphatic topicality of the play—"never before had he [i.e., Jonson] handled a major political issue so effectively. . . . Whereas *Volpone* had been concerned with attitudes and impulses permanent in human nature, though liberated and enforced by contemporary events, *The Devil Is an Ass* brings the events themselves upon the stage."[4] The terse epilogue of the play suggests that gentle enforcement and liberation of another contemporaneity also impinges on the play:

> Thus, the *Projector,* here, is over-throwne.
> But I have now a *Project* of mine owne,
> If it may passe:

—the epilogue of the play has only a single joke to make, but its "project" is to indicate the personal, professional coordinates of his subject—

> that no man would invite
> The *Poet* from us, to sup forth to night,
> If the play please. If it displeasant be,
> We doe presume, that no man will: nor wee.

Unusually, the actor who speaks the epilogue speaks neither for the author nor for the "limited partnership" of author and acting company, but for the actors *as opposed to* the author. The actor has learned the lesson of *Bartholomew Fair,* in the prologue of which representatives of the poet appear to make a contract, unmediated by the actors, between the poet and the audience. The actor who speaks here at the end of *The Devil Is an Ass* also proposes, albeit casually, a kind of contract with the audience, a regulation of courtesy: the actors wish to forestall any competition for the poet's company should the play succeed; if it fails, he'll naturally be foresaken. The tone is not much changed from that of the prologue to *Bartholomew Fair*—if anything it is more genial. Nor is Jonson's point any less searching:

that even in the theater, professional relations, even professional courtesy, are collusive; that in the most unlikely places the deck is stacked; that the theater is itself a "project." It is hardly coincidental that monopolistic competition should have occupied Jonson's attention at this moment, in the wake of the preparation of the folio *Works*. The various efforts to "repossess" his text—Jonson's editorial labors and Stansby and Burre's negotiations for lease or purchase of copyrights—had further sharpened the poet's sense of the network of competing proprietary interests and advantages that hedged his plays. There is considerable charm to the epilogue to *The Devil Is an Ass:* I want to emphasize the charm of Jonson's graceful and shrewdly knowing capitulation to the monopolistic character even of the literary economy, an economy of competing projects.

Early in his career Jonson can adopt a fairly simple, fairly popular antimonopolistic stance, as he does in *Poetaster,* when the braggart Tucca promises the Crispinus, the satirist, a monopoly of playing as a reward for his assistance in humiliating Horace; but as Jonson became more and more jealous of his own works and of their reception, his stance became more contorted.[5] In *Jonson and Possessive Authorship,* I have followed how Jonson's desire to dictate the terms of his own critical reception expressed itself in exceptional proprietary interventions in the dissemination of his printed works. When Owen Felltham responded to Jonson's "Come, leave the loathèd stage," he reads Jonson's critical imperiousness as a kind of magically abusive monopolistic competition:

> 'Tis known it is not fit,
> That a sale Poet, just contempt once thrown,
> Should cry up thus his own.
> I wonder by what Dowre
> Or Patent you had power
> From all to rap't a judgment.[6]

This is especially stinging because especially apt: despite Jonson's protestations of having "departed his right" in his plays, he yearns toward a continuing and inexhaustible property—perpetually renewed despite continuing sales.

The narrative of Jonson's career in England's public and published sphere is a constant scramble for vantage, from theater to press, from theater to banqueting house, from banqueting house to press, from quarto to folio—all of which can be described as a constant flight from publicity to privacy. That the flight from publicity is itself so very public might be dismissed as bad faith, but the cultural historian will not be dismissive, for Jonson's obsessive

and various self-display is a revealing historical phenomenon. He was profoundly alert to the conditions of literary practice, to the variety of media and
to the habits of consumption associated with those media, and he yearned to
control his own reception; as a result, his writing and his behavior register
crucial adjustments in the economic and cultural organization of intellectual
property.

The Author as Publisher, II:
Samuel Daniel and Simon Waterson

It's a project, a designement of his owne.
                                    Every Man Out of His Humour,
                                                        II.ii. 35–36

Jonson involved himself in a number of functions "proper to" the stationer:
he was probably involved in providing the paper and determining the page
layout for *Sejanus;* he probably initiated the publication of several of his early
masques and arranged that those masques written after the folio was published be printed for private circulation only; he sometimes took great pains
over the work of revising texts specifically for print and sometimes took comparable pains over the work of press correction. It is important to recognize
that *analogous* involvement of authors in preparing their texts was quite normal in the medium of scribal publication, as Harold Love has recently reminded us, and one could easily speak of Jonson's practice as a strenuous and,
sometimes, blunt attempt to force the printed book to function like the scribal
codex and the trade in printed books to recapitulate the commerce in manuscripts: we could say that Jonson, long recognized as one of seventeenth-
century England's most interesting neoconservative ideologues, is equally
interesting as a neoconservative artisan. And when we refer to Jonson as "neoconservative," the emphasis should fall on the prefix, for his attempt to make
the culture of print function as a version of scribal culture is *neo*conservative,
a forceful novelty. But the cultural force of this artisanal neoconservatism
depends on the fact that Jonson's practices were by no means unique.

Across the spectrum of English book culture, a set of practices that I have
generally grouped under the rubric of "editorial repossession" accumulated,
occasionally disrupting stationer's intellectual property (albeit usually quite
inadvertently) but eventually quite explicitly resisting that property. Jonson's
practice was not egregious; he was one of several authors whose engagement
with book production eventually compromised the extraordinary freedoms

that had been confirmed on the English press in its infancy. His involvement in book production, although sustained and reflective, was seldom if ever as extreme as, for example, that monumentalized in the large-format pageant volume for James's coronation entertainment folio, *The Arch's of Triumph . . . Invented and published by Stephen Harrison Joyner and Architect* (1604). Jonson's entertainment volume barely recognizes the other contributors to the event, yet his power over the event and its record is only, as it were, imaginary. Harrison's, by comparison, is quite real. Harrison can afford generously to recognize the contributing poets and collectives (guilds and communities of aliens), for in recognition of his own preeminent contribution, the City of London paid the printing costs for this lavish illustrated volume, leaving the printed stock "to be sold at the Authors house in Lime-street."[7] The volume was not entered, but no stationer would have contested the arrangement. Neither were rights formally vested in Harrison, but of course his monopoly was beyond challenge, for as long as he or his printer possessed the engraved plates for the illustrations, the volume was inimitable—or could only have been imitated at great expense.

Even this arrangement is less egregious than it seems. Although we know surprisingly little about the conventions of authorial compensation, we do know that stationers often paid authors in kind for their manuscripts, by providing them with a number of copies of the finished printed book. We customarily speak of these as presentation copies, but in fact at least one author simply sold a certain number of these copies, presumably in a consignment arrangement with a bookseller, who might well have been the original publisher.[8] Harrison simply extends the practice, securing his reward by selling not just a few but all of his books; by selling the books himself, rather than through a professional bookseller.

Others in the circle of Jonson's experience and on its periphery similarly crowded the stationers' business. Savile reportedly subsidized the printing of his great edition of Chrysostom (published from 1610 to 1613) to the tune of 8,000 pounds, an astonishing sum, some of which went for the production of a typeface specially designed for the edition. Jonson contributed a series of poems for the front matter of *Coryat's Crudities,* a book published by William Stansby, the stationer who would become Jonson's most important publisher, although in 1611, Coryat would have bulked larger in Jonson's imagination than Stansby. Coryat was a friend and Jonson had many reasons to find his volume fascinating: it is a kind of picaresque travel narrative, and travel had the status of a moral threat in Jonson's imagination; the book is dominated by the figure of episode-as-salad, as "raw" experience, which would have tickled Jonson's eager culinary imagination; it is a reckless, hastily prepared autobiographical gesture, spilling from Stansby's press during the years in which Jonson was preparing his folio *Workes,* a classical gesture of composed literary self-presentation. But Jonson betrays another object of fascination in his acrostic poem on Thomas Coryat's name:

> O f travel he discourseth so at large,
> M arry he sets it out at his owne charge;
> A nd therein (which is worth his valour too)
> S hewes he dares more then *Paules Church-yard* durst do.[9]

The financing for this book was certainly unusual: Charles Cotton remembered it as late as 1676, when he wrote, "I will sit down and write my Travels, and like *Tom Coriate* print them at my own charge."[10] It is difficult to make sense of the attribution of *daring,* for the book was racy and would therefore sell, and it was duly entered, to Blount and Barrett, and so presumably had been licensed or was expected to be licensed shortly. That the stationers had reservations about publication may be a catchpenny fiction, an earnest of the raciness of the book, but there may have been some initial trouble over its licensing.[11] It seems that Coryat was engaged in a whirlwind of self-promotion: "he hath bene conveniently able to visite Towne and Countrie, Fayres and Mercats, to all places and all societies a *Spectacle* gratefull, above that of *Nineveh* or the Citie of *Norwich,*" Jonson wrote in the "character" he composed for the *Crudities,* "and he is now become the better *Motion,* by having this his Booke his *Interpreter:* which yet hath exprest his purse more then him."[12] Allowing for Jonson's exaggeration it would seem that Coryat really was attempting to make himself a popular phenomenon—"Topographicall Typographicall Thomas," as Hugo Holland called him; a cosmopolitan Will Kemp, according to John Strangwayes.[13] With its dozens of comic panegyrics, in several languages, the book was part of a waggish campaign of self-marketing and, although the long-promised publication apparently won the interest of Prince Henry, Coryat seems to have "dared" to pay for the printing in order to profit directly from the sales of the book, an eager embrace of the new mass market in books in preference to the differently chancy pursuit of traditional patronage.

Although publication by nonstationers could be accommodated, it was recognized as a potential disruption and was, technically speaking, an abuse of company regulations. As has been mentioned above, the Stationers' Court made a general ruling "against printinge for forens to the Company" as early as January 1598:

> ffor Remedie thereof, yt is ordered that if any person or persons
> of this Company shall hereafter print or cause to be printed any
> copie or booke which shall not be proper to hym self and whereof
> he shall not reape the whole Benefit to his own use by sellinge it
> in the Companye but shall suffer any other person or persons that
> shall not be of this companye to have the benefit of the sale or
> disposition thereof. Then in every suche case all and every suche
> bookes and copies shall and may be disposed & printed againe
> accordinge to the discretion of the m^r. wardens, and Assistentes
> pf this Companye. . . . And the partie or parties offendinge herein
> shall ipso facto Lose &forfait all his and their Right & interest in
> all & every suche booke & bookes.[14]

Naturally, exceptions to this strict rule would have *had* to have been made
in cases like that of Harrison's *Arch's of Triumph*. There is no documentary
record of instances in which the rule was enforced, though we shall see at
least one important occasion, from 1612, in which the rule seems to have
been brought to bear. It was no doubt hoped that the mere existence of the
rule would curb the shortsighted cooperation of individual stationers with
infringing "forens," but the practice persisted.

As in the case of Harrison's *Arch's of Triumph*, the authorial publication
of *Coryat's Crudities* barely disturbed the normal structures of stationer's
copyright. Neither Blount's name nor Barrett's appears on the imprint—it
was printed "by William Stansby for the author, 1611"—but there is nothing about their entrance to excite suspicion. The copyright seems to have
been a normal one; at least it satisfies one of the usual criteria of regularity, to wit, evidence of transfer of copyright at a later date: Barrett's widow
assigned the book to another stationer in 1626 (IV:158). But the copyright
was not absolutely secure. In the same year in which the *Crudities* was issued, Eld printed the *Odcombian Banquet* for Thorpe, a book that stripped
away Coryat's portion of the *Crudities*, leaving "only" the 120 quarto pages
of panegyrics that had made up the front matter of the *Crudities*. If Blount
and Barrett challenged the edition, no record of the challenge survives, and
one can imagine that Thorpe might have claimed in defense that Blount and
Barrett had entered *Coryat's* book, and not the (more interesting) material
prefixed to it. In a casual, but not a trivial way, Thorpe's action raises the same
question that Jonson had raised a year or two earlier in his printed masques,
the question of the precise object of copyright, with its even more difficult
subtending question, the question of how that objectification properly takes

place. Thorpe is not likely to have made a similar "interrogation" of a text not only "entered to" but also "printed for" his company brethren; his daring was almost certainly provoked and facilitated by Coryat's. Here, then, is a sign of tension, a sign that ad hoc arrangements with authors could disturb relations within the company of stationers.

In the following year a far less flamboyant figure than Coryat provoked a far more important instance of such disturbance: once again, it is Samuel Daniel who cuts the most distinctive figure in the history of authorship. If his 1601 *Works* is a milestone in the general *cultural* history of English authorship, *The First Part of the Historie of England* is an equally important landmark in the specifically institutional history of English intellectual property. This time it was Nicholas Okes who was guilty of "printinge for forens to the Company"; the book was printed in 1612, for the author's ostensibly private distribution. In his prefatory "Advertisements to the Reader," Daniel reports having paid for the printing of a "few copies only" of what was, in effect, a partial first draft of the *History* "which I heere divulge not, but impart privately to such Worthy Persons as have favored my indeavors herein."[15] As it turns out, this description is at least a little bit disingenuous, though the facts of the matter would have remained obscure had it not been for the documentary trail left by subsequent maneuvers for control of the copyright. Okes had entered the *History* in April, but on June 22 the entrance was canceled by order of the Stationers' Court. No reason for the cancellation is given, but because the book was reentered to Simon Waterson, it seems fair to assume that Daniel objected to Oke's entrance as not having been part of the original bargain. It will be recalled that Waterson had been Daniel's publisher for two decades: the reentrance was meant either to restore the circulation of the book to Daniel's control or to ensure that the potentially valuable copyright be vested with Daniel's friend—indeed, these two motives may blur into each other.

There was a brief lag of five days between the voiding of Oke's entrance and the entrance to Waterson. The court was willing to accept the objections to Oke's entrance, but Okes would have had his own colorable objections to any request that the copyright be vested with someone else, since his entrance had presumably been formally unimpeachable.[16] No doubt the Stationers' Court would have been a very sympathetic audience. We have here a dry run for Hayward's complaint of 1614 that Garbrand and Stansby were bringing out a new edition of his *Sanctuary of a Troubled Soul* "without his privitie"— only in Daniel's earlier case, the author's rights were even less secure. Daniel and Waterson were obliged to bring supervenient influence to bear, hence, presumably, the five-day delay and the unusual warrant for the June 27 entrance, "under th'andes of Master Doktor Mokett and Thwardens, and by the relacon of master Norton under his handwytinge that my Lord grace his [i.e., the archbishop of Canterbury's] pleasure is soe."[17] This did not end the matter: at least some of the stationers must have been annoyed by the high-handedness of the proceedings, and as many would have recognized that the reentrance posed some degree of threat to their own convenient monopolistic traditions. They kept their eyes on Daniel, and an entry in the Stationers' *Court Book C* indicates that they had had reason to suspect his good faith. The entry, dated 2 January 1613, settled what may have been a slightly protracted investigation:

> Mr. Samuell Daniell yt is agreed that he shall deliver into the hall
> 200 perfect bookes. whereof 40 be in thandes of wydowe Crosley
> of Oxford which the Companie shall receave of her as parcell of
> the said 200 bookes. And also that he shalbe presently paid for the
> said bookes .xx^{li}. Also he promiseth that yf he mend or add any
> thing to the book hereafter. That then yt shalbe prynted according
> to thorders of the Companie.[18]

The complaints that led to this are easy enough to reconstruct: during the previous June it would have been argued that Daniel had had no intention of vesting copyright in Okes when he hired him to print this portion of the *History*, that he was hardly interfering with the stationers' business, since this was to be a private edition, no competition whatsoever. Okes would have had his doubts, having printed upwards of two hundred copies for Daniel. Inquiries had been made and it was discovered that Daniel had indeed consigned a stock of copies with the Oxford bookseller Elizabeth Crosley: Daniel *was* competing on the stationers' turf. As if he himself were a refractory stationer, Daniel was therefore ordered to turn over what must have been a sizable portion, perhaps all, of the remaining stock of the *History*. Moreover, because Waterson had colluded with him, the company retaliated by effectively voiding his copyright, in accordance with the ordinance of January 1598: within a few months the 1612 edition was reprinted "for the Company of Stationers."[19] Considering the authority that had been brought to bear on Daniel's behalf during the confrontation of the previous June, the combination of the forced sale of Daniel's stocks and the corporate publication of the work constitutes a fairly bold assertion of company prerogatives. Strictly speaking, the archbishop of Canterbury could claim jurisdiction only over license, and that had already been conferred, yet the stationers must have felt that they must make a decisive stand at this juncture. They would not have risked offending the archbishop, however, had they believed their position to be in any way uncertain.

There is a bit more to this story, but before proceeding further it will be useful to reflect on one of the final stipulations of the January 1613 agreement, the proviso that if the *History* should be altered or enlarged, the copyright should vest with the company at large—or rather, since on the evidence of the 1613 reissue of *The First Part of the Historie* the copyright in the first part had already been settled on the company, *even if* Daniel should alter or enlarge the *History,* copyright would *continue* to vest with the company. The stipulation seems to protect against a dodge that may have been sporadically attempted as a means of relocating or, at least, challenging a settled copyright: the attempted claim that a revised version of a text be considered as a new work and thus be newly entered. The issue of continuity of copyright is a disputed area of historical bibliography, disputed largely because the evidence implies that conflicting practices operated simultaneously—one of the most obvious signs of the ferment in the sphere of intellectual property. Generally speaking a stationer could not hope to wrest copyright from a colleague simply on the grounds that the version originally entered and printed was somehow defective. When Edward White printed a "newly corrected and amended" text of *The Spanish Tragedy* in 1592, he was fined for infringing Abel Jeffes's original copyright. (Actually they were both fined, since White claimed that, earlier, Jeffes had infringed his rights in *Arden of Feversham.*) The stationers frequently sought to accommodate the competing interests of stable property and quality control: in this case, when the market presented itself for a new edition, Jeffes printed White's good text "for" White, but no transfer of copyright is recorded.[20] Although this accommodation seems to concede rival claims, the company usually gave the highest priority to maintaining continuity of copyright, which safeguarded capital and preserved the corporate authority, the crude anchor of "fellowship." In Kirschbaum's formulation, entrance or publication of a bad text could secure copyright, even copyright in a good text.[21]

This general rule, that copyright subsisted across widely variant texts, obtained in nondramatic publishing as well, as the example of Bacon's *Essays* will show clearly enough. The *Essays* were entered in 1597—there were difficulties over this first entrance, but they are not germane to this phase of our analysis—and Jaggard's second edition of this text, in 1606, was presumably protected by the initial copyright. (It was originally entered to Humphrey Hooper, and although there is no record of transfer, Hooper was still in business and there must have been an unrecorded arrangement between Jaggard and Hooper.) In 1612, however, John Beale entered and published a new edition of the *Essays:* nine of the original ten essays had been revised and twenty-nine had been added. It would appear at first that Bacon's revisions had helped Beale to a new property, that authorial industry had again usurped the Stationers' internal regulatory control, but this turns out not to have been the case. Almost as soon as Beale printed the new edition, Jaggard reissued his text, with the twenty-nine new essays appended on continuous sheets. Some haggling ensued, with the result that Beale printed subsequent editions of the *Essays,* but printed them *for* Jaggard.[22] This diplomatic arrangement is worked out along the same lines as those used to settle Jeffes and White's claims to *The Spanish Tragedy* twenty years earlier.

The principle of continuity could operate quite oddly in extreme cases. When Jaggard and Blount went to register those "Copies as are not formerly entred to other men" as part of their scrupulous commercial preparations for publishing the first Shakespeare folio, they did *not* enter Parts 2 and 3 of *Henry VI,* nor *The Taming of the Shrew.* Copyright in the very bad texts of *2 and 3 Henry VI* had already been established—they belonged to Thomas Pavier—and, since copyright in a bad text was a good copyright, Jaggard and Blount knew that they would need to settle things with Pavier. *The Taming of the Shrew* is an even more extreme case. Copyright in a play originally entered and thrice printed as *The Taming of a Shrowe* had descended to Smethwicke; that play may have been Shakespeare's first version of the play, or a garbled version of the same play that Jaggard eventually printed, or a play based on the play Jaggard eventually printed—it may even have been Shakespeare's *source*—but as the object of stationer's copyright it was effectively the same as the play that Jaggard intended to print and thus could not be made the object of a new entrance.[23] The principle of continuity was sometimes almost comically stretched, as in 1655, when Jane Bell printed Shakespeare's *King Lear* (in a text based on the second quarto of 1608) by virtue of the fact that she owned the rights, by transfer, in the anonymous play *King Leir.*

An instance of the sort of diplomacy used to resolve the competing claims on *The Spanish Tragedy* and Bacon's *Essays* may be usefully adduced here, since it suggests a degree of historical drift. In 1635, Daniel Frere entered William Lambard's legal treatise, *Archion,* and had it swiftly printed, to the apparent annoyance of Lambard's grandson, Thomas. The Stationers' Register records a new entrance of the work three months later, to Frere *and* to Henry Seile, specifying that the text being thus entered was "the true original Copie from the Authors executor. The former Entry of this booke to Daniell ffrere being hereby made void" (IV:341). Lambard's *Archion* brings us to the era of Jonson's second folio, and the competition between Frere's text and that which Seile acquired from Lambard's executor anticipates the legal dispute over Jonson's unpublished works between Benson and Crooke, on the one hand, and Walkley, on the other, a dispute between what might be called "stationer's copy" and "author's copy."

Although author's copy was asserted with novel vigor during the 1630s, it had made appearances earlier. It may be observed that this assertion was only very infrequently made by the author on his own behalf: Hayward, for example, is exceptional. Instead the author (or his executor) provides leverage in a struggle between stationers. This pattern is already observable late in 1586, in that early confrontation between author's and stationer's copy already discussed, when Waterson's brother-in-law, William Ponsonby, warned Fulke Greville that a manuscript of Sidney's *Arcadia* had been submitted for licensing—this, it seems, as part of a campaign to arrogate rights in *The New* (and "authorized") *Arcadia* to himself.[24]

When Ponsonby died, in 1604, Waterson inherited Ponsonby's rights in the *Arcadia* and in *The Faerie Queene*, but this is hardly the deepest aspect of the continuity between their careers. The collaboration of Greville and Ponsonby resembles the slightly simpler relationship between Daniel and Waterson; both these collaborations began at roughly the same time. From the *Arcadia* episode forward, such alliances functioned to hedge the works of the Sidney circle with unusual protections. Thomas Newman published *Astrophel and Stella* in 1591 without registration and, although it behooves the publisher to proclaim his solicitude for Sidney's reputation, one can perhaps detect some excess in his dedicatory epistle:

> I have been very carefull in the Printing of it, and where as
> being spred abroade in written Coppies, it had gathered much
> corruption by ill Writers: I have used their helpe in correcting
> and restoring it to his first dignitie, that I knowe were of skill and
> experience in those matters. And the rather was I moved to sett
> it forth, because I thought it pittie anie thing proceeding from so
> rare a man, shoulde bee obscured.

Perhaps hindsight makes one read this suspiciously: in September, Burghley commanded that Newman's edition be confiscated (Arber, *Transcript,* I:555). It may be that those interested in Sidney's reputation objected to the poor quality of Newman's text, for a better edition of *Astrophel and Stella* appeared before the year was out. Yet the principle of continuous copyright seems at first glance to have remained inviolate, since the revised text was also published by Newman. In fact, however, Newman's *Astrophel and Stella* is a boundary case; from one perspective, the continuity of copyright therein appears to have been slightly eroded. The erosion has to do with the inclusion, in the first edition, of "sundry other rare Sonnets of divers Noblemen and Gentlemen," among them twenty-eight sonnets from Daniel's *Delia*. Daniel protested the publication—

> Although I rather desired to keep in the private passions of my
> youth . . . : yet seeing I was betraide by the indiscretion of a
> greedie Printer, and had some of my secrets bewraide to the
> world, uncorrected: doubting the like of the rest, I am forced to
> publish that which I never ment.

Although this seems formulaic, it does sort with the external record. He goes on, "But this wrong was not onely doone to mee, but to him whose unmatchable lines have indured the like misfortune"—which makes sense of the suppression of the first edition of *Astrophel and Stella* and of the publication of the revised edition. It also helps explain a fact that should, at this point in our discussion, seem somewhat surprising—that Daniel lodged this protest in a 1592 edition of all fifty poems of *Delia,* an edition published not by Newman—who *might* be said to have established his right to these sonnets by virtue of having published the greater part of the sequence in his first edition of *Astrophel and Stella*—but by the man who would become Daniel's lifelong collaborator, Simon Waterson. Waterson had entered the book in February 1592 (II:603). When he and Daniel wrested copyright in *The First Part of the Historie of England* from Okes, who had registered that work, they were reusing a device that they had employed twenty years earlier.[25]

The narratives of most successful relocations of copy share a common feature. Rights to the *Arcadia* were turned over to Ponsonby only after an appeal to the licensers; Waterson secured the rights to *Delia* after Burghley's confiscation of the Sidney/Daniel collection of sonnets: the best hope of a stationer seeking to publish a revised, or better, or otherwise "more authorized" text was by means of an appeal to supervenient authority.[26] We have seen sporadic traces of such intervention in dramatic publishing—staying registrations from the late 1590s forward may function this way, to enable an acting company to select the publisher and control the timing of publication by deferring issue until some unusual sanction for publication be secured. And when Walkley wished to supplant Crooke's and Benson's claims to Jonson's unpublished works, he was obliged to appeal, first, to a secretary of state and, thereafter, to the Court of Chancery. When Daniel and Waterson sought to loosen Okes's grasp on the *History of England,* they turned to the archbishop of Canterbury. To my knowledge, only one author prior to

Hayward succeeded in relocating a copyright by direct intervention, but he is an exception who proves and so confirms the rule. On January 23, Bacon's *Essays* were entered to Richard Serger in the Stationers' Register; and on February 5, the exception makes itself felt at Stationers' Hall. The Register is laconic, as usual:

> *Humfrey hooper* Entred for his copie under thandes of Master
> FRAUNCIS BACON. Master Doctor STANHOPE master BAR-
> LOWE, and master warden *Dawson*, A booke intituled *Essaies,*
> *Religious meditations, Places of Perswasion and Disswation* by
> master FRAUNCIS BACON. (3:79)

Would that the Register were a bit more forthcoming. The entry tells us that Hooper's was an authorized edition, though we might have learned as much from the prefatory epistle that Bacon addressed to his brother, in which he informs the reader that

> These fragments of my conceites were going to print; To labour
> the staie of them had bin troublesome, and subject to interpre-
> tation; to let them passe had beene to adventure the wrong they
> mought receive by untrue Coppies, or by some garnishment.
> Therefore I helde it best discreation to publish them my selfe as
> they passed long ago from my pen. . . . And as I did ever hold,
> there mought be as great a vanities in retiring an withdrawing
> mens conceites (except they bee of some nature) from the world,
> as in obtruding them

he commits them to print.[27] It is unclear from this whether the untrue or garnished version to which Bacon refers here had fallen into Serger's hands or Hooper's. Hooper may have been given a good text in order to forestall Serger's unauthorized publication or he may himself have been prepared to go to press with a text that Bacon chose to supplant. We know that Hooper's edition was printed and available for sale two days after his 5 February entrance and from this we can infer that Serger's entrance was an attempt to forestall *Hooper's* edition, on the technicality that Hooper had neglected to make formal entrance of his own copy of Bacon's book—a stationer's power play.[28] Hooper will have appealed to Bacon himself, who impressively inter-vened against Serger's entrance by presenting himself at Stationers' Hall. (It must have been a quietly dazzling event: the essays were entered to Hooper that day, but the court did not steady itself to make a formal cancellation of Serger's entry until two days later.)[29] It would have been quite unclear to those present whether this was an *author's* power play—that is, whether Bacon claimed the right to stay that edition as an author or as an M.P. rapidly rising in his queen's esteem. At any rate, the evidence suggests that in 1597 only the authorial M.P. could make such a claim.

I have already argued that presenting texts as corrected, revised, augmented, or otherwise "under thandes of" the author was an important aspect of marketing in the late Elizabethan book trade. It may now be added that this significant feature of marketing, however important it is for many authors' sense of their own place in a developing book culture, does not impinge much on the calculus of property relations internal to the company. However much an individual author might wish to replace a bad text, the company continued its resistance to authorial intrusion.[30] Waterson and Ponsonby were unusually sympathetic and they had two good reasons for their advocacy of authors' texts. First, such authorial loyalties gave them continuing access to a coherent and valuable body of manuscripts, the works of Sidney, Spenser, Daniel, and the Countess of Pembroke. Moreover, their abiding ties to the Herberts gave them a base of power distinguishable from that constituted by company regulations and trade fellowship.

Waterson and Daniel leave an unusual documentary trail in the Stationers' Register. Kirschbaum discusses the next such extraordinary episode, another apparent relocation of copy, this from 1604, along the lines of that for *Delia.*[31] Important as was Daniel's *Vision of the Twelve Goddesses* in shaping the unfolding competition between Daniel and Jonson, it is even more intriguing as part of the slow erosion of the principle of continuous copyright. Edward Allde brought out a first edition without entrance soon after its January performance; Waterson's edition followed within the year: its dedication, by Daniel, to the Countess of Bedford contains what by now we have come to expect:

> In respect of the unmannerly presumption of an indiscreet
> Printer, who without warrant hath divulged the late shewe at
> Court, presented the eight of *January,* by the Queenes Majestie
> and her Ladies; and the same verie disorderly set forth: I thought
> it not amisse, seeing it would otherwise passe abroad, to the
> prejudice both of the Maske and the invention, to describe the
> whole forme thereof in all points as it was then performed.[32]

No dispute before the Stationers' Court is recorded, but copyright evidently vested with Waterson, who published the *Vision* again in 1623—although he may, of course, have reached the kind of accommodation with Allde that Stansby and Burre reached with the holders of copyright in works published in the Jonson folio of 1616. On the basis of a letter from Lord Worcester to Lord Shrewsbury, it was once thought that Allde's edition was actually called in, but the evidence is at best ambiguous; nonetheless the fact that the revised version was published for Waterson and not for Allde marks a break with the pattern we have observed for such publications as *The Spanish Tragedy,* Bacon's *Essays,* or Lewkenor's *Usage of the English Fugitives.*

Here is the bibliographic context from which Daniel's *History* emerged in 1612. Daniel had published the first edition of the work: unlike most authors he was accustomed to having his way with those stationers with whom he worked. Okes, the original printer, had registered the work: he was the only stationer involved in the publication and, since copyright was a privilege internal to the Stationers' Company, he could hardly have supposed that any would find his registration objectionable. Daniel and Waterson did object and the copyright was relocated, but they had to bring external pressure to bear to effect the relocation: most of the instances of such relocation on behalf of authorial will required such extraordinary measures. When it was discovered that Daniel's agents were secretly *selling* the *History,* the relocation was itself effectively voided: although the company could bow to pressure and give limited indulgence to authorial will, it could hardly acquiesce when an author surreptitiously laid claim to a large share of trade privileges. When the relocation of copyright was voided, copyright did not revert to the original entrant, but was instead vested in the company: Okes was neither to derive singular benefit nor to suffer singular risk from a defense of principle—and the risk might have been substantial, since it was the archbishop of Canterbury who had endorsed the original relocation of copyright. Moreover, this was a company matter, as had been recognized in the ordinance of 1598. Casual as they might be about day-to-day record keeping, the company often acted sharply and firmly when fundamental questions of corporate privilege were at stake. The new entrance stipulated that copyright in Daniel's *History* should stay with the company even "yf he mend or add any thing to the book hereafter": the stationers were slowly coming to recognize, and to defend against, a structural weakness in their system of copyright, that their protections were imperfectly suited to such otherwise unremarkable practices as revision, adaptation, augmentation, excision, sequel, and (the extreme case) minimal variation. In the burgeoning culture of writing that print had fostered, these practices had flourished, effectively challenging trade practices that had subsisted under a regime of habit and common sense, of impure practical reason.

I do not wish to overgeneralize from this particular case. The proviso may simply recognize that Daniel's history of mending and adding had, in the cases of *Delia* and *The Vision of the Twelve Goddesses,* irregularly constituted new copyrights for Waterson and had enabled him to publish books that made prior editions less marketable. Daniel and Waterson may have constituted a special case, but their methods were ready-to-hand. Authorial protests against indiscreet, careless, or greedy printers long antedate the publication of *Delia;* if these protests had originally served to demonstrate an author's modest disposition to privacy and to draw attention to corrections and expansions in second editions, these protests were now working to disadvantage some printers and to favor others. From this time forward, London's stationers might well regard this old authorial rhetoric with a new wariness, for it had unsettled their property.[33]

The narrative of Daniel's bibliographic career may now be carried a step further. Neither he nor Waterson attempted to dispute the company's appropriation of copyright in January 1613, nor did they protest the subsequent reprinting of the 1612 edition "for the Company of stationers." But when Daniel finally completed the *History of England* several years later, he proceeded in what should now be a more or less predictable fashion. The book was printed in 1618 with a page, preceding the title page, that announces how he managed to evade the terms of the 1613 agreement:

> A Speciall Priviledge, Licence and Authority, is granted by the
> Kings Majesties Letters Patents, unto the Author *Samuel Daniel,*
> one of the Groomes of the Queenes Majesties most Honorable
> Privy Chamber, for him, his Executors, Administrators, Assignes
> or Deputies, to Print, or cause to bee Imprinted, and to sell
> assigne and dispose, to his, or their benefit, This Booke, intituled,
> *The Collection of the History of England.* Streightly forbidding
> any other to Imprint or cause to be Imprinted, to Import, utter
> or sell, or cause to be Imported, uttered, or sold, the sayd Booke
> or Bookes, or any part thereof, within any of his Majestyes
> Dominions, upon payne of his Majesties high displeasure, and to
> forfeit Five pounds Lawfull *English* Mony for every such Booke or
> Bookes, or any part thereof . . . , besides the Forfeiture of the sayd
> Booke, Bookes, &c. (sig. [ ]₁ᵛ).

This is not quite as unaccommodating as it seems at first glance: the book was printed "for the Author" by Nicholas Okes. But the privilege is not simply an ad hoc arrangement between the Crown and a loyal retainer; it is not disarticulated from the institutional history of the book trade. It emerges, rather, from a history of continuous and coherent interaction between an author and a company deliberately at odds over where the rights to control the reproduction and distribution of writing ought properly to be located.

This is hardly to suggest that the granting of such patents to nonstationers was unprecedented.[34] Though not a member of the Stationers' Company, Francis Flower became the queen's printer for books in Latin, Greek, and Hebrew in 1573. I have already had occasion to refer to the patent granted to Byrd and Tallis two years later affording them control of all music publishing; of course, neither of these composers were stationers. The music patent was a source of friction early in its history: although neither Tallis nor Byrd seem to have meddled in the lucrative trade in singing psalters, Byrd apparently attempted to monopolize all printing of lined paper.[35] But the friction soon relaxed. In 1598 the patent passed to Thomas Morley, who, though not a stationer, not only farmed his patent to assignees within the company, but established his own press as well, apparently without company protest. As we shall see, such grants as that to Byrd and Tallis or to Daniel were not isolated. The grant to Daniel is unusual insofar as it was a *calculated* response to commercial arrangements about which he was well-informed and which he was decorously but firmly resisting; yet even less well-informed patentees threatened the institution of stationer's copyright, albeit less deliberately. The clash of patent and copyright now commands our attention, and not only because it was one of the most powerful engines of change in the evolution of early modern intellectual property. The history of copyright finds its proper context within the larger history of economic monopolies.[36]

Henry Tudor's dual legacy to Elizabeth was a sturdily elaborated administrative structure and a time bomb of debt.[37] The grant of patents of monopoly was one of Elizabeth's characteristic responses to the fiscal crisis of her reign. As that crisis deepened during the last years of her reign and through the reign of her successor, the patent became one of the leading objects of protest: in the lop-sided public debate on monopoly some of the key themes of revolutionary politics were articulated. This ferment has obvious implications for both the history of authorship and the history of the book trade, the microhistories that I have been reconstructing. Those implications may be quickly sketched. Printing patents such as that granted to Daniel are rather small fry when compared with, say, the alum monopoly, yet they enabled Daniel and others like him to beat the stationers at their own game. On a different flank, the broadly diffused popular hostility to patents emboldens an author like George Wither to hazard a more or less principled attack on stationer's copyright and provides him with a vital vocabulary of protest. The stationers, for their part, recognized that their own prerogatives would need shoring up in the face of a developed antimonopolistic climate of opinion, and this led them to a renewed emphasis on their status as ideological workers. This is how they presented themselves to a skeptical parliament in the early 1640s and how they would continue to present themselves throughout the seventeenth century.

The Growth of Monopolies and the Semantics of Invention

The state was both the subject and object of mercantilist economic policy.
The state had to assert itself in two opposing directions. On the one hand, the demands of the social institutions of the confined territories had to be defended against the universalism characteristic of the Middle Ages. . . . But this aspect was altogether of lesser importance, for in most practical matters the Middle Ages were cast in the mould of particularism rather than in that of universalism. For this reason, undoubtedly the greater power of mercantilism was directed inwards and not outwards, against the still more narrowly confined social institutions, cities, provinces and corporations which had dominated medieval social activity.

Eli F. Heckscher, *Mercantilism*

Phylarchus, in the twenty-fifth book of his History, . . . states "the Sybarites, having given loose to their luxury, made a law that . . . if any confectioner or cook invented any peculiar and excellent dish, no other artist was allowed to make this for a year, but he alone who invented it was entitled to all the profit to be derived from the manufacture of it for that time; in order that others might be induced to labour at excelling in such pursuits. And in the same way, it was provided that those who sold eels were not to be liable to pay tribute, nor those who caught them either. And in the same way the laws exempted from all burdens those who dyed the marine purple and those who imported it."

Athenaeus, *Deipnosophistae*

Protected printing of the early and mid-sixteenth century occupies an important place in the prehistory of the Stuart monopoly culture. Several lines in the genealogy of the Stuart patent have been traced—to Sabellicus's printing monopoly in mid-fifteenth-century Venice, to Aldus's unenforcable monopolies of Greek printing and of printing in italics, to Tallis and Byrd's music patent, and to Day's *A.B.C.* In the course of examining these vignettes, the early patent has been shown to elaborate, specify, and, in some instances, confound a variety of older institutional protections. The protection of individual craftsmen—of printers or of other manufacturers—specifies monopolies traditionally proper to corporate institutions (market towns, guilds) and although such protections originate as occasional political interventions designed to attract and naturalize new forms of luxury production, they develop into protomercantilist *habits* of protectionism and emerge as crucial to royal fiscal policy. The protection of authorized texts, in particular, adapts not only ecclesiastical canonization of texts but also the *pecia* system, by means of which university monopolies on education were extended to enable the controlled production and distribution of study-texts. In a pungent instance of the recoil of individualized protection upon the corporate privileges from which it, at least partly, descends, we have seen the printing patent clash with traditional guild monopolies and privileges as early as the 1570s, in the class struggle that erupted within the Stationers' Company.

It will be useful to trace this eruption to its roots in the 1530s, recurring to the somewhat cryptic message that Cromwell bundled with a letter to Richard Grafton in 1538, the copy of a royal proclamation stipulating that the words *"cum privilegio regali"* not be printed "without adding *ad imprimendum solum.*" I return to this moment in order to indicate the emergence of the trade *itself* as an object of state concern distinguishable from the crude ideological policing per se. Recall that Grafton, hard at work on production of the Great Bible, took this proclamation as a warning that license and privilege were not identical and should not be represented as mutually entailed. The interrelation of these two regulatory functions remains to be charted.

The gnomic news from Cromwell shocked Grafton since, as he saw it, the 1538 proclamation split economic from ideological policy. Of course, privilege—like stationer's copyright a few decades later—may usually be assumed to entail royal or ecclesiastical sanction; privileges were not likely to be conferred in subversive or heterodox books. At this especially nervous juncture, however, privilege was to be treated merely as a commercial guarantee and licensing, the mechanism of ideological regulation, was technically splintered off from the elementary commercial monopoly. However frequently the two functions would be reunited—and it was very much in the stationers' corporate interest to obscure the distinction between them—their tendency to diverge critically distinguishes English book culture. The remarkable powers conferred on the London Stationers' Company, their powers of commercial self-regulation, had the effect of maintaining an appreciable degree of distinction between the commercial status of books and their ideological charge. This may be contrasted with the situation in, say, France, where the absence of a deliberate mechanism for self-regulation within the book trade kept the two forms of regulation somewhat less distinct; in France, therefore, the recognition of issues of intellectual property lagged that recognition in England and, thence, *authorial* involvement in the competition for commercial control of texts was somewhat retarded.

Of course, crude state ideological control and state economic control were never fully disarticulated under Henry. Grafton's shock at the inhibition of his monopoly was no doubt compounded when Cromwell insisted that the Great Bible be sold at ten shillings per unbound copy, so that the 1536 injunction requiring each parish to purchase a copy of the authorized English Bible could be satisfied easily. The price threatened Grafton and his associates with real hardship.[38] Cranmer took up their case in a letter to Cromwell, urging that they be allowed to sell the book for 13s. 4d. and then proposing a compromise: "Nevertheles they ar right well contented to sell theym for x s., so that you wolbe so good lorde unto theym, as to graunte hensforth none other Lycence to any other printer, saving to theym, for the printyng of the said bible."[39] Eventually Cromwell himself received a grant by letter patent "that no manner of persone or persones within this oure realme shall enterprise attempt or sett in hande to print any bible in the english tonge of any maner of volume duryng the space of fyve yeres next ensuyng after the date hereof, but only suche as shalbe deputid assignid and admytted by the said lorde Crumwell."[40] So Grafton's initial shock, the threat of a severing of exclusive privilege from permission, was compounded by price control and, finally, the displacement of the privilege itself. Worse was coming: in 1541 he was jailed for publishing an attack by Melancthon on the Six Articles and thenceforth was deprived of his "deputed" privilege in Bible printing. His fortunes improved, however, three years later.

As mentioned in chapter 3, in 1544 Henry had granted a monopoly in the printing of all service books to Grafton and Whitchurch.[41] One may plausibly argue that the grant of this patent was ideologically motivated, for service books, perhaps even more than the Bible, were particularly vulnerable to adjustments conducing to heretical doctrine. And yet the terms of the initial grant to Grafton and Whitchurch emphasize mercantile as well as ideological policy, with perhaps slightly greater emphasis on the former. Certainly, Henry VIII had no reason to obscure or misrepresent his intent:

> Where in tymes past it hathe been usualsy [*sic*] accustumed that
> thies Bookes of Divine service, that is to sey, the *Masse Booke,*
> the *Graill,* the *Antyphoner,* the *Himptuall,* the *Portans,* and
> the *Prymer,* bothe in Latyn and in Englyshe of *Sarum use,* for
> the Province of Canterbury have been Prynted by Strangers in
> other and strange Countreys, partely to the greate Losse and
> Hynderaunce of our Subjects, who bothe have the sufficient Arte
> Feate and Trade of Printing, and by Imprintyng suche Bookes
> might profitably and to th'use of the Common Welthe be set
> on worke, and partely to the setting forthe of the *Byshopp of
> Romes* usurped Auctoritie and keping the same in contynuall
> Memorye, contrary to the Decrees Statutes and Lawes of this our
> Realme, . . . to th'entent that hereafter We woll have theym more
> perfectely and faithfully and truely doon to the high Honour of
> Almyghty God, . . . We of our Grace especiall have Graunted and
> Geven Privilege, etc.[42]

This is perfectly accurate: the preponderance of service books, and particularly of primers, had been produced abroad. The grant to Grafton and
Whitchurch not only fosters native industry, it restrains the tendency, increasingly a source of royal alarm, of English currency to migrate south. This
sort of generalized grant, a grant in a whole class of books, may have been
somehow associated with the office of king's printer. When Grafton received
that title in the next reign it carried with it the exclusive right to print official acts and proclamations. The contemporaneous creation of the office of
King's Typographer and Bookseller (granted to Reynold Wolfe) also carried
such a class monopoly.[43] Wolfe became the official printer of maps and of
books in Latin, Greek, or Hebrew, including Greek and Latin grammars;
in addition to an annual salary Wolfe received exclusive printing rights in
whatever he should choose to print. Wolfe's patent evolved into clearer form
as it passed to Francis Flower, for during Flower's tenure the office of Royal
Latin Printer was understood to carry with it a monopoly in grammar and
accidence books.[44]

Royal privileges in particular books continued to be granted sporadically
to stationers, yet the development of the stationers' formal registration system at least partly obviated the usefulness of such privileges. The phrase "cum
privilegio" soon lost even the limited commercial specificity it had once had:
by the second half of the century it functions as a general warrant of propriety, signifying approval by the licensing authorities, allowance by the Stationers' Company, and, occasionally, the protection of the king's privilege. In

effect, the royal power to enforce a monopoly was delegated to the Stationers' Company and so reinforced the municipal monopoly that was the customary perquisite of its guild status. But the privilege was never fully displaced by stationer's copyright—the latter was easier to acquire but the former could cover whole classes of books and, in the case of particular works obviously of exceptional commercial value, was no doubt thought a particularly sturdy form of protection. The survival of the blanket monopolies carried by the offices of Royal Printer and Royal Latin Printer remained as signs of the reserve of royal economic power ultimately disruptive to guild stability (and, implicitly, to municipal trade regulation).[45]

This pattern of delegation and reservation may be traced clearly in one of the first grants of blanket or class monopolies, the grant to Richard Tottel in 1553 of the patent in all law books.[46] Mary awarded the patent for seven years; when it was about to lapse, Tottel, perhaps hesitant about asking Elizabeth to continue even a small feature of Marian policy, appealed to his peers for confirmation of the patent, applying to the Stationers' Company itself for extension of his charter.[47] But in January of 1559, he managed to acquire a grant for life of this broad monopoly, this time from Elizabeth herself.[48] That year, in fact, saw several lucrative grants by letters patent as Elizabeth sought ways to make the press especially responsive to her own will. Jugge and Cawood were named queen's printers in March, Seres received a lifetime patent in the primer and in all books of private devotion, and John Daye received a seven-year privilege in Cunningham's *Cosmographical Glass* and in any other book he chose to print thenceforth.[49] Though the number of these blanket monopolies was never great, they constituted a significant economic force within the book trade, as the case of John Wolfe's "reformation" clearly shows. Moreover, the significance of these trade monopolies extends far beyond the sphere of the book trade.

The year 1559 was decisive in the history of English economic policy. A set of related recommendations were brought in to Parliament (probably in April) aimed primarily at discouraging currency outflows and restraining inflation.[50] These essentially monetarist recommendations are part of a general royal and parliamentary effort to implement a systematic economic policy. They anticipate the currency reform of the next year, the official crackdown on economic offenses in 1561, and, eventually, the massively influential employment and wage intervention: the Statute of Artificers of 1563.[51] Parliamentary policy in these years is distinctively conservative, concerned with preserving traditional industrial structures; the Crown, on the other hand, had an interest in encouraging new enterprises. Both parliamentary and royal policy seem to have been guided by Cecil, but they do not originate with him. Certainly the royal interest in development is characteristically Tudor, a continuation of Henrician policy, though it is pursued with a new intensity characteristically Elizabethan.

I began my discussion of local protectionism by referring to the short-term monopoly granted to John of Speyer, a mid-fifteenth century grant calculated to establish a press and perhaps to foster a printing industry within the Venetian republic. Although the Italian states had long led Europe in such efforts to attract foreign expertise, English monarchs, beginning with Edward III, had occasionally made similar efforts.[52] Under the Tudors, this practice was invigorated. Though the monopolies most frequently attacked toward the end of the sixteenth century constrained freedom to import foreign goods, the original form of monopoly consisted of exclusive rights of manufacture, not of trade: it was designed to encourage native industry, and this seems to have been the motive behind most of the Henrician and Edwardian grants.[53] Sometimes the Crown was pressured into such "modernizing" policies, as in the early 1540s when Henry VIII sought out foreign expertise in iron mining and manufacture because of rumours of a Dutch export ban.[54] Foreign pressure and practice must have stimulated the proliferation of monopoly grants to a fairly significant degree, for before the middle of the sixteenth century, alien craftsmen clearly expected such favors from European monarchs: in 1537, Antonio Guidotti, a Venetian, wrote to Cromwell asking him to intercede with the Crown on behalf of some Italian silk weavers who were willing to set up shop in England provided that they be awarded by a "privilege for 15 or 20 years that no man may make such work except under him."[55] Such protection was becoming one of the characteristic instruments of international economic competition. It is worth remembering here that denization, the grant of rights to immigrate, is usually as important a component of these grants as is the monopoly, for the patent protects alien experts not only from competition but from the local constraints of guilds engaged in related production and of municipalities jealous of the economic rights of its burgesses. Such privileges consolidate royal authority over the economy and erode local jurisdictions; they are critical instruments of nationalization.

Grants to aliens on behalf of native industrial growth were extended in two important ways during the first part of the century. First, the favoritism shown to continental experts was tentatively extended to native specialists: a protection once granted almost exclusively to aliens was now being sought and secured by native entrepreneurs, who customarily offer the Crown an interest in the undertaking as part of their petition for the privilege.[56] One can speak of a real shift in the function of this form of protection under Elizabeth, who (according to a count that excludes printing patents) granted twenty-one monopolies by letters patent to foreigners in the course of her reign, and thirty to English natives.[57] The evolution of the printing privilege provides one of the earliest and most telling examples of this extension. Because the press was crucial for the promotion of Tudor political and ecclesiastical policy, protection of the native book trade and its leading members was particularly convenient; tendencies in economic policy were reinforced by interest in a specifically national ideological regulation. Elizabeth and Cecil recognized that the importation of dissenting religious books had consistently threatened England's various orthodoxies; and one of the easiest ways to impede such imports was to accede to the petitions of the stationers, collectively and, in particular cases, individually.

In the wake of the printing patents granted in 1559 come a variety of patents to experts in other areas—makers of soap, of gunpowder and saltpeter, of glass, sulfur, and oil; tanners and glassmakers; and, above all, miners, metallurgists, and civil engineers.[58] Pumps for clearing mines and devices for draining wetlands are particularly favored—half a century before the boom in such patents was lampooned in *The Devil Is an Ass*—for the Crown used these patents to encourage large-scale enterprises.[59] The grants, then, favor *projects*, undertakings characterized not only by alien skills but also by economic risk. In the patents for such large public works, moreover, we can discern the second, and perhaps the more remarkable, way in which the protection of alien expertise was extended under Elizabeth: the patent of monopoly shifts its protection from the unfamiliar to the new.

To some extent, the emphasis on novelty is a convenience of political rhetoric. In the face of long-standing local protectionisms, the grant of patents to aliens seemed supererogatory; even grants to natives, emanating from a distant court, could seem an unwonted obtrusion. It therefore behooved the patentee to insist that he was bringing a new industry—or at least an unprecedented technique—along with his monopoly. Thus Jacobus Acontius, a Protestant radical born in Trent, submitted the following appeal to Elizabeth sometime during the first few years of her reign:

> Nothing is more honest than that those who, by searching, have
> found out things useful to the public should have some fruit of
> their rights and labours, as meanwhile they abandon all other
> modes of gain, are at expense in experiments, and often sustain
> much loss, as has happened to me. I have discovered most
> useful things, new kinds of wheel machines, and of furnaces for
> dyers and brewers, which when known, will be used without my

consent, except there be a penalty, and I, poor with expenses and
labour, shall have no returns. Therefore I beg a prohibition against
using any wheel machines, either for grinding or bruising, or any
furnaces like mine, without my consent.[60]

The petition is a semantic gold mine. First, it proposes invention as a "mode
of gain" distinguishable from all other such modes—a particular form of economic labor deserving particular protections. Such a principle acquired no
formal legal standing under Elizabeth, although applications for monopolies
predicated on novelty multiplied (and assertions of invention as a form of
labor continue). Acontius's rhetoric is revealing in other ways, though what
it reveals is a telling degree of uncertainty. His petition presents sketchy versions of both of the two great and competing modern arguments for patent
protection. On the one hand, he appeals for the monopoly as a gracious reward for labor in the public interest; on the other hand, he asserts that innovation creates a kind of natural property: "furnaces like mine." Acontius was
an alien, to be sure, but he makes his claim as a professional innovator, as an
inventor.[61]

As early as 1399, it was established that those seeking *any* form of royal
grant "shall make express Mention in their Petitions of the Value of the Thing
so to be demanded. . . . And in case they make not such Mention in their said
Petitions, and that duely proved, the King's Letters Patents thereof made
shall not be available."[62] Petitions for exclusive exploitation of a new technique or device—for patents of invention—tended to offer some form of
what came to be known as a patent specification, a drawing or a model of
the device or a description of the technique to be protected, representations
intended to distinguish the object of protection from other technologies.[63]
The discipline of such specification, the rhetorical work of individuating the
object of protection, is a crucial precondition for the eventual constitution of
intellectual property as such.

Both transitions under discussion here—from the alien to the native;
from the unfamiliar to the new—leave their traces in the patent granted to
George Cobham in May 1562, around the time of Acontius's petition. Together with his partner, Tomasso Chanata, Cobham had asked the queen for
the right to sole import and exploitation of a new form of dredging machine,
urging the "diligent travel" required to discover the machine. The queen acceded to the petition, though she made the grant to Cobham alone, in order
to "give courage to others to study and seke for the knowledge of like good
engines and devyses."[64] The terms employed in this transaction are in a state
of subtle adjustment: in such uses of "travel" and "seeking" the labor of ex-
ploration (for the purposes of import) shades off toward the labor of practical

imagination. *Discover* and *invent* had long been words with strongly spatial connotations, but that spatial character was being worn away, displaced, as *novelty* moved toward the semantic center of these words. This semantic motion was by no means smooth: all the social, economic, and political tensions that come to a head in the debate on monopolies at the turn of the next century impinge on the uses of such terms. And, naturally, the semantic shift was as slow as it was unsteady.[65] Forty years after Acontius's petition for monopoly protections, when such grants began to suffer sustained scrutiny and attack, Bacon mounted a theoretical apology for the patent in Parliament, but in terms that seem pulled both from the past and toward the future. The vocabulary of discovery was under sufficient semantic pressure that it could be easily parsed into distinguishable forms, into the alien and the native, the uncommon and the unprecedented: "If any man out of his own Wit, industry or indeavour finds out anything beneficial for the Common-wealth, or bring in any new Invention, which every subject of this Kingdom may use; yet in regard of his pains and travel therein, her Majesty perhaps is pleased to grant him a Priviledge to use the same only by himself or his Deputies for a certain time."[66]

Historians of literature will recognize that "invention" was undergoing a similar transformation as a technical rhetorical term. For centuries the science of invention, the methodical probing and elaboration of the topics available for speech or writing, was conceived as a fundamentally spatial system, a trek within mental space—hence the cognates "topic" and "topography," or the connotations of "common*place*."[67] But one of the most powerful upheavals in Renaissance rhetorical theory is the "dislocation" of invention; in fact, it was an upheaval that eventually led to the collapse of traditional rhetoric. Walter Ong has been the important chronicler of this shift, whereby the verbal craftsman was forced to innovation. The distinctions between rhetoric and dialectic were variously challenged: the dialectician was to acquire the rhetorician's intellectual agility and the rhetorician was to submit to ever stricter standards of efficacy, answerability, pertinence, and point. Invention was no longer to be a process of sorting through established categories and recovering received formulae, all imagined as the systematic traversing of a mental edifice or landscape; it was instead to be a method for, well, inventing—an uncertain method for surprising rather than reaffirming, for coming to terms with the unmapped.

Nowhere are the effects of this dislocation of mental effort so striking—and so remarkably unmediated—as in the poetry of Milton. Again and again, Milton stages a crisis of vocation as a crisis of location. "Where may she wander now?" asks the ambitious and despairing young quester of *Comus*, while with false surmise, the uncouth but rising poet wonders

> Whether beyond the stormy *Hebrides*
> Where thou perhaps under the whelming tide
> Visit'st the bottom of the monstrous world;
> Or whether thou to our moist vows denied,
> Sleep'st by the fable of *Bellerus* old,
> Where the great vision of the guarded Mount
> Looks toward *Namancos* and *Bayona's* hold.
>
> ("Lycidas," ll. 156–62)

But the jitter of possible place is most nervous in that hue and cry after the Muse carried out at the opening of *Paradise Lost*.

> Sing Heavenly Muse, that on the secret top
> Of *Oreb,* or of Sinai, didst inspire
> That Shepherd, who first taught the chosen Seed,
> In the Beginning how if Heav'ns and Earth
> Rose out of *Chaos:* Or if *Sion* Hill
> Delight thee more, and *Siloa's* Brook that flow'd
> Fast by the Oracle of God.   (I:6–12)

The strength of the relative constructions flaunted here, the strength of the providential relations that those constructions carry, throws the anxious uncertainty of place into relief. The nervous uncertainty with which the space of poetic imagination, the location of the Muse, is evoked grows calmer as the poem proceeds—

> Yet not the more
> Cease I to wander where the Muses haunt
> Clear Spring, or shady Grove, or Sunny Hill
>
> (III:26–28)

—but it is permanently uncertain nonetheless. And while it may be true that the poem is full of uncertainties, of time, intention, and reference, the "or's" that expand and, often, disperse the poem originate specifically in the dislocation of the Muse.

To account for this dislocation literary historians usually begin by alleging Milton's discomfort over the propriety of adapting the pagan apparatus of poetic inspiration to the higher exigencies of Christian theology. But other motives for this dislocation must be sought in the seismic internalization of intellectual authority, and the concomitant disestablishment of local authority that was felt, in religion, as the Protestant attack on cult, and, in the economy,

as the internationalization of markets and the discrediting of traditional protectionism. These would provide the cultural springs for Ong's history of
rhetoric, with its narrative of the burgeoning importance and transformed understanding of invention, as well as for the shift in poetic practice prefigured
in Milton's poem. Also relevant here is John Guillory's account of the confrontation between inspiration and imagination within the so-called Dante
controversy that bulks so large in sixteenth-century Italian literary criticism,
a controversy over the truth-claims and sanctity of the *Commedia*.[68] Guillory singles out two of Dante's proponents, Bellisario Bulgarini and Jacopo
Mazzoni, the first of whom claimed that the spiritual authority of the epic
depended on Dante's passivity to the genesis of the poem. For Bulgarini, that
is, the poet mediates a spirtual influx, "visitations upon us of powers outside
ourselves, not the workings of our own minds"; for Mazzoni, not inspiration
but imagination, the mind's own powers, makes the *Commedia*. Whereas in
traditional psychological theory, imagination had a mediating and nearly mechanical function, Mazzoni assigns it a more originative and more volatile
potency; Mazzoni's innovation as a theorist of poetry was to insist that to describe a poem as the product of the imaginative faculty, and thus as a willed
creation, was not to denigrate it. In rhetoric, poetics, and poetic practice,
some version of individualized conceptual innovation—answerable only to
practicability and nature—displaces principles of mediation, the verbal artist
as endlessly answerable mediator of inspiration or tradition.

It may be stimulating to allow Baudrillard to gloss this displacement, as
he does when he describes the transition by which "the oeuvre becomes the
original. Its meaning passes from the restitution of appearances to the act
of inventing them. . . . And this new act is temporalized: it is the irreversible
moment of invention to which other irreversible creative moments can only
be subsequent."[69] That the moment under description here is not the late sixteenth century but the late nineteenth or early twentieth century is perhaps
not so surprising. This "birth of the modern" is reenacted at the occasion of
any important struggle for control of a powerful new information technology.
A transformation in the available means of storing and distributing information inevitably requires of a culture that it renegotiate its conception of how
information is *produced*, that it reinvent invention.

The Attack on Monopolies and the Patent in the Subject

> Here's a trim business towards, and as idle as the players going to
> Law with their poets.
>
> Brome, *The Court Beggar*

> I like not those patents. Sirrah, they that have them do, as the
> priests did in old time, buy and sell the sinnes of the people. So
> they make the King believe they mend what's amisse, and for
> money they make the thing worse than it is. There's another thing
> in too. . . . 'Tis pity that one subject should have in his hand that
> might do good to many through the land.
>
> Heywood (?), *1 Edward IV* (*Dramatic Works*)

Acontius, the Tredentine émigré, has been credited with having invented not only a number of useful contrivances, but the idea of a patent system as well. Though this latter claim will not stand up, it is true that patents proliferate from fairly early on in Elizabeth's reign, which is when Acontius wrote the principled petition already quoted. As has already been intimated, the grant of patents and the award of monopolies became an important aspect of Elizabethan fiscal policy, and it was Burghley who presided over this development. Elizabeth had inherited a number of debts with her title: the monopoly grant—of manufacture, trade, or regulation—could function as payment, with no immediate prejudice to her finances. Customary revenues were unstable; the monopoly, on the other hand, could be sold for money up front or for a royal share in future revenues derived from working the patent. Thus, in the 1580s, ingenious artisans almost always applied for monopolies in partnership with rich and noble men. Whereas earlier patentees seem only to have worked their patents to protect against local or regional competition, the patentees of the seventies and eighties attempted to enforce national monopolies.[70] The monopoly grant thus began to reverse one of its key prior functions, for as patentees enforced their rights more stringently and over larger areas, the patent ultimately constrained industrial experiment and growth in some industries.[71] Moreover, by creating a protobureaucracy and extending royal prerogative into markets traditionally semi-autonomous, the monopoly manifests itself as an infringement of custom, of community, of the rights of the subject. Thirsk nicely captures the steady swelling of protest, when she observes that Lord Treasurer "Burghley started a file of documents on proposals *for* projects and complaints *against* projects: its continuation in James's reign was a thick file . . . entitled *Projects, Propositions, and Remonstrances.* The remonstrances grew until they were as voluminous as the propositions."[72]

The development of opposition to monopoly protection has never been fully chronicled.[73] Robert Bell raised a protest in Parliament in 1571, but no one joined his cause. It was not until the 1580s that opposition began to coalesce and to focus not only on a particular disruption of local economies, but on the principles implicit in such grants. The monopoly increased the leverage of capital over labor, amplified it, and thus accelerated the rate of change within an industry (though it seldom transformed its structures). As we have seen, the patents of monopoly effected a similar acceleration of developments in state power, consolidating royal authority over an increasingly national economy with the political radicalizing effect that those protesting the monopolies were forced to describe established royal prerogatives as somehow abusive: as Cecil would put it in 1601, "Two great things had been drawn in question:"—by which he also means "drawn into direct competition"—"first the Princes power; secondly the freedom of Englishmen."[74] During the early years of Elizabeth's reign, low-level tensions began to develop between many English guilds and the Crown.[75] In 1563 the Statute of Artificers conferred the authority to fix wages on J.P.'s, thus powerfully asserting central economic prerogative and unsettling customary local authority, particularly that of individual guilds.[76] It is also the case that Elizabeth encouraged the formation of new guilds, yet her purpose in so doing was to secure industrial quality control and to limit the growth of older guilds whose influence threatened to mushroom as a result of general English industrial expansion.[77]

The disturbance in the Stationers' Company, John Wolfe's "Reformation," is in the vanguard of the protest against monopolies; it articulates this very sense that once-normal structures had somehow suddenly become palpably abusive. William Seres's account of the protest, though no doubt intended to heighten the sense of its scandal, seems to represent the issues at stake fairly:

> certen yo[u]nge men of the saide company . . . pretend that in
> Iustice yt standeth with the best pollicye of this realme that the
> printunge of al good and laufull bokes be at libertye for every man
> to pryunt without grauntinge or allowinge of any priviledge by
> the prynce to the contrary[.] And in dede they doe not onely go
> about to derogate the princes awthoritye aswell for grauntinge of
> suche like priviledges as also of all lycences for the transportacon
> of clothe wolle beare and suche like sayeng in expresse termes
> that the privilege for sole printinge of all bokes is agaynst the lawe
> and that her majestie oughte not to graunte any suche.[78]

Though this anticipates many of the protests that would later erupt in other industries, the book trade was not preeeminently disturbed by the royal privilege. Indeed the relation of the book trade to the development of both monopolies and their discontents is quite complicated. Subject to some degree of ideological regulation throughout Europe, workers in the book trade had long been accustomed to relatively unpredictable governmental interference in its industrial relations. Moreover the printing privilege, although never available to more than a fraction of stationers, had early established itself as a limited and unexceptional form of monopoly within the book trade.

Since privileges had operated continuously within the English book trade since 1517, we must puzzle over how they became objectionable in the early eighties. The exercise of Crown prerogative per se could hardly have been the culprit, since the prerogative was very close to the surface not only of the printing patent but also of the registration system, which rested on the midcentury royal sanction of the stationers' charter. The Stationers' Company enjoyed exceptional benefits in its partnership with Cecil's royalist nationalism. If the freemen of London's guilds were exempt from the commercial constraints of the Statute of Artificers under the Custom of London, and so were still free to poach on others' trade, the Stationers' Company was exempt from the effects of the exemption, its own monopoly intact. The royal interventions that produced the earliest printing privileges had evolved into a general protection of the book trade, and yet, less than two decades into Elizabeth's reign, privilege and copyright begin to face off as opponents. Since the copyright system subjected *all* book production, at least potentially, to communally constrained competition, the royal prerogative so close to the surface in the archaic patent was set at odds with the guild custom that was its descendant, with the paradoxical result that Wolfe and his fellows could now represent the printing patent as an enormity.[79]

The emergence of opposition to privilege can also be understood as a mutation of trade culture, a matter of professional disposition. The press, which had already become competitive by 1517, had learned the techniques, if not the habit, of opposition in the years since then. That Wolfe spoke of his protest movement as a reformation is more than coincidental, for the book trade recognized itself as an important agent of religious change. Protestant doctrine, when it was heresy, had been impressed upon the margins of Bibles; first Protestant books, then Catholic ones, then Protestant books, then Catholic ones had been smuggled in and marketed surreptitiously; books had been produced with false imprints, so that domestic heresy and sedition could at least be disguised as foreign. In the years prior to Wolfe's agitation, virtually every English stationer had participated in one or another of these gambits. The false imprint by no means exhausted the capacity of the press to deceive and mislead: recall that the printing press is a mechanism for counterfeiting. Although it counterfeits handwriting crudely, it could be made to counterfeit the work of other printing presses with considerable success. So the technology of heterodoxy could easily be used competitively and had indeed been so used in the Lyonnaise forgeries discussed earlier. Since that time this technology had become more sophisticated. When the English book trade experienced a labor glut, the monopoly patent was particularly vulnerable to the available technology. As piracy verged on a labor movement, and sought abstract enemies as instruments of group identification, it seized upon the monopoly as the object of principled opposition.

That there is a *general* logic of opposition between print and monopoly is easy enough to see. The press had pioneered in the development of pro-tected production, having substantially elaborated the older protectionism long associated with artisanal "mysteries." But the press was also an ideal sphere for the competitive erosion of the new form of industrial property. The expertise requisite for the printing of a primer was no longer dazzling; the expertise requisite for the counterfeiting of a privileged edition was every bit as unremarkable. Agent of novelty, the press was also an agent of technical dissemination, of industrial demystification. Natalie Davis points out that as early as the 1530s, intense debates arose on the propriety of disseminating the trade "secrets" of medicine in print.[80] Certainly, how-to books were among the most popular productions of the sixteenth-century press. Long before the ages of Defoe or Diderot, then, the press had begun to wreak a kind of deadpan mechanical satire, disrupting the status of artisanal and profes-sional expertise by means of the demystification of practical knowledge. An example: John Medley claimed to have devised a new apparatus for draining mines, for which he received a twenty-year monopoly in 1562. How does the press figure here? First, the protected press provided a model for other pro-tected industries. Second, the press had delivered the new apparatus itself: Medley's "new" contrivance is described and illustrated in Agricola's *De re metallica* of 1556.[81] Finally, although the press gives Medley the idea for his new apparatus, it also takes it away: the idea is *his* and *new* in only the most contingent and temporary senses of those terms. The press puts individual-ization and novelty of technique under severe pressure, and so undermines the groundwork of the monopoly patent.[82]

Having led many English trades in integrating the principle of monopoly-production into its industrial structure, the book trade again led in focusing industrial tensions on that very principle. It would be several years before similar tensions arising within other industrial sectors produced widespread attacks on monopolies. A first provocation came from the renewal of various industrial patents: during the ten years following 1591 the privileges in starch, salt, train oil, paper, glass, and playing cards were renewed.[83] These renewals flaunted the fact that the patent no longer served the original function of enabling the establishment of new industries. In the eighties and nineties the patent of monopoly becomes a magnet for various sources of grievance. The gentry, those without privileges, objected to the capricious royal interference in the workings of capital; consumers, on the other hand, identified the monopolies as a source of inflation.[84] The more powerful members of the municipal guilds saw in the monopolies a limit placed on the traditional scope of their authority and as a result pursued a policy of disenfranchising the smaller masters within their own companies; such fissuring of industrial solidarities was sometimes exacerbated when disgruntled craftsmen chose to defy the guild oligarchy by supporting the patent applications of wealthy outsiders to the trade.[85] The monopoly had become both destructive and structuring—that is, a crucial instrument of economic transition—and the guilds registered its effects most clearly.[86] By 1603, for example, the powerful English Stock had been erected. The patent granted the stockholders a corporate monopoly in psalters, almanacs, primers, and other books—all of which had long been covered by separate patents—and though the 1603 patent confirmed the unifying monopoly, the association of privileged stationers had probably been in existence since the late eighties.[87] In effect, the Stock constituted a company within the company proper: monopoly was reorganizing the guild.

It was also shaping high politics. By 1601, Robert Wroth would complain in Parliament that

> "There have been divers patents granted since the last parliament; these are now in being, viz. the patents for currants, iron, powder, cards, ox-shin bones, train-oil, transportation of leather, lists of cloth, ashes, anniseeds, vinegar, sea-coals, steel, aqua-vitae, brushes, pots, salt-petre, lead, accidences, oil, calamin-stone, oil of blubber, fumachoes, or dried piltchers in the smoak, and divers others." When the list was read to the House, Mr. Hackwell stood up and asked: "Is not bread there[?]" "Bread," cried everyone in astonishment, "this voice seems strange." "No," said Mr. Hackwell, "but if order be not taken for these, bread will be there before the next parliament."[88]

The large-scale granting of monopoly patents is a direct outgrowth, then, of the industrial policy engineered in the early sixties by Sir William Cecil, Sir William Cordell, and Sir Nicholas Bacon; four decades later that policy was under attack, and Nicholas Bacon's youngest son was obliged to defend it in this the last of Elizabeth's parliaments.[89]

In the previous Parliament, a motion had been made "touching sundry enormities growing by patents and monopolies" and a petition of protest was proposed; Cecil managed to soften the manner of address before the petition was presented to the queen. A cautious Elizabeth meanwhile called for conciliar review of all the extant patents; she also determined to let the courts of Common Law adjudicate suits against patentees, withholding the protection of the prerogative courts. She communicated her intentions to the Commons through Lord Keeper Egerton in very careful terms: she agreed that the patents should "abide the trial and true touchstone of the law," but she nonetheless "hoped that her dutiful and loving subjects would not take away her prerogative—which is the chiefest flower in her garland and the principal and head pearl in her crown and diadem—but that they will leave that to her disposition."[90] The mystery here was simply how much steel braced this "hope." In the event, she did not make good on the promised reforms, making this a trial run for her last parliament.

We can now make a deeper sense of the political stresses that unsettle Bacon's rhetoric as he attempts an unobjectionable defense of the patent. The defense is motivated by loyalty to the queen and braced by his technological enthusiasms, and it therefore proceeds by correlating the monopoly privilege with something deeply felt, however imperfectly formulated and unsteadily grounded, the (implied) existence of rudimentary intellectual property rights:

> If any man out of his own Wit, industry or indeavour finds out
> anything beneficial for the Common-wealth, or bring in any new
> Invention, which every subject of this Kingdom may use; yet
> in regard of his pains and travel therein, her Majesty perhaps
> is pleased to grant him a Priviledge to use the same only by
> himself or his Deputies for a certain time. This is one kind of
> monopoly . . .

Since this is the first English sketch of such rights, their self-evidence—on which Bacon clearly relied—is a somewhat mysterious thing. The rights do not originate with the discoverer or inventor; they are created by the Crown as a reward for contributions to the public good—one can feel the kinship with Acontius's rhetoric some thirty years earlier. Its self-evidence is carried by a rhetoric of the rights of *labor* ("in regards of his pains and travel"), though we are a far cry from the reification of intellectual labor per se. There is nothing particularly nervous about the way this description outlines practical imagination, roughing out the domain of finding out and bringing in; if its "or" is as much coordinating as adversative, the ambiguity is not particularly charged. There is nonetheless a charge, a stress, in Bacon's description, though it is not located precisely in the uncertain description of intellectual labor: the sentence proceeds from the conditional ("if") to the gratuitous ("is pleased"), and from proper urgencies ("his own," "anything," "any," "pains and travel") to casual *disinvoltura* ("perhaps is pleased"). What unhinges the syntax and tone of Bacon's description is the difficulty of accommodating a burgeoning capitalist subjectivity and a weakening feudal prerogative, claim and custom. The parliaments of 1597–98 and 1600–1601 were being forced to measure the liberty of the subject against the prerogatives of the sovereign and finding them increasingly incommensurable. For Bacon, the discoverer clearly has his radical and independent deserts, the Crown its transcendence of a logic of desert: this amounts to a paradox, and it leaves its traces on his syntax.

The larger political valence of these parliamentary deliberations deserves attention. Bacon is careful to speak of the subject's deserts in terms of the rights of labor, and not in terms of the rights of property. It would surely have been unusual at this point to speak of a technique or a device as an intellectual property. Yet the royal prerogative was so desperately in need of defense precisely because it was being challenged by the slowly emerging concept of absolute property. Real property, naturally, leads personal property here. The genesis of a land market after the dissolution of the monasteries and the quickening of that market during the 1580s were the primary forms in which the gentry experienced the potential of capital for shearing the feudal polity off from the now more clearly determinant economy. The alienability of land, complemented by the dominance of wage labor, yielded, in the political sphere, the emergence of absolute property and of inalienable rights. This emergence was tense, central, and slow: as late as 1640, during the Short Parliament, Harbottle Grimston preempted a debate on how to assist the king in his war with the Scots by insisting, "Let therefore first our propertye be settled; and all woulde serve the Kinge for the preservation of the kingdome."[91] But as early as 1603, it was possible for the Puritan lawyer, Nicholas Fuller, openly to argue in *Darcy v. Allen,* the famous *Case of Monopolies,* that "Arts, and skill of manual occupations rise not from the King, but from the labour and industry of men, and by the gifts of God to them."[92] Fuller went on to reproduce Bacon's argument for the claims of invention almost word for word, but this time the argument proposes the protection of invention—not as an obvious first domain of the prerogative, but as its outer limit. The patent, then, was the site of a decisive skirmish in the larger battle for the absolutizing of the subject's property.

To repeat a caveat already made in these pages: I am by no means suggesting that the notion that emerges in Bacon's sentence, of a natural property right in ideas, was a novelty at the turn of the seventeenth century—or that the notion of novelty was somehow itself a novelty. As Jonson reenacted Martial's satiric examination of the commerce and culture of book-selling, Bacon may be said to recur more or less inadvertently to the analysis of genius in Martial's sixth book of *Epigrams:*

> ingeniosa tamen Pompulli scripta feruntur:
> "sed famae non est hoc, mihi crede, satis:
> quam multi tineas pascunt blattasque diserti
> et redimunt soli carmina docta coci!
> nescioquid plus est, quod donat saecula chartis:
> victurus genium debet habere liber. "

> [Yet the writings of Pompullus are held to be ingenious. "Well,
> believe me, that is not enough to make him famous. How many
> talented poets are fodder for moths and bookworms, and only
> cooks buy up their learned songs. There is something more that
> endows sheets with the ages: to endure a book must have *genium*."
> (Martial, VI.61.5–10)

Victurus genium debet habere liber: the line is untranslatable because *genium* may designate a property of mind, what we call "genius," or it can denote a *daemon,* an extrapersonal source of inspiration, or even, by extension, a patron. The semantic uncertainty had a long afterlife, but it was especially quick and nervous in the English Renaissance, as when Spenser represents the genesis of his epic both as his own work ("I guyde") and as the gift of the Muses ("guyde ye"). (In "Lycidas," Milton's final address to the dead and sublimated Edward King insists that the genesis of Protestant spirituality must be forever poised between inspiration and imagination, for of King, the poet-priest, he declares, "Henceforth thou art the genius of the shore," where the shore is a boundary between earth and heaven, inner and outer, personal and impersonal, demon and inward wit.) Bacon builds the patent of invention on similarly uncertain semantic ground when he makes it at once the gracious product of the queen's patronage and a right proper to the subject—and the explicit concern with patronage makes Bacon's language far closer to Martial's than is Spenser's. Of course, the uncertainty of Bacon's rhetoric is strategic, momentous, and deeply contingent, conditioned by a parliamentary predicament made especially tense by pressures emanating from the courts of common law.

In many ways, the parliaments of the nineties and after were playing catch-up with the courts. Regular challenges to particular monopolies had already begun in the early nineties, and Elizabeth's decision to let the patents "abide the . . . touchstone of the law" accedes to a movement already well along.[93] Again and again, the courts would cite a judgment in 1376 against John Peachie, who had claimed a monopoly in the sale of sweet wines on the basis of a three-year-old grant from Edward III. Thus it was established long before the *Clothworkers of Ipswich* case (1614) gave the principle its classic formulation that "the common law abhors all monopolies which prohibit any from working in any lawful trade." This somewhat hyperbolic pronouncement was inevitably tempered in application; what actually transpired in the courts was a fairly regular rejection of monopolies based on royal privilege and a somewhat more regular acceptance of monopolies based on parliamentary act (of which there were few) and those based on immemorial custom.[94] Where Crown grant and custom came into conflict, the courts insisted on the preemptive authority of custom.[95] It is precisely for this reason that from this time forward so many new industries and projects constitute themselves as local guilds or corporations: the aspiring patentees can sue for a patent from the Crown, and defend themselves in court on the basis of the immemorial rights of guilds. What is hard to ignore, however, in the case law of this period is the fact that the courts of common law become more and more oppositional, more radically resistant to the idea of royal prerogative.[96] But in 1603 Coke himself comes very close to sacrificing even the authority of local custom in order to frame the antimonopolist case as radically as possible. He is willing to grant that "the customary rights and ordinances of the cities and corporations are legal" but does not refrain from qualifying that legality "although they oppose the common law and the liberty of the subject." This grudging sentence, from his report on the landmark *Case of Monopolies,* suggests how polarizing monopolies had become: even local custom, if it could be used as a hedge for the monopolist, might be seen as a threat to law and liberty.

The Case of Monopolies—it was Coke who assigned it the name—is of particular interest, and not only because it enacts Elizabeth's submission of royal monopoly to common law adjudication. The case attempts to draw a clear line between lawful and unlawful patents, and so lays the groundwork for the future development of patent law as we know it, as a key branch of the law of intellectual property.[97] The case again reminds us of the abiding problem that the technology of printing presented for the regulation of modern industry. No stationers were directly involved in the case—the plaintiff, Edward Darcy, was Groom of the Privy Chamber; the defendant, Thomas Allin, a London haberdasher—but Darcy's patent was for the sole importation, manufacture, and sale of playing cards, an industry by this time relying on many of the materials and methods developed for book production.

The manufacture of playing cards had long been protected. Edward IV had banned their importation in 1463 in order to encourage domestic production.[98] Elizabeth conferred a playing-card monopoly in 1576, renewed it in 1578 and 1588, and transferred the grant to Darcy in 1598, for an annual rent of 100 pounds, after the death of the former patentee. Two years later, Allin infringed the patent: Darcy alleged that Allin had imported a hundred gross and had eighty gross manufactured in Westminster; Allin admitted to a half gross and pleaded the freedom of London.[99] It is intriguing to watch Coke, the enemy of monopolies, arguing for the plaintiff, for he argued the case as narrowly as possible. One can, indeed, hardly imagine him greatly disappointed when the court found for the defendant. Coke maintained that card playing was a mere vanity, and that the Crown had made its grant not to reward Darcy so much as to moderate an abuse. On the other hand, Fuller, speaking for the defense, had a field day, insisting that Crown grants must be tested against common law, natural law, and custom. That portion of his argument destined to have the greatest consequence was his definition of those patents allowable by law, a definition very close to that used by Bacon in Commons to secure a hearing for royal prerogative. Despite the similarity, Fuller's definition is nonetheless quite damaging to the prerogative:

> Now therefore I will shew you how the Judges have heretofore
> allowed of monopoly patents which is that where any man by
> his own charge and industry or by his own wit or invention doth
> bring any new trade into the Realm or any Engine tending to the
> furtherance of a trade that never was used before and that for the
> good of the Realm; that in such cases the King may grant to him a
> monopoly patent for some reasonable time, until the subjects may
> learn the same, in consideration of the good that he doth bring by
> his Invention to the Commonwealth; otherwise not.[100]

Consider the semantics of "invention" in this polemical context. Invention has shed more of its earlier spatial connotations; the acceptable patent retains less of its original association with efforts to attract foreign expertise. There are two reasons for this semantic drift. The first is simply the general shift in Elizabeth's use of the monopoly grant during the course of her reign. The second is Fuller's wish to essentialize the grounds of monopoly. The *emphasis* on wit and invention as a natural property of the subject serves the needs of a campaign to abridge the royal prerogative. For this same reason, the will to narrow the conditions for the grant of a lawful monopoly, Fuller insists on the importance of inventive *novelty*. After making his now-venerated definition, which would become the foundation of modern patent law, he takes up three earlier Elizabethan patents that had been rejected by the courts, the third of which, a patent to William Humphrey for an apparatus for melting lead, had been declared void on the grounds that one could only claim sole use of a method if one were the true and first deviser.[101] Fuller makes the case decisive; in it, the Court of the Exchequer had determined that Humphrey's device was an "improvement" and not an "invention" and the court held that it was "easier to improve than to invent."[102] Humphrey's patent had made possible the founding of the most successful mining company in England; it was one of Elizabeth's oldest (1565) and most profitable grants. The courts had simply qualified, not voided, the grant, but Fuller made that decision an occasion to severely delimit the royal prerogative.[103] In the process, he severely straitened the criteria for true "wit or invention," and he did so in order to construct a notion of invention so firm and compelling that it could subsist as the ground of privilege independent of the (interested) largesse of the Crown.

It must be conceded that Fuller's construction of invention did *not* immediately acquire compelling force, for the history of early Stuart economic development—and particularly of Caroline economic development—is one of increased monopolization. Though the findings of the courts were given statutory support in 1624, monopoly grants proliferated, with inventions—often the merest technological adjustments—serving as the levers by which a variety of long-established industries were reduced to individual control.[104] If Fuller's arguments were inefficacious in the near term, they would have important resonances after the Restoration and therefore mark an important conceptual development within Stuart culture. His differentiation between improving and inventing gives legal articulation to intellectual effort, the same sort of articulation that takes place in literary culture as imitation became a more and more dubious practice—the sort of articulation, that is, that Jonson would undertake in "Inviting a Friend to Supper," in the parerga to *Sejanus,* or in the theoretical filters that hedge the texts of his masques. Poet and jurist undertake the same cultural task, to subject intellection to discriminating evaluation.

Poet and jurist *and stationer:* in this legal, political, and academic milieu, it is no wonder that stationers should begin to use *invention* to denote an object of property. Thus Ling's usage, in his contentious forward to *England's Helicon* (1600):

> No one man, that shall take offence that his name is published
> to any invention of his, but he shall within the reading of a leafe
> or two, meete with another in reputation every way equal with
> himselfe, whose name hath beene before printed to his Poeme,
> which nowe taken away were more then theft: which may satisfie
> him that would faine seeme curious or be intreated for his fame.[105]

Recall that the insouciant purpose of this preface is to excuse, variously, the publication of misattributed poems, the published attribution of poems intended by their authors for anonymous circulation, and the publication of poems registered to other stationers. Ling makes slight, urbane excuses for the first two infractions, but the third is more defiant, a stationer's challenge to the conventions of stationer's copyright. A vigorously antimonopolistic popular climate has made him temporarily forget what side his bread is buttered on.[106]

CHAPTER FIVE

MONOPOLIZING CULTURE: TWO CASE STUDIES

Harington's Toilet and the Critique of Privacy

You prively gird likewise at patents, . . . which beeing priveledges graunted by a prince, fruits of her royall prerogative, rewards of her trustie and honourable servants, actes for humble subjectes to receive wyth thankes, not to examine according to their owne shallow judgements, privat lawe, in being priviledges, as both the legists and schoolemen determine, are not groslie to bee jested at, careleslie to be disgraced, or fondly to be delt withal. Beware of this good *Misacmos.*

Ulysses Upon Ajax

D. H. Sacks has shown how profoundly the struggle over monopolies contributes to the formulation of modern political theory, alleging that "the concept of liberty grew in antithesis to the growth of a theory of state power which had its concrete expression in the creation of economic monopolies."[1] Not surprisingly, one of the central themes of his analysis is the politics of individualization. He points out that medieval liberties were rights that accrued to one as the member of a privileged *collective* and that this is the traditional conception that shapes Coke's jurisprudence. In *Davenant v. Hurdis* (1599), Coke defended Davenant, who was being sued for failure to comply with a rule of the Merchant Taylors' Company, that half of all cloths be put out for dressing by members of the company, on the grounds that the collective rights of the guild here clashed with the collective rights of the nation; Coke resumes this argument in his gloss to clause 29 of Magna Carta.[2] The monopoly figures in the courts, therefore, not only as the (dubious) occasional expression of Crown prerogative, but also as the (dubious) privatization of collective rights: in 1601, William Spicer could define monopoly broadly as "a restraint of anything public, in a city, or commonwealth to a private use."[3]

The protest from which the modern patent system arises had epochal importance, for it was both adjunct and engine of a larger campaign on behalf of common law and parliamentary right.

The protection of invention is that much more remarkable when seen against the background of this powerful and ramifying attack on privatization, on the prerogative, and on economic regulation per se. During the parliamentary sessions of 1621 and 1624, the Committee on Grievances, chaired by Coke, together with the Committee on Trade functioned effectively as courts of commercial law, with an established procedure and attorneys who specialized in pleadings before them. Documents were regularly impounded, to the expressed annoyance of the Crown and its officers.[4] At the end of their investigations, the committees usually judged a patent either "inconvenient," a "grievance in creation," or a "grievance in execution." The judgment was submitted to the House, defended by the committee chairman, and, without exception, confirmed by the House, after which the patent stood condemned. Only two exceptions could clear a monopoly—if it was "necessary for the good of the State" or if it was for a new invention.[5]

Although hindsight confers the aura of inevitability on this exception, it is worth acknowledging that, despite the inflation of esteem accorded all forms of invention, the privatization of invention was not universally sanctioned. Curiously enough, it came under attack from one of the most inventive imaginations of the Elizabethan turn of the century, Sir John Harington. His attack on property in invention is framed with characteristic flippancy, but the attack is no less important for the offhanded and improbable wit with which Harington addresses the ethos and politics of intellectual property. The subject emerges from an aside in the wildly digressive pamphlet *A New Discourse of a Stale Subject, . . . the Metamorphosis of A Jax*, published in 1596 by Richard Field. This pamphlet describes Harington's own invention, a contrivance that he had conceived in the improvisatory heat of a conversation two years earlier at Wardour Castle. There, the elegance of the company in which he found himself had inspired him to improvised outrage. He had imagined a flush toilet.

Harington wrote *The Metamorphosis of A Jax* under the pen name of Misacmos ("Hater-of-filth"), and his opening encomia to Stercutius and Cloacina, the god of dung and goddess of privies, place this copious elaboration on the outrage at Wardour Castle securely within the Erasmian serioludic tradition. If he gives that tradition a characteristic personal inflection, it can be discerned in the fact that, in the interim between the first conversational improvisation and the eventual printed treatise, Harington had actually installed the new invention at his home at Kelston: Harington's signature is to reconfigure the serio-ludic as the practico-fantastic. He had done it before, as the story of Harington's translation of the *Orlando Furioso* suggests. When Elizabeth learned that his rendering of the scurillous story of Iocondo was circulating among her ladies-in-waiting, she banished Harington from court, wittily inflicting on him the penance of translating the entire poem before he should dare to return. His rustication ended with Field's publication of the completed translation in 1591, and the queen sealed her cousin's return to favor by visiting Kelston the following summer. They celebrated their amity by dining beneath an elevated fountain imitated from a prototype in book 42 of the *Furioso*. Ariosto's description had been beyond the capabilities of Harington's engineering and Harington had therefore adapted his translated description to the exigencies of his plumbing. This adequation is what I mean by speaking of the serio-ludic reconfigured as the practico-fantastic.

Harington's toilet is designed with the specific goal of removing not only all waste but also all odors, of eliminating the eliminated. Yet if modesty determines Harington's design, it also informs the rhetoric of his book, albeit paradoxically—because modesty turns out to be itself a kind of waste product. Misacmos's interlocutor, Philostilpnos ("Lover-of-cleanliness"), writes, "Let a publike benefit expell a private bashfulnes," and the verb indicates the brilliance of Harington's book, the startling homologies of his conception.[6] His water closet is a simple plumbed flush toilet, a device for damming and releasing flows in mechanical emulation of the body's expulsions; and Harington's discursive ethics are similarly emulative. A few pages after he adduces the ancient medical principle that bodily flows should not be constrained, he articulates the same principle as a matter of epicurean social ethics.[7] Detailing the various inconvenience of unimproved "conveniences," he challenges his readers to rid themselves of any residual squeamishness: "These inconveniences being so great, and the greater because so generall, if there be a way with little cost, with much cleanlinesse, with greate facilitie, & some pleasure to avoyd them, were it not rather a sinne to conceale it, then a shame to utter it?" Allowing a good toilet design to go unpublished is thus described as a kind of cultural constipation. But the comparison is more than a Rabelaisian assault on overniceness and prejudice. On the one hand, this figure carries an appeal for the free circulation of ideas.[8] On the other hand, Harington is not Winstanley, for whom feces would be a figure of radical good and the publication of ideas is spoofed as fecal display: it is "some pleasure to avoyd them." We may wonder why Harington has thus mobilized the cultural ambivalence to excretion, the dual valence of the manure pile: the local, polemical force of this ambivalence emerges slowly, in the course of the next few pages of the pamphlet, in which Harington first describes rival solutions to the problem of toilet design, digresses on the subject of rivalry itself, on competition between youth and age, and on competition among the Inns of Court, and then calls for the Inns to "gratulate" his own Lincoln's Inn, not only for producing great lawyers and officials but also for having produced such engineers as himself and Hugh Plat.[9]

If the genealogy of the *Metamorphosis* may be traced to Harington's visit to Wardour Castle, Field's publication, in 1593, of *A Brief Apologie of certen Newe Invencions* by Hugh Plat is a second point of origin, perhaps a more interesting one. One of the pioneers of the Great Instauration, Plat became something of a hero to seventeenth-century natural philosophers, principally for his contributions to the improvement of soil fertility. Beginning with the *Apology* of 1593, he published a slew of pamphlets advertising various contrivances to improve the productivity of English agriculture and the efficiency of English domestic economy.[10] Most of these early pamphlets are little better than puffs, for Plat usually withheld details of his inventions in the pamphlets: he was fishing. In *The Jewell House of Art and Nature* (1594) Plat speaks of "new inventions, *which the Author will bee readie* to disclose upon reasonable considerations, *to such as shall be willing to entertain* them, or to procure some Priviledge for them." That Harington found this extremely provoking may be gauged from the intemperance of the lampoon that erupts within the *Metamorphosis*:

> But that you may see M. Plat, I have studied your booke with
> some observation: if you would teach me your secret of making
> artificiall cole, and multiplying barley (though I feare me both
> the meanes will smell a litle kin to M. A Jax) I assure you I would
> take it very kindly: and we two might have a sute together for a
> monapole, you of your cole, as you mention in your book, and I of
> M. reformed A Jax (166–67).

The artificial coal to which Harington here refers is proposed *but not described* in Plat's *Jewell House* (where he speaks of having invented "a new kinde of fire") and again in a pamphlet published in the following year (and this time he refers to "colebals," so clearly he had devised a formula for briquettes); the agricultural invention is advertised in Plat's *Divers new sorts of Soyle* of 1594.[11] Harington's marginal gloss is blunt—"Some conjecture, that stale & cowdung must effect both these multiplications"—and the gloss seems to have stung. In a pamphlet issued within a month of the *Metamorphosis*, Plat refers to the "stale marginal notes" of M. Ajax; he is nettled by the charge of dealing in excrement, but he is perhaps more annoyed at the attack on the manner and goals of his coy publicity. Hurriedly appending "A petition to the curteous Reader" of his *Sundrie new and Artificiall remedies against Famine,* he contrasts Harington's literary manner with his own "plain and naked tearmes," defends his own reluctance to detail his invention, and attacks Harington's "labor to discredite that secret."[12]

Plat may be forgiven for having taken the attack personally, yet, for Harington, Plat's offense is merely synecdochic. What makes the *Metamorphosis* so important an historical document is its attack on monopoly *culture*. Inveighing against a range of what he calls "these paltry concealements & monapolies," Harington adjusts his sarcastic proposal that he and Plat form a cartel in manures. The new proposal is downright eerie:

> Now for my Monapole, I would ask but this trifling sute . . . [that]
> M. A Jax might be allowed for a Saunt by Pope Sisesinke . . . &
> then with some of the mony that you gain with the perfumed
> cole . . . I will erect in London & elsewhere, diverse shrines to this
> new Saint.

Harington's mock encomium on his new invention is here extended by figuring monopolistic competition as a cult, with public toilets as its shrines. The full period is less alarming than it first seems:

> I will erect in London & elsewhere, diverse shrines to this new
> Saint, and all the fat offerings shall bee distributed to such poore
> hungrie fellowes as sue for Monapoles, which being joyned to the
> ashes of your cole, wil be perhaps not uncommodious for land,
> and you and I will begge nothing for our reward. . . . What thinke
> you M. Plat, is not here a good plat layd, that you and I may be
> made for ever? (169–71)

Mobilizing the Protestant hostility to the cultic, Harington's rhetoric veers momentarily out of control: he is suggesting a rustication, with ashes and urban night soil to be spread on fields left fallow by these unproductive monopolists; but for a fleeting clausal moment, he seems to be proposing that "all the fat offerings" made in London's privies be served up to these "poore hungrie fellowes"—a punitive fantasy of coprophagia.[13] Nothing in Dekker, Heywood, Shirley, Jonson, or any of the other dramatists who will satirize monopoly culture on the Jacobean stage can compare with this. Secreted invention and restraint of trade are here imagined as a short-circuit of flows that perverts English economic life into a filthy religion. Plat was right to be disturbed. To the angry defense appended to Plat's *Remedies against Famine,* Harington responded with shrewd publicity: he commissioned his servant, Thomas Combe, to prepare schematic diagrams of the improved privy, and offered his own services, gratis, to those who might wish to install this public toilet. (In his contribution, Combe adduces and translates Persius's adage *"bonum quo communius eo melius"* to articulate the general principle: *"Goodnesse is best, when it is common showne, / Knowledge were vayne, if knowledge were not knowne."*)[14] For Harington, print is deployed in direct opposition to monopolistic competition.[15]

Harington's *Metamorphosis* seems to have earned him yet another banishment from the court of Elizabeth, but to suppose Elizabeth's motive to have been mere overniceness would be a mistake.[16] She may have been put off by Harington's cloacal publicity; she would have been downright annoyed to have her cousin describe her fiscal policy as an imposed cultural constipation. In what may seem a passing move in a digressive moment, Harington had touched a nerve.[17] The queen had recently renewed many of the most lucrative industrial monopolies, and her cousin, perhaps underestimating the importance of industrial patents to royal fiscal policy, failed to anticipate the determined zeal with which she would defend them, particularly in the face of increasingly coherent resistance.

So the confrontation between the two Lincoln's Inn inventors, Harington and Plat, is a good deal more than a diverting vignette: it is broadly intelligible as part of an accumulating struggle over the politics of economic regulation. Harington's position is not only anti-Elizabethan, it is eccentrically so, for he maintains that the engrossing of ideas is an economic abuse utterly continuous with the engrossing of other commodities. Motivated by an aristocratic hostility to new forms of property—especially to a form of property disarticulated not only from land but from other traditional forms of capital—Harington harnesses popular hostility to commercial monopolies for the unusual purpose of discrediting the nascent reification of intellectual property per se. He thus anticipates, by several decades, the Puritan elaboration of antimonopolist sentiment that, during the Interregnum, took in not only *industrial* monopolies but also the institutional protection of the learned professions—the clergy, lawyers, and physicians.[18] Harington's early attack on intellectual engrossing inverts what would be Bacon's pro-Elizabethan strategy, which is to specify and harness an inchoate sense of the justice of intellectual property in order to shore up the embattled cause of the queen's prerogative in economic regulation.[19] Far less committed to the work of royalist apologetics, Plat staked out (or backed himself into) a third position, one that points toward the legal future, by discriminating invention from other objects of protection. In his 1596 treatise, *Sundrie new and Artificiall reme-dies*, he voices the popular position "that the very food of the earth even the blessing of the Lord, should be no longer subject to this copyhold & slav-ish tenure, of such base & unmerciful lords, who . . . set what price they list upon a bushell. Is there no Court of Chauncery, neither in heaven, nor upon earth, to bridle these covetous and unmercifull Lords?" [A₂ᵛ].[20] He then begs the reader's patience, however, since his coal-balls and other inventions "do as yet attend some courtly favours, whereby they cannot so presently as I wish, breake foorth into the publike service of this land." Although Plat's self-interest blazes here, the distinction he makes between *kinds* of monopolistic protection became extremely important in parliamentary discussions during the next two decades. Like other genuine technological innovators, Plat failed in his suit for patent protection, but he makes an important contribution to political debate on technology.[21] He is groping toward the crucial Jacobean construction of intellectual property as a discrete and quite special case in a regulated economy.

Poet-Prophet-Patentee: George Wither against the Stationers

> I proceed to *Ovid* and *Chaucer.* . . . Both writ with wonderful
> Facility and Clearness; neither were great Inventors: for *Ovid* only
> copied the *Grecian* Fables: and most of *Chaucer's* Stories were
> taken from his *Italian* Contemporaries, or their Predecessors:
> *Boccace* his *Decameron* was first publish'd; and from thence our
> *Englishman* has borrow'd many of his *Canterbury Tales:* yet that
> of *Palamon* and *Arcite* was written in all probability by some
> *Italian* Wit, in a former Age: as I shall prove hereafter: The Tale
> of *Grizild* was the Invention of *Petrarch;* by him sent to *Boccace;*
> from whom it came to *Chaucer: Troilus* and *Cressida* was also
> written by a *Lombard* Author; but much amplified by our *English*
> Translatour, as well as beautified; the Genius of our Countrymen
> in general being rather to improve an Invention, than to invent
> themselves; as is evident not only in our Poetry, but in many of our
> Manufactures.
>
> John Dryden, preface to *Fables Ancient and Modern*

Harington's blanket attack on privatization, brilliant and eccentric, indicates how much could be put up for grabs in these years, how radical the con-ception of monopoly could be. *Davenant v. Hurdis* tells a similar tale, insofar as it shows us Coke directing antimonopolistic weapons against even the traditional privileges of an established guild. In this climate of opinion, King James took pains to give the first years of his reign a modestly reforming color. In his proclamation of 7 May 1603, he apologizes for Elizabeth's indiscretion in the "too large extending" of her prerogative in her granting of monopolies and he suspends all except grants to corporations and guilds; he maintained this apologetic posture in a speech at the opening of his first parliament ten months later.[22] The Commissioners of Suits, a permanent body for reviewing applications for patents of monopoly, was established in 1603, with Bacon a prominent member. The Jacobean reform was notoriously shallow and short-lived: however often James might renew his protestations against monopoly—as he would famously do in the *Book of Bounty* of 1610— those protestations, so much belied by his actions, did little to allay the zeal of the courts.[23] In 1615, the landmark *Clothworkers of Ipswich* case powerfully inhibited the prerogative and outlined economic principles in which the essence of the modern patent of invention is clearly promulgated:

> But if a man hath brought in a new invention and a new trade
> within the kingdom, in peril of his life, and consumption of his
> estate and stock, etc., or if a man hath made a new discovery
> of anything, in such cases the King, of his grace and favour, in
> recompense of his costs and travail, may grant by charter unto
> him, that he only shall use a trade or traffic for a certain time,
> because at first the people of the kingdom are ignorant, and
> have not the knowledge or skill to use it; but when that patent
> is expired, the King cannot make a new grant thereof, for when
> the trade has become common, and others have been bound
> apprentices in the same trade, there is no reason why such should
> be forbidden to use it.[24]

The patent, that is, is to serve the economic development of the commonwealth and not, or not directly, the royal treasury.

James continued to assert his authority in the face of such resistance: when Lord Keeper Ellesmere, who had been outspoken in his opposition to monopoly grants, failed to attach the Great Seal to two new grants in 1616, he was promptly removed from office. The seal passed to the more tractable Francis Bacon, but Bacon began to modify his position in 1620, when he urged that the Privy Council undertake an examination of the system (though he had assisted in the defense of the most notorious monopolies); in the autumn of 1620–21, before Parliament was convened, James established a commission to look into all aspects of the problem, probably to defuse anticipated parliamentary complaints. A Committee on Grievances was formed, on Coke's motion, giving Parliament a mechanism for systematic assault on monopolistic competition. The session engaged in some very powerful assaults on monopoly—though a bill, passed in the Commons, summarily revoking all monopolies and endowing the courts with the ultimate authority in identifying what might be classed as monopolies, was killed in the House of Lords. The parliamentary position on the matter was reformulated in the 1623–24 session and on 25 March 1624 the Statute of Monopolies was passed, giving legislative reinforcement to the key principles already worked out in the courts.[25] This included special provisions (articles 5 and 6) sanctioning patents "to the first and true inventor or inventors of such manufactures which others att the tyme of makinge of such letters patents and graunts did not use so they be not contrary to the lawe nor mischievous to the State by raisinge of the prices of commodities at home, or hurt of trade, or generally inconvenient."[26]

As we have seen, many of the tensions that yielded the parliamentary challenges of the 1620s had already been palpable before the turn of the century and felt in London's guildhalls. In such a politico-juridical atmosphere, in which a chartered company could be represented as a corporate monopoly (as the Merchant Taylors' Company had been in *Davenant v. Hurdis*), even a corporation as generously protected as the Stationers' Company must have felt the need for some discretion in the exercise of its own prerogatives.[27] Article 9 of the Statute of Monopolies would carefully exempt the customary privileges of municipalities together with those of "any corporacions companies or fellowshipps of any art trade occupacion or mistery, or to any companies or societies of merchants within this Realme, erected for the mayntenance enlargement or ordering of any trade of merchandize," but here Parliament was being more conservative than the courts, which had exerted registered pressure for more sweeping restraints.[28]

This most radical development, the sporadic challenge to guild monopolies per se, was hardly necessary to put the stationers on notice. A network of patents was as important to the London stationers as was the denser web of copyrights. The wealthiest figures in the Stationers' Company were sharers in the English Stock, which had been built from some of the earliest of Elizabethan printing patents, and it behooved them to leave uncontested many of the new patents awarded to other stationers and even to nonstationers under James. Those who feared for the Stock could have taken some comfort from the Statute of Monopolies: it exempted "any letters patents or grants of privileges heretofore made or hereafter made of, for, or concerning printing" (article 10), yet the statute gave stockholders and older patentees no conspicuous advantage over new patentees from outside the company.[29] An uneasy tolerance of such patentees therefore animates the book trade during the early seventeenth century.[30] We have seen that the struggle between Daniel and the stationers for control of his *History of England* was brought to conclusion in 1618 when Daniel secured a patent in the work. We can now appreciate the complexity of the stationers' acquiescence to such a royal intervention. Best not to challenge such occasional interventions; certainly it would have been dangerous for the stationers to cry "monopoly" in such a case.

The patent persists as a site of tension, however, and the tension was not always checked. Daniel is not the only nonstationer who used the patent as a pointed instrument for securing advantage over the stationers, but the stationers began to contest the device.[31] They made it difficult, for example, for John Minsheu to publish his polyglot dictionary, *Ductor in Linguas,* on which he claimed to have spent 1,000 pounds. Minsheu secured a twenty-one-year patent in the work in 1611 and immediately turned to the Stationers' Company, hoping that they would buy the patent, but they refused. This may not be an instance of deliberate industrial resistance, of course—Minsheu may have set too high a price on the patent—but neither side seems to have been much willing to accommodate the other.[32] Minsheu eventually found printers for the work (Bradwood did the bulk of the work, but Stansby eventually took over) and a few booksellers who would agree to stock it, but it took him six years and considerable ingenuity to arrange financing for the first edition of the dictionary: he appealed to the Inns of Court, seeking a subsidy to defray the printing costs, and he offered printed sheets of the first few pages of the dictionary to those wealthy individuals from whom he sought production loans. Once the work was complete and ready for issue in 1617, Minsheu had separate dedications printed for binding into presentation copies, and, most ingeniously, he also arranged that a regularly updated list of purchasers be bound into the dictionary. Newly revised copies of this list were still issuing from Stansby's shop in 1619, when Jonson pronounced Minsheu "a rogue" in the course of his conversations with William Drummond, yet one supposes that Jonson speaks enviously of one who had mustered so much control of the dissemination of his own work. Jonson's envy would have sharpened in 1625 when Minsheu published the second edition of his dictionary, the first English book published by subscription, a work in which an author had secured complete control of copyright, substantial control of production and distribution, and a rare degree of commercial intimacy with his consumers: the social structures of patronage had been wrung from and imposed on market institutions of very different tendency.[33]

The challenge of the patent to the structure of the book trade may have been exacerbated after 1617 and 1618, when the number of such grants suddenly began to increase, and this seems to have provoked the stationers to less equivocal resistance.[34] One of the first important struggles involves William Fulke's *Confutation of the Rhemish Testament,* which had been a kind of lightning rod for trade conflict since its entrance in 1588 to George Bishop and Ralph Newberry. The queen's printer, Christopher Barker, claimed a right in the work by virtue of his monopoly on the Bishops' Bible, extracts from which make up the largest portion of Fulke's text. This particular intra-industrial tension, a competition between copyright and patent, had been settled by compromise, and rights in the text had descended to a small consortium including the king's printers and one of Bishop's assigns; but in 1619 authorial pressures interfered when Fulke's daughter secured a patent in the work.[35] This had the effect of pitting one patent, the venerable patent of the king's printer, against another, that of the daughter, Mrs. Ogden. The matter was referred to the ecclesiastical authorities—presumably at the instigation of the king's printers—whereupon Mrs. Ogden's patent was rescinded. She persisted, however, and managed to have the matter referred to Bacon, then Lord Chancellor, and to Secretary Naunton. In this case, where no challenge to the prerogative could be suspected, Bacon finds on behalf of Mrs. Ogden, confirming her patent for twenty-one years: as in the case of Minsheu's dictionary, the patent was threatening the book trade with the birth of *authorial* publication.[36] But even this instance may seem a small matter compared to the battle that soon erupted, when the Stationers' Company found its boldest authorial adversary in George Wither.

Wither initiates his campaign on behalf of authorial intellectual property in the modest and exploratory idiom of pastoral.[37] In his second publication, *The Shepherd's Hunting* (1615), a collection of plaintive eclogues, he falls quite casually into an argument on behalf of the rights of literary labor:

> But, thou know'st, I am but young,
> And the pastoral I sung,
> Is by some supposed to be
> By a strain too high for me:
> So they kindly let me gain
> Not my labour for my pain.[38]

According to its title page, *The Shepherd's Hunting* was "written during the authors imprisonment in the Marshalsey," where he had been confined as a punishment for his *first* publication, *Abuses stript, and whipt.*[39] Wither will not be constrained to mere complaint here, or anywhere; again and again, *The Shepherd's Hunting* gets a lift from the way satire sharpens pastoral. Thus the snide "kindly" of the penultimate line above; thus the ensuing "Trust me" that faintly curls the lip of Wither's speaker, Willy:

> So they kindly let me gain
> Not my labour for my pain
> Trust me, I do wonder why
> They should me my own deny
> Though I'm young, I scorn to flit
> On the wings of borrowed wit.

It's interesting that Wither's argument should not come properly into focus until this last couplet. The language of "kindly" misappropriated labor, so unexpected in pastoral (however appropriate to the actualities of the rural economy), only serves, we finally gather, to counter the accusation that Willy, the pastoral figure for Wither's friend William Browne, is a plagiarist.[40] The brilliance of this moment is its discovery of the economic tensions that subtend literary culture: Wither anticipates my own analyses by announcing that the heightened stigma on plagiarism is functional, that it serves as an industrial convenience.

The Shepherd's Hunting was written in 1614, fairly early in Wither's career, but this passage in its fourth eclogue initiates a distinctive line of argument and action that would carry right through that career. There is, of course, nothing particularly distinctive about rebutting a charge of plagiarism: as we have seen, such charges and such rebuttals had become staples of English literary culture during the previous two decades. Nonetheless, the emphasis on *poesis* as labor, on attribution as a wage, and on contested attribution as a mask for the misappropriation of labor power whereby the accusers "let me gain / Not my labour for my pain"—this sharp survey of the literary economy is pure George Wither, whether or not it is what Charles Lamb was thinking of when he wrote that Wither's "poems are full . . . of a generous self-seeking."[41]

A decade after *The Shepherd's Hunting*, Wither elaborated its rudimentary assertion of the rights proper to poetic labor in the far more strenuously polemical work, *The Scholler's Purgatory*. He addresses it to the Convocation of 1624, asking the bishops to take his part in the struggle that erupted the previous year between himself and the Stationers' Company.[42] He had been walking a very thin line since at least 1621, when *Wither's Motto* was first printed. The wardens of the Stationers' Company, in their semi-official status as licensers, apparently refused to allow it; and when one of their company did print the book and then went on to print a second impression despite an explicit injunction not to do so, the printer was fined. Nor had the matter ended there. Because the book seemed to exult over the death of Northampton and to cast some aspersions on Buckingham, Wither was called in for interrogation, together with several of the stationers involved in producing the book. As a result, Wither landed again in the Marshalsea, where he endured what was apparently a particularly rigorous confinement. Jonson kept the matter alive by lampooning Wither in *Time Vindicated*, his masque for the 1622–23 Christmas season—this part of the story is particularly choice since it gives us *Jonson* attacking a writer for overearnestness, self-righteousness, and presumption to moral superiority. The attack backfired—nothing new for Jonson—but it backfired in a revealing way. John Chamberlain reported that "Ben Johnson . . . is like to heare of yt on both sides of the head for personating George withers," evidence that Wither had at least some influential supporters—Pembroke certainly, but also, quite possibly, the king himself—and could just get away with the pose of chrono-mastix. By that time *Wither's Motto* had gone through several more or less surreptitious editions and had won Wither an impressive popular audience; and despite the suspicions it had aroused we soon have decisive evidence that Wither had won royal approval and favor.[43]

Five weeks after the performance of Jonson's masque, James extended his support by granting to Wither, his assigns, and heirs a fifty-one-year patent in Wither's *Hymns and Songs of the Church*. Wither had advertised his interest in biblical poetry as early as 1619, when he published his *Preparation to the Psalter*—a long treatise in which Wither defends vernacular psalm translation, argues its tactics, and details the devotional uses of an English Psalter.[44] He had offered the work as a demonstration of his own qualifications as a biblical translator and as a prospectus for the serial publication of fifteen "decades" of Englished psalms suitable for singing and thus presumably designed to compete with Sternhold and Hopkins.[45] The promised collections were slow in coming. Although the next year saw the publication of a volume of commentaries, verse and prose translations, meditations and variations on the first psalm, Wither's complete psalter didn't appear until 1632. Yet he assumed the mantle of biblical poesy otherwise with *The Hymns and Songs of the Church,* in which he translates all the other lyrics in the canonical Scriptures, including the Song of Songs, for melodies by Orlando Gibbons. Vocational ambition partners with commercial savvy, for the English audience had a deep attachment to the Sternhold and Hopkins psalter, which was not to be easily displaced, even by the most popular of contemporary poets. But the *Hymns* could make for an apt complement, and given Wither's popularity, *its* market would be large, so James's patent would have been a very substantial financial boon.

As we have seen, the royal grant of something like authorial copyright was unusual, though not unprecedented: a small number of authors had secured patents in the sale of nontechnical works—not only Daniel but, before him, John Norden, who was granted a patent for his *Speculum Brittaniae* in 1592; Arthur Golding, near the end of his life, for all his works; Thomas Middleton, for *The Peacemaker* in 1618.[46] The grant to Wither was particularly disruptive, however, for it contained the unusual stipulation "that no English *Psalme-Booke* in Meeter, shall be bound up alone, or with any other Booke or Bookes, unless the said *Hymnes* and *Songs* of the *Church* be annexed thereunto."[47] The stationers' outrage at the grant hardly needs explication: the psalter was one of the major texts of English devotional practice, perhaps *the* major text of *private* devotional practice. Along with the Primer and the Catechism, it was one of the crucial matrices of popular literacy—and, therefore, a mainstay of the English book trade.[48] Those with an interest in the psalter patent had therefore devoted considerable energy to protecting their monopoly. Remembering the struggles of the seventies and eighties for control of this lucrative copy, the leading figures of the company had petitioned for renewal of the old patents within three days after Elizabeth's death. In the terms of the Jacobean renewal, which no doubt reflects the language of their petition, we can detect all the cunning of the petitioners' bad faith: the patent was awarded to the company as a whole, which functioned as a general agent of the English Stock, but ostensibly "for the benefit of the poore of the same" company.[49] Nor does one need hindsight to perceive the bad faith. Wither details the imposture in *The Scholler's Purgatory* as he moves from the ironic prayer that he might be the only man alive who sought his "owne glory, and inriching," to a well-informed and sharply focused exposure of the stationers' own humbug:

> And whereas they object I have compassed a priveledge to the
> publike greevance . . . I did not, as some of the Stationers have
> done, in the name of many, and by pretending the reliefe of
> the poore (whome they may be prooved therby to oppresse)
> monopolize the principall bookes of Sale within this Realme (even
> those wherein the whole commonwealth have a j[u]st interest)
> which is really one of those Monopolies that our State abhores.[50]

—that the state abhorred and the stationers cultivated, sometimes at considerable cost: in 1614, when one William Alley challenged the sharers' rights to the psalter, the company had had to petition for a new version of the patent grant, and the sharers settled with Alley for 600 pounds.[51]

After a similar, but fruitless, attempt to make terms with Wither, the stationers determined on a simple and ill-judged course of noncompliance.[52] They not only refused to sell or even to print Wither's *Hymns* (so that he was forced to hire George Wood, who—as one of the book trade's most notorious renegade printers—was in and out of prison as frequently as was Wither), they mounted a campaign for the withdrawal of Wither's grant.[53] In November 1623, they addressed a petition to James; when he proved unresponsive, they turned to the Commons early in its session of 1624, as that house pursued the second of its two great assaults on economic monopolies. By March, the Statute of Monopolies had been passed and both the Committee on Grievances and the Committee on Trade were busily regularly investigating royal grants, as they had been since the session of 1621—so it is not extraordinarily surprising that in May it was commanded that Wither's patent be "brought in."[54] No action on the matter is recorded. Wither might have sought protection for his own patent under the Statute of Monopolies, article 10 of which protected printing patents from challenge, but—at least according to Wither—the stationers were assiduously lobbying Commons against his grant. Wither may have decided to finesse the parliamentary inquiry by presenting himself before the Privy Council a few weeks after his summons to Parliament. The council willingly endorsed the patent: the two sites of jurisdiction instance the epochal polarization of parliamentary rights and royal prerogative. But the support of the Privy Council only slightly alleviated his difficulties in exploiting the patent, hence his strident supplementary appeal to the Convocation in *The Schollers Purgatory*.[55]

The larger political battle over monopolies crucially determines Wither's argument. From the outset he takes pains to counter the charge that his own patent amounts to a monopoly and to expose the monopolistic character of normal commercial practice within the book trade. This gesture of tu quoque turns out to be extremely incisive, since Wither not only indicates how frequently stationers themselves have been the recipients of printing patents, but he also protests—and for the first time, to my knowledge, in the history of the English book trade—the whole system of registration whereby the members "of their Corporation . . . can and do setle upon the particular members thereof, a perpetuall interest in such Bookes as are Registred by them at their Hall, in their severall Names: and are secured in taking the ful benefit of those books, better then any Author can be by vertue of the Kings Grant, notwithstanding their first Coppies were purloyned from the true owner, or imprinted without his leave" ($B_6{}^v$–B_7). The analysis is both shrewd and prescient, since it registers the implicit competition between printing patent and stationer's copyright, and anticipates how that friction would lead to the formulation of an authorial copyright based, however incoherently, on features of these its two ancestors.[56]

Wither was well aware of the structural tensions within early English publishing. Not only does he discern the stresses between the various forms of monopolistic competition in the book trade, but he is alert to its stratification.[57] He casts himself as a spokesperson for the disadvantaged among the company: "And verily, if you had heard, as I have done, how many of the Printers, of the Bookebynders, and of the yonger Bookesellers among them, do complaine against most of their Governors, and how many matters of great consequence they do probably object: You would thinke it were unsufferable" ($G_7{}^v$). This is astute enough, yet Wither has his limits as a tactician: he attacks the more fully capitalized monopolists, the publishers, and seeks to ally himself with the binders against them, yet his patent was at least as detrimental to binders as to publishers.[58] Small wonder, then, that the binders declined the proffered alliance, as demonstrated by their broadside against Wither's patent.[59] In *The Schollers Purgatory* (F_8–$F_8{}^v$), Wither claims that they had been compelled to lobby against him in Parliament, yet he surely underestimated the willingness of groups within the book trade to rally in solidarity when the company's general monopoly was publicly challenged.

Wither's argument murmurs with an intriguing new vocabulary, a rhetoric of authorial labor, anticipated, for example, in Bacon's defense of the prerogative before Parliament. I am not a monopolist, Wither tells us, the booksellers are; I am an author, and that is to say I am a worker. Or, to quote Wither precisely, "the Stationers have . . . usurped upon the labours of all writers, that . . . have consumed their youth and fortunes in perfiting some laborious worke."[60] For Wither, the poet-prophet, poetry is a vocation and a *job:* "I did not leape on a suddaine, or irreverently into this employment; but haveing consumed almost the yeares of an Apprenticeshipp in studies of this kind, I entred therinto conscionably" (36); he then goes on to give a concise analysis of the specific technical difficulties of translating Hebrew verse into English—again with the goal of describing the translator's work *as* work.[61] The intrinsic claims of effort animate the defense of his patent against which "there can be no publike grievance truely named . . . except it bee a griefe to some fewe Idle drones, to behould the laborious lyving upon the sweate of their owne browes."[62] This rhetoric of labor receives an odd but characteristic inflection, for as Wither goes on the offensive, his stance recalls that of his idiosyncratic pastoral persona.[63] Philarete, the authorial persona of Wither's early works, was not a lyric shepherd, but a satiric hunter; so too is the strenuous author of *The Schollers Purgatory:*

> The Booke-sellers do peremptorily challenge an interest in every
> mans labour of this kind [i.e., authorial labor]; and a worshipfull
> Lawyer was latelie pleased on their behalfe to say, that the benifit
> arising from the sale of bookes, was their ancient, and lawfull
> birthright. But . . . unlesse he can prove, the Author hath sold
> them his birth-right (as often he doth, for lesse then a messe of
> pottage) he being the elder brother, the right first . . . falleth unto
> him [and he goes on to instance other heirs—"the Printer, and
> Booke-binder"] that clayme just title before the booke-seller."
> (B_6^v)

Thus Esau speaks against the Jacobean printer.

For all the force of this language of property, Esau speaks on behalf of Jacobean prerogative, for he claims to seek nothing more than "repossession by the royall power" (B_6). Wither's ideological location lies somewhere in this no man's land between authorial right and royal prerogative.[64] He tells us that the booksellers have "cast upon me the unjust imputation of a base Monopolist: whereas I doubt not but I shalbe able to prove that his Majestie hath vouchsafed me nothing, but what was, IUS REGALE, and in his Lawfull power to confer" (B_6^v). No doubt this was good tactics. An author's common law property in his manuscript works had not been directly tested, whereas the king's prerogative was a talking point, a highly developed legal position. Moreover, Wither knew quite well that the stationers' own privileges rested on that prerogative, and he wields this knowledge with fair exultance:

> If his Majesty hath not Authority to commaund the addition of a
> fewe leaves (for Gods glory, and the peoples edification) to such a
> booke, as hath allowance from the Prerogative Royall onely; Then,
> either the Stationers are very presumptious, in anexing the singing
> Psalmes and Robert Wisdomes Songs to the Bible and booke
> of Common prayer, at their owne pleasures, and for their owne
> profit: Or els their Prerogative is more absolute then the Kings.
> (B_6)

This defense of the prerogative neutralizes the stationers' charge of monopoly, but it does not exhaust Wither's argument. Under cover of this defense,

Wither asserts a natural authorial property: "yf his Majestie hath not a legall power to confirme unto me that which is naturally myne owne, By what right then, doe they and others enjoy priviledges for those books wherein every man hath as good property as they" (B6ᵛ). This assertion of legal property constitutes a breakthrough in the history of authorship. Wither was no doubt aware of the fragile novelty of this line of argument: although the assertion of natural property is, by definition, absolute, it functions in *The Schollers Purgatory* as a token of his relative merit, a device for bolstering his claim to be the *preferable* recipient of rights originating with the Crown.

The Schollers Purgatory thus dances on the brink of authorial property, a brink that, admittedly, would be traversed very slowly. A decade later, another psalmodist, George Sandys, could more confidently petition King Charles for a patent in his own translations of the psalms and other biblical hymns: "whereas the Company of Stationers have an order, that no Printer shall print any booke but for one of their own Societie, thereby to ingrosse to themselves the whole profitt of other mens Labours."[65] By 1677 a challenge to the almanac patent was rebuffed in *Stationers' Company v. Seymour* (one of a series of skirmishes between Seymour and the company over patented books) when the court held that the Crown had a right to grant this patent because *"there is no particular author of an almanack."*[66] The decision can only be loosely affiliated with Wither's protest: on the one hand, the author is here counterpoised to royal prerogative, not allied to it; on the other hand, the decision implicitly recognizes the legal priority and preeminence of authorial property, since in this case it is implied that only an intellectual "commons" like the almanac is available to Crown grant. Yet as had so often been the case, this crucial development in the legal history of authorial property unfolded by negation. Authorial property, indeed modern proprietary authorship, is a kind of improvisation in the *Seymour* case, almost inadvertently conjured as a confirming *and* delimiting boundary on the royal prerogative.[67] What is an author? Wither contends that an author is the most deserving recipient of patent protection; in *Seymour,* half a century later, an author is he or she whose writings could not properly be made the object of such protection.

In Wither's day, commercial norms were such that he could not confidently rest an argument on the self-evidence of claims of natural property—which explains why he takes such pains over dismantling those of the stationers.[68] Yet despite the generally unarticulated, merely implied reference to the natural rights of authors, Wither does sketch one aspect of what would become the suite of modern intellectual property. Among the offenses of stationers, Wither recurs to misattribution and to publication without the consent of authors. Of course, he operates here in a venerable tradition of complaint, for protests against unauthorized publication became a staple of prefatory epistles by the 1570s and protests against both misattribution and plagiarism come into vogue at the turn of the seventeenth century—and both, of course, have classical antecedents. Only Heywood can be said to have anticipated Wither's sensitivity to such "crimes against signature," but Wither outstrips Heywood. As Willy's proud self-defense in *The Shepherd's Hunting* ("I scorn to flit / On the wings of borrowed wit") makes clear, even Wither's early pastorals had been hardened by plagiarism, real and imputed. *The Schollers Purgatory* is as sensitive to such matters, and far more explicit. Toward its conclusion Wither imagines a typical stationer—"a mere Stationer," he calls him—going about his typically degraded business, and he surmises that the mere stationer's response to *The Schollers Purgatory* would be to deny its authenticity. This imagined slight provokes Wither to a strenuous insistence on the internal consistency of his oeuvre: the conceptual apparatus of Renaissance philology, with its flourishing science of attribution, is here reflected back onto authorial *self*-consciousness, the author's authority confirmed by the demonstrable serial coherence of the oeuvre. Even before writing *The Schollers Purgatory*, Wither had sought an unusual degree of control over a printed volume, and an even more unusual *form* of such control. When John Marriott asked permission to publish *Faire-Virtue*, Wither's last book of pastoral poetry, the poet refused; when Marriott was importunate, Wither agreed to the publication, but stipulated that Marriott report his reluctance in a prefatory epistle that is strange enough to deserve quoting here:

> And (if you looked for a *Prologue;* thus much he wished me to
> tell you, in stead thereof: because (as he sayd) he himselfe had
> somewhat else to do. Yet, (to acknowledge the truth) I was so
> earnest with him, that, as busie as he would seeme to be, I got
> him to write this *Epistle* for me: And have therunto set my *Name*.
> Which, he wished me to confesse . . .

This peculiar authorial revenge on an industrial culture of misattribution is small but crucial nonetheless, at least insofar as it *insists* upon the subordination of the stationer's to the author's name: as Wither would argue throughout *The Schollers Purgatory*, "the reputation of Schollers, is as deare unto him [i.e., the ideal bookseller] as his owne: For, he acknowledgeth, that from them, his Mystery had both begining and meanes of continuance" (117). Wither thus advocates what has become a modern orthodoxy: authorized publication and accurate attribution as a kind of trademark, a warrant of merchantability. Except in very unusual circumstances—one thinks of Martial—these "crimes of signature" are almost always described as offenses against honor and reputation. The novelty of Wither's protest—besides the novelty of sheer animus—is that he gives these crimes an unvarnished description as economic offenses, as stolen labor. *The Schollers Purgatory*, therefore, comes close to enacting a rhetorical revolution, if not a conceptual one.

CHAPTER SIX

PERSONALITY AND PRINT:
Areopagitica AND THE
GENETICS OF INTELLECTUAL PROPERTY

Whence, then, the enigmatic character of the product of labour?

Marx, *Capital*

❧❧

Arguing for the defendant in the Case of Monopolies, Dodderidge conceded that "le case fuit tender concernant le prerogative del Prince et liberty
del subject, duissoit etre argue ove bone caution; car 'he that hews above
his hand, chips will fall into his eyes.' "[1] Dodderidge's caution led him to
more, and more substantive, concessions, yet although he was arguing against
Darcy's playing-card patent, he managed to assert one of the fundamental arguments on behalf of the patent of invention. He insisted that an artificer's
skill and occupation were his "patrimony, which is as land to a gentleman."[2]
His case against Darcy could afford this assertion of craft-knowledge, know-
how, as an object of property: Darcy's patent was not what we would call
a patent of invention, but was instead a commercial monopoly, the right to
import and sell playing cards and to exclude their native manufacture. The
traditional commercial privileges of London citizenship had emboldened the
defendant, Thomas Allin, to infringe Darcy's patent; sensing the fragility of
those privileges, Dodderidge attempted to bolster the defendant's position by
asserting a natural property in artisanal knowledge. It is a revealing maneuver:
Dodderidge models the property in know-how on that property most securely
lodged in English law, on real property itself—"as land to a gentleman."

A revealing maneuver, although not a brilliant one: Thomas Allin was
a haberdasher and could hardly claim specialist knowledge in playing-card
manufacture. Know-how functions in this case simply as a discriminant, a

defensible object of protection; "invention" has an analogous function in Bacon's defense of the prerogative. In tender cases, such defensible objects are used to discriminate against that far larger group of monopolies that inhibit technical development and commercial growth. Sometimes these defensible monopolies are distinguished from commercial monopolies granted by the Crown; on other, less frequent, occasions they are distinguished from those objects of the increasingly dubitable protectionism implicit in the freedom of London. To understand know-how and invention simply as levers in the complex struggle over patent and prerogative is not to minimize the importance of their emergence into legal and political discourse. The same must be said of the emergence of a vocabulary of authorial *labor* in Wither's poetry and prose: although Wither's vocabulary may be traced to origins in pastoral and georgic, to the traditional image of poet as ploughman, his use of this vocabulary in an attack on the stationers' monopoly is epochal. We may speak of the reification of know-how, invention, and writing in these tender cases. The debate on the patent is both an occasion and an instrument of that reification; that this reification redounded upon and unsettled the book trade is clear from the property disputes that erupted within it in the ensuing decades.

The legal history of the second folio edition of Ben Jonson's *Works* can tell at least part of this tale. Thomas Walkley's efforts in the late 1630s to secure control of Jonson's texts depend on a principle of natural authorial property in literary works—an unarticulated, but not unarticulable, principle. These texts had been more or less conventionally vested in other stationers by means of registration, yet Walkley's bill in Chancery, following upon an appeal to the secretary of state, sets this traditional mechanism of vesting copyright at odds with a less formal genealogy of property, one that Walkley characterizes both as legally prior and as extrinsic to the institutional arrangements of the Stationers' Company:

> Whereas severall of the writings and workes of Benjamin Johnson late deceased and not before printed were some short tyme before his decease presented unto & given by the same Benjamin to Sr Kenelme Digby to dipose thereof at his will and pleasure.
>
> To whose care & trust the said Benjamin left the publishing and printing of them . . . , And the said Benjamin shortly after dyeing, the said Sr Kenelme Digby in pursuance of the said truste reposed in him delivered the same Copies to yor Orato^r to have them published and printed according to the intencon of the said Benjamin Johnson.[3]

Walkley here indicates his partial deference to the conventions of stationer's copyright, for he is careful to note that the works for which he seeks protection had not been previously printed. But he bases his claim to copy protection, unconventionally, on a chain of transmission tethered by care and trust to Jonson's intentions. The claims of Walkley's adversaries to copyright in these works are denigrated in terms that may seem somewhat familiar: "having obtayned by some casuall or other indirect meanes false and imperfect Copies of the same works [they] did make an Entry in the Hall of the Company of Stationers of London in their owne name for the printing & publishing of the same workes."[4] This is not far from, say, the protestations of Heminges and Condell against the publication of "stolne and surreptitious copies" of Shakespeare's plays, but the difference between Walkley's complaint and the epistle of Shakespeare's fellows is not trivial. The specificity of reference—to particular printers, to the particulars of registration—and the implied collusion of "the Company of Stationers of London" bring us some distance from the rhetoric of Shakespeare's fellows. Moreover, Heminges and Condell were apologizing to *readers* ostensibly abused by "maimed, and deformed" texts; Walkley protests an offense against himself and Jonson. Heminges and Condell allege theft to explain textual corruption, but in an atmosphere in which "theft" must be regarded as largely figurative. In 1623, when the Shakespeare folio was printed, what Walkley would later describe as the casual and indirect transmission of manuscripts to printers was by no means an industrial abnormality, though it had become accessible to a criminalizing rhetoric; in 1640, Walkley pressed the case farther, attempting to confirm at law the distinction between the indirect and the authorized, between casual and intentional transmission.

The front matter to the Shakespeare folio adumbrates other aspects of Walkley's bill of complaint. In the intentional sequence that Walkley describes, Digby functions as what we would now call Jonson's literary executor, although Walkley does not employ the term; in their dedication to William and Philip Herbert, Heminges and Condell muse over the fact that Shakespeare's works have outlived him, over his "not having the fate, common with some, to be exequutor to his owne writings." The terminology is quite unstable—"executor to" seems to have been used interchangeably with "executor of" so that the literary manuscripts can be supposed here to be both (figuratively) a kind of will as well as (perhaps less figuratively) a heritable property. But a deeper conceptual insecurity has to do with the idea of a testator-author who lives to be his own executor—and the phrase is tangled in a sentence dominated by the more traditional figures of the author as parent and the writings as progeny, figures quite imperfectly coordinated with that of the author as executor. Heminges and Condell are groping for terms to describe their own sense of responsibility to an author whom they believe would be concerned with the posthumous disposition of his writings, and they record their sense of the loose relevance of the privileged responsibilities of executor to testator. By the time Walkley came to assert his claim to copyright in Jonson's works, he believed that those responsibilities and privileges might be invoked—not figuratively, but actually. When Greville and Walsingham had sought to shape the posthumous publication of Sidney's *Arcadia,* they appealed to those who controlled licensing.[5] On the other hand, by the time that Walkley attempts to circumvent the norms of stationer's copyright in order to secure control of the posthumous publication of Jonsonian materials, he can imagine other lines of intercession. He directs his complaint first to a secretary of state and then to Chancery, for Walkley makes an issue of authorial rights, rights that are specifically heritable, alleged to survive the author as a matter of will. Moreover, those rights are more or less confidently counterpoised to the trade rights of those stationers who happen merely to have acquired alternative manuscripts; he asserts that his manuscripts, still tethered to Jonson's intentions, have a different legal status from Crooke's and Benson's copies. Admittedly, Walkley is somewhat irresolute, for he denigrates his rivals' manuscripts on philological-editorial grounds—the old charge of "false and imperfect Copies"—as well as on intentional-stemmatic grounds—the newer charge that the rival manuscripts were "obtayned by some casuall or other indirect meanes." The editorial argument, drawing upon the rhetoric of prefaces, a language of marketing, must be regarded as largely supplementary; the intentional argument, drawing on the discourse of property and contract, is what enables Walkley to present a colorable appeal outside the Stationers' Company and into the jurisdiction of the courts of equity.[6]

Walkley is as much a beneficiary of Wither as he is of Jonson, for it is Wither who had most clearly asserted that an author may "clayme just title before the booke-seller." For Walkley as for Wither, there is an authorial copyright prior to stationer's copyright, and distinct therefrom. Wither grounds that right in authorial labor, while Walkley traces it to authorial intention, but the rhetorical differences here are relatively minor in import, since both formulations work by denigrating a copyright deriving from the institutional arrangements of a monopolistic company. In Walkley's case, the self-interest of the litigant was shortsighted: here was a stationer inadvertently undermining part of the foundations of his own industrial privileges. As it turns out, Walkley's complaint is a type, an anticipation of undertakings by the Stationers' Company in the next few years, in which the company would concede many of the principles on which their traditional privileges rested in order to salvage the practical advantages of those privileges—a gambit useful only in the short term.

"Propriety Confounded": Licensing and Authorship, I

We have not yet exhausted what might be called the generative self-seeking of Wither's struggle with the stationers. Of course, the most important individual product of that struggle was the formulation of an authorial "just title" contradistinguished from stationers' copyright; yet a more general achievement, that Wither opened the economic structure of the book trade to public criticism, is quite as important. In the course of his eager exposure of the humbug of company officials, Wither drew attention to a persistent strategy of the stationers, one on which they would rely for at least another century: the trick was to evade or conceal an argument about property by flaunting an argument about values. In the first few sentences of *The Schollers Purgatory* Wither pungently charges that the stationers had "vilified his Hymnes, rather as Censurers then sellers of Bookes" (sig. i₂). He devotes much of the rest of his book to ridiculing the stationers' claims to ideological scruple.[7]

The accumulating sense of authorial disadvantage within book culture is no doubt what released Wither's satiric outrage, but it is perhaps a bit remarkable that others had not provoked similar attacks in earlier decades, since the stationers' ploy was hardly new. It would be perverse to say that, at bottom, censorship had always been an instrument of industrial monopoly and that monopoly had never been an instrument of censorship. Elizabeth's first effort to control censorship, the injunctions of 1559 for the regulation of religion, had established an unwieldy system for licensing of printed books; the stationers were simply subjected to this system, charged dutifully to aid in the effort to control unlicensed printing. Thus charged, however, they had begun representing themselves as leading defenders of orthodoxy, couching any number of subsequent appeals for augmented monopolistic privileges as requests for weapons in a battle against heresy and treason. In the months prior to the promulgation of the Star Chamber decree of 1586, which so substantially strengthened the position of the wealthiest members of the Stationers' Company, the company patentees petitioned Star Chamber to protect their privileges against the piracies of Wolfe, Warde, and their followers. Employing a vocabulary that would grow even more contested during the following decade, the patentees defended "her majesties Prerogative" against the "greate bouldnes in those which nowe impugne her majestie herein" (Arber,

2:804). They went on to promote the patent as a weapon in the battle against heterodoxy:

> But for the conveniency of privileges It were very necessary for
> the common welth, that none shoulde prynt at all, but suche as
> are authorised from her majestie beinge knowne men. For if every
> man maie print, that is so disposed, it maie be a meanes, that
> heresies, treasons, and seditious Libelles shall often bee dispersed,
> whereas if onelie knowne men doo prynte this inconvenience is
> avoided. (Arber, II:805)

Such arguments were crucial props of the monopoly culture of the Stationers' Company. They provide the basic structure for the ruling handed down in the Star Chamber decree of June 23 for repressing the activities of "dyvers contentyous and disorderlye persons professing the arte or mysterye of Pryntinge or selling of bookes." Their

> Abuses and enormyties are nothinge abated: but (as is found
> by experience) doe rather daylye more and more encrease to
> the wilfull and manifeste breache and contempte of the said
> ordinances and decrees to the great dyspleasure and offence
> of the Quenes most excellent majestie by reason whereof
> sondrye intollerable offences and troubles and disturbances have
> happened aswell in the Churche, as in the Civill governement of
> the state and common wealthe of this Realme.[8]

Section 4 of the decree spells out new penalties, but the list of violations thus punishable is quite strikingly augmented. It includes not only books published without license "accordinge to thorder appoynted by the Queenes majesties *Injunctions,* And . . . first seen and perused by the Archbishop of *Canterbury* and Bishop of *London*," but also books published

> against the fourme and meaninge of any Restraynt or ordon-
> naunce conteyned or to be conteyned in any statute or lawes of
> this Realme, or in any Injunctyon made, or sett foorth by her
> majestie, or her highnes pryvye Councell, or against the true
> intent and meaninge of any Letters patentes, Commissions or
> prohibicons under the great seale of England, or contrary to any
> allowed ordynaunce sett down for the good governaunce of the
> Cumpany of Staconers. (Arber, II:810)

The decree was designed to bolster company control of the book trade against the competition of both nonstationers and those disenfranchised members of the company, but purely economic devices are made colorable by associating them with the structures of licensing. Section 3 of the decree curtailed competition by banning the erection of new presses; attrition was to reduce "to so smal a number of maisters or owners of pryntinge houses, beinge of abylity and good behavyour, As the Archbishop of *Canterbury* and Bishop of *London* for the tyme being shall thereupon thinck requisyte and convenyent for the good service of the Realme."[9]

It would be misleading to urge that monopoly was always in the vanguard of censorship. One manifestation of James I's general bookishness was his alertness to the political consequence of publication. In 1610, he himself drafted a proclamation in which he announced his intention to secure "better oversight of Books of all sorts before they come to the Presse" by appointing "Commissioners that shall looke more narrowly into the nature of all those thinges that shall be put to the Presse, either concerning our Authoritie Royall, or concerning our government."[10] We find one of the important instances in which royal censorship clearly took the lead of the monopolistic contrivances of the Stationers' Company later in James's reign, when he sought to suppress the importation of Dutch corantos, which had been flooding into London since late in 1620, a tide that had provoked Jonson's masque for January 1621, *News from the New World*.[11] Yet the quickened royal interest in regulation was complemented and often anticipated by the stationers' self-serving lobbying. Thus, having observed the king's interest in constricting the flow of news, Nathaniel Butter and Nicholas Bourne apparently presented themselves before the Privy Council sometime in mid-1621 and secured an exclusive right to print news sheets on the proviso that each be authorized by Francis Cottingham, newly appointed to serve as news licenser: the English appetite for news would thus be satisfied by producers directly indebted to the economic protection of the Crown. Most stationers found James's interest in suppressing the import trade particularly heartening, since they had long wished to increase their control over the import trade in books.[12] They therefore appointed a committee to lobby for a royal proclamation to clarify and bolster company authority over the import trade; the proclamation was forthcoming in September 1623. Adverting steadily to the Star Chamber decree of 1586, this "Proclamation against disorderly Printing, uttering, and dispersing of Bookes, Pamphlets, &c" appears to be primarily concerned with censorship, but this primacy is hardly more than a convenient fiction: the proclamation not only bans the production and sale of "any sedi-

tious, schismaticall, or other scandalalous Bookes, or Pamphlets whatsoever"
(which ban was nothing new, after all), it also prohibits commerce in

> any other booke or bookes (though lawfull or allowed to bee
> Printed by such to whom the Printing thereof doth belong) which
> shall be Printed contrary to the true intent of the sayd Decree, or
> shalbe Printed out of this Realme, of purpose to avoyd the said
> Decree, or any prohibition or restraynt conteyned in any Letters
> Patents, Priviledge, or lawfull ordinance.[13]

With very little sleight of hand, state censorship is thus transformed into
monopolistic competition—maddeningly little sleight of hand, it must have
seemed to Wither, whose demystifications may have seemed a bit too easy.

In the next reign, in July 1637, the privileges conferred in the proclamation of 1623 were confirmed and extended in a new decree of Star Chamber.
There is a consensus among historians of the book trade that the 1637 decree
was promoted by the Company for the benefit of Stationers. In fact, with two
exceptions—an unprecedented requirement that new editions of books previously published be licensed and a grant to the university presses to employ
as many apprentices as they wished—everything in the new decree served
the monopolies of the London stationers.[14] The company's rights of search
and seizure were reiterated, as were the old exclusion of nonstationers from
participation in the book trade and the restrictions on the number of masters, presses, apprentices, and, a novelty, typefounders and manufacturers of
presses. The regulation of imported books was strengthened: formal provisions for port searches were made, a new requirement that all imports be
registered was instituted, and the terms of the 1623 proclamation were extended to include a ban on commerce in foreign editions not only of patented
books but also of *any* book under English copyright.[15] Clause 12 of the decree, which stipulated that no books in English whatsoever were to be imported, eloquently testifies to the braid of censorship and monopoly at this
juncture.

> *Item,* for that Printing is, and for many yeers hath been an
> Art and manufacture of this kingdome, for the better incouraging
> of Printers in their honest, and just endeavours in their profession,
> and prevention of divers libels, pamphlets, and seditious books
> printed beyond the seas in English, and thence transported hither;
> It is further Ordered and Decreed, etc.

This is one of the novelties of the decree, but it was evidently devised by Charles's own advisers and not by the stationers: this provision is found in a version of the decree drafted before the stationers proposed additional regulations. Stuart protectionism more than complements censorship.

The Star Chamber decree of 1637 was only in effect for four years, for Parliament dissolved Star Chamber, along with the Courts of High Commission, in July of 1641. However short-lived, the decree served as a kind of Stuart regulatory standard: two years after the Restoration, Parliament would pass a licensing act modeled closely on the 1637 provisions. Press historians have occasionally remarked on the continuity that links this act of 1662, via the 1637 decree, to the original decree of 1586, but the continuity is somewhat less interesting than the decisive adjustments made in 1637. As L. R. Patterson would have it—and he puts the matter in the strongest possible terms—the 1637 decree is marked by a distinctive Stuart political style: "the 1586 Decree was basically a regulatory document designed to safeguard the state religion, . . . but the 1637 Decree made censorship a political instrument of despotic government."[16] The main differences between the two documents are the increased detail of the Stuart decree and the more thorough restriction of participation in the production and marketing of books. Many of the details reflect the frustrations of the censor in the face of a polemical ingenuity that had made the printed book into a manifold medium of complex messages: not only was copy for "body-text" to be licensed, but front matter, illustrative material, and other textual apparatuses were now to be approved. The 1637 decree thus fully politicizes the material and commercial book, for by the extent of its provisions the decree confirms that the literary commodity is saturated with political meanings.

These regulatory developments bring us to the brink of the era of parliamentary press regulation, an era crucial to the development of intellectual property primarily because it saw an irreversible fracture in the independent authority of the Stationers' Company. In the decades prior to the Civil War, rival industrialists (actors or members of other companies), individual stationers, and authors had sought remedies against the company by appealing to supervenient authorities—the courts, the monarch, influential aristocrats or clerics—with the result that the authority of the Stationers' Company seemed increasingly contingent, even to the stationers themselves. The regime of parliamentary regulation confirmed this development. By an act of 1653, the book trade was put under the interventionist control of the Council of State, which was even to control admission to the trade and to adjudicate copyright disputes, while the officers of the Stationers' Company were explicitly

instructed to obey their orders. Cromwell's orders for the regulation of printing, issued in 1655, continued the work of the 1653 Act.[17]

These years constitute what is perhaps the most notorious moment in
early modern English press control. The struggle in the early 1640s over the
institution of parliamentary licensing properly provokes a return to the historiographic challenge that has motivated this book, Foucault's assertion that
the penal, the censorious, is the driving force in the constitution of authorship. As Foucault would have it, the individualizations of modern authorship
are produced by less fully individuated agencies of authority—produced by
"power," in the idiom of the early Foucault—as a means of constraining the
interpretive freedom of the reading subject. Foucault's orientation to censorship as the central determinant of "legalized" authorship was variously
anticipated by liberal historiography, which had long seized on the author
of *Areopagitica* as the great mythographer of early modern authorship. I
have been urging, however, that the author of *The Scholler's Purgatory* must
stand as the great *historiographer* of early modern authorship, of authorship
constituted specifically if not exclusively as a trade function. It would be a
mistake to underestimate the ideological in any account of the sociopolitical
upheaval of the 1640s; what makes the period revolutionary is precisely the
ideological origins and articulations of its struggles. Granting this gladly, we
might at the same time remind ourselves that what brought the jurisdiction
of Star Chamber over press matters to an end was, at bottom, a tax revolt.[18]
In the elections to what came to be the Long Parliament, twelve monopolists
were expelled from the House of Commons, thus consolidating an ideological
position that had emerged over the preceding decades as *definitively* "Parlia-
mentarian."[19]

It should not be surprising, however, that some of the censoriousness
that distinguished the 1637 Star Chamber decree should survive the court
itself. Blagden has asserted that the Long Parliament wished to extend the
freedom to criticise both Crown and church, and there is no question but that
the events of 1641 gave an important boost to the dissenting press: Plattes's
Macaria of that year gives the sort of progressive opinion that stands behind
Blagden's assessment when he anticipates that "the Art of Printing will so
spread knowledge, that the common people, knowing their own rights and
liberties, will not be governed by way of oppression."[20] Yet the abolition of
Star Chamber was hardly motivated by a rejection of censorship. On May 17,
1641, even before the abolition, Commons had established the Committee
on Printing to investigate all complaints against disorderly publication and to
draft legislation for the parliamentary regulation of the press. This committee grew out of four other committees formed earlier in 1641.[21] In February,

the committee pursuing the prosecution of Laud was charged with looking into the archbishop's claim that he had authority to license books; a day later a committee was formed to suppress publication of a particularly inflammatory speech made by the king's solicitor before both houses; in April, a third committee had been appointed to consider the publication of members' speeches; and, since early in the year, a special subcommittee of the Grand Committee for Religion had been appointed to examine all forms of disorderly printing: the Committee on Printing was formed to eliminate the overlapping of these various bodies.[22] But the Commons and its committees were not the only bodies that competed with the doomed Star Chamber for the privilege of controlling the circulation of books. The Upper House had also appointed a committee to investigate unlicensed publication, in March 1641, while the courts of common law also intervened in press regulation.[23] Surveying the regulatory chaos that prevailed as various political institutions jockeyed for preeminence, Siebert observes that "printers arrested by a committee of the Commons were freed by order of the Lords; and occasionally jurisdiction was disputed between committees of the same house."[24] Popular pressure to free the press had some effect on official attitudes and actions, but it was overpowered by the eddying competition for press control.

This nervously kaleidoscopic regulatory atmosphere fostered a small but eventually crucial development in the history of intellectual property, and the single most powerful piece of evidence in support of Foucault's bibliographic hypothesis. On January 29, 1642, as part of its scattershot campaign for control of the press, Commons ordered

> that the Master and Wardens of the Company of Stationers shall
> be required to take especiall Order, that the Printers doe neither
> print, nor reprint any thing without the name and consent of the
> Author.

This is not a belated Witherian reform: the author is marked out not as a producer—the sort of producer who had benefited, for example, from competition between stationers and acting companies or between different stationers—but as a potential object of punishment. "Author," that is, here names that human origin of discourse who is submissible to punitive objectification. Insisting, moreover, that someone bear that name, the censorious Commons ordered

> that if any Printer shall notwithstanding print or reprint any thing
> without the name and consent of the Author, that he shall then be

> proceeded against, as both Printer and Author thereof, and their
> names to be certified to this House.[25]

Siebert is surely quite mistaken when he assesses this as "one of the earliest recognitions of the rights of authors by the English Parliament."[26] (Indeed, a far more important such recognition came and went during these years, the parliamentary granting of a special authorial copyright for fast-day sermons preached before the House of Commons between 1641 and 1643. The grants, which are recorded in the imprimatur of the published sermons, constitute a breakthrough, but a very small one, since there is no evidence that the 1642 order was taken as a generalizing extension of these grants.)[27] This compulsory "authorization" was devised to shore up a tottering regulatory regime.[28] By writing the name and consent of the Author into law, the ordinance makes a small contribution toward the eventual reification of authorial property. The order was perhaps more consequential in other, subtler ways: the emphasis on authorial consent establishes a sociopolitical distinction between manuscript and printed book. Consent helps to discriminate the publication of copy-texts never intended for print from the publication of works either composed with print dissemination in mind or grappled to the print medium later, in a second authorial thought. Recently, Wendy Wall has given a brilliant reading of Anthony Scolocker's mocking reflection on the flaunted modesty of the early modern author who declines "to be a Man in Print": Wall discusses the disruption of gender that, Scolocker cleverly imagines, attends on the immodesty of publication.[29] Wall's achievement in the opening pages of her study, richly elaborated in the book that unfolds from it, is to indicate a crucial aspect of the way print publication refigures subjectivity. This order of Commons reminds us that the effects of publication are reciprocal. To be a man in print was to be a different kind of man than to be a man in manuscript, certainly; it is also true that this differential subjectification elaborated the differentiation between media. The boldness of the man in print (a boldness uncertainly gendered, as Wall has discovered) distinguished print from handwriting; the punishable author of the printed book leaves a faintly bloody smudge on the medium itself.

The regulatory volatility that provoked this penal reification of authorship made many members of the book trade nervous. It particularly threatened the members of the several Stocks, a group that by this time was effectively congruent with the Stationers' Court of Assistants and whose control of the trade, in the years prior to 1641, had been substantially bolstered by their status as de facto regulatory agents of the Crown.[30] The dissolution of Star Chamber undermined the position of the ruling monopolists in the company, the foundation of whose royal patents had crumbled, and so galvanized a resistance movement within the book trade.[31] As had long been the case, the printers represented an unruly industrial faction, and the political disturbances of 1641 enabled a proliferation of unlicensed and sometimes clandestine book production over the next two years—and, of course, this "disorderly" printing contributed to the political ferment and provoked the competition for regulatory authority.[32] Networks for the distribution of pamphlets and broadsides had long existed, but coranto publication in the decades immediately preceding had spurred the further development of these networks and increased their efficiency; these networks made it possible for those printers who wished to do so to circumvent the booksellers, whose long-standing economic and political sway within the book trade had ebbed.[33] Rule after rule was flouted: nonstationers began to invade the trade, unlicensed presses operated, apprentices were bound over in excess of the statutory limit, journeymen opened their own printshops, books were published without license or registration, patents were infringed.[34] In 1641, a group of printers petitioned Parliament (and published the petition) for abolition of all patents conferred on nonprinting stationers, once again drawing attention to the fissuring of the trade.[35]

Such resistance will naturally recall Wolfe's rebellion sixty years earlier, although in this later case the opposition to the industrial status quo was far more articulate than that of Wolfe and his insurgent "reformers." Moreover, this time the complainants were operating in a far more favorable climate of opinion. In *The Compassionate Samaritane* (1644), William Walwyn made freedom of the press an important component of a general argument for religious toleration, and suggested that Parliament had inadvertently betrayed its own intentions by choosing to maintain a licensing system under its own auspices.[36] But more epochal arguments were also propounded. Within this unstable regulatory environment the crucial nexus between religious and political tolerationism and a more broadly diffused antimonopolism began to form, establishing an ideological linkage so durable and so deeply ingrained as to appear natural from our own standpoint. Wither had anticipated the linkage when he exposed how the stationers had hidden monopolistic practices behind the banner of licensing, but the events of the early 1640s provoked the sectaries to the ingenious argument that parliamentary licensing constituted a betrayal of Parliament's own antimonopolist principles. In 1644, at a key point in his strenuous defense of *Liberty of Conscience,* Henry Robinson argued the absurdity of curtailing freedom of religion when other, less spiritual freedoms of thought were defended ("why are not all *Arts* and *Sciences* thus manacled, if *Divinity* may be so much improved thereby"); Robinson extended the *reductio*—it is his most characteristic polemical device—by suggesting that one might as well restrain business and trade as inhibit liberty of conscience:

> We should thinke it a most gross solecisme, and extravagant
> course in any State which did make Laws and Statutes, that the
> Subject might not go about and dispatch his worldly businesse,
> save in one generall prescript form and manner. . . . If the
> redeeming civill rights and priviledges which hath made this
> present Parliament so deare, be acceptable in so high a nature as
> to engage the Kingdome in a war for their defence; how much
> more will the Liberty of Conscience, which transcends the other,
> as far as spirituall liberty does temporall, engage it still further at
> their devotions?[37]

Emphasis falls elsewhere in most of *Liberty of Conscience*, but the swerve to consider economic justice is hardly uncharacteristic. In the course of the 1640s, Robinson emerged as one of the chief ideologues of the Hartlib circle, and much of his work grapples with how to foster economic growth. But *Liberty of Conscience* initiated a sequence of tolerationist works by Robinson, who seems to have regarded religious freedom as an important component of sound economic policy. The principle is important enough, but even without it *Liberty of Conscience* would bulk large in Robinson's intellectual biography, if only because of the difficulties that attended on its publication. According to Prynne, Robinson was obliged to set up his own press staffed with Dutch workmen in order to get this tolerationist work printed: Robinson experienced the unfreedom of the press at close range.

It may be worth observing that the linkage of religious and industrial freedom, freedom of conscience and freedom from monopoly—the linkage so important to Lilburne's *England's Birth-right Justified* of 1645—did not necessarily seem natural to all nor did it develop immediately, since various sorts of interest obstructed the formation. However factionalized Parliament was during the early 1640s, the bulk of parliamentary opinion was that censorship should be sustained and that unauthorized publication should be arrested, and this position was unaffected by antimonopolistic fervor.[38] On the other hand, and even among radical stationers, sectarianism and tolerationism did not necessarily entail a distrust of monopolistic competition. William Prynne lost his ears in 1637—the second time he was thus condemned—for anti-Episcopal publishing, but four years later, in the aftermath of the dissolution of Star Chamber, we find him arguing on behalf of various printing monopolies before the Committee on Printing—this in his capacity as standing counsel to the Stationers' Company.[39] There is no question that Prynne had the courage of his convictions, so the defense of company monopoly must not have seemed inconsistent with his other principles.[40] Within a month, on the other hand, Prynne's own bookseller, Michael Sparke, also a staunch Puritan, anonymously published a scathing attack on the system of stationers' monopolies: *Scintilla, or a Light broken into darke Warehouses,* "printed," according to the title page, "not for *profit,* but for the Common Weles good: and no where to be *sold,* but some where to be given."[41]

In the interim between the Commons' provisional order of January 1642 and the passage of the first parliamentary Licensing Act of the Interregnum in June 1643, the leadership of the Stationers' Company scrambled to protect its interests. They were variously spurred to action—by general regulatory chaos, by the evisceration of their patents, by the embarrassment of *Scintilla,* and by the accumulating threat manifested by a disgruntled faction within the company, more self-serving than Sparke, which had already formally appealed to Parliament for reform of the book trade, including cancellation of extant patents. The company proceeded by making two petitions before Parliament; their tactics in both were by now utterly predictable. First, in January 1643, they repeated Prynne's 1641 appeal, petitioning for cancellation of the Bible patent. They argued that the concentration of rights in the Bible was impoverishing the poor of the company, on whom company leadership could confer, by way of charity, nothing "excepting the benefit of Printing a few small Bookes."[42] According to Blagden, this was quite disingenuous, for "in the years immediately following the publication of *Scintilla* the monopolizing of monopolies in books was carried further than ever before; for a short period the Stationers' Company, through the English Stock, controlled the printing of the Bible and the *Grammars* . . . , regained control of the Law Patent, and owned the printing houses of the king's printers in London and Edinburgh and the printing materials at Cambridge."[43] The second of the stationers' petitions to Parliament was less narrowly focused, longer, and a good deal more elaborate than the first: it called for the substantial restoration of the old licensing system, the bulwark of their monopoly. Once again, the stationers represent their interest in suppressing competition from outside the company as solicitude on behalf of censorship; what is new, of course, is the urgency that the Civil War had brought to matters of ideological regulation, the warmth with which the stationers might hope to have their own remonstrance received.[44] The petition discriminates "well ordered Printing" from "meere Printing"; surveys the state of European press regulation; reviews, quite sketchily, the history of English regulation; and, in a candid description of the logic of protectionism, proposes the two ends of regulation:

> The first and greatest end of Order in the Presse, is the advance-
> ment of wholesome knowledge, and this end is meerly publike:
> But that second end which provides for the prosperity of Printing
> and Printers, is not meerly private, partly because the benefit of
> so considerable a Body is of concernment to the whole: and partly
> because the compassing of the second end does much conduce to
> the accomplishing of the first.[45]

The petitioners praise parliamentary legislation and lament the failures in the enforcement of that legislation, urging "that in matters of the Presse, no man can so effectually prosecute, as Stationers themselves."[46] As in the 1580s, what the stationers sought was external sanction for their own industrial police-work: "if the Stationers at this present do not so zealously prosecute as is desired, it is to be understood, That it is partly for want of full authority, and partly for want of true encouragement."[47]

They sought power to restrain the usual enormities—the proliferation of presses, excessive employment of apprentices, invasion of the trade by non-stationers, underregulated imports, poor workmanship—together with some new ones, like the development of unregulated retail networks ("the shame-full custome of selling Pamphlets by Sempsters, &c. and dispersing them in the streets by Emissaries of such base condition"). But the most closely argued portion of the remonstrance concerns copyright protection, a subject made dangerous by such polemicists as Wither and Sparke:

> As the case now stands, Stationers . . . are so farre from enjoying
> priviledge, that they are abridged of their ancient Right, propriety
> of Copies being now almost taken away and confounded. . . .
> And to instance onely propriety of Copies, that in some mens
> understanding, is the same thing as a Monopoly: Though it not be
> so much a free privilege as a necessary right to Stationers; without
> which they cannot at all subsist, Yet some men except against it
> as a publike injury and grievance. . . . An orderly preservation
> of private Interest, and propriety in Copies is a thing many
> wayes beneficiall to the state, and different in nature from the
> engrossing, or Monopolizing some other Commodities into the
> hands of a few.

This latter point was plainly felt to be a fine one, requiring further explanation. The petition first asserts the distinction between books and other objects of protection—a distinction based, it turns out, on the limited market for books: the Bible excepted, books "are not of such general use and necessity, as some staple Commodities are, which feed and colath[e] us, nor are they so perishable." Nonsensically, it is further asserted that unregulated competition would raise book prices; more plausibly, copyright is urged as an incentive for the printing of books that might otherwise seem too great a risk of capital. The petitioners argue that the flow of books across an extensive distribution network and the maintenance of various stocks in England's bookshops depended on copyright, on the confidence of print capitalists that wholesaling and sales on consignment would not put their investments at risk.[48]

We have already seen that authorial assertions of property had grown somewhat more common since the days of Bacon and Daniel's interventions in the business relations of the stationers, and that anticipations of author's property were a good deal more frequently asserted by stationers, as leverage in feuds over copy with other stationers. Here in the petition of April 1643, a far-from-crystallized author's interest in publication is once more opportunistically asserted:

> Community as it discourages Stationers, so it's a great discour-
> agement to the Authors of Books also; Many mens studies carry
> no other profit or recompense with them, but the benefit of their
> Copies

—"benefit": the term may be colored by its specifically theatrical use, a performance in which a playwright would receive a specified fraction of the total gate receipts; certainly it is colored by the sense of gratuity and so cannot be called property. But the future will voice itself nonetheless in the warning that ensues:

> and if this be taken away, many Pieces of great worth and
> excellence will be strangled in the womb, or never conceived at all
> for the future. (Arber, I:587)

It is a powerful figure, though Milton will wield it with even greater force in *Areopagitica*.[49] Still, the authors of the remonstrance could not have realized how much they might be conceding by their eloquence. A censorious

Parliament had had recourse to the author as an instrument of ideological regulation little over a year earlier; now the stationers were going to the same well, as an instrument of their own monopoly.

In the short term, the stationers got more or less what they wanted in the Licensing Act that was finally passed in June 1643: the stationers' registration system received the blessing of Parliament, parliamentary licensers were appointed, and although the Stationers' Company did not recover full control of its police powers, representatives of the company were to number among the officially appointed searchers. As in 1586, legislation produced an immediate increase in the number of copies brought in for registration.[50] Yet the act did not reduce the tensions within the company (which were exacerbated by those of the larger political moment), and, again as in 1586, the leadership cast about for ways of soothing trade factionalism. The Court of Assistants was expanded, but a disaffected group consisting mainly of booksellers protested the exclusion of the commonalty for the election. And a few months later, early in 1645, a similar but better organized group of rebels challenged the very legitimacy of the sitting court and forced the formation of a committee to draw up new electoral procedures and a new means of distributing the work and the profits of Bible printing. The spirit of the parliamentary army had invaded the Stationers' Company. The old leadership of the company asked the lord mayor to intervene, warning that the disturbance in the Stationers' Company could easily spread to other companies; on July 1, the leaders of the protesting group were summoned before the Court of Aldermen and reprimanded. Blagden remarks on "the high proportion of printers who rallied to the support of the establishment" by signing the petition to the mayor.[51]

The year 1645 was a watershed: the defeated rebels were booksellers, long ascendant within the company; the printers, now thriving, had been the company's underdogs during the Elizabethan years. Their experience seems not to have produced abiding complacency, however, for the persistent volatility of the atmosphere emboldened the *printers* to consolidate their successes. They continued to violate company limits on the number of apprentices that might be bound and journeymen employed; and, in 1651, they attempted to secede from the Company by petitioning the press regulatory committee of parliament for permission to form an independent company. Thwarted, they renewed their petition several times in the ensuing decades, but neither Parliament nor a restored Crown would relinquish the relative simplicity of regulation offered by a single Stationers' Company.[52]

I have offered this account of the politics of the book trade during the Interregnum as a way of qualifying the Foucauldian hypothesis. Censorship both leads and lags the less piquant violence of hierarchy and capital in the regulatory struggles that shape book culture in the Civil War, taking its place within a constellation of political events, economic interests, and ideological adjustments that informed the campaign for freedom of the press in the 1640s. We can now gauge Milton's place within these developments and can recognize *Areopagitica*—so important in the history of book culture; so much more important in the historiography of book culture—as an epiphenomenon of tendencies that led, at the same time, to a major upheaval within the book trade during the spring of 1645.

A provisional summary may be useful at this point. The fracture and distribution of regulatory powers in 1641 called into question two customary features of English book culture. First, just as various state authorities began to compete for control of licensing, licensing itself no longer seemed a natural function of the state. Second, just as various producers began to compete for the right to monopolize the Bible, the monopoly in the Bible and in other books became a scandal outside the book trade (having sporadically scandalized many within the book trade for many decades).[53] And this double ideological disturbance was supplemented in two ways that would have consequences for the elaboration of intellectual property. First, it was supplemented by the resurgence of religious reform. Now that various individuals and groups contested one another's spiritual authority, addressing audiences of unprecedented variety and size, the idea of spiritual infallibility had lost its security—hence the tentative theorizing and practice of toleration, and the challenge, if only sometimes implicit, to the very rationale of licensing. As Robinson makes clear, tolerationism began to make common cause with the critique of monopoly culture. Second, it was supplemented by a variety of earlier assertions of authorial prerogative: the humanist argument for the civic privilege of an intelligentsia; the campaign of that intelligentsia, as it failed to secure civic privilege in defense of poetry, of fiction, and, indeed, of writing itself; the competition between the artisans of the theater and those of the press for control of the market in drama; the competition between playwrights and actors and the consequent emergence of an author's theater; the revival and transformation of a classical discourse of plagiarism; and the development of editorial authorship, the sense that it might only be fitting for an author to influence the format in which his work would be read and the channels for its dissemination. And so, again, to *Areopagitica*.

Stillbirth, Reification

este libro, como hijo del entendimiento

Don Quixote, I, Prologue

Long ago, David Masson expressed surprise that the man who wrote *Areopagitica* in 1644 should have found himself serving as a press licenser five years later.[54] Abbe Blum casts her description of this apparent paradox in Milton's biography in psychological terms, as a "desire to restrict and be restricted, to embrace and repudiate the language of powerful prohibitive authority," a formulation that seems calculated to clarify the political, religious, but above all psychological continuities running from *Areopagitica* to *Paradise Lost.*[55] Other continuities may now be brought into focus. Consider, after all, with what rich accuracy we might also describe the stationers' petition to Parliament in April 1643 as expressing a "desire to restrict and be restricted, to embrace and repudiate the language of powerful prohibitive [economic] authority." To put these phrases to such use may seem (at worst) a clumsy parlor trick and (a bit better, perhaps) a way of suggesting the psychological substrate of monopoly capitalism—albeit at the risk of sacrificing the idiosyncrasy that Masson and Blum seem to discern in Milton's ideological position. I think it would be more instructive to construe the resemblance between the stationers' desires and those of the poet somewhat differently, as evidence of the economic substrate of Milton's imagination. Both *Areopagitica* and *Paradise Lost* offer images of heroic contest between principles or ideological representatives, a battlefield of ideas; but the conflicted desire that motivates these works, the desire to restrict and to be restricted, is imbued with the logic of post-Caroline economic and ideological regulation— if the term "logic" can refer to a formation so scarred by contradiction and bad faith.

What is Milton's place in the history of English press regulation? How is *Areopagitica* shaped by that history, and what does it contribute to it? Milton had written an inflammatory treatise in defense of divorce that was published only a few weeks after the Licensing Act became law. *The Doctrine and Discipline of Divorce* had been published anonymously, though the author was easily identifiable; six months later, however, the tract was published in a second unlicensed edition, this time prefaced with a dedicatory letter over Milton's name, a provocation. It so provoked the Reverend Herbert Palmer that, six more months later, in August 1644, he singled it out in an antitolerationist sermon he preached before Parliament: "a wicked book is abroad and uncensored, though deserving to be burnt, whose Author hath been so impudent as to set his name to it and dedicate it to yourselves."[56] Eleven days later the Stationers' Company formally dissociated itself from Milton's pamphlet (among other books), noting that its publication was quite irregular. That same day, Commons directed that those involved in publishing works "against the Immortality of the Soul and concerning Divorce" be rounded up and punished. Though Milton is not likely to have approved of the Licensing Act at the moment of its promulgation, the threat carried in the August 1644 order must have galvanized his opposition and set him to work on *Areopagitica*. More than the timing of its publication suggests this genetic account of *Areopagitica*. One feels nervousness and reaction in the extravagant personality of the treatise, in the sense of a self-regarding temperament in its argument, in its inflation of ethical appeal. "They who to States and Governours of the Commonwealth direct their Speech, High Court of Parliament, . . . I suppose them as at the beginning of no meane endeavour, not a little altered in their mindes," he begins, and then directs attention to his own alteration, "the very attempt of this addresse thus made, and the thought of whom it hath recourse to, hath got the power within me to a passion" (II:486–87). Impassioned by the insult and danger that the divorce pamphlets had elicited, *Areopagitica* is suffused with animus; the inflation of the ethical is central to both its tactics and its influence.

The inflation of the ethical makes itself felt in a variety of ways, though perhaps in no way so insistently as in Milton's handling of the Isocratic fiction of oral presentation.[57]

> When complaints are freely heard, deeply consider'd, and speedily
> reform'd, then is the utmost bound of civill liberty attain'd, that
> wise men looke for. To which if I now manifest by the very sound
> of this which I shall utter, that wee are already in good part
> arriv'd . . .
>   . . . and how farre you excell them [i.e., the Athenian
> Parliament as well as other "cities and Siniories"], be assur'd,
> Lords and Commons, there can no greater testimony appear, then
> when your prudent spirit acknowledges and obeyes the voice of
> reason from what quarter soever it be heard speaking . . . (487;
> 490; and see also 491)

Among other things, the oral residue, the spokenness of the pamphlet accords with a will to erase the mechanical-industrial mediation of the book trade, to efface anything that might disrupt the dream of complete intimacy between composition and reception.[58] This erasure is more than a mere rhetorical device; the resistance to mediation makes itself felt in the argument proper. Take, for example, the moment when Milton comes to the *propositio* of his oration, calling upon Parliament to judge

> over again that Order which ye have ordain'd to regulate Printing.
> That no Book pamphlet, or paper shall be henceforth Printed,
> unlesse the same be first approv'd and licenc't by such, or at least
> one of such as shall be thereto appointed. For that part which
> preserves justly every mans Copy to himselfe, or provides for the
> poor, I touch not, only wish they be not made pretenses to abuse
> and persecute honest and painfull Men, who offend not in either
> of these particulars.

The fiction of oral presentation, in which the written is figured as the spoken, is complemented by that most celebrated cluster of figures in *Areopagitica*, in which the written is figured as the animate.

> I deny not, but that it is of greatest concernment in the Church
> and Commonwealth, to have a vigilant eye how Bookes demeane
> themselves, as well as men; and thereafter to confine, imprison,
> and do sharpest justice upon them as malefactors: For Books are
> not absolutely dead things . . .

The figurative animation of books has a long and complex history.[59] At the root of any such figuration lies the function of writing as substitution for personal presence—in letters, wills, proclamations, contracts, epitaphs, and so forth.[60] Thus Ovid:

> Frost-fearing myrtle shall impale my head,
> And of sad lovers Ile be often read.
> . . . .
> Then, when this bodie fals in funerall fire
> My name shall live, and my best part aspire

or, rather, thus Jonson adjusting (in *Poetaster*) Marlowe's rendering of the last lines of the first book of Ovid's *Amores:* Jonson here does homage to Marlowe's homage to Ovid's conjoined figure of literary reputation as perdurable and of one's writing as a soul that survives the mortal body. Milton works in this tradition, which can be traced from Ovid back to Horace, Ennius, and their Greek predecessors, but his principles and tactics put the figure under considerable stress. Writing is again a perdurable stand-in for the writer, but in his curious attempt to impose a nearly physiological precision on his figure of the relation between writer and writing, Milton succeeds only in mystifying the relationship:

> For Books are not absolutely dead things, but doe contain a
> potencie of life in them to be as active as that soule was whose
> progeny they are; nay they do preserve as in a violl the purest
> efficacie and extraction of that living intellect that bred them.

Whatever the relation proposed here between the writer and written, the written is certainly not here abstracted or detached. Books are a sort of sperm bank; in his edition, Sirluck refers us to Bacon's *Advancement of Learning*, where Bacon urges that "the images of men's wits and knowledges remain in books." Bacon then corrects himself, shifting briefly to the more technical, neoplatonic vocabulary on which Milton will linger, "Neither are they fit to be called images, because they generate still, and cast their seeds in the minds of others." Bacon, however, quickly surrenders the figure of the dissemina- tive book—"they . . . cast their seeds in the minds of others, provoking and causing infinite actions and opinions in succeeding ages" (2:492)—whereas Milton lingers over the disseminative figure. Thus, only a few lines after books are said to preserve the extraction of the intellect that bred them, they are again physiologized:

> Many a man lives a burden to the Earth; but a good Booke is
> the pretious life-blood of a master spirit, imbalm'd and treasur'd
> up on purpose to a life beyond life. 'Tis true, no age can restore
> a life, whereof perhaps there is no great loss; and revolutions
> of ages doe not oft recover the losse of a rejected truth, for the
> want of which whole Nations fare the worse. We should be wary
> therefore what persecution we raise against the living labours
> of public men, how we spill that season'd life of a man preserv'd
> and stor'd up in Books; since we see a kind of homicide may be
> thus committed, sometimes a martyrdome, and if it extend to the
> whole impression, a kinde of massacre.[61]

A variety of conceptual pressures constrain the argument here. The impres- sion of Milton's mortalism and monism, first, may be discerned in the distinc- tively physiological character of the aftereffect of writing, its potency embalmed as a nearly material immortality.[62] On the other hand, the tactical project of denigrating the industrial mediation of the press inhibits the representation of the book as independent and fully embodied. Even in figure, the potency of books is not specified to their materiality—which is why the figurative cadenza comes to rest as it does, with licencing an assault on a most mysteriously hedged materiality: "a kinde of massacre, whereof the execution ends not in the slaying of elemental life, but strikes at that ethereall and fift essence, the breath of reason it selfe." Of course, Milton had another motive for inhibiting the materialism of the figure. By means of abstraction, etherealization, he sought to untether books from local, particular, and momentary interest.[63]

Still, it is the materiality, the physiology, of Milton's figure that strikes one as most curious, and neither the inspiration of Bacon's *Advancement of Learning* nor the pressure of monism will explain it. The relation of writer and written is expressed as a genetics, an affiliation as intimate as that of father and son and more so (if also more ethereal). This is no casual formulation. Milton's imagination is evidently fully engaged here, for the figure of genetics ramifies throughout the treatise.[64] It reemerges, for example, in Milton's account of how the tradition of papal censorship was transformed during the Counter-Reformation:

> *Martin* the 5. by his Bull not only prohibited, but was the first
> that excommunicated the reading of hereticall Books; for about
> that time *Wicklef* and *Husse* growing terrible, were they who first
> drove the Papall Court to a stricter policy of prohibiting. Which
> cours *Leo* the 10., and his successors follow'd, untill the Councell
> of Trent, and the Spanish Inquisition engendring together brought
> forth, or perfeted those Catalogues, and expurging Indexes that
> rake through the entralls of many an old good Author, with a
> violation wors than any could be offer'd to his tomb.[65]

The genesis of the Indexes anticipates the genesis of Death, in *Paradise Lost*, from the copulation of Satan and his daughter, Sin: Milton had a special interest in perverse copulation. The evil bastards of *Areopagitica*, the catalogues of prohibited books, parody the traditional figure of the book as child of the author. These censoring books do violence to other books, here figured as "the entralls of many an old good Author": the written is again intimate, even consubstantial, with the writer.[66]

In *Areopagitica* the imaginative habits marked theologically by Milton's mortalism yield physiological and genetic figurations of the book and sadistic figurations of licensing—necrophiliac or dys-seminative, as we have seen, or abortifacient, as when Milton concludes his history of licensing by recalling the golden age that preceded it:

> Till then Books were ever freely admitted into the World as
> any other birth; the issue of the brain was no more stifl'd then
> the issue of the womb; no envious *Juno* sate cros-leg'd over the
> nativity of any mans intellectuall off spring; but if it proved a
> Monster, who denies but that it was justly burnt, or sunk into the
> Sea. (II:505)

The passage would be important enough as a reminder of the limits of Milton's liberalism, since it gives epigrammatic force to the statement of his belief in the value of postpublication censorship, a belief that he represents as widely accepted ("who denies but that . . ."). Once again, books figure within an excited but mystified genetics. The book justly burned is a monster, at once biologically connected to its authorial progenitor and also uncannily aberrant, a freak of nature. This disconnective aberrance carries forward into the ensuing sentence, where human pathos hovers over the book unjustly stifled, but the pathos is deployed without any reference to authorial-"parental" interest: "But that a Book in wors condition then a peccant soul, should be to stand before a Jury ere it be borne to the World, and undergo yet in darknesse the judgement of *Radamanth* and his Collegues ere it can pass the ferry backward into light, was never heard before."[67] Here the excited genetics of the book are most fully mystified. Filled with the potency of authors, books are nonetheless purified and nearly independent of individual interest; in this case, the birth of the book is blocked not at the womb but at the grave, as if licensed writing were a mere regress.[68]

In opposition to this excited and scrambled genetics of books, Milton will associate licensing with a perverse, antireproductive, or monster-producing sexuality. "But that a Book . . . should be to stand before a Jury ere it be borne to the World . . . was never heard before, till that mysterious iniquity provokt and troubl'd at the first entrance of Reformation, sought out new limbo's and new hells wherein they might include our Books also within the number of their damned." Sirluck points out that the "mysterious iniquity" is the great whore, with whom the kings of the earth have committed fornication, and upon whose head was written "Mystery" (Rev. 17:1–5). Mystery, the whore, is also the mother of abominations: Milton here gives us an alternative version to the earlier genealogy of licensing, in which Leo X fathers the Index on the Council of Trent. Abortifacient Juno, Leo, and Trent, and the Mysterious Iniquity form a linked mythological node opposed to the cluster of the seminal author, the book as vial of potency, Truth as virgin, and the reader or nation as athlete-warrior.[69] Of course, this opposition brings the biographical determinants of Milton's argument into focus. *Areopagitica* does private business for Milton, further managing the disruptions of the past few years of his life—his transgression of his own virginity, which he had made sacred to an anticipated career as England's prophetic poet; the failure of his marriage; the psychologically labored transformation of private divorce into public doctrine; being made to suffer censorious attacks on his divorce tracts, the publication of which had been taken as proof of the dangers of allowing a lapse in press licensing.

Infused as it is with private animus, engaged as it is with private labor, *Areopagitica* nonetheless does a good deal of public work in these genetic figures, resuming projects begun both by Wither and by Robinson. Milton seems to have been following the public debate on press regulation fairly closely, for the choice of Juno—the cross-legged anti-midwife—as a figure of licensing seems a direct response to the stationers' petition of 1643. Milton has appropriated and redeployed the rhetoric of the stationers' own warning concerning the danger of a lapse in the rights of registration, that "many pieces of great worth and excellence will be strangled in the womb, or never conceived at all for the future" if stationer's copyright should fall victim to indiscriminate antimonopolism. If nothing else, Milton's redeployment of this figure as part of an argument against licensing indicates his intuition that licensing and the stationers' monopoly are related matters, the one a prop to the other. This is, to be sure, a rather pallid reflection of Wither's protest against the stationers for "how unchristianly" (and how hypocritically) they had "vilified his Hymnes, rather as Censurers then sellers of Bookes" (i²). Milton is somewhat more attuned to the themes of authorial labor that emerge in Wither's poetry and polemics; and although he marshals the rhetoric of popular antimonopolism to very different ends, Milton has learned, perhaps from Wither, to see how deeply book culture has been permeated by protectionisms:

> And as it [i.e., licensing] is a particular disesteem of every
> knowing person alive, and most injurious to the writt'n labours
> and monuments of the dead, so to me it seems an undervaluing
> and vilifying of the whole Nation. I cannot set so light by all the
> invention, the art, the wit, the grave and solid judgement which
> is in England, as that it can be comprehended in any twenty
> capacities how good soever, much lesse that it should not passe

> except their superintendence be over it, except it be sifted and
> strain'd with their strainers, that it should be uncurrant without
> their manuall stamp. Truth and understanding are not such wares
> as to be monopoliz'd and traded in by tickets and statutes, and
> standards. We must not think to make a staple commodity of all
> the knowledge in the Land, to mark and licence it like our broad
> cloath, and our wool packs.[70]

The economic register obtrudes sharply here, just over halfway through *Are-opagitica,* emerging from the language of esteem and evaluation and coming into focus with the figure of the book as coin of the realm, authenticated by the stamp of the licenser's imprimatur. But in the culminating sentences, with their crucial appropriation of antimonopolism, the place of the economic is confused. Kendrick has brilliantly probed how Milton's figurative practices *disturb* his argument, how they heighten and exceed it, and certainly the figure of license as monopoly must be a leading instance of such disturbance. First of all, it is not clear whether it invites us to recoil from the transformation of truth and understanding into monopolized commodities or from the transformation of truth and understanding into commodities per se—such wares as to be *monopolized,* or such *wares* as to be monopolized. It would seem unlikely for Milton the pragmatic politician to project this latter fantasy, in which writing is somehow forcibly degraded to the commodity form; but an idealist Milton, polemicist for the heroic disinterest of intellectual life, is as strong a presence in *Areopagitica* as is the politician. The irresolution, which blurs the difference between a populist antimonopolism and an idealist, even aristocratic, disdain for the marketplace, may have been conceived as part of the coalitionist project of *Areopagitica,* but it has deep roots in Milton's self-conception.

But this only begins to expose the irresolution of Milton's economic language, for at this juncture it is also unclear how fully his sentences are meant as a *figurative* argument. It is uncertain, that is, whether Milton is here probing an analogy between licensing and monopolistic competition; or whether he is arguing, as Wither had, that licensing was an actual instrument of monopolistic competition (enabling the elaboration of monopolistic protections by concealing them behind the smokescreen of moral regulation); or whether, indeed, he is arguing that licensing by its very nature imposes the structure and the effects of monopoly (or perhaps simply the effects of commodification) upon book culture. In this instance irresolution is probably not strategic, but a site of Milton's genuine inconclusion. Moreover, the degree to which the polemic against licensing is inhabited by economic concerns remains irresolute. The licenser will reappear in the figure of the monopolist in the balance of the treatise: "all things shall be order'd, all things regulated and setl'd; nothing writt'n but what passes through the custom-house of certain Publicans [i.e., tax-collectors] that have the tunaging and pundaging of all free spok'n truth" (2:545). It is unclear how deeply this is felt—unclear, that is, whether Milton is seriously making common cause with popular antimonopolism and identifying his polemic against licensing with it, or whether popular antimonopolism is simply a convenient rhetorical club, a polemical *topos*. The uncertainty persists through the last sentences of *Areopagitica*, where Milton rises closest to full-throated Witherian denunciation of monopolistic aims underwriting the institution of licensing. He has described the 1643 Licensing Act as "the immediate image of a Star-chamber decree" from the regime of Luciferian Charles, the decree of 1637,

> Whereby ye may guess what kinde of State prudence, what love of
> the people, what care of Religion, or good manners there was at
> the contriving, although with singular hypocrisie it pretended to
> bind books to their good behavior

—a nice turn in which books, animated by the criminalizing energies of ideological regulation, are subjected, bound, within the juridical personae of *suspects*—

> . . . with singular hypocrisie it pretended to bind books to their
> good behavior. And how it got the upper hand of your precedent
> Order so well constituted before [i.e., the January order of 1642],
> if we may beleeve those men whose profession gives them cause
> to enquire most, it may be doubted there was in it the fraud of
> some old *patentees* and *monopolizers* in the trade of book-selling;
> who under pretence of the poor in their Company not to be
> defrauded, and the just retaining of each man his several copy,
> which God forbid should be gainsaid, brought divers glosing
> colours to the House.

At this last moment the monopolist is no longer a figure for the licenser; instead, in a Witherian exposé, license is a figure, a strategic screen for monopoly.

Milton here betrays his alert outsider's attention to the tradition of debunking protest that had emerged from within the Stationers' Company in the anxious aftermath of the dissolution of Star Chamber. Yet indebted as he is to the analyses of Sparke and his immediate heirs, Milton will not affiliate his arguments with theirs. He begins the final sentence of *Areopagitica* with a tactically judicious attempt to put the rhetoric of economic protest back in its place, to distance himself and his argument from its clamor—without, in fact, silencing it:

> Another end is thought was aym'd at by some of them in procur-
> ing by petition this Order, that having power in their hands,
> malignant books might the easier scape abroad, as the event
> shews. But of these *Sophisms* and *Elenchs* of marchandize I skill
> not: This I know, that errors in a good government and in a bad
> are equally almost incident . . .

At least some features of this concluding gesture might be explained by the coalitionist logic that, according to Sirluck, motivates so much of Milton's argument. By settling the focus of the argument upon the tactics and tech-niques of government, Milton makes a final appeal to the Erastian elements of the parliamentary center, which Milton sought to sheer off from the Pres-byterian right. Yet even the passing sneer at the frauds and connivances of monopolistic stationers could have little appeal to this group, and the embrace of a prominent idiom of trade factionalism might even have been slightly off-putting; moreover, these sentences belatedly obtrude arguments that find a home nowhere else in *Areopagitica*. The political tactics of this rhetorical moment were imperfect—though this in itself should be unsur-prising, for *Areopagitica* was hardly an effective political document—and its contemporary influence was slight. Still, to consider Milton's tactics, and to alert oneself to the lapse of political acumen here, is to confront conceptual urgencies that Sirluck's coalitionist analysis has missed.

Albeit disavowed, subordinated, and irresolutely deployed, the concerns of stationers' protest appear to have established a presence in Milton's imag-ination, for its language shoulders its way insistently into *Areopagitica*. If the inhibiting humbug of "marchandise" concludes the treatise, the figuration of inhibited merchandise opens its final section. Indeed, it initiates the move-ment toward one of the rhetorical climaxes of the treatise, the description of the virgin Truth hewed into pieces and scattered, her full reintegration impossible before the Second Coming, her partial reassembly inhibited by licensing. At this transitional juncture, remarkably, the evocation of merchan-dise is neither irresolute nor aloof:

> There is yet behind of what I purpos'd to lay open, the incredible
> loss, and detriment that this plot of licensing puts us to, more
> then if som enemy at sea should stop up all our hav'ns and ports,
> and creeks, it hinders and retards the importation of our richest
> Marchandize, Truth. (II:548)

There is, in fact, very little yet behind to lay open: what follows is a forceful reiteration of arguments that Milton has already advanced concerning the specific dangers of press licensing. The increasingly dense figurative texture and heightened sonorities of the ensuing pages are new, and there is novelty, too, in the invigorated chauvinism of these pages; but even more striking is Milton's new emphasis on unfettered labor, production, and commerce. Announcing this shift in the sentence above, Milton seems to ally himself practically with Robinson's free-trade and free-press tolerationism and to af-filiate himself imaginatively with Harington's critique of the constipated fluid mechanics of secrecy. Much less guarded here than at the conclusion of the pamphlet, Milton embraces the analogy between unfettered commercial cir-culation and unfettered discursive circulation.[71]

It is difficult to register the force of this analogy, the nonobviousness and rhetorical éclat of the dictum that "Truth and understanding are not such wares as to be monopoliz'd." In the aftermath of the conceptual revolution and historical transformation from which *Areopagitica* so eloquently speaks, these rhetorical discoveries and the conceptual intuition that underwrites them may now seem slightly pallid. But the analogy between intellectual de-bate and commerce was not inevitable, though they may now appear to be so. Wither, Sparke, the insurgent booksellers of the 1640s, and, much earlier, Harington and Bacon had helped raise the question of whether truth and un-derstanding were or should be wares and, if so, wares of what kind; Wither and Milton bring these incipient questionings to the brink of theory. Since I think it useful to be fastidious in describing the degree to which Milton's understanding of licensing entails a theory of the commodity, I am obliged to quibble with what I take to be the most strenuous critical discussion of this problem. Kendrick is, I think, a significant shade wrong when he urges that "part of Milton's rhetorical strategy is to make all human activities appear in the light of the commodity form. Each sphere of activity is capable of being monopolized, its natural movements bottled up and stapled, and the monop-olization of books logically leads to or implies the fetishism of other areas." Kendrick is quite right to sum up the negative argument of Milton's penul-timate section thus—"If books are to be licensed, the third part of Milton's

argument goes, then manners, recreation, music, balconies must also be regulated. The regulation of these areas is regarded as a patent impossibility"—
exactly, but here the argument goes awry—"since they are not really commodities, not really 'things' offering themselves to monopoly." Milton's plain
argument at this juncture is that licensing of these "areas" is merely a practical impossibility, though the project had been undertaken by means of a
variety of sumptuary regulations, sabbatarian laws, and proclamations governing theatrical entertainment. He does not argue that licensing is not possible because these areas are not commodities: the *analogy* Milton makes
between license and monopoly, the interdependence between license and
monopoly that Wither exposes and Milton reflects, all but collapses into *identity* in Kendrick's argument.[72] This identification explains Kendrick's earlier
imprecision. It is not Milton's strategy "to make all human activities appear
in the light of the commodity form"; he makes all human activities appear
in the (fire)light of the license form, itself a curiously pathetic, bodily form.
And because industrial politics had begun to probe the relation between the
license form and the commodity form, the dim light of the latter—dim because it was intuited more than understood—shines glancingly on manners,
recreation, music, and so on. I do not think this can be described as a matter
of strategy: the figures of merchandise or monopoly are deployed with too
little resolution to be strategic.

Nor Absolutely Dead Things: Blooded Books

Commodification was the destiny of thought, but as that fate was being
sealed, commodification appeared as a figure of thought, a metaphor. Because we now have property in ideas, it is easy to misread the language of
commodification in *Areopagitica* as mere description or mere protestation,
and so to miss its speculative force. I have been emphasizing both the irresolution and the energy with which Milton figures books and thought in
order to recover the predestinational moment of intellectual property, the
moment when property in ideas could still present itself as imaginable, but
not as a given.

    In the final section of *Areopagitica* Milton introduces the image of an
athletic and militant national body, "rousing herself like a strong man after
sleep" (2:558); she is rousing herself to renew the disputatious work of reformation, an intense physicalization of intellectual contest. The physiological
potencies evoked earlier in the pamphlet are unleashed here in the description of England, "a Nation not slow and dull, but of a quick, ingenious, and

piercing spirit, acute to invent, suttle and sinewy to discours, not beneath the reach of any point the highest that human capacity can soar to" (2:551). From this description, Milton proceeds to the evocation of an ideally *healthy* intellectual culture, and this evocation suggests that the analogy between commercial and discursive freedoms of circulation supplements and extends the arc of physiological figuration:

> For as in a body, when the blood is fresh, the spirits pure and
> vigorous, not only to vital, but to rationall faculties, and those in
> the acutest, and pertest operations of wit and suttlety, it argues
> in what good plight and constitution the body is, so when the
> cheerfulnesse of the people is so sprightly up, as that it has, not
> only wherewith to guard well its own freedom and safety, but to
> spare, and to bestow, upon the solidest and sublimest points of
> controversie, and new invention, it betok'ns us not degenerated,
> nor drooping to a fatall decay, but casting off the old and wrincl'd
> skin of corruption to outlive these pangs and wax young again,
> entring the glorious waies of Truth and prosperous vertue.

Two matters of rhetorical coherence may be observed here. First, that the representation of healthy intellectual culture, with its fountainlike fullness and swelling overflow into idealized body-receptacles (at once solid and sublime), is precisely loyal to the representation of the inseminative relation in the figure of the book as vial of potency. And second, that both book and contestatory intellectual culture are pitched against morbidity. (The extreme instance of the threat of licensing to the specifically vital aspect of the book is the description, already cited, of licensing as prenatal death.) The chief function of the heroic body-receptacle, the book or the nation, is to outlive. Like a phoenix or a snake, though more prodigal than either, the nation must slough a moribund spiritual body; the book, for its part, must survive and surpass its author, like . . . what?

It will be useful to recall Ovid's figure of the literary text as the partial afterlife of an author:

> Then, when this bodie fals in funerall fire
> My name shall live, and my best part aspire.

One thread in the knot of aspirations, fears, and speculations that secures this durable topos is the idea that the death of an author is a deeply pathetic figure of *editio*: at death, all of an author's writings are unintentionally sent forth from his or her private control. This may help us understand why this topos exerted a particular fascination in early modern England at a moment when the rights and regulation of publication were steadily contested. One crucial stratagem in this contest was the attempt to control or constrain posthumous publication by recourse to the idea that an author's physical life might be given posthumous extension. The formal, legal device by which a person's control might survive him or her was by means of the will and since the chief use of the will was to transfer property, both posthumous authorial control and posthumous edition were frequently articulated as transfers of property. The contest over posthumous publication thus functions as an important stimulus to the development of intellectual property as such. At the beginning of this chapter we examined several instances of tension over posthumous publication; in two of these instances, the publication of the first Shakespeare Folio and the publication of the second Jonson Folio, the tension receives articulation as a struggle over something like heritable property. In the former case, the articulation is figurative: Shakespeare is described as having failed to be "exequutor to his owne writings," the phrase understood to imply a complex of hybrid functions—author-as-testator, editor-as-executor; "writings"-as-will, "writings"-as-property. In the case of the Jonson Folio, the articulation is actual, worked out about four or five years before *Areopagitica:* the quarrel between stationers for control of Jonson's unpublished work was manifested as a struggle between the rights of registration and the heritable rights of property.

How else, besides as property, might writing be made the object of posthumous authorial will, or be made to figure as such; how else might writing be made resistant to inadvertent posthumous edition? This is to ask how the dead contrive to outlive themselves, besides by writing wills. There are other, less formal devices that enable personal will to survive persons, a whole spectrum, from the oaths of survivors, to their promises, to less formal understandings, to that vaporous empathy expressed in the confident announcement that the deceased "would have wanted it that way." As law and conventional stricture withdraw their influence, intimacies of affect, introjections and identifications, must replace their binding force. This end of the spectrum is populated by apprentices, friends, spouses, and, above all children, identified with the living body of the deceased by genetics and identified with the will of the deceased by nurture. Hence, then, a complex of topoi: the child as extension of parent (sometimes as a particular body part), the child as parent reborn, the child as parental utterance—for Jonson, the child as "his best piece of *poetrie.*" By a further figurative extension, the durable text, written or printed, may be spliced to these figures. The text is a body part—"my best part," for Jonson's Ovid; "this living hand," for Keats ("Look, I hold it toward you"); the text is a child—

> Goe little booke, thy selfe present
> As child whose parent is unkent

—the child of a persona, Immerito, the Spenserian "speaker" of *The Shepheardes Calender.* In *Areopagitica,* Milton represents books in ways that are related to both the figures of the book-as-property and the book-as-child. Yet we have already noticed—it is perhaps the most fundamental critical remark one could make about the treatise—how the figures of *Areopagitica* exceed themselves, displacing and all but exploding simplicity of reference. Milton's descriptions of books are related to the book-as-child, or the-book-as-property, but only anamorphically so. He stipulates that books are not properly monopolizable wares, but does not specify the scope of the stipulation; he begins a sentence by describing scholarship as mining, and at the moment at which polemical writing is to be represented as the product of this labor (a direct conversion of real property into commodity), the figurative register slips, and the miner emerges into sunlight having "drawn forth his reasons as it were a battle raung'd" (2:562).[73] In these and in the description of books as the "writt'n labours and monuments of the dead" we can discern a will to describe books as *not quite* property. As survivalist effort on the brink of commodification, thought and writing are made to seem uncomfortably but inevitably economic objects—not *such* wares.

Not quite property and, similarly, not quite children: "For Books are not absolutely dead things, but doe contain a potencie of life in them to be as active as that soule was whose progeny they are." The "life beyond life" of books is personified only to evoke the possibility of homicide or massacre; otherwise it is abstracted or sublimated, a living soul, but living prior to or beyond individual life. In the recurrent emphasis on the book as vial and conduit of potency, material and sublime, the eccentricity of Milton's mortalism is emphasized almost to the point of paradox. I have already suggested the tactics of Milton's rendering of books as not quite children, but we can now take up the historical, but pretactical, ground of Milton's hedged figuration of books.

It may be approached via one more observation about tactics. Milton mollifies Parliament even as he attacks the Licensing Act:

> And as for regulating the Presse, let no man think to have the
> honour of advising ye better then your selves have done in that

> Order publisht next before this, that no book be Printed, unlesse
> the Printers and the Authors name, or at least the Printers be
> register'd. Those which otherwise come forth, if they be found
> mischievous and libellous, the fire and the executioner will be the
> timeliest and the most effectuall remedy, that mans prevention
> can use.

Praising the order of January 1642, Milton finds a remarkably ominous way of representing its arrangements.[74] One last inquisitorial animation: the book that ventures forth without its surnames, should it misbehave, will be treated like a capital criminal or heretic. The double condition leaves room for a good deal of uncertainty, and it is difficult to construe the uncertainty as altogether tactical. Is the fully *attributed* book, however mischievous and libelous, to be spared the fire and the executioner, on the grounds that an element of the transgression—if not its essence—is unacknowledged publication? This would be a strong reprise of Milton's central argument, that published heresy and error, printed mischief and libel, are themselves no threat to a reforming nation.[75] Or is attributed mischief and libel to be punished as always, the executioner's violence to be visited on author and printer? Thus construed, the 1642 order merely maps a procedure for the special case of anonymous publication, an animating, scapegoating procedure to be used against the mischievous and unattributed book. This double interpretation to Parliament of its own order of January 1642 thus seems to stay within the realm of arguably strategic utterance. The double condition enables a radical tolerationist to suppose that all utterance is to be allowed while granting an Erastian centrist the confidence that all print culture is still to be submitted to strict state oversight.

Because of the stressed logic of the double condition, both of these constructions leave problems in their wake. The latter construction, that the order is concerned only with regulating anonymous publication and leaves the regulation of attributed books to be handled, as it were, at a distance, trails a residue of political illogic. For Milton has spoken of the punishment of mischievous books, not of their practical removal from circulation. The threatening rhetoric of punishment implies that the order is coercive, a means of inhibiting future mischief, but fire and executioner can hardly inhibit in the specific instance of books dislocated from their makers. Or, rather, it cannot be inhibiting unless—and this is the fantasy that Milton's rhetoric is poised to release—book culture might propagate itself without human intervention. The effect is to vitiate the rhetorical force of symbolic violence, reconstituting it merely as violence against symbols. There is, moreover, a blunter difficulty with the latter construction, the simple difficulty that this construction of the 1642 order is severely antitolerationist—a profound limitation of the argument of the treatise, if not, effectively, an implied retraction. The alternative construction, that the attributed book can pose no threat to a reforming nation, introduces a curious qualification, that mischief and libel are no threat, are perhaps not even criminal, provided they be tethered to an originating agent or agents. Certainly the order of 1642 made anonymous and "unauthorized" publication a crime, a crime for which the printer could be doubly punished "as both Printer and Author thereof"—though the remedy was left unspecified. A distorted inversion of this principle haunts Milton's venerating reference to the order, the politico-juridical fantasy that attribution mitigates, even neutralizes, transgression: the attributed text is not only harmless, but a privileged instrument of Reformation; the unattributed text is a scapegoat, alienable and manageable.[76] At the same time that it achieves a strategic, coalition-building ambiguity, Milton's double condition fosters an attributive mystique.

This aggrandizement of attribution, however vague and fantastic, is propped and invigorated by many other aspects of *Areopagitica*. Milton's insistence on the seminal potencies of thought and the genetics of books exaggerates the personifying habits of a culture of licensing to the point at which genetics detaches itself from its origins in ideological regulation to become something like an independent principle, as natural as biology and as fundamental as the relationship between body and soul. The treatise thus repudiates licensing while retaining attribution, which is transformed from a practical instrument into a structure of thought, what we might call an ideologeme. In the event, the aggrandizement of attribution has had a powerful and specific influence. As will be seen in the next chapter, a few key texts by Milton have had an inordinate power over subsequent developments in book culture—and of these *Areopagitica* has been the most important. As lawyers and philosophers developed models of the political subject as a bearer of rights, historians and literary scholars would look back at *Areopagitica* and construe its celebration of attribution as an assertion of authorial rights over the circulation of books, or, sometimes, as a reassertion of rights *ostensibly* originating with the 1642 order. Hence, to recur to an example already cited, Siebert's description of that order as "one of the earliest recognitions of the rights of authors by the English Parliament." As has already been shown, that order "recognizes" no rights; it simply seizes on the author for a registry of potential malefactors—yet as shrewd a political analyst as Milton's editor, Sirluck, could be misled into referring to the 1642 regulations as "the Signature Order." And a more recent study of the politics of the 1644s, equally shrewd, could promulgate a version of Siebert's and Sirluck's misunderstanding, finding in *Areopagitica* roughly what they had read into the 1642 order: "Milton's argument is not based upon a notion of Truth or knowledge as something which is separated, like the Spirit, from the world. Rather, it is a property argument based partly upon the limitation of monopoly to the author's ownership of his copy."[77] This is a traditional misreading—but a misreading nonetheless—of a couple of passages from *Areopagitica,* most notably Milton's disparaging summary assessment of the 1643 act:

> And how it got the upper hand of your precedent Order so well
> constituted before, if we may beleeve those men whose profession
> gives them cause to enquire most, it may be doubted there was in
> it the fraud of some old *patentees* and *monopolizers* in the trade of
> book-selling; who under pretence of the poor in their Company
> not to be defrauded, and the just retaining of each man his several
> copy, which God forbid should be gainsaid, brought divers glosing
> colours to the House.

It has been easy enough to suppose that this refers to authors' retention of (something like) copyright, though that is certainly not the primary sense of the passage. The historical context makes it clear that Milton is defending each stationer's retention of (stationer's) copyright, and opposing that community of stationer's copyright that extremists within the company were said to have been urging. The "old *patentees* and *monopolizers* in the trade" had said rather little about author's prerogatives during the early 1640s, though their petition for the renewal of licensing in April 1643 had pleaded on behalf of the poor of the company and warned against the threat of "confusion" of copy.[78] Despite Wither's assertions that an author's writings are his birthright and that authors are the "true owners" of printers' copy, the proprietary standing of authors had not acquired such currency as to confound the stationers' position.[79] For Milton, "copy" was inchoate and uninstitutionalized (though it had cropped up now and again), and it was therefore unnecessary that God should forbid *its* being gainsaid.[80]

It may be useful to take a reading of Milton's precise position in *Areopagitica*. Once we are disabused of the idea that he is making what would have been a surprising (and, thus, suprisingly casual) defense of authorial copyright, we confront the less surprising but still curious fact of Milton's repeated and emphatic defense of stationer's copyright. In the *propositio* of the treatise, when he exhorts Parliament to reconsider its recent ill-advised Licensing Act, he shields a portion of the act from his general denunciation:

"that part which preserves justly every mans Copy to himselfe, or provides for the poor, I touch not." Again, he can only be speaking of stationers here, for there is nothing authorial to touch on in the 1643 act, except for a single provision for the arrest of "Authors, Printers, and other Persons" involved in the production of scandalous or unlicensed books.[81] In fact, even the requirement that stationers secure an author's consent prior to printing had been dropped between January 1642 and 1643. Milton, however, makes nothing of this change, a change that an *advocate* for authorial property might be expected bitterly to lament. As far as Milton was concerned, the rights of copy had been justly preserved in the 1643 act, which is to say that parliamentary protection of stationer's copyright had not flagged. This exposes what I take to be the least intuitive aspect of the analysis I have been offering: that Milton endorses the tethering of copy to stationer (in the interests as much of jurisdictional stability as of economic justice) and powerfully figures a tethering of book to author (both in the interests of a pathetic argument for the free circulation of ideas and as part of a variously motivated corporealization of thought), but without much apparent interference between these two polemical activities.[82]

It is important to notice what the figure of intellectual paternity accomplishes. If books "contain a potencie of life in them to be as active as that soule was whose progeny they are," if "they do preserve as in a violl the purest efficacie and extraction of that living intellect that bred them," paternity begets not property but more paternity. The figure of genetics argues the case for no *authorial* rights whatsoever, deploying its animated pathos on behalf of a quite unindividualized intellectual life. The Hartlibians, perhaps the most intellectually sturdy of Milton's early colleagues, eventually came to feel that Milton was too old-fashioned to suit them, too interested in rhetoric, but the mark of their influence may be felt in the metaphoric core of the above passage, with its impersonal biogenetics. Milton presents *Areopagitica* not as "the disburdening of a particular fancie, but the common grievance of all those who had prepar'd their minds and studies above the vulgar pitch to advance truth in others, and from others to entertain it." Antipopulist, of course, but this is also casually anti-individualist: the Hartlib circle thought in terms of collective intellectual work and so, at this point, did Milton.[83] The utopian image offered in *Areopagitica* of a nation rousing itself to spiritual struggle sustains just this interest in collectivity, a deep conceptual undertow to Milton's passing defense of stationers' property, that defense itself pitched against the abusive hyper-individualism of the monopolistic printing patent. However vividly biogenetic his representations of the relation of author and book may be, they are also quite curiously impersonal or, more precisely,

improper—and that, I believe, bespeaks his deliberate resistance to any regulatory argument that is structured, explicitly or implicitly, by monopoly. His
limited attack on licensing rests on a recoil from monopoly that seems almost instinctive, but is conditioned both by Hartlibian collectivism and by
four decades of articulate protest against the royal institutions of monopolistic competition.

The sharpest apparent contribution of *Areopagitica* to the history of intellectual property, then, is inadvertent, since it has to do with the subsequent misreading of the treatise as an essay on authors' rights; its subtler but
certainly remarkable contribution is the eloquence and extravagance of its
attributive mystique. The industrial history of the personality of books must
include *Areopagitica* as one of its cultural monuments, though it may not
usefully be included in a chronicle of the law of property.[84] That said, it may
be conceded that the nebulous formation of authorial rights does haunt this
polemical moment. To prop their case for the protection of stationer's copyright, the old monopolizers *had*, after all, alluded to something like derivative
authorial rights. For Milton, as I have already suggested, the allusion was perhaps the most the striking of the several arguments that spurred his polemical imagination: "Many mens studies carry no other profit or recompense
with them, but the benefit of their Copies; and if this be taken away, many
Pieces of great worth and excellence will be strangled in the womb, or never
conceived at all for the future." Following immediately on their analysis of
the importance of copyright in mitigating capital risk within the book trade,
the monopolists' evocation of the "benefit of copies" displays the process by
which authorial copyright evolved, as a back-formation, from stationer's. We
can now gauge the attention with which Milton read the petition, and the particular imaginative inflammation that the old monopolists had kindled in this
corner of their appeal to Parliament. Although his references to retaining and
preserving of copies certainly refer to stationer's copyright, Milton has almost
as certainly been struck by the stationers' description of benefit of copy as a
means of protecting the genetics of books from Junonian licensers. Benefit of
copy, as the stationers represent it, is hardly a formal authorial property, but
its adjacency to stationer's copyright, and its dependence on it, give us what
might be called the last stage in the prehistory of authorial property. Milton's
appropriation of the language of the stationers' petition, like the recurrence to
figures of production and commerce, registers the *range* of stresses informing
the English revolutionary moment. But the treatise is distinguished, scarred
rather, by a refusal of economic assertion and argument: intellectual production and commerce appear as obtrusively metaphoric, not fully to be thought.
And now another aspect of Milton's influence comes into view. That partial

historiography of authorship, with its repressions of industrial history in favor of a history of censorship—the historiography that culminates in Foucault's "What is an Author?"—is a historiography that *Areopagitica* initiates, and the partiality of which *Areopagitica* betrays.

Enacting the radicalism of its political moment, *Areopagitica* remaps the early modern market, and particularly the book trade, breaking down several of their key structures into constituent features, and reassembling them, sometimes as unstable composites. The struggle within the book trade to redistribute the fruits of monopoly (a struggle in which the "reformers" were making opportunistic use of popular antimonopolism) appears, changed, in *Areopagitica* as a struggle for ideological freedom of publication. More generally, the market in books is remapped as a market—and, more often, as a battlefield—of ideas, purged of private interest by the transformed energy of antimonopolism (so that we are offered, in the ideological sphere, an anticipation of the economist utopia of the autonomous market). Equally generally, the national economy of early mercantilism is refigured in the spiritual chauvinisms of a reforming Elect Nation. (Though here one must make a concession and a distinction: that English religious reform had provided some of the ideological starch and structure of English mercantilism, so that Milton's use of mercantilist nationalism as a map for reformation nationalism is a kind of ideological homecoming; and that Milton seeks a far more qualified protectionism for the intellectual market than was customarily found in state regulation of international trade, though both forms of protectionism were similarly capricious.) Those who risk capital on book production, including authors—who may now write in hopes of the benefits of copy rather than out of aspiration for patronage—appear in the figurative guise of "reason it selfe, . . . the Image of God," so that spiritual and intellectual venture are conceived as a distinctively capitalist incarnation of Divinity. And the anticompetitive and protoproprietary structures within the book trade appear, deinstitutionalized and idealized, as an attributive mystique, an intense genetics, simultaneously spiritual and corporeal, that links the laboring producers of books to their valiant and fiercely personal products.

CHAPTER SEVEN

MILTON'S TALENT:
THE EMERGENCE OF AUTHORIAL COPYRIGHT

> Then he which had received the one talent came and said, Lord, I
> knew thee that thou art an hard man, reaping where thou hast not
> sown, and gathering where thou hast not strawed: And I was afraid,
> and went and hid thy talent in the earth: lo, there thou hast that
> is thine. His lord answered and said unto him, Thou wicked and
> slothful servant, thou knewest that I reap where I sowed not, and
> gather where I have not strawed: Thou oughtest therefore to have
> put my money to the exchangers, and then at my coming I should
> have received mine own with usury. Take therefore the talent from
> him, and give it unto him which hath ten talents. For unto every one
> that hath shall be given, and he shall have abundance: but from him
> that hath not shall be taken away even that which he hath.
>
> Matthew 25:24–9 (KJV)

> When I consider how my light is spent
> Ere half my days, in this dark world and wide,
> And that one Talent which is death to hide,
> Lodg'd with me useless . . .
>
> Sonnet 19 in *John Milton: The*
> *Complete Poems and Major Prose*
> (ed. Merritt Y. Hughes)

The brute facts of Milton's blindness—the date of its onset and the pace of its
development—and the complex commensuration of bodily and spiritual vi-

sion have tended to dominate the decent project of explicating Milton's nineteenth sonnet. Those who date the poem by dating Milton's blindness (or date Milton's blindness by dating the poem) assume that "light" means (or means, at least) "eyesight." It may also mean "vitality," "grace," or "the resources of a literary tradition." "Spent" is easier: biographical criticism will allege that Milton's light was spent on the Commonwealth, that at least eyesight and vitality were spent on reading and writing polemics on ecclesiastical polity, licensing, and regicide; that they were spent on prose. Yet "*is* spent" introduces a small uncertainty, the slight progressive nudge of the construction raising the question of whether the light is *being* depleted, or is already exhausted. And the anxious uncertainty of this inventory of light is compounded with the turn from the light to the Talent. How is "Talent" to be construed? To begin to answer: although it is unclear whether the husbanding of light is failing or has failed, what has been firmly established already is that this is a poem of pinched economics, which is to say that its goals are, particularly, measurement rather than description. So "that one Talent" is not another name for "light." (Obviously not: the light is spent, the Talent is lodg'd uselessly, and even the most hapless accountant can distinguish such different ways of handling capital.) But what, then, is this Talent, which is not eyesight, vitality, or the resources of a literary tradition?

The naive and sentimental biographer's answer—premature, though not necessarily wrong—is "a gift for writing poetry." Milton might plausibly have conceived of such a gift as "useless" on the grounds that he had not been writing much poetry in the late forties and early fifties: some sonnets, an epistle about (personified) copies of his books that he had sent to the Bodleian but which had been lost in transit, a handful of psalm translations. It is hard to imagine why it might be "death to hide" such a gift, though the imaginative challenge is probably greater for us than for Milton's contemporaries, if only because, for them, the term "talent" would quickly call up associations with its context in Matthew 25. It is, of course, from the parable of the servants entrusted with five, two, and a single *talanton* (a Greek coin, the name of which is derived from a term for a particular measure of weight, itself derived from the term for a scale) that Milton takes his figure. The parable (like its variant in Luke 19, where the gift is denominated in pounds) is both uncanny and harsh in its evocation of the perils of spiritual—and, more specifically, evangelical—caution in the *use* of the gift of revelation, and the King James Version respects the uncanniness by having the returning lord protest his servant's failure to secure what is specified as a *usurious* increase on the gifts of the spirit.[1] The parabolic exaltation of spiritual meanness is painfully impressive, and it may be that that impressive force alone warrants the extravagant fatality of Milton's phrasing. A sophisticated and unsentimental biographer might now chime in with a suspicion that the reference to "that one Talent which is death to hide" (with all its uncanny associations, including the endorsement of usury) is also the latest in Milton's several guilty recollections of his debts to his earthly father, the money-lending scrivener who financed the young poet's protracted and perhaps useless education. This talented, musical father had died just over a year after Milton's first volume of poems appeared, and after that death, Milton had become almost exclusively a writer of prose. This gives us another way of accounting for the extravagant phrasing, that it is heated by familial pressures and frictions, and another gloss for "talent," that it is not just a "gift" for writing poetry analogous to the gift of revelation, but a gift of money, one with many implied, but perhaps unspecified, strings attached.

Since they cannot be securely inventoried, the residual unspecificity of "light" and "Talent," and the unspecifying voice of the verbal constructions ("is spent," "is death to hide," "lodg'd," "though more bent") arouse and frustrate the soul's accountancy. So the cognitive serenity of consideration and the spiritual poise of patience is disturbed by more than a murmur that cannot be prevented: both are fundamentally disrupted by something very like the spirit of capitalism—a parsimony of light, a talent-pinching meanness. At least in one very crucial aspect, then, we are dealing with the same cultural or conjunctural imagination that expresses itself in *Areopagitica*. In both cases, mental and spiritual strivings are submitted to economic assessment, but obsessively, as if such accounting were a kind of curse. Although "Truth and understanding are not such wares as to be monopoliz'd and traded in by tickets and statutes, and standards," *Areopagitica* will not relinquish economic argument; indeed, the treatise is so committed to economic figures that it invents, on behalf of Reformation, the crucial ideological fantasy of a marketplace of ideas, a fantasy that firmly represses its material base. The more private economic idiom of Sonnet XIX is a good deal more haunted, the intimate material base of that idiom less securely repressed. But in neither case can Milton speak of mental effort without representing it as a form of capital.

The seventeenth century is a watershed in the semantic history of "talent" as it is in the semantic history of "genius." As we have seen, "genius" is undergoing what might be called a transmythologization as the antique daemon is assimilated and transformed into a mysterious inward property of individuals, their distinguishing essence. Modern "talent" is also an inward property, and is well on its inward way in Milton's sonnet, though it is considerably less mysterious than "genius," and for reasons that can be genetically traced, since the parable emphasizes the accommodations of the spirit by representing revelation in terms of human currency. Semantic drift in the use of "talent" transforms the idea of *accommodated* divinity, by exaggerating the accommodation at the expense of the divinity—hence William Watson's reference in 1600 to "sorie fellowes of no talent gift or ability." In effect, "talent" undergoes its secularization by taking the parable at its word.

The full internalization of "genius" is, at the earliest, a nineteenth-century phenomenon, prior to which the meaning of the term remained suspended, "of the shore" as Milton would have it in "Lycidas," between inner and outer, between intrinsic property and daemonic possession. The internalization of "talent" has come about even more slowly: even now we speak of talent as a "natural gift," and if we are only barely conscious of the semantic complexities of the formulation, a sense of sacred obligation stalks the talented nonetheless. The semantic career of "talent" is thus much constrained by the original use of the term, for the talent of the parable is never proper to the servant. In this regard, Watson's largely secular use of the term still preserves a good deal of the original connotations: "talent gift or ability" seems to describe a spectrum of increasing properness to the subject, with "talent" originating in some outer source of capital, and coming to the subject not as if it were a gift from a patron, but as if it were a temporary loan from some master. But other uses of the term emerge in the early decades of the seventeenth century, uses not only secular but also less loanlike, even less gift-like, which is to say more proper to the subject.[2] By 1656, Blount's dictionary could instance as a colloquial use of the term, "We say, a man of good talents, i.e. of good parts or abilities"; during the second half of the century, and as early as 1669, the term could be used simply to refer to a personal or national characteristic.[3] The development of these "proper" meanings involves the influence of a different philological strand, traceable to Old French and other Romance usages, in which "talent" means a wish, inclination, or disposition, though not, apparently, of a *distinctive* sort. By the seventeenth century, a talent is almost always distinctive and individualizing, but the supposed origin of the distinctive feature, the degree of its property to the subject, was variable. Milton's use of the term is tethered closely to its biblical origins, as Milton's talent is tethered to the Master who conferred it; it may be that his use of the term implies a rebuke to those who could think and speak of talent as the coinage merely of the brain.

The semantic conversion of talent into a distinguishing characteristic of the subject, and Milton's psychological engagement in the work of this conversion, are fully imbricated in the legal and economic history of intellectual property, of course; the decades during which "talent" undergoes crucial semantic change are also crucial to the history of copyright. We might now speak of "talent" as an important member of the lexicon of secular humanism, a term retaining only vestiges of the sacred or the grateful, but in the seventeenth century the term had two different meanings: the one old and sacred and the other new and secular; the former imbued with the ideology of clientage (though briskly engaged in modern fiscalism) and the latter probing the emergent ideology of possessive individualism. By the end of the seventeenth century, to mean the term one way was probably to treat the other meaning as tendentious. One of the ironies of the history of intellectual property is that in the ensuing decades Milton was made into the champion of a possessive individualist "talent." We have seen that possessive individualism animates his imagination—I use each of these terms advisedly—when he considers how his light is spent or when he presumes to instruct Parliament on the sociology of Reformation, so it was a sensitive misunderstanding, historically inevitable, by means of which Milton's parabolic "talent" became ours. My purpose in what follows is to articulate the continuous complex participation of Milton's texts and reputation in the unfolding of this crucial transformation.

"The Authority of the Author"

As has already been mentioned, parliamentary activism during the Interregnum fractured the relatively independent authority of the Stationers' Company over the book trade.[4] Ideological regulation of the press had once been supervised by the officers of the company, who served as powerful if fitfully dutiful delegates of church and state and whose decisions were only occasionally corrected by those they represented; but in the 1640s Parliament had insisted on the primacy of its own supervisory prerogatives. Parliament was unequal to the task it had set itself—press censorship never having been very efficient—but its persistent legislative and administrative efforts transformed English book culture.

The progressive inhibition of the stationers' authority was variously effected; eventually the constitution of authorial property became one of the most important instruments of that inhibition. At midcentury, however, the possibility of a constitutive analysis of authorial property was inhibited by the same public concerns as had held the foreground of discussions of press regulation in the 1630s and 1640s. Public reflection on press regulation continued throughout the century, but until the eighties it was most often conducted as an evaluation of censorship. As we have seen, the anti-Stuart critique of monopolistic competition, so important to the period leading up to the Civil War, had briefly taken the press as an object of scrutiny, but as the Caroline state collapsed, the interrogation of censorship occluded at least some such explicitly economic disputes. Still, important industrial difficulties *did* surface within the book trade and thence emerged into public attention, although they were usually dealt with as problems pertaining primarily to censorship. This is, of course, the political logic that had provoked Milton to his sometimes jeering analysis of press regulation in *Areopagitica:* that because the granting of new printing patents had ceased with the revolution, leaving older patents virtually unprotected, the richest stationers had been transformed into outspoken proponents of licensing. The rationale of ideological regulation quite consistently served the interests of capital within the book trade.[5] Those interests were threatened by the rumblings of faction, but when dissident printers petitioned Parliament in 1651 for permission to form their own company and directed a similar appeal to the king twelve years later, they were, both times, rebuffed—and rebuffed because Parliament and, later, both Parliament and Crown felt that a single company would be easier to supervise.[6]

The immediate provocation for the 1663 petition was the Licensing Act that had restored censorship the year before. In response to petitions from a company leadership alarmed by the printers' secessionist grumblings, the number of master printers was capped at the then current limit of fifty-nine, with a target for the reduction of that number set at twenty, while strict regulations aimed at securing full employment for all journeymen in authorized shops was also promulgated.[7] The company's monopoly and its mechanisms of self-government had been and would continue to be sustained as an instrumental convenience for a censorious government, but its autonomy was steadily compromised—first by the parliamentary Council of State, and, now, in the Restoration, by the royal surveyors of the press.

Yet questions of industrial freedom and industrial property were not utterly dissolved into questions of censorship. A vocal and persistent faction of printers continued to lobby for separate incorporation, apparently finding a cautiously sympathetic ear in Surveyor L'Estrange, who seems to have entertained the possibility of a regulatory regime coordinated specifically with the manufacturing sector of the book trade.[8] Nothing much came of this long-standing resistance movement, which seems finally to have died out in 1679—at the moment, oddly enough, at which L'Estrange gave the petitioning printers his strongest endorsement—but their continued and vocal dissatisfaction meant that unreconciled economic tensions within the book trade remained fully visible and articulate for those most concerned with regulating the supply and circulation of printed books. A striking document from this tradition of protest shows the emergence of copyright as an object of particular contest: in *A Brief Discourse Concerning Printing and Printers* (1663) the aggrieved printers alleged that the booksellers had grown so powerful and, in particular, had so monopolized stationer's copyright that "it is become a question among them, whether a Printer ought to have any Copy or no" (B_4). More pertinent to the development of legal inquiry into intellectual property than this incipient class struggle was the revival of contest over monopolies in books. The most lucrative patents had been variously leased and traded in the 1630s, so that by the 1640s, the rights in those patents were the object of a tangle of lawsuits, stock negotiations, and infringements.[9] The Civil Wars had put a crack in the foundation of the patents, and it remained to be seen whether they had irreparably damaged the standing of the patentees: with the Restoration, rival claimants struggled vigorously both for the restitution of the patents and for the clarification of their own titles to them.[10] As before, quarrels over patents escaped the jurisdiction of the Stationers' Company; the primary site of this struggle was the courts. Richard Atkyns, heir to a patent in books of the common law, however, also tried to take his case to the reading public.

The Original and Growth of Printing (1664) may be taken as a Restoration update to Wither's *Scholler's Purgatory* and as perhaps the first attempt to present the history of the press as a history of printing rights. Writing early in the Restoration, Atkyns alleges that Henry VI was directly responsible for introducing printing into England, that printing was therefore a royal "invention," and that all rights to print therefore properly derived directly from the Crown.[11] Atkyns offered enough evidence for his account that it seemed plausible—so plausible, indeed, that some aspects of his history were honored with a refutation in 1735.[12] As successor to a privilege for the printing of law books, Atkyns made it his purpose to establish the printing patent as the normative form of intellectual property, normative as opposed, naturally, not to authorial property but to stationer's copyright, which he made out to be quite derivative, secondary at best.[13] Here was a last-ditch attempt to derive all monopoly practices in the book trade from the prerogative, with no intervention of customary industrial monopolies. (This ancient derivation, however, depends on a modern logic, since the prerogative is supplemented by the rights of innovation: monopoly rights begin with Henry VI both as monarch *and* as inventor.) It was, in one sense, a doomed undertaking, for by December 1689, the prerogative would be crippled by the Bill of Rights— and not only in the sphere of monopoly practices. In the closest reprisal of Wither's efforts, Atkyns supplemented his etiology of publication rights with an attack on those rights claimed by the stationers.[14] The stationers claimed

special privileges—including, presumably, some freedoms to invade printing patents—by virtue of their charter; he challenged that the terms of the
charter should be carefully looked into. This challenge must have been more
than coincidentally pointed, for about this time the stationers discovered that
they could not put their hands on the original manuscript of the charter on
which they had staked so much. We may suppose that Atkyns had been tipped
off. In 1665, the Stationers' Court turned to William Prynne, now Keeper of
Records at the Tower, for assistance in securing a copy, which was transcribed
from a version enrolled there. If nothing else, such contest over the "original"
of printing rights indicates the potential radicalism of the moment.

On the basis of his royalist historiography, Atkyns not only reasserted his
claim to the law patent, he also proposed that press regulation might best
be made the responsibility of the patentees themselves.[15] Like several other
patentees outside the company, he was struggling against various intrusions
on his privilege by members of the company and fearful that the institution of
the printing patent might not in fact recover from the disruptions of the Interregnum. The Restoration Licensing Act of 1662 had offered at least nominal
protection of traditional monopolistic structures: both patents and stationer's
copyrights had been confirmed by the act, and the penalties for infringement
were to be split between the injured patentee or copyright holder and the
Crown.[16] Of course, the act did not clarify the standing of either monopoly
form, and, moreover, it had been limited to an effective duration of only two
years, which left all interested parties maneuvering for position. The act was
renewed in 1664, the year of Atkyns's *Original and Growth;* it was renewed
again the following year, this time until 1679 (after which the act was allowed
to lapse until 1685). The long-term renewal should have reassured the stationers, but Atkyns continued to nettle them. In fact, legal disputes pitting
him—or other nonstationers who claimed large patents—against the stationers dragged on into the next decade and beyond.[17]

Within the context of the Restoration moment, the contest over the law
patent provoked some amateur legal thinking that reprises, sharpens, and
specifies themes from the Elizabethan and Jacobean struggles over monopolies. Atkyns's royalist historiography is interesting enough, but the rhetoric
of his final pages is especially telling, for there he likens the patent to an
act of royal agricultural enclosure, a particular assertion of the Crown's more
general property (E_1). The analogy is motivated by Atkyns's special interest
in publishing the *law,* a complex of texts that might have presented itself
as a common cultural domain, particularly during the Interregnum. Atkyns's
argument founds his exclusive rights to exploit this apparently public domain on the model of the monarch's exclusive rights to Crown lands, even

to those on which custom had conferred the appearance of common property. In the context of the highly visible activity of ajudicating property in
lands that had been sequestered during the Civil War, of recovering royal
property to the Crown and, in some cases, compensating the disappointed
purchasers, Atkyns's choice of analogy could not have seemed poised, but
that is perhaps the point.[18] He is not only defending intellectual property
by "realizing" it; he is at the same time loyally reasserting the Crown's real
property in a contested area.[19] I take it that a threshold is crossed here, and
with much fanfare, for real property lies at the center of the English law of
property—it might be argued that it occupied the center of all of English law;
certainly 90 percent of the curriculum at the Inns of Court concerned land
law—and the comparison of the printable object to land thus constitutes a
key "moment of theory" for intellectual property as such. The moment has
its ironies, of course, for Atkyns actually specifies arguments that enemies of
monopolies like Nicholas Fuller had begun to sketch in the 1610s. As Clive
Holmes has observed, the Jacobean antimonopolists had begun to extend the
law of property in ways "that permitted the incorporation of lands, goods, and
occupations into a single privileged class"; the Restoration monopolist now
facilitates the incorporation of inventions, like printing, within that same large
legal class.[20]

Of the responses to Atkyns's campaign, one contains a formulation as
ingenious and as momentous as this "realizing" of industrial practice. Two
years after the publication of *The Original and Growth*, a broadside appeared
that sought to discredit Atkyn's argument; *The Case of the Booksellers and
Printers Stated* opens with a polemical maneuver that turns out to forecast
the subsequent legal history of copyright. The maneuver had been crudely
anticipated on several occasions in the history of the English book trade, but
it had never been formulated quite so clearly:

> It is humbly conceived, First, That the Author of every *Manu-
> script* or *Copy* hath (in all reason) as good right thereunto, as
> any Man hath to the Estate wherein he has the most absolute
> property, and consequently the taking from him the one (without
> his own consent) will be equivalent to the bereaving him of the
> other, contrary to his Will.

—note the obliging recurrence to the idiom of land law—

> Secondly, Those who purchased such Copies for valuable
> considerations, having the Authors right thereby transferred to
> them (and a due Licence and Entrance according to Law) 'twill be

> as prejudicial to deprive them of the benefit of their Purchase, as
> to Disseise them of their Freehold.

This advances and formalizes devices by which, for example, authors had served individual stationers in their efforts to secure copyrights against the claims of rivals within their own company. In those earlier instances, the author assists, diacritically, in confirming one stationer's claim against that of another. Here, on the other hand, it is claimed that the author's activity *founds* the property, which is then merely transferred to the manufacturing stationer. The author of *The Case of the Booksellers* simply refuses Atkyns's premise that the contested property lies in the printing itself, which is to say that the tactics of the moment conduce to the reification of authorial property. This engagement reenacts the struggles over monopolies from half a century earlier, with the author of *The Case of the Booksellers* reiterating a stationer's version of Nicholas Fuller's insistence on the absolute character of the subject's property, impregnable to attempted prerogative invasions. But thanks to Atkyns, the struggle was carried out, at least for a time, as if it were a contest over real estate.[21]

The emergence of property in books as a theoretical problem, shadowy in *Areopagitica* and sharper in *The Original and Growth*, is by no means an isolated phenomenon, but takes its place in a general ferment within seventeenth-century political self-consciousness. If the argument that an address to real property should have a founding status for understanding and adjudicating political relations is remembered as Locke's decisive innovation, worked out at the end of the 1670s, this small skirmish of the sixties reminds us that such address is hardly new.[22] In fact, Atkyns and his opponents recall James Harrington's political writing of the early 1650s.[23] But to look back from *The Original and Growth* to Harrington's *Oceana* and forward to Locke's *Two Treatises on Government* is to remind ourselves how richly the political practices of the Protectorate and Restoration stimulated the theory of property: in the various aftermaths of the English revolution, Harrington, Wren, Atkyns, Locke, and many others variously engaged themselves in investigations of what property was, what its normative form might be. The particular—and distinctive—problem of commensuration between real property and more moveable, more marketable property is the great work of late seventeenth-century political thought, but it had been anticipated not only in revolutionary constitutional argument but here in this skirmish over intellectual property.[24]

Yet the struggle for the restitution and clarification of patents must itself be regarded as revolutionary if only insofar as it constitutes a moment in which control of the book trade was not submitted to the rhetoric of censorship. Granted that the proprietary argument of *The Case of the Book-sellers* reflected practices that had been asserted—if only sporadically—since the beginning of the century; still, the purity of its address to rights should be weighed and appreciated. Wither had long before verged on a language of property that we can find enunciated frequently at midcentury. In December 1660, for example, a Lord Powess had brought a complaint before the Stationers' Court against the widow of a printer named Griffin. Griffin had entered a romance by Powess and printed it at the author's charge; having added to the work, Lord Powess found Mrs. Griffin obstructing his intent to finance a second printing. Lord Powess swore "that he never contracted with Mr. Griffin for, or gave him a right in the said Originall, & Mrs. Griffin (now attending) haveing only the entrance of the said booke to offer in behalf of her title," the Court referred the matter to the master of the company for adjudication.[25] The difficulties of the case are obvious: entrance and "widow's property" confront aristocracy, the occasionally asserted relocative rights of revision, and the sketchy conventions of privately financed publication. Yet it should be noted that even this proprietary argument is in fact shaped by the practical logic of censorship: the case offers telling evidence of the negative effect of the public obsession with licensing. Entrance is now so specified to the mechanisms of censorship that Lord Powess can concede Griffin's entrance without (ostensibly) even imagining that he might have conferred "a right in the said Originall"; whereas Mrs. Griffin understands entrance as securing just such a right. This uncertainty over the force of entrance persists and is, during the next three decades, as determining as the emergence of a political science of property: the muddle of this dispute heralds the persistent muddle in the career of authorial property as it proceeds toward full reification in the Statute of Anne of 1710—a complex career worked out in relation both to a public sphere in which the regulation of books appeared as a problem of ideological control and to an industry desperately seeking to sustain its monopolies.

The Restoration moment is marked in the book trade not only by an increasing recourse to the rhetoric of property, but also by increased codification of trade practices and by the continued erosion of the stationers' powers of self-regulation. To some extent, these developments depended on the zeal of Roger L'Estrange, in whose hands the power of press regulation was so notoriously concentrated. Yet the history of the Restoration book trade is not to be reduced to a biography of L'Estrange: he did not, after all, accumulate all the regulatory power that seeped away from the stationers, for a good deal shifted to the law courts.[26] Litigation over such privileges as the law, Bible, and almanac patents recurred so insistently that it changed the regulatory climate: an incoherent body of case law began to coalesce concerning the institution of the patent.[27] Many of the relevant suits were brought by the company itself, in attempts to secure external props for their conventions and interests, but many of these suits backfired.[28] The stationers were therefore obliged to campaign on various fronts. In 1667, for example, they sought to renovate their standing by securing a new charter from the Crown, itself exactly reproducing the original of 1557; but the new charter was quickly challenged in Parliament, challenged as a feeble document that protected the industry without safeguarding the interest of the state in suppressing libels.[29] The charter would have been forfeit in 1670 had L'Estrange not interceded on behalf of the company, promising on its behalf that a new set of bylaws would be forthcoming.[30] They were slow in coming, however, and the regulations that were finally produced, in 1678, seem more optative than confidently imperative. The new bylaws stipulated that no presses be set up without company approval, that no unlicensed books were to be printed, and so forth.[31] At L'Estrange's insistence, a fine of 200 pounds was set for infringements on Atkyns's law patent. It may be that the struggle over Atkyns's patent left other traces on the new charter, which is introduced with a careful acknowledgment that no industrial charter may abridge royal prerogatives and concluded with signatures of the lord keeper and the lord chief justices confirming that this charter did not constitute any such abridgment.[32] This jealous marking of the limit and extent of company privileges is no more telling than in the stipulation that the Court of Assistants be the court of first instance in all copyright disputes. What this tells us is how insecure company self-governance had become: aggrieved tradesmen had been powerfully tempted of late to seek the less fragile, more disinterested adjudication of the courts, and the bylaws make an ineffectual effort to restore company authority over properties no longer conceived as emerging from within intra-industrial relations.

Still, we cannot speak of this as a proto-Lockean moment, nor as a post-Witherian moment either. Questions of authorial rights, and particularly of authorial property, do not often surface within the rhetoric of this long season of codification, neither in the stationers' new charter or bylaws, nor in Restoration patent litigation. Yet as the traditions and powers of industrial self-regulation deteriorate, there are signs of increasing authorial propriety observable in practices that disturb traditional relations within the book trade. As earlier, authorial claims confound property relations. In 1688, for example, Edward Vize sold Joseph Watts his interest in Milton's *Judgement of Martin Bucer,* which Vize had purchased from Simmons, the son of the original registrant of the volume; but by 1695 Watts apparently had come to feel that his title might be rendered insecure by residual authorial interests, for in that year he paid Milton's widow ten guineas, in return for which she sold him "All that my Book or Coppy entituled The Judgment of Martin Bucer." This was, to be sure, part of a larger settlement: Watts's ten guineas bought him not only Elizabeth Milton's property in *Martin Bucer* but "alsoe all other the Coppyes and Writings which were the Works of the said John Milton."[33] Elsewhere on the document is a list of what seem to be the titles comprised by the sale, twenty-four works in prose. Watts may have made the initial purchase in order to compete against—or to collaborate with— the bookseller Awnsham Churchill, who had registered Milton's prose works a few weeks earlier, though no edition was immediately forthcoming from Watts or Churchill.[34] Editions of the prose works do appear in 1698 and 1699, though neither man can be securely connected with either edition, but Watts's turn to Milton's widow may have been an attempt to shore up his title as part of the preparations for one of these two editions. At any rate, the purchase from Vize was plainly felt to be fragile, and the purchase from Elizabeth Milton was at least supplementary; the terms of the contract, however are hardly so modest, for Mrs. Milton claims to "Grant bargain and sell" the works in question.[35] The contract concedes that registration does not itself secure a title. Milton's 1667 contract with Samuel Simmons for *Paradise Lost* transfers "All that Booke Copy or Manuscript . . . Togeather with the full benefitt profitt & advantage thereof or which shall or may arise thereby"—a comprehensive list, proof that by the latter part of his career Milton could conceive of authorial rights in ways *not* registered in *Areopagitica*. Although the contract seems so decisively to transfer Milton's claims to Simmons, Simmons nonetheless secured from Mrs. Milton a kind of quit claim deed to the poem in 1681, four months after having made his final payment on the contract.[36] These arrangements, taken together with Watts's payment for the prose works in 1695, suggest that Mrs. Milton's claims haunt the stationers—not surprisingly, as we shall see.

One important trade development during this period offered some practical reinforcement for the idea of originative authorial property advanced in *The Case of the Booksellers*. We have already observed how the early Stuart market in newsbooks and, more generally, in small pamphlets entailed the elaboration of extensive distribution networks. These networks unsettled the traditional organization of the trade if only because they depended on the work of a great number of petty laborers excluded from the formal structure of the Stationers' Company—the Mercury-women who handled much of the wholesaling of newsbooks, and the street-hawkers who handled so much of the retail trade in ephemera. The market in ephemera also reorganized the internal structure of the company. By the eighties, imprints might advertise a book as printed for X and "published" by Y, and McKenzie determined that in such instances Y is charged with large-scale dispersal of the book or pamphlet to a variety of booksellers. This publisher is not necessarily the capitalist who is coordinating all aspects of book production and marketing; indeed he is certainly not so where the imprint declares a pamphlet to have been "printed for the Author and published by . . ." In this instance the "publisher" functions like those stationers who assisted the likes of Minsheu or Wither, authors who had taken on the expense of the production and distribution of *their* books and who sought thereby to reap most of the profits of the venture. The development of this new trade function turns out to have had some effect on authors, for the trade publisher facilitated their control of book production—"they could, if they wished, deal direct with a printer, by-pass the book-sellers, and yet have the publishing taken care of."[37] The increased specialization of trade functions brought new tensions to a book trade already unsettled by patent disputes and by printers' low-level discontent: in 1684, the bookseller petitioned against the new dispersers of books.[38]

This form of specialization was as consequential as the development of partisan printing and bookselling in the 1640s. Threatened by an increasingly efficient market in ephemera, some members of the book trade began to concentrate their energies elsewhere, developing an upscale list. Such "literary" publishing had been anticipated, to be sure, by the likes of Ponsonby, Stansby, and, more emphatically, by Moseley, but a career like Jacob Tonson's was the product of a pressure to niche marketing that had never before been as powerful as it became in the 1680s.[39] We may speak of his close relations with individual authors, his instigation of important literary projects, and his sponsorship of subscription publication as a decisive displacement of aristocratic by commercial patronage; we may speak of his unusually close relations with particular printers, which relations fostered something that anticipates the modern "house style," as a decisive transformation of trade fellowship by a logic of cartelization. These developments also involved such authors as Dryden and Congreve in book production and marketing in ways anticipated by Jonson's idiosyncratic relations with the press, more hesitantly, but just as creatively anticipated by Daniel's, Minsheu's, or Wither's involvements with the stationers.[40] As is well-known, Tonson's "list"—Congreve, Etheredge, Shakespeare, Rochester, Dryden, Beaumont and Fletcher, Otway, Jonson, Shadwell, Pope, Vanbrugh, Gay, Addison, Spenser, Cibber, Prior, and Milton—also powerfully contributed to the large national enterprise of English literary canon formation. Indeed, the list transformed the conception of authorship, one aspect of which comes to include "being part of a distinguished list": if,

as I have argued above, Ponsonby established himself as stationer to the Sidneys, Tonson's practice makes Congreve into "a Tonson man."[41] Reciprocally,
the author, who now figures as part of a product line, acquires clarity as a site
of commercial value—hence, I think, the inflated respect even for the claims
of a distinctive poet's widow.

If trade developments thus make a significant contribution to the recon-
figuration of authorship, a sequence of political skirmishes was at least as
consequential. Here the issue of licensing once more leads.[42] Late in 1675,
stung by a flourishing traffic in libels, the House of Lords had prepared itself
to institute press restraints of unprecedented severity, though it did not follow
through; in 1677, L'Estrange had sought for new powers to control abuses by
the most influential members of the Stationers' Company. Freedom of the
press therefore became a Whig rallying cry in the censorious atmosphere of
the last years of the Cavalier Parliament. "You had almost as good kill a Man,
as a good book," Parliament was instructed, "for he that kills a Man, kills but
a Reasonable Creature, Gods Image: Whereas he that destroys a good Book,
kills Reason it self, which is as it were the very Eye of God": this was Charles
Blount's admonition, more attuned to parliamentary will in 1679 than Milton's original had been in 1644.[43] In the flush of Whig success following the
Popish Plot, the new Parliament not only passed its first Exclusion bill—it
also deliberately allowed the Licensing Act to lapse.[44]

It is instructive to reflect on how Blount recycled *Areopagitica*. Although
his quotation seems less the work of an imperfect copyist than a quotation
from memory, faulty but appreciative, he could not have been working from
memory. We might notice that Milton's treatise was so little regarded as a
defense of authorial *property* that Blount appropriates its argument with im-
punity, closely reproducing its structure, cutting and condensing here and
there, but also quoting word for word, and often at great length; and although
he is careful to attribute the source of the formulation here at the beginning
of his *Vindication of Learning*, he is not so careful in what follows.[45] Nor was
Blount the only polemicist to draw on *Areopagitica* in defense of a free press;
William Denton, more interested in the anti-Catholic vein in Milton's treatise, digested much of Milton's argument in his *Apology for the Liberty of the
Press* in 1681.[46] In the aftermath of the Popish Plot, the resistance to licensing
became a prominent manifestation of resistance to the royal prerogative. The
author of *Areopagitica* was once more the revolutionary ideologue, his arguments for freedom of the press now construed, retrospectively, as part of a
thoroughgoing revolutionary program that included *The Tenure of Kings and
Magistrates*, the *First and Second Defense*, the 1681 *Character of the Long
Parliament* (a portion of the *History of Britain* that had been suppressed in

the original edition of 1671), and, soon to be added to this revolutionary suite, *Eikonoklastes*.[47] The *Areopagitica* of the 1680s addressed a Parliament that had at long last responded to Milton's exhortations by disrupting the history of licensing—not simply on behalf of the free circulation of ideas, but also on behalf of a specific abridgment of royal authority. But the Whig moment reshaped *Areopagitica* even more profoundly, initiating a modern misrecognition that finds in Milton's figures of a genetic affiliation between author and text an assertion of authorial property *over against* that of the stationer.

This is not to suggest that the assertion of authorial property would inevitably carry a Whig charge, only that it could be made to do so. Like many other late seventeenth-century constructions of property, the construction of authorial property is at least in part a polemical convenience. It accumulated considerable utility during the 1680s. As we have seen, in the 1660s, when patented outsiders mounted court challenges to the stationers' monopoly, and to their copyright in particular, the stationers' response anticipated the determinations of the Mansfield court a century later, by claiming that what patents really threatened was not stationer's copyright but an authorial property that subsisted beneath it. A few years later, the printers would adapt this same argument against the booksellers, as a way of disabling any sense of the natural origins of copyright in stationers' capital. But perhaps the most fantastic assertion of authorial property dates from the 1680s, when England was without a Licensing Act and the surveyor of the press, Roger L'Estrange, was out of a job. For L'Estrange, the person most dedicated to the abridgment of press freedom in the latter half of the seventeenth century, authorial prerogatives and authorial property could function, similarly, as stays against the stationers' irregularities.

No longer allowed to spend his days searching out seditious printing, L'Estrange had turned his hand to a history of the Popish Plot, but when he published it, he discovered that the industry that he had so cunningly manipulated was beyond his control. I *"made a* Legal Assignment *of my* Right *to a* Bookseller," he tells us. *"I* Authorized *him to* Print *it, and he* Imprinted *it by the* Authority *of the* Author." But it seems that a consortium of stationers who had published narratives of the Popish Plot and of the ensuing trials had attempted to interfere in the publication of L'Estrange's *History: "Some of the* Pretenders *to the* Formal [former?] Trials, Arrest *my* Bookseller, *as an* Invader of their Propriety, *and Threaten him most wonderfully into the Bargain."* With the exception of Henry Chettle, no English author since Robert Crowley and William Baldwin had known so much about the workings of the book trade, its norms and regulations, so L'Estrange's outrage is especially telling. Deprived of his authority over the press by the lapse of the Licensing

Act, L'Estrange is grasping at regulatory straws. He pits something even more radical than authorial property against the chaos that lurks behind the threats of the "Pretenders": "*They do not complain of any* Imitation *of their* Copy, *but take upon them, as if no man else were to write upon* That Subject"— that is, as if they held rights in an entire class of books, something perhaps analogous to the law patent. What follows is a spluttering argument against the exorbitation of stationer's copyright that L'Estrange must have felt as a potential danger of the freedoms of an unregulated press—

> *At this rate, we shall have all* Sermons *forfeited to the* Kings
> Printers, *for the Descanting upon* Their Bibles, *and all* Books
> whatsoever, *to the* Company of Stationers, *because they are*
> *made out of the* Four and Twenty Letters; *and the* A B C *is* Their
> Copy.[48]

The very sketchiness with which this protest maps the territory of intellectual property is striking: cast as an appeal to common sense, the protest suggests the unexamined familiarity of this landscape. L'Estrange implies that the intellectual territory has been abusively enclosed, and he here attempts to reclaim its commons—the Bible, the alphabet. The extravagance of his arguments here implies a radical question: "What *did* stationer's copyright protect and were there not interests that should limit that protection?" And, in the language of satiric hyperbole, one can see the rationale of fair use and public domain beginning to emerge:

> *What a* Scandal *is this to the* Commonwealth of Letters? *What*
> a Cramp *to* Learning, *and Industry? That if I have a mind to*
> Compile *a* History, I must go to Forty little Fellows

—one cannot tell whether the author's heat or the compositor's apprehension of a shortage of italics controls the typography at this point—

> I must go to Forty little Fellows for leave, forsooth, to Write the
> Narrative of the Proceedings upon our Blessed King and Martyr,
> the Brave Earl of *Strafford*, Archbishop of *Canterbury*; with a
> hundred more Instances of the like nature, because some or other
> *of them has lurched, perhaps, a* Copy *of* Their Trials.
>   What if a man should write the Battle of *Worcester*, and
> the Kings miraculous Escape, after the Defeat; must he not
> mention the *Thousand Pound* that was set upon his Majesties

> Head, without leave of the *Printer* that had the *Propriety* of the
> *Proclamation* that offered it?

(The typography is nicely witty, here introducing as an emphatic type the black letter used for proclamations and acts of Parliament.)

> Or if a Body would draw up a Systeme of Treason and Sedi-
> tion; must he go to the Publisher of Bacons Government for a
> License?[49]

L'Estrange is straining, but he protests here on behalf of what approximates to a modern conception of the rightful relations between author and the book trade, in which stationers are seen as "properly" the industrial servants of authors, as the beneficiaries of an authorial property. If we search more deeply into L'Estrange's splenetic imagination, we glimpse an authorial property that originates with writing, and is neither conferred upon authors as an act of royal or state patronage nor extruded from an industrial monopoly. Which is to say that the sometime surveyor of the press has forgotten what he knows of the history of printing in order to imagine the origins of literary property.[50]

It must be conceded that this did not require a tremendous leap of the imagination—and it may be useful to describe the trajectory of that leap quite carefully. What is remarkable is that the stationers should be described as *usurping* on the intimacy, the property, that constitutes the book as *of* its author. A few years later, in 1694, we find Locke annotating excerpts of the draft of a new licensing act, wherein he expresses his resistance to prepublication licensing in a modern idiom that resembles L'Estrange's: "I know not why a man should not have liberty to print whatever he would speak; and to be answerable for the one, just as he is for the other, if he transgresses the law in either."[51] That licensing is illogical is predicated on the resemblance of printing to speaking, both understood here as properly unmediated forms of utterance: printing is something that an *author* does. Although this use of "to print" to denote an author's "edition" (OED 7b and perhaps 7a) may be found in the sixteenth century (and it may derive from much earlier uses that denote especially purposive *scribal* activity [OED 4]), it gained currency in the seventeenth century. Locke's use is casual—remarkable for being unmarked, as it were; L'Estrange, more alert to the industrial actualities of publication, protests industrial mediation as a violation of the natural (that is, natural*ized*) intimacy of author and printed text, the natural (that is natural*ized*) printerliness of authorship.

L'Estrange asserts his own prerogatives over against those that had been vested by custom with the stationers—that is the primary force of his argument here. But his argument does ancillary work as well, when he takes on the proper claims of Nathaniel Bacon's publishers. It may be useful to recall the special cases within the field of modern authorship as Foucault describes it, the case of "founders of discursivity"—the likes of Radcliffe, Marx, and Freud.[52] We can see these unusual configurations of authorship as throwbacks, historical descendants of the classical and medieval *auctores,* the breadth of whose authority could not survive the early modern revolutions in philology and in the making and selling of books. It may be that Bacon's *Government* preserved some vestiges of such large authority. But within the logic of L'Estrange's polemic, this cultural authority is formed less on the model of medieval *auctoritas* than on that discursive formation—call it a commercial genre or topic—protected by the early modern patent. The patent is a different kind of throwback, an emanation of royal prerogatives that resists and disrupts the specifying regime of commodification. It is ironic, of course, to find L'Estrange arguing for the commodity form and against the archaic prerogatives of a "royalist" discursivity, rejecting royal discursivity simply because it had been hijacked by the forty little fellows who seem to have taken shares in the notional Bacon patent. The commodity of thought is being narrowed and mapped by an angry surveyor.

The Authorial Icon in the Tonson Era

> He had too much good Sense to value himself upon any Qualities
> except those of his Mind, and which only he could properly call
> his own: for all external and adventitious Titles, as they may at
> the pleasure of a Tyrant, or by an unfortunat Attemt against his
> Government, be quite abolish'd . . .
>
> John Toland, *The Life of John Milton*

> King Charles's head has too often been found at the end of some
> intriguing little avenue of specialized enthusiasm.
>
> John Carter, *Taste and Technique in Book-Collecting*

L'Estrange's protest, pitched against unlimited stationer's copyright and implicitly advancing both authorial property and fair use, nicely registers the technical regulatory issues that came to the fore in the lapse of the Licensing Act, but the subtext of his complaint is equally illuminating. "I must go to

Forty little Fellows for leave, forsooth, to Write the Narrative of the Proceedings upon our Blessed King and Martyr." Now Atkyns had argued for the preemptive immanence of royal authority in all lawful monopolies, but the head that wore the crown haunts L'Estrange's argument in a very different way. L'Estrange's nostalgia none too subtly suggests that the disarray of property enabled by the lapse of licensing is another usurping act of Parliament. Say stationer, say Whig; say Whig, say regicide; say Blessed King and Martyr (or Earl of Strafford or Battle of Worcester), say author—honest, witty, and reverently nostalgic author. Say Charles and, says L'Estrange, say self-possessed and *propertied* author. The idea of authorial property functions more or less explicitly as a lever for abridging the leading stationers' various monopolies, but it also serves L'Estrange as part of a complex ideological constellation of neo-Cavalier individualism. The range of polemical services that authorial property could perform may be what eventually secured its legal reification.

It comes into its own in the siege against licensing. After its long lapse the Licensing Act had been renewed in 1685 for seven years, and it came up for what would be its last renewal in 1692; on this occasion a number of stationers who were relatively disenfranchised within the company petitioned both houses against renewal. They complained to the House of Lords that licensing "subjects all Learning and true Information to the arbitrary Will and Pleasure of a mercenary, and perhaps ignorant, Licenser; destroys the Properties of Authors in their Copies; and sets up many Monopolies."[53] This argument from property rights became crucial to future opposition to licensing: in 1695, for example, Commons protested that the act, then up for renewal, "prohibits printing anything before Entry thereof in the Register of the Company of Stationers . . . whereby . . . the said Company are empowered to hinder the printing all innocent and useful Books; and have an opportunity to enter a Title to themselves, and their Friends, for what belongs to, and is the Labour and Right of, others."[54]

The determination not to renew licensing in 1695 is a high point in Macauley's great *History of England,* though he deplores what he takes to be the politically vacuous, nearly unprincipled character of the event.[55] The Journal of the House of Lords preserves a list of the Commons' objections to their amended version of the act, a list possibly composed by none other than John Locke (though perhaps more plausibly attributable to Edward Clarke, writing under his friend the philosopher's influence).[56] The third of the eighteen objections, that registration violates "the Labour and Right of, others," though it can be found in Wither, has a decisively Lockean resonance and dignity, yet Macauley offers a dismissive summary of the list and concludes, "Such were the arguments which did what Milton's Areopagitica had failed to do" (V:2482).[57] It is true that the objections hew far closer to those of *The Schollers Purgatory* than to those of *Areopagitica*. If Locke did compose these objections, we should not be surprised at the Witherian tendency, for Locke began his campaign against licensing in 1693 at least partly in response to the unpleasant experience of having an edition of his own bilingual *Aesop* subjected to the stationers' price-fixing. If Macauley found the Witherian pragmatism of these arguments off-putting, he was nonetheless unwise to imply that the high-mindedness of *Areopagitica* exerted no influence on the nonrenewal of 1695.[58] Five of the objections concern themselves with preserving an international free market in books: the protest against stopping all ports of entry but London and the caveat over custom-house delays that leave the importer's stock to "lie dead" more than faintly recall Milton's own "address to Parliament." Nor is the resemblance surprising. In 1693 Charles Blount had issued his second adaptation of *Areopagitica,* titled *Reasons Humbly offered for the Liberty of Unlicensed Printing:* Milton's treatise was not only in the air but in the bookstalls.[59] I contend that the debates on licensing between 1692 and 1710, and particularly those aspects of the debate that addressed questions of literary property, deeply affect and are affected by the memory of Milton, who became at this juncture one of the preeminent polemicists on behalf of authorial prerogatives, a *Whig* champion of authorship.

What follows is a political history of authorship in the Tonson era, the formative years of statutory copyright. A word about the period term will suggest a bit more about the topology of this history. The termini of this historical sketch may be paired variously: 1692, the final renewal of the 1662 Licensing Act, and 1774, the decision in the House of Lords on the case of *Donaldson v. Beckett;* or 1698, Toland's *Life of Milton,* and 1780, Johnson's *Lives of the Poets;* or again, 1691, when Jacob Tonson acquired full copyright in *Paradise Lost,* and 1767, the year of the last Tonson Milton, published by Jacob Tonson's grandnephew, Richard; 1688, the birth of Milton's granddaughter Elizabeth, and 1771, the death of William Lauder, who had claimed that Milton had *translated*, not written, much of *Paradise Lost*. To summarize the sketch: during this period, when authorial copyright received its most sustained and consequential public scrutiny to date, Milton was the exemplary authorial instance; as the printed book became a truly mass medium and the book trade struggled to defend its monopoly, Milton was instrumental, a public discursive means, to the constitution of modern authorial property.[60]

Press regulation was transformed during the Tonson era, although hindsight suggests that the transformation was anything but revolutionary.[61] While both the stationers and the Crown made several efforts to revive licensing after its lapse in 1595, parliamentary resistance (usually centered in the House of Commons), prevented the institution of any form of parliamentary press regulation in the near term. By this time tensions between Commons and the monopolizing stationers had the nearly cozy familiarity of routinized conflict.[62] Still, the rhetoric of persuasion and deliberation shifted in important ways, if not in unprecedented ones, for the traditional and congenial representation of trade regulation as ideological now gives way to that primarily economic idiom—we might call it a "Lockean" idiom—which had become a dominant strain in Restoration political theorizing. When a licensing bill was prepared during the first session of the 1695 Parliament, the stationers, desperately vigilant in the defense of the monopolies around which the book trade had been organized for nearly a century and a half, petitioned with uncharacteristic candor that "their Property . . . be provided for."[63]

Perhaps they felt that this was no time for beating around the bush.[64] The proposed bill would have abolished the monopoly of the London stationers and put an end to the registration system: such legislation would have been nearly as disastrous as no legislation.[65] Trade confidence in traditional protections virtually collapsed with the end of licensing: there was a brief upsurge in the number of registrations in 1694, but there was a substantial dropping off thereafter. A bill for press regulation drafted early in 1699 in the House of Lords provided for compulsory entrance (and for a number of traditional regulatory mechanisms), but it was severely amended: out went much of the extravagant language concerning the threat represented by unlicensed printing, out went the provisions for import controls, and, most strikingly, out went the requirement that all books be entered in the Stationers' Register before being printed.[66] Without legislative support, the registration system collapsed: in 1701, only three books were entered in the Stationers' Register.[67] Meanwhile, untrammeled by the legal risk that had long inhibited those who might challenge the London monopoly, provincial printing enterprises began to prosper—whereas between the charter of 1557 and 1692, printing outside of London was concentrated largely in Oxford, Cambridge, and such renegade outposts as York and Chester.[68] Trade solidarity, long merely nominal, was no longer even a talking point. The company—or its officers— had once lobbied on behalf of capital in the language of liveried brotherhood and censorship, but it did so no longer; now the booksellers petition Parliament independently as often as do the company officers, and nearly everyone speaks in the language of propertied self-interest.

They were taking their cue from Parliament, which was in a demystifying mood. Commons had rejected the Licensing Act on the grounds that it "in no Wise answered the End for which it was made," to wit, the restraint of treasonable and seditious printing, the responsibility for which, they recognized, had been effectively shifted to the courts of common law.[69] Glancing retrospection reveals that this jurisdictional shift had long been underway, and so was no more striking than was the rhetorical one. In 1692, during the debates that led to the last renewal of licensing, the House of Lords had adopted an amendment that would have suspended the requirement of prepublication licensing for all books that printed the names of both author and printer: the licenser's judgment was thus to be displaced by the more methodical constraints of the laws of libel, seditious libel, and treason. The amendment was killed during debates in conference with the Lower House, but this near miss anticipates the regulatory displacement that would soon ensue; it also indicates that the courts had long been preparing to shoulder this burden.[70]

The Tonson era is an increasingly judicial period in the history of public discourse. Since midcentury, the law of treason had been elaborated to include among traitors authors and printers whose words betray the intent not only to kill but also to restrain or defame the Crown; the law of seditious libel was also given a wider application, with publication with seditious intent displaced by publication of material judged to be seditious.[71] Verbal practice became more dangerous, for the courts were now capable of casting a far wider net than the licenser had ever done.[72] Although there was some slight retrenchment in the last years of the seventeenth century, we can speak, nonetheless, of a general development in the hundred years following the Restoration: the judicial apparatus became an efficient instrument of quiet terror, forcing each ideologue to internalize his or her own censor, reducing what was felt to be the fundamental need for official license.[73] That is why when Defoe entered the public debate on licensing, his attention fastened on the courts and how to mitigate the anxious uncertainties that their jurisdiction had produced. In his *Essay on the Regulation of the Press* (1704), he urged that what constitutes libel be rendered explicit by law so that "all Men will know when they Transgress, which at present, they do not; for as the Case now stands, 'tis in the Breast of the Courts of Justice to make any Book a Scandalous and Seditious Libel."[74] Clarification was not forthcoming, and Defoe and his fellows were left with a fearful psycho-political conjuncture in which "the Crime of an Author is not known. . . . There are many ways to commit this Crime, and lie conceal'd" (20–21).

It may be worth musing on the eloquence of Defoe's protest. To write and to be published were no more dangerous at the turn of the eighteenth century than at earlier moments in the history of print. Defoe attests, nonetheless, to a powerful sense of authorial implication in the printed book, an implication variously produced—by a culture of libel, by the development of the author as trademark, and by the proliferation of sites and occasions at which the assertion of authorial property in stationer's copy and, residually, even in printed books was made to carry significant polemical and practical weight. It is not surprising that Defoe partnered his plea for an explication of libel with an assertion of authorial property, an assertion that, while less strenuous than Wither's, is more intricately specified to the particulars of marketing. He proposed a law of publication to protect authors not only from inadvertent commission of libel but also from "a sort of Thieving which is now in full practice in *England*, and which no Law extends to punish, *viz.* some Printers and Booksellers printing Copies none of their own. . . . It robs Men of the due Reward of Industry, the Prize of Learning, and the Benefit of their Studies" (25). This theft is variously detailed, and includes not only unauthorized printing, but also unauthorized abridgment and various forms of careless printing, including printing in reduced-format editions on poor-quality paper.

> As soon as a Book is publish'd by the Author, a raskally Fellow
> buys it, and immediately falls to work on it, and if it was a Book
> of a Crown, he will contract it so as to sell it for two Shillings, a
> Book of three Shillings for one Shilling, a Pamphlet of a Shilling,
> for 2*d.*, a Six-penny Book in a penny Sheet, and the like. This is
> down-right Robbing on the High-way, or cutting a Purse. (27)

The protest against market derogation, one of the leading features of the "moral rights" worked out in modern intellectual property law, illuminates the turn-of-the-century author's sense of continuing psychological attachment to the sequence of printed editions, an attachment that we may call, after Defoe, "possessiveness." For here is the remedy he proposes in the next sentence:

> The law we are upon, effectually suppresses this most villainous
> Practice, for every Author being most oblig'd to set his Name
> to the Book he writes, has, by this Law, an undoubted exclusive
> Right to the Property of it. The Clause in the Law is a Patent
> to the Author and settles the Propriety of the Work wholly in
> himself, or in such to whom he shall assign it; and 'tis reasonable it
> should be so: For if an Author has not the right of a Book, after he
> has made it, and the benefit be not his own, and the Law will not
> protect him in that Benefit, 'twould be very hard the Law should
> pretend to punish him for it.

Here, finally, is a requirement of signature that binds book to author as property to possessor. This corresponds most closely to Foucault's narrative etiology of intellectual property whereby property succeeds from punishment—though, of course, Defoe's argument is a late development within an elaborate and evolving system of proprietary rights, and not an etiology proper. Moreover, property is here asserted *both* as a recompense for peril and as a defense against derogation, a means by which an author can stay the dispersal, over his name, of books in unanticipated and unauthorized printed forms. His phrasing is a bit ambiguous—"a Book, after he has made it" may mean a book *once* it has reached publishable form (and until it is transferred to a stationer) or it may mean a book from the moment of its completion forward (until the end of time)—but the logic of his proposal is not: an author's control of the form in which a book circulates should be as durable as his culpability: " 'Twould be unaccountably severe, to make a Man answerable for the Miscarriages of a thing which he shall not reap the benefit of if well perform'd."[75] The rhetoric, the culture of authorial property, has now developed to the point that authorial copyright (and the ancillary moral right of protection against derogation) can be represented as an actual *absence* in the legal system:

> 'Twould be unaccountably severe, to make a Man answerable for
> the Miscarriages of a thing which he shall not reap the benefit
> of if well perform'd; there is no Law so much wanting in the
> Nation, relating to Trade and Civil Property, as this, nor is there a
> greater Abuse in any Civil Employment, than the printing of other
> Mens Copies, every jot as unjust as lying with their Wives, and
> breaking-up their Houses. (28)

In this rhetorical climate even the stationers were frequently obliged to represent themselves as defenders of authorial property; it was the only remaining shield for self-interest of any durability and weight. Thus, when the booksellers sought permission to bring copyright bills before Parliament in 1707 and 1709, they did not petition only for themselves—they also spoke for authors. The 1707 bill "for the better securing the Rights of Copies of printed Books" was read once and died in committee, but the initial petition deserves inspection, since it proposes legislation on behalf of those "many learned Men [who] have spent much Time, and been at great Charges, in composing Books" and these authors are proprieters: they "used to dispose of their Copies upon valuable Considerations, to be printed by the Purchasers, or have reserved some Part, for the Benefit of themselves, and Families."[76]

Without such explicit "reservation," no residual property is ascribed to authors; there is nothing in the booksellers' petition, that is, that implies the sort of lingering, quasi natural authorial property implied by Simmons's and Watts's dealings with Mrs. Milton and explicitly advocated in Defoe's *Essay:* once they have paid for their copies, the stationer-purchasers "also have, by such their property, made provisions for *their* widows, or children" (emphasis mine).[77] Linked by the earnest pathos of family obligation, authors and stationers are perhaps too similar, and the petitioners weakly attempted to conjure some difference between them, between an author's copy and a stationer's property: infringement is said to work "to the great discouragement of persons from writing matters that might be of great use to the public, and to the great damage of the proprietors," but the difference between *persons* and *proprietors* is thin, almost vaporous.[78] In the booksellers' 1709 petition, in which they sought permission to bring in a successor bill, infringement is said to operate according to the same differentia, discouraging *writers* (a vocabulary of extralegal amateurism) and injuring *proprieters* (a very different vocabulary).[79] They therefore proposed a bill for "securing to them the property of books, bought and obtained by them." They achieved mixed success in pursuit of that goal, but even that mitigated success was short-lived.

Claims of a disinterested desire to assist in ideological policing are replaced by solicitude for authors, for heirs, and for property, but it should already be clear that at this juncture the rhetoric of these petitions teeters. Where does property emerge? Whose is it? The 1709 petition recurs with convenient accuracy to the way the economics of publishing *had* been organized, with property an industrial production: "it has been the constant usage for the writers of books to sell their copies to booksellers, or printers, to the end they might hold those copies as their property, and enjoy the profit of making, and vending, impressions of them." This is roughly accurate: the early book trade converted copies into property. But the idea of a genesis of property *by sale* seems a kind of conceptual embarrassment that authorial property seems poised effortlessly to relieve. The bill received by the House of Commons on January 11, 1710, embraces the new solution, its preamble indicating an intent to restrain all publication of

> Books, and other Writings, without the Consent of the Authors
> thereof, in whom the undoubted Property of such Books and
> Writing as the product of their learning and labour remains[,] or
> of such persons to whom such Authors for good Consideracions
> have lawfully transferred their Right and title therein. . . . [Such
> infringement] is not only a real discouragement to learning

> in generll [*sic*] which in all Civilized Nations ought to receive
> the greatest Countenance and Encouragement but it is also a
> notorious Invasion of the property of the rightful Proprietors of
> such Books and Writings, to their very great Detriment, and too
> often to the Ruin of them and their Families.[80]

An extreme—one might say "extremely Witherian"—statement, but the bill did not pass in this form. The stationers must have brought some pressure to bear, though the mechanism of persuasion has not been traced, for the preamble was carefully cut and dramatically transformed by a committee of the whole, so that it restored the distinction so crucial to the stationers; the bill now seeks to restrain publication of

> Books, and other Writings, without the Consent of the Authors
> or Proprietors of such Books and Writings, to their very great
> Detriment, and too often to the Ruin of them and their Families.

Once more, though, in the long run, ineffectually, "Authors *or* Proprietors."[81]

In the final form of the bill, the stationers achieved some of their goals. To be sure, they lost perpetual copyright, and a roster of state officials were designated to adjudicate public complaints against particular stationers for unfair pricing.[82] But the institution of the patent was left undisturbed, the principle of exclusive copyright went unchallenged, and books already in print on April 10, 1710, including books by ancient authors, were to receive twenty-one years' copyright protection. Above all, the customary authority of registration was confirmed, for

> nothing in this Act contained shall be construed to subject any
> Bookseller, Printer, or other Person whatsoever, to the Forfeitures
> or Penalties therein mentioned, for or by reason of the Printing
> or Reprinting of any Book or Books without such Consent, as
> aforesaid, unless the Title to the Copy of such Book or Books be
> Entred, in the Register-Book of the Company of the Stationers, in
> such manner as hath been usual.[83]

This was a pyrrhic victory for the stationers: although the obvious purpose of this limitation was to preserve and fortify the traditional mechanism by which they parceled out their monopoly, the limitation apparently included authors as well as stationers. The wording of the bill is a bit sloppy on this point, but if authors who failed to make entrance were also to be deprived of remedy,

the stationers would have to arrange for their access to the register.[84] The bill
creeps up on this problem, first requiring that "said Register-Book may, at
all Seasonable and Convenient times, be Resorted to, and inspected by any
Bookseller, Printer or other Person" and then, more tellingly, detailing remedies against the company clerk, should he "Refuse or Neglect to Register,
or make such Entry or Entries, or to give such Certificate, being thereunto
Required by the Author or Proprietor."[85] If the Statute of Anne was revolutionary for putting an end to perpetual copyright, it was equally so for opening
the stationers' register to nonstationers, transforming it into the instrument of
a national system of legally limited privileges. These are irresolute sentences,
informed by two distinct legislative sensibilities, the one responsive to the petitions of the stationers, the other resistant to those petitions and hesitantly
promoting authorship as a bulwark of that resistance.[86] More than any others
in the bill, these sentences bear the fossilized traces of a competition that had
finally reorganized the very ground of competition: the phrase distinguishing
"author" from "proprietor" derives from a tradition of stationers' petitions;
the absence of specific reference to the "author" in the list of likely victims of
infringement (or in the list of possible infringers) derives from a tradition of
controlling books by exclusively regulating stationers; the insistence that the
register remain open to all derives from a tradition of antimonopolism that
had finally ceased to except the book trade from its purview.

It will now be useful to ask what Milton contributes to the legal recognition of authorship and to the riddle of textual personalization, both to its
mystery and its solution. What is his contribution to the search for rightful
ownership of ideas? What figure does he cut in the Tonson era, in a culture
of forced ideological privatization and improvised proprietary redress?

John Toland's *Life of Milton* offers one answer. A biography of Milton
the controversialist, the *Life* was originally published, in 1698, as an introduction to the first nearly complete edition of Milton's collected prose, the first
substantial collection of Milton's prose having been published only the year
before. Although it is technically inaccurate to refer to the 1698 edition of
the prose as "Toland's Edition"—Toland denied having prepared it, though
the editor has never been identified—the designation is apt nonetheless.[87]
Certainly there is good reason for thinking that he wrote the *Life for* this
particular edition, that he was trying to produce an author conformable to
the accompanying texts. Elaborating the literary portrait lightly sketched in
Edward Phillips's biography, itself written to introduce the 1694 collection
of Milton's *Letters of State,* Toland's biography cultivates the still subsistent
public memory of a political Milton; to some extent, it resists the relatively de-
politicized representation of the author that might have been inferred from

Tonson's collection of *The Poetical Works* in 1695.[88] Toland was a political radical, a deist and a Socinian, and he takes Milton as his cultural model; his *Life* and the volume in which it first appeared are a monument to Milton the anti-Presbyterian and, above all, to Milton the regicide.

That Toland discusses *Eikonoklastes* (1649) with particular energy is therefore not surprising.[89] Vigorously and personally anti-Stuart, Milton's attack on the *Eikon Basilike* (1649) of Charles I is for Toland a key text. Not that Toland's *Life* rediscovered *Eikonoklastes* for the late seventeenth century: in 1690 a new edition of Milton's tract had appeared, pointedly engaged against the Jacobite backlash to the revolutionary settlement.[90] The anonymous editor had published, as an unsigned addendum, what remains the chief piece of evidence against Charles's authorship of *Eikon Basilike,* a scrap of paper now known as the Anglesey Memorandum. First discovered in 1686, it assigned authorship to John Gauden, chaplain to Charles II.[91] Of course, challenges to the king's authorship were not new; they had begun crackling round the *Eikon Basilike* within weeks of its first appearance.[92] On the title page of *The Princely Pelican* of 1649, the first royalist defender of the king's book promised specifically to authenticate the text by offering *Choice Observations Extracted from His Majesties Divine Meditations: With Satisfactory Reasons to the Whole Kingdom, That His Sacred Person Was the Only Author of Them:* he was responding to allegations of plagiarism first published by Milton himself.

If Milton had offered an impersonal critique of the prerogative in *The Tenure of Kings and Magistrates,* he had personalized the attack in *Eikonoklastes.* The main object of scorn in this latter work was the inauthenticity of Charles's piety: he brings special relish to the conclusion of the first section of his treatise when he observes that one of Charles's customary prayers, published in *Eikon Basilike,* was in fact taken from Sidney's *Arcadia.* He describes the appropriation of this "vain amatorious Poem," first as a lapse in taste and then as "a trespass more than usual against human right, which commands that every author should have the property of his own work reserved to him after death, as well as living."[93] This constitutes a striking shift from the argument of *Areopagitica:* here, for the first time, Milton speaks of writing as authorial property, and a natural property at that, not one that rebounds from industrial custom or derives from the largesse of the state. Of course, his argument is heated by the polemical occasion, but if it constitutes a departure from the position taken in *Areopagitica,* the departure is not, I think, a heedless one. Rehearsing the market engagements of *Areopagitica* with a high disdain that marks the discontinuity between the two treatises, Milton reviews Charles's "privat Psalter": "Which they who so much admire, either for the matter or the manner, may as well admire the Arch-Bishops late Breviary"—Laud's new prayer-book—

> and many other as good *Manuals,* and *Handmaids of Devotion,*
> the lip-work of every Prelatical Liturgist, clapt together, and
> quilted out of Scripture phrase, with as much ease, and as little
> need of Christian diligence, or judgement, as belongs to the
> compiling of any ord'nary and salable peece of English Divinity,
> that the Shops value (III:360).

These lines (which Toland quotes) implicitly link true religiosity with an originality distinguished from the quilted compositional habits and the psychological dispositions of the "notebook method." But it should be observed that the privacies here endorsed and the property here defended are also alloyed to a denigration of the market, so that in contradistinction from *Areopagitica, Eikonoklastes* offers a Protestant ethic almost opposed to the spirit of capitalism: *Eikonoklastes* does not offer a middle stage in a progress from *Areopagitica* to the contract with Simmons for *Paradise Lost.*[94] If the sketch of a natural authorial property right gestures toward a politico-economic future, it does so ambiguously: not only does Milton disdain the salable, but the property he sketches seems to be inalienable and therefore structurally inimical to economic practice.

This ambiguous assertion of "natural rights" in intellectual property assumed a special prominence in the 1690 reissue of *Eikonoklastes,* where it resonates with the unknown editor's profoundly anti-Jacobite bibliography. By publishing the Anglesey Memorandum, Milton's editor threatened Charles's authorial reputation with greater damage than even Milton had attempted, for now the *entire* text was in danger of alienation from the king's hand. Milton's remarks on Pamela's prayer could now serve as a clairvoyant gloss on this larger royal imposture, and the new prominence of those remarks produced an exceedingly important theoretical ligature. In *Areopagitica,* Milton had championed those intimacies of attribution that evolve into the modern "paternity right." According to the Anglesey Memorandum, these were the same intimacies that had been so notoriously flouted in the publication of *Eikon Basilike.* In *Eikonoklastes,* Milton refers to the misattribution of Pamela's prayer not as a violation of figurative paternity (or as some analogous disruption of genetics) but as a trespass on property. In this most notorious controversial context, with the nature of royal authorship and even royal identity at stake, Milton was found describing misattribution itself as *theft.*

Like Valla's *Treatise on the Donation of Constantine,* the 1690 *Eikonoklastes* must stand as a monumental example of the political clout sometimes accruing to critical bibliography. A considerable amount of correspondence and personal testimony was published during the early nineties in efforts to establish or disestablish Charles's authorship of *Eikon Basilike,* and the presentation of this data was often the merest pretext for defense of or attack on Stuart monarchy. Consider the first royalist response to the corrosive bibliography of the 1690 *Eikonoklastes,* the 1691 *Restitution to the Royal Author.* It begins its shrewd defense of Charles's authorship by challenging the authenticity of the Anglesey Memorandum; it goes on to point out that *none* of the prayers usually included in *Eikon Basilike* were printed in its earliest editions, Pamela's prayer not excepted. Then comes the countercharge: the author of the *Restitution* proposes that the prayers were actually interpolated, in order to discredit the king, by a meddlesome but well-meaning bookseller. The next Tory response was to force the resignation of L'Estrange's successor, James Fraser, who had licensed not only the 1690 *Eikonoklastes* but also, in 1692, a book by Anthony Walker arguing the case for Gauden's authorship of *Eikon Basilike;* if Macauley is correct, the Whig response to *this* event was a device of the indefatigable Blount, who seems to have written an inflammatory, anonymous, pseudo-Tory treatise, *King William and Queen Mary Conquerors,* which Edmund Bohun, Fraser's Tory replacement and the editor of Filmer, duly licensed. At one point Blount claimed that Bohun had *written* the tract—for which gaffe he was soon expelled from office.[95]

Late seventeenth-century politics had fostered a good deal of anonymous and pseudonymous authorship. The controversy over *Eikon Basilike,* electrified by the political context and, specifically, by a political contest over the historical record, rapidly made Milton the focus of heated attention to the proprieties of authorial identification.[96] Milton's challenge to Charles's authorship had coded a challenge to the legitimacy of his rule and now, in the milieu of the Glorious Revolution, both counterfeit authorship and its detection had become crucial tools of delegitimation. Yet another Tory counterattack, more emphatic even than that of the 1691 *Restitution,* came in 1697, when Thomas Wagstaffe raised the stakes. Wagstaffe partners his *Vindication of King Charles the Martyr* with an attack on Milton, affirming the king's authorship of *Eikon Basilike* while alleging that the interpolation of Pamela's prayer was *Milton's* idea. He proposed that Milton had secured the release from prison of the printer, William Dugard, on the condition that Dugard assist in the imposture, so that Milton could then level an accusation of plagiarism against the martyred king.[97]

Toland's 1698 biography intervenes in this swirl of highly politicized, highly partisan, bibliography. In the *Life* Toland restates the case for Gauden's authorship, quotes the Anglesey Memorandum, and recounts the details of its discovery. He then goes on to suggest that Gauden had proffered the king's book in the jussive, as it were, as a means of exhorting the young prince Charles to purge himself of inherited papist taint and to return to that true English piety that Gauden had modeled for him in the *Eikon Basilike*. Toland argues that Milton had not only discovered "a piece of Royal Plagiarism, or (to be more charitable) of his Chaplains Priestcraft" but must also have suspected that the *rest* of the king's book was an imposture: "One of *Milton's* sagacity could not but perceive by the Composition, Stile, and timing of this Book, that it was rather the production of som idle Clergyman, than the Work of a distrest Prince."[98] Toland takes some pains to suggest how many people had colluded in Gauden's imposture. Given the polemical context, it is easy to say how this discussion of *Eikon Basilike*—somewhat longer than his discussion of *Paradise Lost*—could come to seem the central moment of Toland's *Life of Milton;* that it was so received may be gleaned from the exchange that ensued in 1699: Offspring Blackall's anniversary sermon preached before the House of Commons; Toland's response to the sermon, *Amyntor: or, a Defence of Milton's Life. Containing . . . A Complete History of the Book, Entitul'd Icon Basilike;* and the counterresponse, *Mr. Blackall's Reasons for Not Replying to a Book Lately Published, Entituled, Amyntor.*[99] These are central texts in the swarm of pamphlets from these years that compete to evaluate the regicide (and to measure it against the attempt on King William's life).

The debate between Wagstaffe and Blackall on the one hand and Toland on the other puts Milton at the center of late seventeenth-century contests over authentic and responsible textuality.[100] Toward the end of his discussion of *Eikonoklastes,* Toland generalizes with freethinking glee:

> When I seriously consider how all this happen'd among our selves
> within the compass of forty years, in a time of great Learning
> and Politeness . . . I cease to wonder any longer how so many
> supposititious [*sic*] pieces under the name of Christ, his Apostles,
> and other great Persons, should be publish'd and approv'd in
> those primitive times, when it was of so much importance to
> have 'em believ'd; when the Cheats were too many on all sides
> for them to reproach one another, which yet they often did;
> when Commerce was not near so general, and the whole Earth
> intirely overspread the darkness of Superstition. I doubt rather the
> Spuriousness of several more such Books is yet undiscover'd, thro

the remoteness of those Ages, the death of the Persons concern'd,
and the decay of other Monuments which might give us true
Information. (150)

Say *Eikon Basilike,* say the Bible. Faced with this insupportable dislocation
of venerable texts and venerable authors, Blackall addressed a House that
had failed to pass four bills for press regulation; here was what happened,
he warned, when "without Controul or Censure," the foundations of religion
were "suffered to be called in Question."[101] Toland responded more expan-
sively to Blackall in *Amyntor,* where, for some twenty-six pages, he mused
on the threat to religion by providing a survey of textual decanonizations
that had disrupted and embarrassed the Christian tradition.[102] This exchange
presages a full-fledged ferment over attribution, as the implications of critical bibliography broached in these years were elaborated. But at this late-
seventeenth-century juncture, the struggle over the king's book gives a deep
political and historical resonance to the rather shallower attributive struggles
that emerged from the book trade into public debate on licensing and press
regulation, the commercial struggles that would make attribution into an issue of property law.

"The Name of the Author": Ludlow, Crusoe, Gulliver...

Toland does not make the modern scholarly error of representing Milton
as a champion of individual intellectual property rights, though this crucial
transformation was underway. What remained to be accomplished before-
hand was, first, that the Milton of the Whig *Eikonoklastes,* Toland's hero of
authentic textuality, should be recruited to assist the Milton of the Whig *Areopagitica,* Blount's hero of unlicensed printing, and that this composite Milton should be taken up by those engaged in finally disabling the stationers'
monopoly. What could the Milton of *Eikonoklastes* contribute? His usefulness in the assault on the stationers' monopoly is fairly easy to describe. The
proprietary claims of the stationers could be trumped by alleging a tie that
bound text and author more closely than that which bound text and stationer.
The rich biogenetic figures that link text and author in *Areopagitica* have an
undeniable power (despite the fact that they had not been originally deployed
to disable the stationers' proprietary claims), but the intimacies of author
and text urged by *Eikonoklastes* had taken on far greater signifying power
in the course of the late seventeenth century, summing a potent complex of
political and spiritual obligations. It was as if regicide and revolution could

be explained and justified merely by proving Charles to have plagiarized, or Gauden to have pseudonymized.

But the textual politics of the moment are tangled, worth remembering lest we assume an unproblematic march, a simple *progress* toward attribution and property. If the textual inauthenticities ascribed to *Eikon Basilike* were stigmatized, they were also variously indulged, for printed imposture was the political topos of the age. In 1691, the pseudonymous *Letter from Major General Ludlow to Sir E. S.* had appeared, ostensibly printed in Amsterdam, summarizing, without acknowledgment, the attack on Charles I from *Eikonoklastes* and concluding, by way of postscript, with a comparison of Pamela's prayer to that passed off as Charles's in *Eikon Basilike*.[103] In the following year, a sequel appeared, *A Letter from General Ludlow to Dr. Holingworth*, which follows *Eikonoklastes* in great detail, after the fashion of Blount's recyclings of *Areopagitica*. During the nineties Hollingworth wrote several defenses of Charles I, including a refutation of Walker's attack on Charles's authorship of *Eikon Basilike,* and this latter provoked "Ludlow" to a third anti-Caroline tract, *Ludlow No Lyar* (1692), in which he again paraphrased substantial portions of *Eikonoklastes*. The concluding pages rehearse Milton's attack on Charles's plagiarism from the *Arcadia*. So much is "Ludlow's" attention fixed on the crime of inauthentic authorship that he *both* taxes Charles with plagiarism and charges Gauden with imposture.[104]

This "Ludlow," then, this most insistent detractor of the king's book and the inauthentic king who (in one way or another) did not write it, is thus himself deeply unoriginal. How are we to explain the inconsistent attitude to misattribution thus manifest? We might suppose the inconsistency to have been deliberate, that attributing this handful of anti-Caroline pamphlets to Ludlow was meant to parody the misattributions of the regicide moment. Of course, the misattributions are of very different kinds; certainly "Charles" performs a different function for *Eikon Basilike* than that which "Ludlow" performs for *Ludlow no Lyar*. The prayers in *Eikon Basilike* have social force as an "edition" of Charles, the printed "icon" of a particular author, particularly situated; the impostures that Milton and Anglesey describe reverse the book's social force by making the book into a misrepresentation of a person. The attribution of *A Letter from General Ludlow to Dr. Holingworth* is quite different, for the force of the *Letter* depends on its argument, and its ostensible origin in a particular author is, as it were, ornamental: like the names "Corydon" or "Lycidas," "Sh—" or "Mr. W. H.," "Ludlow" establishes significant associations (Ludlow was in exile, a hero of the Revolution, whose name had most notoriously been affixed to the orders for the execution of Charles I).[105] If such ornamental authorship was not thought to interfere with the dogged

assault on the royal authorial icon, it is because the likes of "Ludlow," Immerito, and Lycidas had become archaic, vestigial. Although such "persons" have
never disappeared from public discourse, they would be all but swept away
by a composite set of pressures to individuated self-consistency that might be
summed up as compulsory identity. The whelming tide of proprietary authorship is one of the pressures driving the development of compulsory identity, a
massive one. Protests against *Eikon Basilike* and the backlash against Milton
and *Eikonoklastes* make more modest contributions. But to remark the contribution of the Ludlow pamphlets returns us to the original problem: how
could the actual author of these pamphlets, a lobbyist of identity, commit a
pseudonymy? And to allege that "Ludlow" is a vestigial and merely ornamental author-effect, comparable to "Charles" in quite a limited sense, is only a
part of an answer.

The Licensing Act had not lapsed when the Ludlow pamphlets went into
print; if "Ludlow" is allusive and ornamental, it is also evasive and protective,
a response to a regime of censorship.[106] We could say that the inconsistency
in *Ludlow no Lyar,* the stigma attached to misattribution and the coincident
indulgence in misattribution, points to a seismic transformation taking place
in the politics of discourse at the end of the century and that transformation is
as easy to trace in the parliamentary record as it is in the Ludlow pamphlets.
Returning to that record, it is important to remember that disabling the stationers' monopoly was not the only goal that Parliament set itself as it rumi-
nated over press regulation between 1695 and 1710. For most M.P.'s, indeed,
this was a secondary concern; the question of licensing remained paramount,
with control of information and opinion concerning matters of high politics
remaining the focal regulatory issue. Legislation proceeded slowly, however,
because orthodox opinion on the subject of political expression was giving
way. One source of that weakening has already been noticed: many MPs felt
that the courts already possessed the requisite tools for ideological policing.
Early in the century, the Crown had taken pains first to suppress and later
to control the circulation of news; in the early 1640s, Parliament had appropriated such practices.[107] This was not understood as a threat to "freedom of
speech" for, as originally understood, that freedom was a right claimed only
for Parliament (at first, only for the speaker, but by the reign of Elizabeth, for
all members of the House); it was specifically a right to initiate discussion on
any subject.[108] Parliament had long been jealous of the secrecy of its deliberations, hence its resistance, early in the century, not only to the circulation
of news, but especially to parliamentary reporting. This control of news was
slowly, if not very steadily, relaxing, but the value of freedom of *public* expression in matters of high politics, a new freedom, was still a subject of serious

debate: it appears that at least some of the M.P.'s who opposed the renewal of licensing wanted to protect the new independent political journals that were almost indiscriminately disseminating political news, whereas Fielding would argue the case against such freedoms of political publication as late at 1747.[109] The advocates of a free press were themselves divided over the value of anonymous or pseudonymous publication. In his *Essay on the Regulation of the Press,* the future author of the pseudo-autobiographical *Robinson Crusoe* would argue that the compulsory identification of authors on the title pages of printed books, a feature of many proposed bills for press regulation, could serve as a preferable regulatory alternative to a licensing system.[110] He was answered in the following year by Matthew Tindal, who objected that "compulsory imprint" would inhibit political criticism that would be useful to the commonwealth.[111] By providing protection for the most heterodox writers, Tindal takes the more radical position, but it entails a conservative resistance to compulsory identity. His position maintains a kinship with the old notion of *vox populi, vox dei,* a special sanction for utterance of indefinite origin. The pseudonymy of "Ludlow" is similarly affiliated: it bears a relationship both to politico-prophetic anonymity and collectivism. Thus a faction of those seeking freedom to publish political news and commentary could deliberately oppose the compulsory identification of author and utterance.

"He thinks it no fair Proceeding, that any Person should offer determinately to fix a name upon the Author of the Discourse," writes the author of "An Apology for the, &c," prefixed in 1708 to the fifth edition of *A Tale of A Tub:* "He" is the anonymous author of the *Tale.*[112] It was once thought that Swift had himself drafted the Statute of Anne, and although this is pure fantasy, he was deeply interested in the regulation of the book trade: he had warm relations with the warehouse-keeper of the English Stock, Benjamin Tooke; and his work for the Harley ministry as editor of the political *Examiner* had brought him close to the day-to-day workings of a Parliament wrestling with the problems of press regulation.[113] But the biographical facts only corroborate what may be gleaned from *A Tale of A Tub* itself; on that evidence alone we might assert that not even Defoe was so alert to the topical and aesthetic interest of what might be called disattribution. The unsigned "Apology" defends the anonymity of the *Tale;* it complains against those who have "pronounced another Book to have been the Work of the same Hand with this; which the Author directly affirms to be a thorough mistake" (3); it argues against the accusation made by one of the "Answerers" of the *Tale,* that *"this Author's Wit is not his own in many Places"* (7); and it takes pains to dissociate certain portions of the *Tale* from the author by associating them with others, as "Parodies, where the Author personates the Style and Manner of other Writers, whom he has a mind to expose. I shall produce one Instance," he goes on, with intricate attributive glee, "it is in the *51st Page. Dryden, L'Estrange,* and some others I shall not name, are here levelled at, who having spent their Lives in Faction, and Apostacies, and all manner of Vice, pretended to be Sufferers for Loyalty and Religion" (3). Who writes this, if not the anonymous apologist? On that fifty-first page, a footnote printed for the first time in this fifth edition indicates that "Here the Author seems to personate *L'Estrange, Dryden,* and some others, who after having past their Lives in Vices, Faction and Falshood have the Impudence to talk of Merit and Innocence and Sufferings" (42). And who writes *this*? At the end of the "Apology," the apologist explains that the bookseller has arranged for "several Gentlemen" to provide notes to the *Tale,* "for the goodness of which he [i.e., "the Author," one supposes] is not to answer, having never seen any of them" (11). If the Gentlemen seem to overlap the Apologist, so too does the Author (who knows nothing of the Gentlemen): "The Author cannot conclude this Apology, without making this one Reflection . . ." (10).

The diffraction and condensation of authorial identities may not be traceable or reducible to the struggle over imprint, but it is difficult to imagine that the aesthetic gaiety of this authorial instability is not responsive to the various pressures that marketing and regulation had brought to bear on attribution. To be sure, the pleasant instability of authorial identity takes a topical tumble in the "Postscript" to the "Apology."

> Since the writing of this which was about a Year ago; a Prostitute Bookseller hath publish'd a foolish Paper, under the Name of Notes on the *Tale of A Tub,* with some Account of the Author, and with an Insolence which I suppose is punishable by Law, hath presumed to assign certain Names. (12)

The Prostitute Bookseller was Edmund Curll, who had begun his *Complete Key to The Tale of A Tub* (1710) by working out a split attribution:

> The Dedication to my Lord *Sommers,* the Preface, Epistle to Prince *Posterity,* the four Digressions, *viz.* 1. Concerning *Criticks.* 2. In the Modern Kind. 3. In Praise of *Digressions* 4. In Praise of *Madness* and *the Battle of the Books* are assign'd to Dr. *Jonathan Swift;* and the *Tale of a Tub* and the *Fragment* containing a Mechanical Account of the *Operation of the Spirit,* to *Thomas Swift.* [114]

Swift believed that Curll had been misled by "that little Parson-cousin of mine," Thomas, who seems to have been pleased to let speculation about the authorship of the *Tale* circle around himself. Swift's correspondence on the matter place him at a cultural-historical threshold: in a letter to Tooke written two months after passage of the Statute of Anne, he protests that "it is strange that there can be no satisfaction against a Bookseller for publishing names in so bold a manner. I wish some lawyer could advise you how I might have satisfaction."[115] What Swift longs for here is a *law* of attribution to give force and shape to disseminative practices now felt to be somehow destabilizing. But the site of Swift's irritation is itself unstable.[116] The Apologist for the *Tale* (now all but identified with the Author) adopts what we might take as a predictable attitude—"The Author . . . asserts that the whole Work is entirely of one Hand"; but in the letter to Tooke, Swift indicates a provocation different from that of the partial attribution to Thomas—"I wish some lawyer could advise you how I might have satisfaction: For, at this rate, there is no book, however so vile, which may not be fastened on me."[117] Not misattribution but attribution nettles Swift. The protection he imagines, the right *not* to be identified—whether accurately or inaccurately— as the author of a given work had never and has never been codified. In a paradox as expressive of the uncertain but excited regulatory climate as of Swift's notoriously disordered character, Swift longs for a law of attribution, at the same time resisting the climate of compulsory authorship, a climate that not only heated the market in books but had heated Swift's own imagination.

If the printed book was being cautiously tied to its author during these years, the knot was not yet secure, and the likes of Swift and Tindal can be found resisting its bindings, each for very different reason. Legislation in the matter proceeded irresolutely. The bill passed by the House of Lords in 1699, the one that the Commons rejected despite Blackall's exhortations, stipulated that publisher and printer should have *their* names printed in all books and that they be prepared to furnish authors' names upon demand; that rather modest provision was repeated in a virtually identical bill of 1702.[118] But Defoe's regulatory proposals of 1704, which move closer to requiring compulsory authorial imprint, at the same time uncover an overwhelming concern with property that now plainly determines the logic of licensing. To ensure that "no Book can be published, but there will be some body to answer for it," he urges that "a law be made to make the last Seller the Author, unless the Name of Author, Printer, or Bookseller, be affix'd to the Book." This effectively reprises the terms of the old 1642 order issued by the House of Commons that would make an author *of* an unauthorized printer—reprises and transforms it: Defoe proposes that subjection to punishment be dictated by economic positions.[119]

Defoe's *Essay* does more than shine a light on the process by which proprietary issues were intruding on crudely ideological ones. As Defoe frames his proposal, when an author's body is unavailable to the law, the merchant is *made into* the author; this way of putting it illuminates a transformation in the relation of author and stationer:

> If the Name of the Author, or of the Printer, or of the Bookseller,
> for whom it is printed, be affix'd, every Man is safe that sells a
> Book; but if not, then no Man will sell it, but he that hath some
> private Reason for propagating what the Book treats of, and such a
> Man has some Title to pass for the Author.

Here is a law of authorship, a law, that is, that renders authorship compulsory, even in uncertain cases. The stationer provides a kind of raw human material onto which authorship may be imposed—for punitive purposes, of course, though the language of *entitlement* asserts a proprietary principle that now subtends the penal: the subject-object of punishment must be a possessive author. If no imprinted name indicates such an author, then the possessive stationer becomes entitled to authorial punishment. The stationer is to be situated as a secondary subject within a law of compulsory authorship.

More than imprint was to tether the book to its author; we have seen that the competition over property itself was binding the printed book to authors in other ways. Once again, the author was used to limit the economic power of the stationers—although in this case, the object of limitation is a new one, the term of copyright. In the *Memorandum* of 1694 in which Locke criticized the Licensing Act then still being considered for renewal, he particularly inveighed against the "absurd and ridiculous" institution of perpetual stationer's copyright in the works of ancient writers and proposed as an alternative that copyright endure only for some fixed term, fifty years, or seventy, past the date of the first printing of a book.[120] (The inspiration for this sort of term-limited privilege is, of course, the old institution of the patent.) The opposition to perpetual copright is one of the most consequential aspects of Locke's critique of licensing: similar provisions for abridgment find their way into the next draft of the licensing bill considered by the Commons.[121] Locke's proposal implies a sense of a public domain, a nascent one perhaps, but far richer than that which informs L'Estrange's protest against those forty little fellows who might seek to monopolize, say, the alphabet. The regulatory logic for an extensive term may seem to derive from the by then traditional argument that copyright existed to protect the widows and children of stationers, but Locke's proposal is more radical in tendency—as becomes clearer when we consider that he also advocated a copyright in the works of modern authors limited to fifty years, or seventy, past the death of the author. Locke has devised a copyright that protects widows and children—of authors, when they are alive to "authorize" publication; of stationers, where such living authority is lacking. In Locke's commercial system, as in Defoe's slightly later proposal, the stationer has assumed his modern form as an authorial surrogate, a delegate at best.

Nor was this an erratic mutation; the stationer begins to conform to this shape even in the legislative history, despite the petitions of the company. In both the first draft and the revised version of the licensing bill worked out by the House of Lords in 1699, the author is the primary subject of regulation: the importer of seditious, heretical, or treasonable works, the printer or publisher of such works "shall be subject and liable to the same punishment as by law might have been inflicted upon the author thereof."[122] And the *proprietary* precedence of authors became a key feature of the law that was eventually passed in 1710 to provide some stability for the book trade. As has already been shown, the draft version of the Statute of Anne was prolix on the subject, its preamble insisting that it was "the Authors thereof, in whom the undoubted Property of . . . Books and Writing as the product of their learning and labour remains" and stipulating in its early paragraphs, if not in those on registration, that this property could only come secondarily to "such persons to whom such Authors for good Consideracions have lawfully transferred their Right and title therein."[123] More significantly, and despite the booksellers' petitions, the act follows Locke's lead by eliminating perpetual copyright and establishing the life of the author as one of the key variables in a system of limited copyrights.[124] Besides the twenty-one-year limited copyright in books already in print, the Statute of Anne provided a fourteen-year copyright both on books already composed but not yet printed, and on books not yet composed, that term "to commence from the Day of the First Publishing" of such works—and although the meaning of this phrase is imprecise, nothing here seems to disrupt the traditional organization of copyright around industrial arrangements. But a very last clause, added when the bill was sent up to the House of Lords, does disrupt that tradition, for it provides

> That after the Expiration of the said Term of Fourteen Years,
> the sole Right of Printing or Disposing of Copies shall Return to
> the Authors thereof, if they are then Living, for another Term of
> Fourteen Years.[125]

Books already in print were to be systematically referred to the life of the author: the body that had answered for a book was to be a body that could continue to profit from it. Defoe had gotten his wish.

The reversion clause, an afterthought, may be obtrusive, but it also highlights the incoherence installed elsewhere in the act. At the same time that it seems to constitute an authorial copyright tentatively predicated on authorial ownership of a text, it also cramps that ownership, giving it the disjointed termini characteristic of patent privileges; that this privilege was term limited and also proprietary constituted a fracture in the idea of property itself. Indeed, the general structure of the Copyright Act seems almost certainly to have been modeled on the restricted patents provided for in the Statute of Monopolies of 1624, which maintained extant patents for twenty-one years and limited new ones to terms of fourteen years. And in this regard we might say that Defoe, who had called for "A Patent to the Author," had gotten his wish in regrettable form. This, the coarse assimilation of patent conventions into the very structure of literary property, is a key field of incoherence within the structure of copyright, second only to the persistent identification and differentiation of author and proprietor. This second disruption within the legislation transmits intellectual property as a composite, originating with the author but manifest in the form of a royal handout: if the old competition between the patent and the copyright is drastically transformed by the Statute of Anne, it could hardly be said to have been laid to rest.[126]

Reactive and composite, statutory copyright was a blunt instrument, difficult to adjust to impending circumstance, though the difficulty was not immediately apparent. Because old and lucrative copyrights—like those in Shakespeare, Dryden, and Milton—were renewed for twenty-one years and, because the Stocks continued to operate unconstrained, the most powerful members of the book trade preserved their monopolistic position and no drastic reorganization of the industry ensued. Although there would be continuing parliamentary deliberations on licensing, the immediate effect of the act was to produce a more stable regulatory climate concerning property than had prevailed for as long as any living stationer or politician could remember.[127] Still, infringements of copyright—sporadic but persistent throughout the history of the book trade—begin to multiply during the 1720s: Tonson's monopoly of *Paradise Lost,* for example, was at least twice transgressed. The booksellers occasionally attempted injunctions against pirates, but they had little luck in enforcing them. The infringements of the early twenties and the mild upheaval of 1724–25, when the first of the statutory copyrights in works of *living* authors began to fall free, made 1731 ominous: when the older copyrights lapsed, the classics were to suffer exposure to competition.

It is worth noticing how the effort expended during these decades in litigation, petition, and collusion to secure or to recover monopolistic protections
of certain books helped to generate that aura associated with the modern
literary classic: we are here observing a crucial juncture in the commercial
reification of bourgeois literary art.

Gulliver, Scriblerus, Milton: Typography and Talent

As Foxon, Rogers, and Rose have variously demonstrated, the author most
responsive to the new legal and commercial climate is Pope.[128] We can now
see him as a litigant, resisting infringement; as an entrepreneur, rounding
up subscriptions; and as a maker of contracts, careful to secure for himself
the protections and benefits of the latest legal developments. The *market*
in books becomes, for Pope, a sensitive and articulate register of his literary abilities, his talents. In the course of a meticulous account of a subscription campaign that Pope mounted in the aftermath of the Statute of Anne,
Rogers pauses to remark, "One perceives that the young poet really was
able to use the *Iliad* subscription to take stock of his career: to estimate
how far he had arrived, to sort our [*sic*] varying reactions in his audience,
to get a line on his own ambiguous situation in politics and religion."[129] By
1728 he knows the trade well enough to take charge himself as publisher of
The Dunciad and to set himself up as a kind of commercial patron to the
young and, he hoped, tractable, printer, Lawton Gilliver.[130] He takes care
with the assignment of copyrights, contriving to retain the maximum personal leverage in resisting piracies; he delays publishing his *Letters* in 1737
until the disposition of a new copyright bill should be clarified.[131] Dr. Johnson remembers Pope as having learned to write by imitating the layout and
letterforms of printed books, so it is not surprising that Pope went on to close
the circle—for we can also observe Pope as a compositorial author (in the
line of, say Jonson and Congreve), hovering over the details of punctuation,
capitalization, typeface, and page layout.[132] If Jonson was torn between allegiance to a culture of intimate patronage and a fascination with a marketplace in things that was, through the agency of the theater and the press,
drawing phrase and attitude, plot and idea into the circle of commercial
reification; if the forces of reification only occasionally flash upon Jonson's
artistic consciousness—it is otherwise with Pope. He is fully conscious of the
marketplace in books and the way that law had reshaped it; and this busi-
nesslike consciousness in no way interferes with his career as a poet of arch
composure. Here is reification achieved, such that no tension plays between

poem and contract: we have, in Pope, a commercial nostalgist, a talented typographer.

In 1740, late in his career, Pope made a detailed set of notes on the current disposition of his literary property, making specific reference to the terms of contracts he had made and to the then current state of copyright law.[133] That state was in flux. Once the terms of the copyrights began to lapse, the courts had been faced with the task of construing the statute. As we have seen, its mixed language betrays no simple intention of recognizing or constituting an author's right; its primary purpose was to place monopolistic competition within the book trade under stringent, codified state regulation. But as litigation forced the courts to interpretive construction of the statute, they eventually came close to articulating the principle that copyright originates in the author's intellectual labor, the ostensibly effortful *conception* of an abstract work of the imagination or intellect. Though this now seems an intuitive concept, it was not then an obvious legal formulation (moreover, as I understand it, it is not at *present* a legally defensible definition). This is a territory of legal and literary culture that has been well described by Mark Rose, and there is no reason to retrace it in detail, but I want to pursue the figure of Milton's talent as it rolls through this landscape.

The historiography of these years is by no means simple: neither legal historians nor historians of the book trade, for example, have explained why it is that legislative maneuverings and litigation did not begin in earnest until about three years after the 1731 lapse of statutory protections. That they were spearheaded by Jacob Tonson the younger is no surprise. Most interesting for us is the fact that this Tonson, who had owned the *stationer's* copyright in *Paradise Lost,* brought out a new edition of the poem in 1732, within nine months of the lapse of the statutory copyright in his previous editions. Much has been made of the fact of Queen Caroline's alleged interest in the edition, but Tonson was, of course, equally eager in his sponsorship, for he seems to have been hoping to publish an edition so substantially revised that it might arguably be represented as a new work, in some sense technically untethered from Milton and therefore capable of new statutory protection.[134] He found the perfect editor for this project in Richard Bentley.[135]

It is well-known that Bentley rewrote *Paradise Lost;* it has recently been argued that Bentley was entirely disingenuous in his claims to be restoring the poem to some ostensibly original status.[136] But the historical analysis of Bentley's edition need not content itself with evaluations of Bentley's taste, theological acuity, or good faith. Hugh Kenner is, as often, on a wonderfully right track when he suggests that Bentley "may stand as synecdoche for the scholars, who removed from behind the classical texts the persons whose moral authority had drawn men's minds to those texts for more than a thousand years: the classics were consistently read as moral authorities, and authority stems from a person."[137] Kenner is actually referring here to Bentley's great scholarly achievement from the period of authorial imposture, the proof in 1699 that the *Letters of Phalaris,* thought to have been among the most ancient examples of Greek prose, were in fact first- or second-century forgeries; Kenner's analysis is equally applicable to Bentley's Milton. When Elijah Fenton undertook some unusually heavy emendation in his 1725 edition of *Paradise Lost, The Traveller* accused him of "ignorance, want of taste, and silly officiousness" and protested equally against "the privilege that rich booksellers [in this case, of course, Tonson] have of putting it in the power of any ignorant editor to murder the finest authors."[138]

"Murder" puts it very strongly in the case of Milton, though not, perhaps, too strongly in the case of Phalaris. *The Traveller* marks the degree to which early eighteenth-century editorial practice puts authoriality under stress. Certainly Bentley's analytic dispersal of Milton into "(1) a blind poet,"—this is Kenner's list—"(2) an ill-lettered amanuensis, and (3) an officious interpolator who wrote all the illogical bits"—to which I think should be added (4) a fallible printer—this analytic dispersal erodes the intimacy between *auctor* and book that it had once been the function of textual scholarship to protect, but which such scholarship as Bentley's was beginning to threaten.[139] Such erosion had begun as early as *The Life of Milton,* when Toland had imagined similar dismantlings of authorship and canon. Inspired by Milton and Anglesey's critiques of *Eikon Basilike,* he had darted a similarly disattributive glance at the central structures of orthodoxy, disdaining that "so many suppositious pieces under the name of Christ, his Apostles, and other great Persons should be publish'd and approv'd in those primitive times," and calling for a more critical understanding of authorship. The Statute of Anne had issued a similar call, to which both Tonson and Bentley would idiosyncratically respond.

As the effects of the Statute of Anne began to reveal themselves, this new, crude institution for regulating the book trade provoked new reflections on the ties that bind author to text. Naturally, it was the booksellers who were most interested in practical tests of the nature and strength of the authorial suture. Once such test arose in 1734, when Tonson, together with those other booksellers who had theretofore shared the copyright in Shakespeare's works, sought and secured an injunction in Chancery against Jeffrey Walker, who had challenged their property by bringing out his own edition of Shakespeare. It may at first seem odd that the booksellers took this route, for the procedure in Chancery was fairly complex, but the choice was crucial, since a Chancery injunction was only available in assistance to a common law right. The case, then, rested on the question of whether an author had a common law property in his or her compositions distinct from the property created by the 1710 statute; if such a property did exist, then it could conceivably be assigned to a bookseller, without being impinged upon by the statute. The booksellers were at the same time urging a petition in Parliament to extend the protections of the Statute of Anne for another twenty-one years, and although the bill passed Commons it was defeated in the House of Lords. What might be called the Chancery maneuver turned out to work much more effectively, and the booksellers most threatened by the lapse in statutory copyright used it relentlessly during the next two decades. Their strategy was to split the property in books between a "natural" property, constituted within the private "manuscript culture" of the author, and a statutory property, constituted by statute within the public sphere of "book culture." The analysis of literary property undertaken in Chancery shares the distributive habits of Bentley's textual scholarship.

The stationers continued to force a public anatomy of authoriality in Parliament and, more successfully, in Chancery during the next two decades. When Walker, who made it his particular business to challenge monopolies in the English popular "classics," went after the Tonson Milton in 1739, he encountered judicial opposition in what had become the bookseller's familiar turf, the Court of Chancery. The chancellor affirmed, on behalf of the booksellers, the deathlessness of Milton's proprietary claims. That the Statute of Anne places the focus in these disputes on *assigned* property, on such property as had been conferred on stationers by authors long dead, is particularly important, for it gives the interrogation of textuality something of the quality of a revenge play: economic competition is configured as a defense of the dead. Bentley had strengthened Tonson's control of Milton's text quite differently, dislocating the received text from the venerated author and making quite a new text as a bibliographically aggressive act of pious restoration. In a sense, the received text is denigrated on behalf of an authorial mystique that serves, above all, the editor and publisher. (That these connotations had not been lost is evident in the *Grub Street Journal:* a reviewer of the prospectus to Bentley's edition assures the dead Charles that "the murd'rous critic has avenged thy murder.")[140] The authorial mystique operates with similar potency, but by means of a different logic, in Chancery: for there, on the other hand, Tonson made the received text his own by making it into an alienable icon in which the venerated author perpetually inheres. In a different polemical context Milton had argued "books are not absolutely dead things, but do contain a potency of life in them to be as active as the soul was whose progeny they are; nay they do preserve as in a vial the purest efficacy and extraction of that living intellect that bred them"; the encounters in Chancery in the thirties strengthen this potency by endowing it with legal as well as ideological force.

Milton's status in this polemical context receives quite specific inflection, for the question of his authoriality still retained the particular ideological connotations confirmed within the battle over the bibliography of *Eikon Basilike*. Nowhere do those connotations persist more strangely than in the so-called Lauder affair, which places Milton firmly at the center of a crisis of authoriality. We can now trace the roots of Lauder's attack on Milton's authorship to frustrated Jacobite zeal, an etiology that indicates the continuity of Lauder's project with that of Wagstaffe: the method of attack remains the allegation of plagiarism.[141] What has changed, I think, is the heft of the allegation, and this change has a good deal to do with the fact that authoriality has become more and more a legal matter. Which is to say that the context in which the Lauder affair signifies includes the habit of the Chancery maneuver; includes Warburton's *Letter from an Author to a Member of Parliament* (1747) on behalf of perpetual copyright; includes *Millar v. Kincaid,* as well, a case in which an appeal to the common law protections customary in Chancery was nonsuited in a Scottish Court in 1743 and similarly treated by the House of Lords in a 1750 appeal. This polemical atmosphere conditions Lauder's treatment of Milton by shifting the rhetoric of the accusation of plagiarism from a loosely conceived stigmatization to an allegation of quasi criminality, as if literalizing Martial's old metaphor. The Lauder affair begins in January 1747 with an article in the *Gentleman's Magazine* in which Lauder pointed out that *Paradise Lost* was as indebted to some little-known sixteenth- and seventeenth-century Latin poems as it was to Homer and Virgil. Early in the article Lauder announces that *"by this Essay on Milton's Imitation of the moderns,* I no way intend to derogate from the glory or merit of that noble poet, who certainly is intitled to highest praise"(25). Here and in subsequent letters to the *Gentleman's Magazine,* Lauder quotes a variety of neo-Latin poems to which Milton was surely indebted, and as his correspondence proceeds he allows his scorn to break forth. In his June letter to the magazine Lauder appeals to the *court* of public opinion, offering examples of plagiarized passages, as he puts it, "in further prosecution of my charge against Milton" (285). That the language is hyperbolic, like, say, that of the charge that Bentley had "murdered" Milton, is surely the case, but the language persists. Two years later, Lauder, much encouraged by Dr. Johnson, published an expanded version of the articles in pamphlet form, and this time his accusation is unbridled: "His industrious concealment of his helps, his peremptory disclaiming all manner

of assistance, is highly ungenerous, nay criminal to the last degree, and absolutely unworthy of any man of common probity and honour." [142] The idiom
of this die-hard Jacobite attack is conditioned by the increased pressure on
the bond of author and text, a pressure applied both in the courts and in
Parliament.

Milton retains a central position during this fascinating moment in the
history of English intellectual property. A century later, on February 5, 1841,
Macauley recalls a very different aspect of the moment in a speech in Parliament against a bill to extend the duration of copyright to sixty years:

> As often as this bill has been under discussion, the fate of Milton's
> granddaughter has been brought forward by the advocates of
> monopoly. My honorable and learned friend [Serjeant Talfourd]
> has repeatedly told the story with great eloquence and effect. He
> has dilated on the sufferings, on the abject poverty, of this ill-fated
> woman, the last of an illustrious race. He tells us that, in the
> extremity of her distress, Garrick gave her a benefit, that Johnson
> wrote a prologue, and that the public contributed some hundreds
> of pounds. . . . At the time at which Milton's granddaughter asked
> charity, Milton's works were the exclusive property of a bookseller.
> Within a few months of the day on which the benefit was given at
> Garrick's theatre, the holder of the copyright of Paradise Lost—I
> think it was Tonson—applied to the Court of Chancery for an
> injunction against a bookseller, who had published a cheap edition
> of the great epic poem, and obtained the injunction.

Macauley dwells "with great eloquence and effect" on the irony of the moment at which the Chancery maneuver, grounded on natural right, necessi-
tated a charity based on a belief in the very same natural right. But he only
begins to chart the irony of the occasion; to do so, we need to consider further
the position of one of the sponsors of the *Comus* benefit, Dr. Johnson himself.

Johnson made his first efforts on behalf of Elizabeth Foster, Milton's
granddaughter, in a postscript (pp. 165–68) to Lauder's 1750 *Essay on Milton's Use and Imitation of the Moderns*. Marcuse has discussed how Johnson
became involved in the Lauder affair: though Johnson's politics were not as
extreme as Lauder's, nor his dislike for Milton quite so vehement, his enthusiasm for modern Latin poetry was on a par with Lauder's; as soon as he got
wind of Lauder's project Johnson seems to have thought it a useful means of
drumming up subscriptions for an anthology of neo-Latin verse. [143] But the
violence of Lauder's attack seems to have given even Johnson pause, and his

1750 postscript urging aid to Milton's granddaughter enabled him to moderate the vehemence of the attack.

To situate this more precisely in the political bibliography of Milton: Johnson adapted his pathetic account of Milton's granddaughter from Newton's edition of *Paradise Lost,* published only a few months earlier, the first variorum edition of an English poet ever published. By adopting variorum format, with its foregrounding of the industrial mediation of the literary text, Newton perfects that anatomy of literary production undertaken by Bentley in the sphere of criticism and by the booksellers in Chancery. Yet if the moment of Bentley coincides with the origins of the Chancery maneuver, the moment of Lauder, which subjects Miltonic authoriality to the most heated public controversy of the Tonson era, coincides with the breakdown of the Chancery maneuver. When Walker made his second attempt on *Paradise Lost,* Tonson again sought an injunction in Chancery. In this second case of *Tonson v. Walker* (1752), twenty years after the first—and with the text of *Paradise Lost* now twenty *more* years outside the protection of the Statute of Anne—the case for the plaintiff had to stand on the novelty of Newton's apparatus: Milton's text was to be protected by his editors.[144] The chancellor, Lord Hardwicke, granted the preliminary injunction, but his order was so ominous, so dubious about Tonson's common law rights, that Tonson dropped the case before it could come to trial.[145]

To return to Milton's granddaughter: reference to her poverty became one of the commonplaces of public discourse on the rights of authors— Talfourd and Macauley were still at it almost a hundred years later.[146] One of the recurrent themes of Bentley's anatomy of authoriality had been the poverty of Milton and his printer; he makes of this fragility of personal circumstance an explanation of the vulnerability of the text to corruption. Though this account has a dubious bearing on Bentley's textual argument, its pathos seems to have been extremely taking. The topos may derive from the rhetoric of the booksellers' petitions to Parliament: one might recall their appeal in 1694 when, seeking renewal of the Licensing Act, they adverted to "Widows, and others, whose whole Livelihood depends upon the Petitioners Property."[147] Such language leads to that specifically commercial reification of authoriality by which Pope and Johnson would eventually come to know themself as men of letters. For Johnson, pathos and accounting are mutual supplements: it bears remarking that his most detailed account of the commercial reification of authoriality may be found in his essay on the "Life of Milton," in which Johnson details the terms of Milton's sale of *Paradise Lost* to the printer Samuel Simmons, the history of the sales of the epic, the changes in the demography of the reading public, and the transformation of literary marketing. Though the fate of Elizabeth Foster might be urged, in the short term, against the booksellers' treatment of authors, it inevitably functions as a means of resisting statutory inhibition of a trade operating according to common law right. The pathetic account of Miltonic authorship is complemented by Lauder's renewal of Martial's rhetoric, his campaign against a figuratively criminal plagiarism: although the accusation of plagiarism might serve, in the short term, to discredit Milton, the criminalization of plagiarism supports and promotes the case for natural property in ideas.

But it is precisely here, where pathos and criminalization participate in the rhetorical heightening of authoriality, that the ironies of the Lauder affair and its debts to the *Eikon* tradition come into focus. Johnson supported Lauder's claims, but both his prefatory letter and postscript were circulated as Lauder's. And when it came out, to Johnson's indignation, that a great number of Lauder's "sources" for *Paradise Lost* had been trumped up—that, indeed, several of the Latin poems from which Milton had allegedly stolen were actually seventeenth-century Latin translations of Milton's *own* poem—Johnson forced Lauder to make a public apology. And here is the punch line: he *dictated* the retraction. Authoriality is not simply examined in the Lauder affair, it is policed; yet, like quicksilver, the more one presses it, the more slippery it becomes. All literary personhood, all verbally possessive individualism wanders off in a flurry of scare quotes: "Lauder" is as fugitive as is "his" "Milton."

The Lauder affair brings this account back to the controversy over *Eikon Basilike*, for in 1754 Lauder attempted something of a comeback, publishing yet another attack on Milton titled *Charles I Vindicated*. He revives the Wagstaffe theory that Milton arranged for a doctoring of *Eikon Basilike* in order to accuse Charles I of plagiarism—and so shifts his own charge against Milton from that of plagiarism, still only rhetorically criminalized, to forgery, a capital crime since 1729. Perhaps nothing had so compromised this not untenable theory as did Lauder's espousal of it; certainly, no version of Wagstaffe's case was again seriously advanced until 1915. But the embarrassing waving of hands with which Lauder passes from the historical record should not obscure the serious effects of his challenge.

Consider the terms of Richard Richardson's early response to Lauder's charges: "I must observe, that *Virgil* himself was not free from the like calumnies. Macrobius positively taxes that most noble poet with having translated, almost *word for word,* the whole 2d book of the *Aeneis* from *Pisander,* and the 4th from *Apollonius Rhodius.*"[148] Richardson points to the difficulty of distinguishing the stigmatized modern practice of plagiarism from the venerable technique of classical imitation. In 1751, Richard Hurd elaborated

Richardson's observation in his *Discourse on Poetical Imitation,* one of the first systematic inquiries into the methods of source study. In the shadow of Lauder, Hurd sets himself the hardest of cases:

> The genius of Virgil never suffers more in the opinion of his critics, than when his *book of games* comes into consideration and is confronted with Homer's. It is not unpleasant to observe the difficulties an advocate for his fame is put to in this nice point, to secure his honour from the imputation of *plagiarism.* . . . What shall we say, then, to this charge? Shall we, in defiance of truth and fact, endeavour to confute it? Or, if allowed, is there any method of supporting the reputation of the poet? I think there is, if prejudice will but suspend its determinations a few minutes and afford his advocate a fair hearing.[149]

Hurd goes on to distinguish between influence, imitation, and plagiarism—to discriminate, that is, the modes of intellectual individuation. And there is no doubt of Lauder's compulsive influence here, for Hurd busies himself over Milton, whom he characterizes as particularly "ambitious of this fame of *invention*":

> He was so averse from resting in the old imagery of Homer, and the other epic poets, that he appears to have taken infinite pains in the investigation of new *allusions,* which he picked up out of the rubbish of every silly legend or romance, that had come to his knowledge, or extracted from the dry and rugged materials of the sciences, and even the mechanic arts. Yet, in comparison of the genuine treasures of nature, which he found himself obliged to make use of, in common with other writers, his own proper stock of *images,* imported from the regions of *art,* is very poor and scanty; and, as might be expected, makes the least agreeable part of his divine work. (202)

In defense of a modern authoriality constructed within a crowded discursive field, Hurd metes out the degrees of intellectual privacy and gauges the precise heft of genius. Lauder also put new pressure on annotation: whereas Newton had been content to record Milton's classical sources, henceforth the model status of the Moderns had to be seriously addressed. Hurd's *Discourse* responds to precisely this pressure, for his analysis allows for the possibility—even considers the inevitability—of a modern *imitatio.*

Hurd is not the only critic who rose to Lauder's challenge: in *Rambler* 121 and 143 and *Adventurer* 95, Johnson also takes up the problem of describing how authoriality might subsist within inevitably redundant discursive systems. He shies away from the definitive description; certainly he would have envied Justice Wedderburn's evasion of the problem in *Tonson v. Collins*, who insisted, "When I speak of the [author's] right of property, I mean in the profits of his book, not in the sentiments, style, etc." Certainly Johnson came more and more to regard authoriality in just this light, as something irreducibly commercial and proprietary. I think it could be maintained that his experience of the Lauder affair helped to drive him to this position.

Having written for and as Lauder, Johnson bore his scars. He is more urbane, less nervous than Hurd, but thirty years after Lauder, Johnson seems still to be going over the same ground in the "Life of Milton" (1779) and his resistance to Milton must now dodge the shameful memory of his participation in Lauder's assault. Of *Comus* Johnson now observes, "the fiction is derived from Homer's Circe; but we never can refuse to any modern the liberty of borrowing from Homer." He accuses the Milton of *Eikonoklastes*, the Milton who alleges plagiarism, of excessive harshness. And the last paragraph of the "Life of Milton" seems truly *haunted* by Lauder, the memory of whom forces Johnson first to a compensatory generosity—"of all the borrowers from Homer, Milton is, perhaps, the least indebted"—and then to a muted statement of the old thesis of Miltonic secondarity—"his work is not the greatest of heroick poems, only because it is not the first."

That Johnson's "Life of Milton" is grudging, even angry, is a commonplace; the memory of Lauder can explain a good deal of this. I am not the first to discover the pentimenti of the Lauder affair in the "Life"; that honor goes to Francis Blackburne. Blackburne begins his response to the "Life" with a succinct summary of Johnson's argument: "Milton was a Whig, and therefore must be a Plagiary."[150] Moreover Blackburne intuits Johnson's dark secret, that Lauder's campaign had threatened Johnson's own authoriality; he divines the original authorial slippage: "There is at least a HIGH DEGREE OF PROPOLLENT PROBABILITY that the Letter in that Magazine [the *Gentleman's Magazine*], signed WILLIAM LAUDER, came from the amicable hand of Mr. Samuel Johnson" (536). Blackburne seems to suggest that this sort of erosion of personality in print is quintessentially Tory; certainly he holds out for a Whig liberty that is particularly devoted to natural authoriality and particularly hostile to the commercial reifications of the press. Consider his handling of a bit of Johnsonian wit:

> "The Life of Milton," says Dr. Johnson, "has been already written
> in so many forms, with such minute enquiry, that I might perhaps
> more properly have contented myself with the addition of a
> few notes to Mr. Fenton's elegant Abridgement, but that a new
> narrative was thought necessary to the uniformity of this edition."
>
> The uniformity of editions is commonly the bookseller's care,
> and the necessity of such uniformity generally arises from the taste
> of the public, of which, among the number of names exhibited in
> the title-pages of these volumes, there must be competent judges.
> It would be a pity however that a conformity to this taste should
> engage Dr. Johnson, in writing this Life, to go beyond what would
> *more properly* have contented himself. (540–41)

Blackburne's accusation is that Johnson has become a market effect. It is a
shrewd attack, for surely the tendency of the "Life" is to represent Milton
in precisely that form.[151] Johnson's "Life" is at once a celebration and a small
act of revenge: it celebrates the commercial and judicial reification of authorship within the Tonson era—celebrates, that is, Johnsonian authorship—and
secures its revenge by carefully measuring the historical distance that separates and secludes Milton *from* that era.[152] It calculates the exchange value
of Milton's talent.

Ten years before Jonson wrote "The Life of Milton," Milton had been a
witness in a very different historiography of authorship. In *Millar v. Taylor*
(1769), the question of the existence of common law intellectual property had
been carefully probed, and the court had determined both that such property existed and that this property had not been taken away by the Statute of
Anne.[153] Speaking for the court, Aston had declared that "the rules attending
property" were obliged to bend to its historical mutability, that they "must
keep pace with its increase and improvement."[154] But the case was difficult,
it produced the first dissenting opinion (Yates's) in the history of the Mansfield court, and Lord Mansfield expressed a kind of weariness as he surveyed
the legislative history of author's property:

> I have had frequent opportunities to consider of it. I have
> travelled in it for many years. I was counsel in most of the cases
> which have been cited from Chancery. . . . The first case of
> Milton's Paradise Lost was upon my motion. I argued the second:
> which was solemnly argued, by one on each side. I argued the case
> of *Millar* against *Kincaid* in the House of Lords.[155]

Mansfield reduced the case to "whether it is agreeable to natural principles, moral justice and fitness, to allow him [i.e., the author] the copy, after publication, as well as before."[156] And this experienced litigant and judge was confident that it *was* agreeable to allow this. He based his determination, inaccurately (not surprisingly), on "the general consent of this kingdom, for ages"— the disagreeing Yates having insisted, notwithstanding, that the kingdom had long consented to regulations that recognized only stationers' property—but Mansfield adduced yet another authority, which he regards even more highly:

> The single opinion of such a man as Milton, speaking, after much
> consideration, upon the very point is stronger than any inferences
> from gathering acorns and seizing a vacant piece of ground; when
> the writers, so far from thinking of the very point, speak of an
> imaginary state of nature before the invention of letters.[157]

Mansfield here resists one line in the plaintiff's arguments, a line reflected in the deliberations of his fellow justices, to wit, the description of intellectual property in terms derived from Locke. Such a description was apparently too much shackled to the language of property and labor, too densely material. With the supposed sanction of Milton to ratify his instinct, Mansfield seems to have concluded that there was an irreducibly special aspect to copyright and authorship that would be vulgarized and obscured by attempts to understand them by analogy, respectively, to property and to other forms of labor. *Millar vs. Taylor* is deeply imbued with the spirit of the Chancery maneuver, this time not only shearing off statutory from common law property, but also blessing the latter by denigrating the former. At this juncture the Milton of *Areopagitica* is enlisted to deliver the benediction.

The contest over Miltonic authoriality sustained throughout the Tonson era has its last skirmish in Johnson's *Life*, which resists the tendencies of *Millar v. Taylor*. In the oedipal work of the sonnet on his blindness, Milton had hidden the material conditions of his talent—the expensive education that his father had financed—and, although Justice Yates had protested such concealments, his fellow justices had accepted the deft repression. Johnson lines up with Yates, insisting on the commercial measure of authorial talent, in a final attempt to murder the suavely murderous Miltonic repression— but he cannot bury it deeply. A Milton fully redeemed from material and political conditions is resurrected within romanticism. His eloquence having first descended upon Lord Mansfield, his fine immaterial ghost later appears to Cowper in a dream in 1793, at the end of the Tonson era. "He was very gravely but very neatly attired in the fashion of his day and had a countenance which fill'd me with those feelings that an affectionate child has for a beloved father."[158] Neither Johnson nor Yates were alive to sigh, "Ay me, thou fondly dreamst," and so neither King Charles's plagiaristical head nor the gory and plagiaristical visage of the poet of possessive individualism are to be found at the end of *this* little avenue of specialized enthusiasm. Both wash far away.

III

THE LAUGHABLE TERM

Chapter Eight

Authentic Reproductions

The time has now come when the English Printer and the English
Publisher must take their due places in the national estimation.
Hitherto the Author has had it all his own way.

Edward Arber, *A Transcript of the Registers of the
Company of the Stationers of London,
1554–1640 A.D.*

The term Literary Property, he in a manner laughed at.

From the Old Law to the New Bibliography, II

Most legal historians have contemplated the Statute of Anne with an obstructed hindsight, coming at it through the sometimes deliberately confusing record of the case law it provoked, and they have therefore assessed it harshly. Although the Statute of Anne carries traces of competing regulatory traditions and of the mixed motives of the legislators who prepared it, it is not as confused as it has been made to seem. So much was made to hang on it, naturally, in the course of eighteenth-century litigation that it came to seem more irresolute and opaque than it is. For Augustine Birrell, like Copinger, one of the great lawyer-bibliophiles of the last fin-de-siècle, it was a "perfidious measure 'rigged with curses dark.'"[1]

How seriously to take this Miltonism of 1899? Birrell's *Seven Lectures on Copyright* emanate, certainly, from an erudite culture struggling to defend authorship against modern iterabilities, from phonograph and photograph, collotype and typewriter. He had prepared these lectures for publication "chiefly because the Law on the subject is expected before long to engage what is sometimes called 'the attention of Parliament'" (p.3): all this patient urbanity seems to insinuate that History has something to teach Legislation, that it could have taught Anne's parliament a crucial thing or two, but Birrell is not so very forthcoming about the lessons to have been and to be learned. His lectures emanate from a British legal culture that had only just come to feel, thanks to the passage of the Chace Bill (1891) in America, that its own system of intellectual property could be made secure from devastating infringements; but the British system was still felt to be hopelessly composite and besieged. Contemplating a founding legal moment of complex unclarity, Birrell resorts to the xenophobia, the nostalgia, and the sanctification of poetry and the poet so fervidly prosecuted in "Lycidas."

I began this book by recalling the historiographic impulses that arose in 1909, when the Berne Convention for international copyright protection was revised in Berlin. When Parliament confirmed the Copyright Act of 1911 and so acceded to the revision, it transformed English copyright law as Birrell had known it. The law was still composite, but a lawyer-cum-historian-of-authorship could approve of a formulation that made the author's life the sole measure of protection.

The law was composite because the technology of copying and markets for copies were heterogeneous—heterogeneous and ramifying—and law could not rationalize this vast field of differences. To recall the bemused despair with which the *Encyclopedia Brittanica* surveyed this broken terrain in 1911:

> we find five British acts, three dealing with engraving, one with
> sculpture, and one with painting, drawing and photography, and
> between them very little relation. We have three terms of duration
> of copyright. . . . There are two different relations of the artist to
> his copyright. . . . The engraver and the sculptor are not required
> to register. . . . The painter cannot protect his copyright without
> registration, but this registration as it is now required is merely a
> pitfall for the unwary. Designed to give the public information as
> to the ownership and duration of copyrights, the uncertainty of its
> operation results in the prevention of information on these very
> points.[2]

This last point should have special force in these pages, since it betrays a curious pressure on the law of intellectual property. At the beginning of this century—as occasionally before—the law of copyright was felt to be under some obligation to inform the public concerning key features of a reified cultural field, obliged to answer such questions (and subsets of such questions) as "What is an author?"; "What is an object of art?"; or "What is the work of art?" I take it that such questions take urgency from new market structures and new reproductive practices, from the early *twentieth*-century antecedents of the Internet and the photocopying machine, of DNA manipulation and the CD-R drive—to which law and historical scholarship variously respond. As a way of reflecting on the historiographic project that this book advances, let me reconsider the material origins of the New Bibliography, from which the modern study of book culture derives.

It would be easy enough to situate this scholarly movement in a tradition of Shakespearean editing, much as McKerrow did in his 1933 British Academy lecture, or in a tradition of nineteenth-century classical editing, as did Greg in his 1945 retrospective for the Bibliographical Society.[3] Indeed, it would be accurate to describe the central project of what we call the New Bibliography as "the disciplined reconstruction of manuscript copy-texts for printed books," a bibliographic project of uncertain Newness. When Greg formulated his "Principles of Emendation in Shakespeare" in 1928, he summarized two decades of practice in the editing of Elizabethan texts and seventy years of classical editing with the simple dictum "no emendation can or ought to be considered *in vacuo*, but criticism must always proceed in relation to what we know, or what we surmise, respecting the history of the text."[4] It was the crucial work of a great triumvirate—Pollard, McKerrow, and Greg— to tease out the full implications of the phrase "history of the text" by an analytic multiplication of the possible sources of textual variation informed by concentrated attention to the mechanics of printing (McKerrow's specialty) and to the history of the book trade (the centers of interest for Pollard and Greg). It is certainly true that Pollard spent the first phase of his scholarly career as an editor of medieval texts (McKerrow, similarly, began with an edition, still reliable, of Thomas Nashe), but Pollard and McKerrow began to distinguish themselves when they shifted their attention to the industrial regularities and regulations that determine the printed text. Shakespeareans understandably locate the New Bibliography in the history of Shakespeare reception at the end of a tradition of enthusiastic but opportunistic emendation, but it would be more illuminating to describe the New Bibliography as a research program in industrial history.

But not just any industrial history. I have been suggesting that a new information technology and a legal crisis which that technology exacerbated were somehow determining for twentieth-century bibliographical scholarship, that problems in modern intellectual property somehow motivate research into *early* modern information technologies and *early* modern intellectual property. Pollard's *Shakespeare's Folios and Quartos* is now remembered as the first work in which the crucial distinction between what we now call the Good and Bad Quartos was proposed, but for Pollard drawing that distinction was merely a stage in a more complex argument that linked textual "purity" with industrial regularity: in his words, "Finding, as we do, that quartos which have good texts and agree with the First Folio are entered regularly in the Stationers' Registers, and that quartos which have bad texts, not agreeing at all with the First Folio, are entered in the Stationers' Register either irregularly or not at all, we are surely justified in arguing . . . that there is some causal relation at work which connects a good text with regular entry prior to publication in the Stationers' Register" (65). The idealized "good" text may be among the least egregious of the lapses here; *many* aspects of Pollard's argument are wrong. However inaccurate, Pollard's formulation is the founding myth of the New Bibliography—that textual integrity and regulated intellectual property are somehow mutually entailed: in this dream the choice of "best text" and the location of intellectual property rights are identical labors. The dream was a recurrent one. Confirmed in a historiographic project that had enveloped all editorial motives, Pollard began his Sandars Lectures of 1915 with an echo of Greg's 1903 review of Lee: "Legal writers on English copyright have not shown much interest in the steps by which the conception of literary property was gradually built up." One year later, the revised lectures, Pollard's reconstructions of the legal history that Parliament had blotted in 1909, were published as *Shakespeare's Fight with the Pirates and the Problem of the Transmission of his Text*.[5]

I emphasize Pollard's idée fixe in order to remark the attunement of the New Bibliography to disturbances in contemporary legal culture. But Pollard's interest in printing *history* and specifically his interest in literary property must be given a plural etiology: to attend more closely to his professional biography will be to reveal other strata in the archaeology of New Bibliographic knowledge. When Pollard became secretary of the Bibliographical Society in 1893, a year after it was founded, the society included a loose coalition of scholars, librarians, and booksellers, but its founding members were men like Copinger and A.H. Huth.[6] They were collectors: Huth, the first secretary of the society, had amassed one of the most important of late nineteenth-century collections. Acquisition was as important a context for New Bibliographic practice as was the editorial tradition.[7] One reason why bibliography was in flux at the turn of this century is that the market in rare books was changing drastically.

According to John Carter, "the overriding importance attached to chronological priority—first edition, first issue, etc.—as a criterion of the interest of a book . . . is actually of quite modern development, for the average nineteenth-century collector was as much interested in the finest-looking or the best-edited edition as in the first."[8] At the turn of the century, however, purely aesthetic criteria were giving way among bibliophile collectors. The emphasis on priority may be best explained in economic terms, as the rationalization of an older rare-book market in which value had been subject to no calculus susceptible to simple codification. This is an oddly democratic development, an appreciable if partial solvent to the control over market values exerted by eminent, often aristocratic, collectors for whom the mysteries of taste had been the primary determinant of value. Whatever its scholarly utility, modern scientific bibliography regularizes, and even deliberately enlarges, the bibliophile market. The founding of such institutions as the Browning, Ruskin, Wordsworth, and Shelley societies and the proliferation of enumerative bibliographies of modern authors, both phenomena of the 1870s and 1880s, fostered new areas of collecting: the rare-book market expanded, and the bibliographies managed that expansion by establishing degrees of rarity, the essential criteria of value in this market.[9] If, as William Roberts remarked in 1894, "the book market [is] itself a stock exchange in miniature," late nineteenth-century bibliographers were providing investment profiles.[10]

The evolution of the Bibliographical Society tellingly registers the antiquarian turn in bibliophile practice. Greg's 1945 retrospective shudders over the society's early interest in what he calls "embellishment," that is, in those sites of aesthetic value—bindings, illustrations, type ornaments—that had been the concern of older collectors.[11] But the society quickly settled into a decade dominated by incunabular research, that is, into books of irreducible priority. A shrewd and cantankerous borough librarian, J. D. Brown, raised a fuss over the prevailing character of research enshrined in the Bibliographical Society in a 1903 letter to *The Library*:

> It may be safely said that modern bibliography is exactly the same old egotistical hobby which it was a hundred years ago, when it became a fad for rich collectors. . . . We have elaborate lists of the incunabula arranged in the order of the authors' names; then someone comes along and and rearranges these lists under the names of towns, and the names of printers.[12]

Brown may not clearly see the real novelty of new bibliographic research, but he correctly intuits its motives: he concludes his intemperate diatribe,

"In short, the modern bibliographer is a kind of hack for the second-hand bookseller and book collector" (148).

If Brown had a hard time getting a hearing, there is no doubt that Pollard took the attack seriously, since he made sure that his response was published as a companion piece to Brown's. Moreover, he remembered such accusations. In a 1913 address to the Bibliographical Society, near the beginning of a decade and a half of unprecedented inflation in the market value of Elizabethan books, Pollard reflects, "It is sometimes said of this Society that its existence has helped to raise the price of the books about which we write. That is very inconvenient for us individually or for the libraries which we represent."[13] "We" dissipates some of the archness of "inconvenient": when Pollard made this remark, he had been on the staff of the British Museum Department of Printed Books for thirty years, had been setting purchasing policy for the B.M. library for ten, and was therefore extraordinarily sensitive to trends and fluctuations in bibliophile value.

Pollard's feel for the market in books remained with him to the end of his career, reasserting itself even as his audience changed from a group of wealthy amateurs to a cadre of specialist academics. His involvement in the rare-book market was in large measure responsible for the first analytical triumph of the New Bibliographers, the identification of the true provenance of the Pavier quartos. Experienced bibliographers have this story by heart— how Greg and Pollard together demonstrated that nine Shakespeare quartos, bearing dates ranging from 1600 to 1615 and attributed to various printers and publishers, were in fact printed more or less together, in 1619, by William Jaggard, for Thomas Pavier, a collection no doubt inspired by the 1616 Jonson Folio. Pollard had identified the quartos as a group in 1906, when, in his capacity as chief purchasing officer for the British Library, he was shown (for the second time in three or four years) bound collections of the same nine plays. In 1907, Greg made the technical breakthrough of linking the quartos by layout, typography, and watermark; whereas Pollard, for his part, continued to consult the market, noting in a 1908 review of Slater's *Book-Prices Current* that these particular quartos were relatively easy to come by, not at all rare when compared to other Shakespeare quartos, just what one might expect of books issued simultaneously for binding as a collection.[14]

Not that Greg was oblivious to the influence of the market on scholarship, though he felt that influence differently. He reported, with ill-concealed disdain, on how subscribers to *The Library* reacted to his typographic arguments: "A number of readers, with their heads full of modern book prices, jumped to the conclusion that I must mean that Pavier was endeavouring to obtain higher prices for his books by pretending that they were first editions, and they hastened solemnly to inform me that the desire for first editions was inoperative in the seventeenth century." Greg's own assessment of Pavier's motives will come as no surprise. Writing on the eve of the Berlin revisions to the Berne Convention, he proposed that what Pavier "wanted to avoid was the charge of having printed plays, to the copyright of some of which he had no conceivable right."[15] Pollard had his mind on book prices; Greg had his mind on property rights. For both men, literary history was now irreversibly bound up with the history of industrial organization and law.

Look Homeward, Angel Now

The New Bibliographic project was shaped by one more feature of the early twentieth-century rare-book market, perhaps its most distinctive feature, which is that the market had tilted suddenly westward. When the Britwell, Huth, and Hoe collections were sold off, between 1910 and 1915, the principal buyers were the Henrys Huntington and Folger, but even before those most spectacular purchases, British collectors noticed that their American counterparts had begun to dominate the major auctions. I suspect that this trans-Atlantic drift motivated the gentle chauvinism of Pollard's efforts at the Bibliographical Society early in this century. In the society's June 1900 *News Sheet,* Pollard observed that "so many of the Society's publications have dealt with foreign subjects, that papers on points of English book-lore would be especially welcome."[16] In his 1913 address, in the midst of a major American purchasing frenzy, Pollard described as an "undeniable and very awkward fact" the internationalism of the Bibliographical Society's early work— international because of its orientation to incunabulae. He called upon his fellow members "to set in order our own English bibliographical house."[17]

To expose how richly Englishness shaped the New Bibliographic project, Sidney Lee is, once again, a name to conjure with. Sole editor of the *Dictionary of National Biography* since 1892, Lee had established himself as a great popularizer of Shakespeare a few years later, when he expanded his *DNB* entry on Shakespeare into an extremely successful book. His 1902 facsimile of the folio, the book that had so nettled Greg, hardly contributed to his status as a popularizer—the facsimile was produced in a limited edition of one thousand—but it did make him seem Shakespeare's great Americanizer. Published on the eve of Lee's yearlong lecture tour of the United States, the facsimile seems to have been published with the tour in mind. Lee's introduction appealed to the pride of "English-speaking peoples," but an irate bibliophile, protesting to the London *Standard* that one hundred copies had been set aside for the publisher, while five hundred copies had been reserved for American subscription sales, winced under the oppression of "Yankee plutocracy."[18]

This is no doubt an extreme response; certainly Pollard's notice in *The Library* was more measured—he neither blames nor praises Lee's introduction. Greg's fuller discussion of the volume, a few months later, is closer in tone to the letter to the *Standard:* "I wish it to be understood that this article is not intended as a review, since I do not propose to make any mention of the many excellences of the volume, but merely to call attention to certain points which must, I think, be excepted from the general praise."[19] Greg excepts these points for nearly thirty pages, and the idiom of scholarly condescension predominates: he refers to "certain obvious errors which cannot escape the attention of any reader familiar with Shakespearian bibliography" (259) and then coolly retrenches, "even the expert is apt to be misled by Mr. Lee's cheerful confidence of assertion" (260). What Greg stigmatizes is the popularizer's genial disregard for the evidentiary. When Pollard got round to fully digesting Lee's arguments, he was similarly disdainful of Lee's slapdash methods, but his criticism, worked out in full in *Shakespeare Folios and Quartos,* carries a charge nowhere anticipated in Greg's earlier review:

> I find myself opposed to him at almost every point. The [bibli-
> ographical] pessimists, of whom Mr. Lee has made himself the
> champion, seem to me to have piracy on the brain. They depict
> it as the ruling element in the book-market in Shakespeare's
> day, Shakespeare and his fellows as submitting to it with what
> I should account a craven and contemptible helpessness, and
> the early edition of his plays as so deeply tainted with fraud and
> carelessness that we can never say where the mischief ends. As
> for the Elizabethan printers and publishers they are set down as
> equally stupid and dishonest, and none escape condemnation.

There is much to say about Pollard's disposition to the archival record, but the first and most obvious thing to say about the project of Pollard's book is that it frames bibliographic research as a character defense. "To me," he writes, "the printers and publishers seem as a rule to have been honest men."[20] Note the elegance and economy: the carelessness and dishonesty attributed to Elizabethan book producers is shifted to Lee, whose "theory," Pollard tells us, "when extended to cover not an isolated instance but a whole series of depredations, conflicts with . . . common sense and the English character" (10). So to Greg's hostility to Lee's vulgar carelessness, Pollard adds indignation over

Lee's dearth of patriotism. The editor of the *DNB* was betraying an English folio to a Yankee plutocracy, and the honest Elizabethans who had printed the quartos were being traduced by their most eminent historian.[21]

Lee's facsimile was highly disseminative, in every poststructuralist sense of the word. The work of the New Bibliographers, on the other hand, confers on the transmission from autograph to playhouse to Stationers' Hall to compositor, pressman, proof-corrector and binder, confers on the material mediation of literary imagination, a calculus. Though he is not so hardy as to suppose what Shakespeare *meant,* much less precisely what he *wrote,* Pollard is confident that he can tell good quarto from bad, that he can read textual authority from Arber's *Transcript of the Stationers' Register.* Lee had not only denigrated, but had *mystified,* production; his facsimile sends the Shakespearean text on a book tour into the wilderness.

Greg ended up siding with Lee, despite the scandal of Lee's lack of method, whereas Pollard became ever more "optimistic" in his textual theories. In his 1915 Sandars Lectures and again in his British Academy lecture for 1923 (*The Foundations of Shakespeare's Text*), he undertook to prove that many of the quarto and Folio copy-texts were based on autograph promptbooks. Thus the dense historical field, so richly mapped in the first two decades of this century, comfortably fades as the Folio text recovers its proximity to the author's pen. For Pollard, Shakespeare's autograph is distinctive, knowable, known, and Pollard's introduction to the essays he collected in 1923 as *Shakespeare's Hand in the Play of Sir Thomas More* therefore grows fervent and tart as he sets Sir E. M. Thompson's work on Shakespeare's handwriting against the assertions of the disseminator: "According to Sir Sidney Lee (preface to 1922 edition of his *Life of William Shakespeare,* p. xiii) Elizabethan handwriting 'runs in a common mould which lacks clearly discernible traces of the writer's individuality.' Cockneys have been heard to say the same of sheep, and yet the shepherd knows each sheep in his flock from every other."[22] By 1934, the year that he gave over editing *The Library,* Pollard advanced the theory that several of the quarto texts were printed from foul papers—effectively, drafts (he had somewhat casually suggested this of some of the Folio texts in the Sandars Lectures)—so that we have texts closer still to some originary authorial, autographic moment.

From our own perspective, the friction between Lee and Pollard had as its most enduring effect the genesis of Greg's fruitfully moderate position. He shared Pollard's early commitment to the methodical reconstruction of a regulated past—he had, of course, been instrumental in promulgating the reconstructive method—but from Lee he learned to regard the Shakespearean texts with anauthorial (or is the term "unoriginative"?) disenchantment. He eventually developed a bracing vision of a vigorously disseminative textual history: transmission makes meanings. In the prolegomena to *The Editorial Problem in Shakespeare* he wrote, "I feel that a particular edition, and far more a particular manuscript in the case of a medieval work, possesses a certain individuality of its own, which makes it a sort of minor literary creation, whose integrity I am loath to violate."[23] This has a somewhat settled aestheticist feel to it, but his note refers us to a more rambunctious version of the argument, that in his enormously canny 1932 essay "Bibliography—an Apologia." There in a gesture of great critical insouciance, Greg devalues the metacritical assumptions underlying the textual criticism of the Vulgate itself:

> An enormous amount of labour has been expended in successive
> attempts to determine what St. Jerome actually wrote, or what
> the divine spirit prompted him to write. . . . It would be foolish to
> depreciate the work which centuries of scholarship have devoted
> to this unending task.

But he then goes blithely on with the work of depreciation:

> We have in fact to recognize that a text is not a fixed and formal
> thing, that needs only to be purged of the imperfections of
> transmission and restored once and for all to its pristine purity.

This is dangerous ground and he knows it, so he shifts to the mildly anxious rhetoric of sacred history: "a text is not a fixed and formal thing . . . but a living organism which in its descent through the ages . . ." The pious rhetoric betrays Greg's nervousness as he prepares to inflict a devastating blow on originative authoriality, by asserting the historical itineracy of the text, which

> . . . while it departs more and more from the form impressed
> upon it by its original author, exerts, through its imperfections,
> as much as through its perfections, its own influence upon its
> surroundings.

He has hedged, retreated from the representation of authorship as a mere impress of form. The retreat is temporary: once again he will assert the authoriality of transmission itself, the scribal power of inscription, the power of compositors to impose their own "original impression":

> At each stage of its descent a literary work is in some sense a new
> creation. . . . In some limited sense, each scribe is a subsidiary
> author, even when he is doing his best to be a faithful copyist, still
> more when he indulges in emendations and improvements of his
> own. And this is just what bibliography, with its impartial outlook,
> recognizes, when it treats each step in the history of the text as
> potentially of equal importance.[24]

Thus Greg's prolegomenon to the New Cultural History, to Gadamer, Jauss, and McGann. When we casually attribute a monological, idealized, and stipulative attitude to textuality to pre-postmodern critics, we should not suppose ourselves to be referring to Greg.

From this distance it will seem odd that a facsimile edition, promising some terminus of textual variation, should have occasioned so complex and, in Pollard's case, so anxious a reaction. But Lee's facsimile constituted a dual assault on Pollard's bibliographic calculus. The first aspect of the assault is obvious: Lee had imagined a bibliographic past full of pirates, a past in which texts proliferate in violation of authorial, censorious, proprietary, or industrial control. But the second violation of the bibliographic calculus has to do with the reproductive technology itself, and its disruption of the bibliophile foundations of New Bibliography. Consider one more passage from the eleventh edition of the *Encyclopedia Brittanica,* this from Pollard's article on "Bibliography and Bibliology." He is discussing "the correction of mis-statements in early books as to their place and origin":

> A special case of this problem of piracies and spurious imprints
> is that of the modern photographic or type facsimile forgery of
> small books possessing a high commercial value. . . . Bad forgeries
> of this kind can be detected by the tendency of all photographic
> processes of reproduction to thicken letters and exaggerate every
> kind of defect, but the best of these imitations when printed on
> old paper require a specific knowledge of the originals and often
> cause great trouble. The type-facsimile forgeries are mostly of
> short pieces by Tennyson, George Eliot and A. C. Swinburne,
> printed (or supposed to have been printed—for it is doubtful if
> any of these "forgeries" ever had originals) for circulation among
> friends. These trifles should never be purchased without a written
> guarantee.

There is of course no such imposture in the Clarendon facsimile. Yet Lee's collotype facsimile constitutes a strange boundary creature, a manufactured rarity, neither old nor new. Is it live or is it Memorex?

The new reproductive technologies were crucial, of course, to the New Bibliography. Photography had played an essential role in identifying the types and ornaments of the Pavier quartos. The photograph and collotype not only satisfied an expanded bibliophile market, they also made possible what the type facsimiles of the old bibliophile author-societies could not: they fostered a cohort of far-flung academic investigators engaged in systematic typographic research and exhaustive investigation of press variants. But as Pollard's article on "Bibliography and Bibliology" suggests—and as the article on "Copyright" cited earlier had suggested—the new technology also constituted an assault on authorship as a stabilizing market force. Once again we confront the complex relation between bibliography and the rare-book market.

I have already suggested some aspects of this relation: widening interest in historical bibliography was stimulated by a rare-book market quickened and shaped by single-author enumerative bibliographies. The immediate effect of such enumerative bibliographies was to foster a taste, by which I mean a market, for books in "original condition." If Buxton Forman's *Shelley Library* (1886) is the landmark single-author bibliography, the new market emphasis on "original condition" was especially encouraged in the bibliographies of modern Victorians produced by T. J. Wise. Book collectors will recognize these names as, perhaps, literary historians will not: Forman and Wise were two of the greatest forgers of all time. What they did was to select individual pieces of poetry or prose from published volumes by the Brownings, Dickens, Eliot, Rossetti, Thackeray, Arnold, Tennyson, Stevenson, Morris, Ruskin, Kipling, and Swinburne, print them as pamphlets, and thus create a first edition.[25] Trained bibliographers, they stayed away from watermarked paper, invented plausible imprints (or omitted them), and imitated the layout of books of the imputed dates. Wise and Forman would then authenticate the pamphlets by describing them in the single-author bibliographies in which they specialized, often with remarks about their interesting provenance and great rarity and with suggestions of appropriate sale prices. The whole episode, with its alliance of scholarship and price-fixing, bibliophilia and bibliography, reached a wonderful conclusion when Wise began to write a column on modern collecting for *The Bookman* in 1893. Or perhaps the crowning glory was when he took over the presidency of the Bibliographical Society in 1922. At any rate, suspicions of some of these pamphlets began to be raised around 1898, and although Wise and Forman had covered their tracks, they did stop the manufacture of these small books before the century ended, at which point Wise began to amuse himself by stealing pages from Restoration plays in the British Museum—about two hundred in all—in order to "perfect" copies of his own. It wasn't until 1903, the year when Lee's collotype came under review from Pollard and Greg, that the two bibliographers managed persuasively to discredit two of the Ruskin forgeries by a collation that proved that these Buxton-Wise "originals" had been set up from late editions.

Much later, in 1934, John Carter and Graham Pollard would multiply the bibliographic tests available to discredit the forgeries—type identification, research into the distribution of copies—precisely the tests that Pollard and Greg had applied in 1907 to the Pavier quartos. Greg had clinched his case with a study of the Pavier watermarks, as Carter and Pollard would clinch theirs with a chemical analysis of the paper used in the Wise-Forman forgeries. What I mean to suggest is that in both instances bibliography was inventing new tests, new ways of mapping the bibliographic past, that scholarship advanced by policing a market in which both authorship and property, as they were casually understood, had been scandalized.[26] Of course this could be reframed from a different perspective: it would be equally fair to say that a forgery is simply bibliography's way of producing a New Bibliography. In each instance the page was held up to the light in such a way that the investigator was relieved of the seductive distractions of the printed word itself. Authorship could only be enforced by looking past its *literal* traces.

None of this *quite* reflects on Lee, yet the first suspicions of the Wise-Forman forgeries may help explain why Pollard responded to Lee's facsimile with an animus that would never leave him. His encyclopedia article suggests the connoisseur's proud zeal for the authentic, but even that seems hardly to justify the strength and persistence of Pollard's disapproval. There is no intent to deceive in Lee's *facsimile:* such intention he exported to a distant and piratical past. But Pollard believed that such a disseminated past was itself an imposture, an intolerable fiction. And Lee's collotype was an accessory after the fact: like the photolithographic facsimiles of his great predecessor, Collier, Lee's collotype was being used, as it were, to authenticate his bibliography—a photograph that generates the truth of its caption.

My meditation on origins might end here, though I think it appropriate to measure just how far the reaction against Lee carried bibliography, and how its reactive energy was deflected toward new intellectual production. In the opening of his *magnum opus* on the presswork of the First Folio, Charlton Hinman shrewdly characterized his great predecessor—"Greg's primary concern, in *The Shakespeare First Folio* as in earlier works, is with copy"—and he thus summarizes the retrospective bibliographic calculus of the New Bibliography.[27] The essential preoccupation of both Greg and McKerrow, even when the task at hand is the preparation of a serviceable edition, is with printer's copy; but this retrospection, this seeing back through the printed text, hardly stops with the assessment of copy. What Greg claims as his goal, in the prolegomena to *The Editorial Problem in Shakespeare,* is "to present the text . . . in the form in which we may suppose that it would have stood in a fair copy, made by the author himself, of the work as he finally intended it" (x). But if this sounds like a Pollardian calculus, it is allowed to veer off toward Lee's disseminative textuality: "In the case of Shakespeare—and the same applies to the Elizabethan drama generally—we cannot hope to achieve a certainly correct text, not so much on account of the uncertainties of transmission— though they are sometimes serious—as because the author may never have produced a definitive text for us to recover" (ix). Things fall apart. Of course, textuality is still to be regulated by an originative personhood, the same foundational person who, since 1911, had stood at the origin of copyright, though in Greg's account a variable person yields a variant text. Hinman is only a step away, accounting for textual variants by distinguishing individual compositors. But not to designate the compositor nor describe his habits of mind, not to name and characterize the authorial mood, that would be to consign the text to the bottom of Lee's monstrous world: it would be decades before bibliography would stray so far westward again.[28]

CHAPTER ONE

1. William Briggs, *The Law of International Copyright* (London: Stevens and Hayes, 1906), 234–42, 264–72, and 435–65; and see also Victor Bonham-Carter, *Authors By Profession* vol. 1 (Los Altos: William Kaufman, 1978), 215–16.

An earlier version of these pages on the New Bibliography appeared in "Authentic Reproductions: The Material Origins of the New Bibliography," in *Textual Formations and Reformations,* ed. Laurie E. Maguire and Thomas L. Berger (Newark: University of Delaware Press, 1998), 23–26.

2. W. R. Cornish, *Intellectual Property: Patents, Copyright, Trade Marks, and Allied Rights,* 3rd edition (London: Sweet and Maxwell, 1981), 301–2. American protectionism was one of the most important stimuli to the Berne Convention, the European agreement constituting a closing of ranks. The enduring tensions produced by nineteenth-century American copyright may be gauged from Frank MacKinnon's wonderfully revealing remark in his appendix, "Notes on the History of English Copyright," for the *Oxford Companion to English Literature,* 2nd ed. (compiled and edited by Paul Harvey, Oxford: Oxford University Press, 1937], 884): "In 1885, the Berne Convention providing for a uniform international system was arranged, and this was given effect to by the Act of 1886. Most States with any pretensions to civilization and culture became parties to the Convention, but the United States (with whom no arrangement under the Act of 1844 had been possible) did not."

3. *The Encyclopaedia Brittanica,* 11th ed., 29 vols. (Cambridge: Cambridge University Press, 1910–11), 7:127a, s.v. "Copyright."

4. Direct authorial access to the Register was mandated in the eighteenth century, for which, see pp. 218–19, below.

5. The statutory nature of this modern form of copyright is itself remarkable. The 1911 act completes a legislative progress that had been initiated in 1709 with the promulgation of the Statute of Anne, the first English copyright statute. The Statute of Anne was by no means clear, but in the course of the eighteenth century litigation conferred upon it the significance of having radically abridged common law copyright, a common law right that it conceived of retrospectively as a perpetual authorial copyright. One of the few vestiges of this common law copyright that "survived" the Statute of Anne

was authorial property in unpublished manuscripts, a property that the Copyright Act of 1911 eliminated, reconstituting it as a statutory right.

6. For a description of the Copyright Act of 1911 that foregrounds its simplicity, see W. R. Cornish, *Intellectual Property* (London: Sweet and Maxwell, 1981), 301–2.

7. *Encyclopaedia Brittanica*, "Copyright," 7:129a.

8. For new forms of unfair competition, specifically the use of false allegations in comparative advertising, see Cornish, *Intellectual Property*, 9–11. The pressures on the patent system were not exactly new, though they took new forms. The Patent Law Amendment Act of 1852 had rationalized the British patent system, with the result that patent applications immediately multiplied. A boon for industry, the surge in patenting activity brought with it a rash of unscrupulous application. By 1883, a new patent office was put in place in hopes of subjecting patent applications to more careful formal scrutiny, though the office was not charged to undertake systematic search of prior patents. In 1901 it was demonstrated that at least 40 percent of all new patents duplicated inventions already under patent protection, so that, beginning in 1905, the office undertook to screen all applications specifically for novelty: thus the beginning of this century saw a considerable expansion of nonjudicial regulation of intellectual property. For more on the evolution of the Patent Office in the aftermath of the Great Exhibition of 1851, see Cornish, 94–97.

9. The problem of photography had been addressed as early as the Fine Arts Copyright Act of 1862, but the solution cobbled together there was so obviously flawed that the original promoters of the act made an effort to stop its passage. Photography remained something of a legal scandal well into this century: the "Copyright" article in the 1910–11 *Encyclopedia Brittanica,* cited above, states flatly that "the great obstacle in the way of securing a really good Artistic Bill has been the introduction into it of photography" (127b). But musical copyright was also an obvious problem. The Copyright Act of 1911 established the principles for the formation of the Performance Right Society in 1914, by which Britain imitated French, Italian, and Spanish arrangements for the enforcement of performance rights.

10. *White-Smith Music Publishing Publishing Co. v. Apollo Co.,* 209 U.S. 1, cited in Lyman Ray Patterson, *Copyright in Historical Perspective* (Nashville: Vanderbilt University Press, 1968), 214.

11. And the Malone Society was founded in 1906, largely at the instigation of the then secretary of the Bibliographical Society, A. W. Pollard. The history of this instauration in bibliography is set forth in F. P. Wilson, *Shakespeare and the New Bibliography,* Helen Gardner, ed. (Oxford: Clarendon, 1970). This expands his very long essay of the same title prepared for the 1942 Jubilee celebration of the Bibliographical Society and published in *The Bibliographical Society, 1892–1942: Studies in Retrospect* (London: Bibliographical Society, 1945), 76–135.

12. *The Library,* 2nd ser., 4 (1903): 267.

13. In Pollard's address to the Bibliographical Society on "Our Twenty-First Birthday" (in 1913), he lays out the New Bibliographic program for historicizing the book: "Between us and the author of any old book stand scribes or printers, publishers, and even binders, and until we have eliminated the errors due to these we cannot reach

the true text in which the author has expressed his thought. Now and again we may eliminate these errors by study only of the book itself with which we are concerned, but more often it needs a general knowledge of the ways of the scribes or printers, or publishers or binders of the day to enable us to see what has been done wrongly, and the accumulation of knowledge as to these ways is one important branch of Bibliography." *Transactions of the Bibliographical Society* 13 (1916): 25.

14. The list of basic texts in English bibliography and in the history of literary culture from these years is remarkable: Duff's *Century of the English Book Trade* (1905), Plomer's *Dictionary of Book Sellers and Printers, 1641–1667* (1907); Greg's "On Certain False Dates in Shakespearian Quartos" (1908) and his edition of *Sir Thomas More* (1911); McKerrow's *Dictionary of Printers and Book sellers, 1557–1640* (1910) and *Printers and Publishers Devices* (1913); Simpson's *Shakespearian Punctuation* (1911); Gildersleeve's *Government Regulation of Elizabethan Drama* (1908); Sheavyn's *The Literary Profession in the Elizabethan Age* (1909).

15. These lectures were published the next year under the now famous title, *Shakespeare's Fight with the Pirates and the Problems of the Transmission of His Text.* The revised second edition of 1920 (Cambridge: Cambridge University Press) contains a new introduction in which Pollard describes his and Dover Wilson's work of those years on the various Shakespeare texts as part of a research project experienced as novel and potent: "what remains to be done is far more important than the little which has so far been accomplished" (xxvi).

16. "The Regulation of the Book-Trade in the Sixteenth Century," *The Library*, 3rd ser., 7 (1916): 18.

17. Ibid., 22–24.

18. "Ad Imprimendum Solum," *Modern Language Notes* 34 (1919) 98. Albright based her argument on a published transcript of a draft of the proclamation, a transcript in which additions to the first draft of the proclamation are marked; she was concerned to show how the additions reveal Henry's desire to confer special precision on precisely the disputed terms. In a paper delivered in December 1918, A. W. Reed had distinguished several layers of revision by an analysis of two draft versions of the proclamation (one of them twice amended). "The Regulation of the Book Trade Before the Proclamation of 1538," *Transactions of the Bibliographical Society* 15 (1917–19): 157–84 (he expands his analysis of the proclamation in his *Early Tudor Drama* [London: Methuen, 1926], 181–84).

19. Albright, "Ad Imprimendum Solum," 100–101.

20. Pollard's response to Albright: "Ad Imprimendum Solum," *The Library*, 3rd ser., 10 (1919): 57–63 (the citation is from p. 59); Albright's counterresponse: "*Ad Imprimendum Solum* Once More," *MLN* 38 (1923): 129–40 (she is far more gracious in acknowledging their substantial agreement than is Pollard; see her p. 130); Greg's reflection on the problem: "Ad Imprimendum Solum," *The Library*, 5th ser., 9 (1954): 242–47 (and he summarizes his position in *Some Aspects and Problems of London Publishing Between 1550 and 1650* [Oxford: Clarendon, 1956], pp. 2 and 65).

21. It is worth pointing out here that although Reed claimed that his analysis of

the various draft versions of the proclamation "confirm Mr. Pollard's reading of the king's phrase in a definite manner" ("Regulation of the Book Trade," 178), it is in fact the case that he was articulating with precision the position that Albright would take a few months later in ostensible opposition to Pollard's (see Reed, p. 179). Pollard seems to have suspected that Albright had simply *misunderstood* his argument ("Ad Imprimendum Solum" [1919]: 63; and see his more cautious and labored discussion in the revised second edition of *Shakespeare's Fight with the Pirates,* pp. 5–7).

22. Pollard, *Shakespeare's Fight with the Pirates,* xxi.

23. It must be admitted that Foucault is anticipated in important ways here by Leo Strauss; see his *Persecution and the Art of Writing* (Glencoe, Ill.: Free Press, 1952). Annabel Patterson has recently subjected the Straussian approach to a sustained historical test; see her fine *Censorship and Interpretation: The Conditions of Writing and Reading in Early Modern England* (Madison: University of Wisconsin Press, 1984).

24. Foucault, "What Is an Author?" *Textual Strategies,* ed. Josue V. Harari (Ithaca: Cornell University Press, 1979), 158–59.

25. Ibid., 148.

26. Ibid.

27. I have used "ideology" and "ideological"—and shall, in the rest of this book, continue to use them—in a restricted sense. Unless otherwise qualified, my use of "ideology" may be taken as a reference to systems of value and belief, systems that, while largely sustained by the "normal" functioning of social institutions, are also accessible to deliberate political manipulation. Such systems perform the work of legitimating or naturalizing the interests of particular groups. This use of the term brackets such larger meanings as are associated with the work of Louis Althusser, for whom "ideology" performs the immense work of interpellating the subject as such; he uses the term in the plural, in phrases like "particular ideologies" to convey the specific sense to which my use of the term will characteristically point (see his "Ideology and Ideological State Apparatuses," *Lenin and Philosophy* [London: New Left Books, 1971], 121–73; as well as the very useful critique and gloss by Terry E. Boswell, Edgar V. Kiser, and Kathryn A. Baker, "Recent Developments in Marxist Theories of Ideology," *Insurgent Socialist* 13 [1986]: 5–22]). I will occasionally invoke such *structural* meanings in what follows, in which case the terms will be specifically qualified. It may be noted that my use of the term also leaves aside the important debate within Marxism concerning the cognitive status of ideology. As I use the term, ideology may be thought of as making possible the misrecognition of social relations, without itself necessarily functioning as the guarantor of misrecognition.

28. This discovery may be taken as part of a disciplined extension of Sartre's quest, monumentalized in *In Search of a Method,* to describe the mechanisms by which the "totality" of the capitalist mode of production is mediated to isolated individual actions and agents.

29. I make the qualification because Foucault himself seeks it: "I shall not offer here a sociohistorical analysis of the author's persona. Certainly it would be worth examining how the author became individualized in a culture like ours, what status he has been given, at what moment studies of authenticity and attribution began, in what kind of system of valorization the author was involved, at what point we began to

recount the lives of authors rather than of heroes, and how this fundamental category of 'the-man-and-his-work criticism' began" ("What Is an Author?" 141). Certainly; but Foucault's casual efforts at such particular examinations are very disappointing. The impressive sentence "Once a system of ownership for texts came into being, once strict rules concerning author's rights, author-publisher relations, rights of reproduction, and related matters were enacted—at the end of the eighteenth century and the beginning of the nineteenth century—the possibility of transgression attached to the act of writing took on, more and more, the form of an imperative peculiar to literature" is misleading, based as it is on false premises concerning the legal and commercial history of authorship.

30. From *The Book of Laughter and Forgetting*, glossed in *NY Times Book Review*, 6 March 1988, and quoted in Jane Marcus, "The Asylums of Antaeus: Women, War, and Madness—Is There a Feminist Fetishism?" in H. Aram Veeser, ed. *The New Historicism* (London: Routledge, 1988), 133.

31. *Parliamentary History*, 36 vols. (London: Longman, 1806–20), vol. 17 (1774), col. 954.

32. My account of *Donaldson v. Becket* is based on *Parliamentary History*, vol. 17 (1774), cols. 953–1003; and on the interpretations offered in MacKinnon, "Notes," 882; Cornish, *Intellectual Property*, 298–99; L. R. Patterson, *Copyright*, 172–78; P. S. Atiyah, *The Rise and Fall of Freedom of Contract* (Oxford: Clarendon, 1979), 108–109; and Ian Parsons, "Copyright and Society," *Essays in the History of Publishing*, ed. Asa Briggs (London: Longman, 1974), 38–40.

33. Legal historians are accustomed to reading and writing "The Statute of Anne (1709)," 1709 being the old-style date; I have given dates in new style throughout this book.

34. *Parliamentary History*, vol. 17, col. 954. When the case finally came to a decision, the second of the eleven judges, Justice Nares, "began by observing that the historical nature of the case had been so learnedly and fully agitated in the hearing of the House that he should wave entering into it" (col. 975). And Justice Aston, who spoke sixth, finally got fed up: "It was not necessary, he observed, for any man to advert either to the Grecians or Romans to discover the principles of the common law of England. Every country had some certain general rules which governed its law: that our common law had its foundation in private justice, moral fitness, and public convenience" (col. 980).

35. In 1693, a minority of the House of Lords sought to block a renewal of the Charles II Licensing Act on the grounds that it "subjects all learning and true information to the arbitrary will and pleasure of a mercenary and perhaps ignorant licenser; destroys the property of authors in their copies; and sets up many monopolies." *Journals of the House of Lords*, 8 March 1693; cited in William Holdsworth, *A History of English Law*, 12 vols. (London: Methuen, 1909–38), 6:375n. It is true, however, that *various* objections to the regulatory scaffolding in and around the book trade were expressed; see the *H. C. Journals, 1660–1745*, 11:305–306. And see John Feather, "From Censorship to Copyright: Aspects of the Government's Role in the English Book Trade, 1695–1775," in *Books and Society in History: Papers of the Association of College and Research Libraries Rare Books and Manuscripts Preconference*, ed. Kenneth E. Carpenter (New York: R. R. Bowker, 1983), whose arguments about the

political context of these regulatory developments I take up at the opening of my fourth chapter.

36. *H. C. Journals,* 15:313.

37. The full text of the statute is given in Harry Ransom, *The First Copyright Statute: An Essay on An Act for the Encouragement of Learning, 1710* (Austin: University of Texas Press, 1956),

38. *Parliamentary History,* vol. 17, col. 954.

39. "Sir John [Dalrymple] . . . made a variety of miscellaneous observations rather foreign to the point, but introduced seemingly to level a stroke of sarcastic humor," *Parliamentary History,* vol. 17, col. 961.

40. Ibid., col. 963.

41. P. S. Atiyah, *The Rise and Fall of Freedom of Contract,* 109.

42. *Parliamentary History,* vol. 17, col. 963.

43. *Burrow's Reports, King's Bench,* 4:2338–40, 98 E. R. 220–21.

44. *Parliamentary History,* vol. 17, col. 963.

45. Ibid., cols. 970–71.

46. Eight of the justices formally found in the affirmative in answer to the first question concerning the existence of common law authorial property—though the eighth, Chief Justice De Grey, exclusively offered arguments against the existence of such property, so that his formal affirmation may be a mistake; certainly he gave a negative answer to the fourth question. There are other examples of apparent inconsistency in the records.

Patterson (*Copyright in Historical Perspective*) gives what are surely inaccurate tallies of the votes taken in the House. He counts ten affirmative answers to the first question, whereas I find only eight, and seven if one discounts the vote of Chief Justice DeGrey. He gives a vote of seven nays in response to the second question, which seems similarly misleading, though allowances must be made for the ambiguity of the phrasing of the question and the eccentricity of the reporting. For those who held that no common law authorial property rights existed prior to publication (Eyre, Perrot, Adams, and perhaps De Grey), question two was mooted; *all* those who held for the existence of prepublication copyright argued that publication did not abridge those rights, although— as mentioned above—Aston and Smythe are reported as giving opinions "in favour of" the second question. The majority opinion that there *had* been a common law copyright prior to the Statute of Anne was sustained in subsequent legal disputes; the vestiges of that common law copyright had practical effects until the Copyright Act of 1911 completed the statutory erasure of common law initiated by the Statute of Anne (see n. 5 above).

47. Justice Adams is precisian: I count his vote on questions three and five as affirmative, as did the court, though he precisely indicates nays in both cases, on the grounds that the Statute of Anne can hardly abridge what never existed.

48. *Parliamentary History,* vol. 17, col. 962.

49. Atiyah goes on to explain that, by this decision, property rights are cast as "artificial creations of law and not themselves physical things which can be picked up in the state of nature." *The Rise and Fall of Freedom of Contract,* 109.

50. *Parliamentary History,* vol. 17, col. 962.

51. Ibid., cols. 971–72.

52. *New York Times,* 20 October 1988, p. 1.

53. *Parliamentary History,* vol. 17, col. 959.

54. Ibid.

55. Ibid.

56. *Parliamentary History,* vol. 17, cols. 960–61. This quite radical historiography is seized upon in the arguments of Justices Eyre and Adams on behalf of the minority opinion against the existence of common law copyright prior to the Statute of Anne.

57. The centrality of this opposition—its foundational status for the case of the appellants—is clearly marked in the opinion of the lord chief justice: referring to one of the important precedents for *Donaldson v. Becket, Basket v. University of Cambridge,* De Grey recalls how "my late hon. and learned friend, Mr. Yorke, who argued that case, endeavoured to shew, that his client's right might arise from the power of the crown; and, to illustrate his argument, said, it might perhaps be 'property founded on prerogative,'— a language, however allowable for counsel, not very admissible by, or intelligible to, a judge." *Parliamentary History,* vol. 17, col. 989. Prerogative and property are safely marked off as exclusive categories.

58. *Parliamentary History,* vol. 17, col. 966. And cf. Justice Willes's discussion of contradictions within the Statute of Anne: "It conveyed to his mind no idea of the legislature entertaining an opinion that, at the time of passing it, there was no common law right; the word 'vesting' appearing in the title had given rise to such an idea, but the preamble contradicted it in the fullest manner; the words of it were, 'Whereas certain printers and booksellers have taken the liberty of printing and reprinting, &c. &c.;' the phraseology of this sentence plainly proved that a known right previous to that statute existed; the legislature would not have termed the exercise of what was common to all, 'taking a liberty,' had they not understood that a right in perpetuity existed at common law." *Parliamentary History,* vol. 17, cols. 979–80. Justice Willes's assessment is simply that "it was . . . an Act very inaccurately penned" (col. 979); more likely it accurately reflects a specific conceptual confusion.

59. *Parliamentary History,* vol. 17, col. 982; and cf. col. 988, where Lord Chief Justice De Grey insists that attention must remain fixed on the *judicial* record.

60. Indeed, the appellants' attempt to cancel the claims of legal history tends toward a dismissal of the past per se, hence the strategic cast of Dalrymple's humor. His description of the Stationers' Company may be instanced: "There were many curious regulations, sir John said, subsisting in this Company; he had read them all, and found the following three. '1. That no two persons should speak at once. 2. That every member should speak with his hat off. 3. That a member should speak seriously.' " *Parliamentary History,* vol. 17, col. 958.

61. *Parliamentary History,* vol. 17, col. 992.

62. McLuhan, *The Gutenburg Galaxy: The Making of Typographical Man* (Toronto: University of Toronto Press, 1962); Ong, *The Presence of the Word* (New Haven: Yale University Press, 1967) (and see also his *Orality and Literacy: The Technologizing of the Word* [London: Methuen, 1982]); Eisenstein, *The Printing Press as*

an Agent of Change: Communications and Cultural Transformations in Early Modern Europe, 2 vols. (Cambridge: Cambridge University Press, 1979); Anderson, Imagined Communities: Reflections on the Origin and Spread of Nationalism (London: Verso, 1983); and Adrian Johns, The Nature of the Book: Print and Knowledge in the Making (Chicago: University of Chicago Press, 1998).

63. S. H. Steinberg's Five Hundred Years of Printing (London: Penguin, 1955) remains an accessible introductory survey; Lucien Febvre and Henri-Jean Martin, L'apparition du livre (Paris: Michel, 1958), offers details of the development of production techniques and of markets for printed books. Johns's superb critique of Eisenstein in The Nature of the Book ultimately ratifies the fundamental importance and utility of her "institutional" approach.

64. Hans R. Jauss, Toward an Aesthetic of Reception, trans. Timothy Bahti (Minneapolis: University of Minnesota Press, 1982); and Williams, The Sociology of Culture. And see also Arthur F. Marotti, Manuscript, Print, and the English Renaissance Lyric (Ithaca: Cornell University Press, 1995); Natalie Z. Davis, "Printing and the People," Society and Culture in Early Modern France (Stanford: Stanford University Press, 1975); Franco Moretti, Signs Taken for Wonders, trans. Susan Fischer, David Forgacs, and David Miller (London: Verso, 1983); Janice A. Radway, A Feeling for Books: The Book-of-the-Month Club, Literary Taste, and Middle-Class Desire (Chapel Hill: University of North Carolina Press, 1997); Roger Chartier, The Cultural Uses of Print in Early Modern France (Princeton: Princeton University Press, 1987); Phillipe Desan, Literature and Social Practice (Chicago: University of Chicago Press, 1989); Margaret Spufford, Small Books and Pleasant Histories: Popular Fiction and Its Readership in Seventeenth-Century England, Past and Present Publications Series (Cambridge: University of Cambridge Press, 1985); and Alexandra Halasz, The Marketplace of Print: Pamphlets and the Public Sphere in Early Modern England, Cambridge Studies in Renaissance Literature and Culture, 17 (Cambridge: Cambridge University Press, 1997).

65. For the early modern period, basic information on the economic and social status of authorship may be gleaned from E. H. Miller, The Professional Writer in Elizabethan England: A Study of Non-Dramatic Literature (Cambridge, 1909); and G. E. Bentley, The Profession of the Dramatist in Shakespeare's Time (Princeton, 1971). Works aspiring to more generalized assertions about the cultural history of authorship are M. T. Jones-Davies, Victimes et rebelles: L'écrivain dans la société élisabethaine (Paris: Aubier Montaigne, 1980); Alain Viala, La naissance de l'écrivain, Le sens commun (Paris: Editions de minuit, 1985); and Raymond Williams, The Sociology of Culture.

66. For stringent and appreciative criticism of the New Bibliography, see D. F. McKenzie, "Printers of the Mind: Some Notes on Bibliographical Theories and Printing-House Practice," Studies in Bibliography 22 (1969): 1–75; McKenzie, The London Book Trade in the Later Seventeenth Century, The Sandars Lectures, 1976 (photocopied typescript); Paul Werstine, "McKerrow's 'Suggestion' and Twentieth-Century Shakespeare Textual Criticism," Renaissance Drama, n.s. 19 (1988): 149–73; and Laurie Maguire's deeply constructive critique, Shakespeare's Suspect Texts: The "Bad" Quartos and Their Contexts (Cambridge: Cambridge University Press, 1996).

67. Jonson and Possessive Authorship (Cambridge: Cambridge University Press, 2002).

68. For a comparable study of a slightly later figure, see Stephen B. Dobranski, *Milton, Authorship, and the Book Trade* (Cambridge: Cambridge University Press, 1999).

Chapter Two

1. For an account of the regulation of English book production before the 1570s, see chapters 3 and 4. The best introduction to the details of Wolfe's career may still be H. R. Hoppe, "John Wolfe, Printer and Publisher," *The Library*, 4th ser., 14 (1933): 241–88, though Hoppe is corrected in several crucial matters by Denis B. Woodfield, *Surreptitious Printing in England, 1550–1640* (New York: Bibliographical Society of New York, 1973), 5–18 and 24–33. A more detailed discussion of Wolfe's career as a printer is Clifford Chalmers Huffman, *Elizabethan Impressions: John Wolfe and His Press* (New York: AMS, 1988). See also Cyril Bathurst Judge, *Elizabethan Book Pirates* (Cambridge: Cambridge University Press, 1934); and my own "For a History of Intellectual Property: John Wolfe's Reformation," *English Literary Renaissance* 18 (winter 1988): 389–412, an earlier version of the following discussion.

2. W. W. Greg, "Samuel Harsnett and Hayward's *Henry IV*," *The Library*, 5th ser., 11 (1956): 1–10. For a particularly interesting account of the reverberations of the Hayward affair in contemporary literary culture, see G. B. Harrison, "Books and Readers, 1599–1603," *The Library*, 4th ser., 14 (1933): 10–16.

3. Of the substantial body of research on the regulation of the English book trade, the following may be recommended as the best introduction to both the facts and the persistent historiographic problems in the field: Alfred W. Pollard, "The Regulation of the Book Trade in the Sixteenth Century," and "*Ad Imprimendum Solum*"; W. W. Greg, "*Ad Imprimendum Solum*," and "Entrance, License, and Publication," *The Library*, 4th ser., 25 (1944): 1–22; Graham Pollard, "The Company of Stationers Before 1557," *The Library*, 4th ser., 18 (1937): 1–38, and "The Early Constitution of the Stationers' Company," *The Library*, 4th ser., 18 (1937), 235–60; Howard W. Winger, "Regulations Relating to the Book Trade in London from 1357 to 1586," *The Library Quarterly* 26 (1956): 157–95; and Cyprian Blagden, *The Stationers' Company: A History, 1403–1959* (London: Allen and Unwin, 1960). For a skeptical response to the historical orthodoxies accumulated in these books, and for the best short introduction to the booksellers' trade and the regulations that shaped it, see Peter W. M. Blayney, "The Publication of Playbooks," in *A New History of Early English Drama*, ed. John D. Cox and David Scott Kastan (New York: Columbia University Press, 1997), 383–422.

4. In *Burned Books*, 2 vols. (New York: Columbia University Press, 1932), Charles Ripley Gillett asserts that Henry made his first direct attempt to regulate the press in 1526, but the 1526 proclamation that Gillett attributes to Henry was in fact issued by the archbishop of Canterbury; *Burned Books*, 1:20. In "The Earliest Evidence for Ecclesiastical Censorship of Printed Books in England," *The Library*, 6th ser., 4 (1982): 135–41, John B. Gleason suggests that a system for scrutinizing religious books printed in England may have existed as early as the first decade of the sixteenth century. Colet seems to have given his approval for the printing of William de Melton's *Sermo Exhortatorius* sometime between 1507 and 1515; Gleason remarks that "the phrases used in Colet's 'decree' . . . suppose a settled machinery of censorship, or at least the

inauguration of one" (140) and supposes that the system was established to control the resurgence of Lollardry in the London area. The system, such as it was, seems to have been short-lived (Gleason, 141; Gleason is wrong, however, in saying that the Colet licensing is the only evidence for the existence of such a system, for Richard Fitz James gave similar approval to the publication of Symon's *Treatise* in 1514). For a careful account of the origins and practice of early Tudor censorship, see Cyndia Susan Clegg, *Press Censorship in Elizabethan England* (Cambridge: Cambridge University Press, 1997), 25–54. Her great contribution to the historiography of the English press has been to show how incoherent was the practice of Elizabethan censorship, how poorly the notion of hegemonic discursive control sorts with the factual record.

On ecclesiastical censorship in the 1520s, see A. W. Reed, "The Regulation of the Book Trade Before the Proclamation of 1538," *Transactions of the Bibliographical Society* 15 (1918): 157–184; D. M. Loades, "The Press Under the Early Tudors: A Study in Censorship and Sedition," *Transactions of the Cambridge Bibliographical Society* 4 (1964): 29–50; and Rudolph Hirsch, "Pre-Reformation Censorship of Printed Books," *The Library Chronicle* (University of Pennsylvania) 21 (1955): 100–105. Attempts to control heretical speech and writing can be traced in England to Ricardian efforts to suppress Lollardry during the 1380s; royal, episcopal, and parliamentary efforts to control Lollardry continue into the fifteenth century.

5. The texts of the two proclamations are given in Paul H. Hughes and James F. Larkin, *Tudor Royal Proclamations,* 3 vols. (New Haven: Yale University Press, 1964–69), *Volume 1: The Early Tudors,* Proclamations nos. 129 and 186; extracts of these proclamations are also given in *A Bibliography of Royal Proclamations of the Tudor and Stuart Sovereigns, 1485–1714,* ed. Robert Steele, 3 vols. (Oxford, 1910), 1: Proclamations nos. 122 and 176.

6. W. W. Greg, *Aspects and Problems,* 6–7; but cf. Winger, "Regulations Relating to the Book Trade," 177, who points out that in the 1540s death penalties were very seldom meted out to printers.

7. See A. W. Pollard, "The Regulation of the Book Trade in the Sixteenth Century"; M. A. Shaaber, "The Meaning of Imprint in Early English Printed Books," *The Library,* 4th ser., 24 (1943): 120–41, W. W. Greg, "Entrance, License, and Publication"; and Leo Kirschbaum, vigorously contesting Shaaber's analysis, "Author's Copyright in England Before 1640," *Papers of the Bibliographical Society of America* 40 (1946): 43–80.

8. In *Shakespeare and the Stationers* (Columbus: Ohio State University Press, 1955), 34–37, Kirschbaum offers a brief but useful survey of the various formulae used in the registers to record entrance and proposes that the various locutions suggest an intelligble drift in the meaning of entrance. See also Clegg, *Press Censorship,* 15–18.

9. On these matters, L. R. Patterson's *Copyright in Historical Perspective* (Nashville: Vanderbilt University Press, 1968) is particularly useful, though his narrative of the development of sixteenth-century regulatory mechanisms has some notable gaps. See also A. A. Renouard, *Traite des droits d'auteurs dans la litterature, les sciences, et les beaux-arts,* 2 vols. (Paris: J. Renouard, 1838); Henri Lemaitre, *Histoire du depot legal* (Paris: A. Picard et fils, 1910); Royce Frederick Whale, *Copyright: Evolution, Theory and Practice* (London: Longman, 1971). For a more general introduction to the jurisprudential issues of copyright, see Benjamin Kaplan, *An Unhurried View of Copyright* (New York: Columbia University Press, 1967).

10. A caveat is necessary at the outset. The records of the stationers and the literature of bibliographical history is rife with terminological confusion. I shall be distinguishing various forms of regulation, but the stationers and their historians often use the same terms to describe different regulatory structures and procedures. Such terms as "license" or "allowance" are used to imply the sanction of a censorious authority in some instances and, in others, the approval of the company of quasi monopoly rights in the production and marketing of a given book; see note 13 below. On the genetic relationship between these two forms of regulation, see chapter 4 following.

11. The first of the "tolerated" entries—they are usually entries for ballads— dates from May 1580. (This comes—not coincidentally—only a few months after the publication of Stubbs's *Gaping Gulf,* for which two stationers were convicted of slander and sentenced to lose their right hands; only one of the two was pardoned.) The remarkable entry "at peril" dates from November 1583, though an entry from 7 May 1582 shows a similar scruple: the latter reads, "*Edward white* Receaved of him for printinge a booke of phisike called *the pathwaie to health for the poore* Translated and gathered by PETER LEVENS And the said *Edward* hathe undertaken to beare and discharge all troubles that maie arise for the printinge thereof. . . . 12d" (Edward Arber, *A Transcript of the Registers of the Company of the Stationers of London, 1554–1640 A.D.,* 5 vols. [London and Birmingham, 1875–94],2:411).

12. "Every boke or thinge to be allowed by the stationers before yt be prynted" (Arber, *Transcript,* 1:350). The language of the register is, however, ambiguous, and this "allowance" may simply be that guild sanction, regulating competition, implied by entrance. At this time, the company was in the habit of fining members "for printing without license," and since such fines were levied in instances of publication of such innocuous books as the *A.B.C.,* it is quite possible that this violation did not involve the sorts of political or doctrinal indiscretion against which eccleciastical or Privy Council licensing was to protect. So the draft regulation requiring "allowance" is suggestive but inconclusive.

Though Elizabeth confirmed the Stationers' Charter on 10 November 1559, the company ordinances seem not to have been approved until 1562. Blagden, *The Stationers' Company,* 40–46.

13. Clegg alleges that entrance was always primarily a record of license, that its function as a means of regulating competition is ancillary, but cannot press her case because the Stationers' original charter no longer exists (14–17).

The entries begin a remarkable change in format in the so-called Register B, begun in 1576, one year into the tenure of Richard Collins as company clerk. Because there is a gap in the record of registrations for copy from July 1571 to July 1576, a full history of the forms of registration is impossible. Nonetheless, it is worth noting that beginning with the new register entrance usually includes the entering stationer, the book title, and the fee paid—as before—as well as a novel notation of the licensing authority, e.g., "aucthorized by the bisshop of LONDON," "lycenced unto him under the Bishop of LLONDON his hande," or "Lycenced unto him under the hand of the wardens," which latter suggests the assumption of responsibilities of ideological censorship by the company itself. The pre-1571 entry format persists on the first few pages of Register B, which suggests that the new format begins with the new register; but the new format replaces it so swiftly that one cannot say with security that it had not been employed, occasionally or even frequently, in the lost entrance records for the years 1571–76. There is simply insufficient documentation for positing, much less dating, a major shift in regulatory procedure during these years, though Greg observes, plausibly, that "after the transference of the book-entries from the Wardens' to the Clerk's Book in 1571 the financial aspect of the entries became subordinate to those of licence and ownership" (*Aspects and Problems*, 32).

Greg gives a helpful account of trends in company licensing in "Entrance, License, and Publication," 7–13; and see also Kirschbaum, *Shakespeare and the Stationers*, 33.

14. For an account of Venetian printing privileges see chapter 3 below. A truly critical account of the dissemination of this regulatory mechanism throughout Europe remains to be written. Relevant documents are collected in R. Fulin, "Documenti per servire alla storia della Tipografia Veneziana," *Archivio veneto* 23 (1882): 84–212; and useful observations may be found in Lemaitre, *Histoire du depot legal;* and G. F. Barwick, "Laws Regulating Printing and Publishing in Italy," *Transactions of the Bibliographical Society* 14 (1915–17): 311–23.

15. A list of privileges extant in 1582 may be found in Arber, *Transcript*, 1:114–16 and 144; a similar list may also be found at 2:775–76. The history of English industrial privilege is taken up in chapter 4.

16. The first entry in the surviving register to mention printing rights regulated by the company dates from the spring of 1556 or 1557. It suggests that these rights had already been regulated for an appreciable period, for they record a violation of recognized convention: "Yt is agreed for an offence Donne by master *wallye* for conselyng of the pryntynge of *a breafe Cronacle* contrary to our ordenances before he Ded presente the Copye to the wardyns" (Arber, *Transcript*, 1:45).

On the internal regulation of printing before 1557, see Graham Pollard, "The Company of Stationers before 1557" and "The Early Constitution of the Stationers' Company."

17. Those familiar with the work of Arber, Greg, both Pollards, and Blagden will recognize the discussion that follows as little more than an interpretive afterword to their accounts of this episode, my purpose being to suggest a fuller range of implication than has traditionally been claimed for the documentary record.

18. *Parliamentary History*, vol. 17 (1774), col. 959.

19. For more on Day's career, see C. L. Oastler, *John Day, The Elizabethan Printer,* Oxford Bibliographical Society Occasional Publications 10 (1975).

20. Day received his first grant of letters patent in September 1552. This grant covered the *Catechism*, but because it overlapped the patent of Reyner Wolfe (no relation to John Wolfe) in the Latin catechism, Day's patent was restricted in March of the following year to the *Catechism* in English. For more on the *A.B.C.*, see Oastler, *John Day;* and H. Anders, "The Elizabethan ABC with the Catechism," *The Library*, 4th ser., 16 (1936): 32–48.

21. Day was seizing a great occasion: Spufford reminds us that there was a literacy explosion at midcentury. *Small Books and Pleasant Histories,* 9.

22. On Wolfe's sojourn in Italy see Maria Grazia Bellorini, "Le pubblicazioni italiane dell'editore londinese John Wolfe (1580–1591)," *Pubbl. Faccolta Lingue*

Universita di Trieste (Sede di Udine, 1971), 17–65; as well as Hoppe, "John Wolfe," 243; and Woodfield, *Surreptitious Printing*, 6.

23. Woodfield, *Surreptitious Printing*, 5–18, 187–88.

24. On the contribution of the Frankfurt Fair to the clandestine book trade, see Paul F. Grendler, *The Roman Inquisition and the Venetian Press, 1540–1605* (Princeton: Princeton University Press, 1977).

25. It has been suggested that this was done simply because of the poor reputation of English printing, yet Wolfe sent other, more reputable Italian texts to the fair, works by Tasso, Pigasetta, della Porta, and Betti, and most of these are given *accurate* imprints.

26. Woodfield, *Surreptitious Printing*, 25–33.

27. Arber, *Transcript*, 2:780. Arber gathers most of the documents relevant to this uprising and to the legislative aftermath in 1:111, 114–16, and 144, and 2:751–812.

28. Ibid., 1:111. For evidence of earlier dissatisfaction among printers, specifically with the administration of the Company, see William Copland's prologue to Robert Copland's *Seven Sorowes That Women Have When Theyr Husbandes Be Deade* (written in 1530), cited in Percy Simpson, *Proofreading in the Sixteenth and Seventeenth Centuries* (London: Oxford University Press, 1935), 55.

29. Ibid.

30. This accusation first appears in the documentary record in Barker's report of December 1582, transcribed in Arber, *Transcript*, 1:144.

31. See Marjorie Plant, *The English Book Trade: An Economic History of the Making and Selling of Books* (New York: G. Allen and Unwin, 1939), 105.

32. Arber, *Transcript*, 2:780.

33. See the two documents reproduced in Arber, *Transcript*, 1:114–16 and 144 and 2:778–82: the former, Barker's December 1582 report, preserved among the Burghley papers; the latter, a supplication to the Privy Council written by Barker and Francis Coldocke, the other of the company wardens.

34. Seres's complaint is reproduced in Arber, *Transcript*, 2:771–73; this sentence appears on p. 772.

35. The full text of the complaint against Norton may be found in Arber, *Transcript*, 2:777–78. Note that Arber mistakenly believes that Norton the barrister and Norton the commissioner were two different men.

36. Arber, *Transcript*, 2:771.

37. Ibid., 2:781–82.

38. On the unruliness of printers as a group, see Rudolf Hirsch, *Printing, Selling, and Reading, 1450–1550* (Wiesbaden: Harrassowitz, 1974), 38f.

39. The report of the expanded commission, the recommendations from which evidentally carried the authority of the Privy Council, are reproduced in Greg's *Companion to Arber* (Oxford: Clarendon Press, 1967), as entry no. 104 (document 3, pp. 126–33); Arber reproduces a hastily written extract from this report, *Transcript*, 2:784–85. According to the fuller text in Greg, the Privy Council undertook "to be meanes that her majestie will not hereafter drawe into previlege after the presente previleges expired any generall title of bokes of any whole arte, nor any bokes extant in copie and

at libertie for others to printe before the previlege specially schole bookes except bokes perteining to her majesties service, and the office of her printer" (*Companion to Arber,* 129).

40. A list of the donated texts can be found in Arber, *Transcript,* 2:786–89.

41. Cyprian Blagden provides a good summary of the cumulative force of the regulatory responses to the rebellion; see *The Stationers' Company,* 71–74; and see also his "The English Stock of the Stationers' Company," *The Library,* 5th ser., 10 (1955): 170—72. A broad program for strengthening the company's regulatory powers is plainly embodied in the report of the expanded Norton-Hammond commission (for which, see the text cited in note above); the 1586 Star Chamber decree simply ratifies—and perhaps slightly elaborates—that program.

42. It should be noted that not all of these regulations immediately benefited the most powerful members of the company. The strictures on books left standing in type and the limitation on the size of editions were in fact established to protect journeymen; see Arber, *Transcript* 2:43–44 and 883.

43. By Blagden's tally, this lobbying "cost the Company the best part of £80," *The Stationers' Company,* 70.

44. Both Arber and Patterson give full texts of the 1586 Star Chamber decree: Arber, *Transcript,* 2:807–12; Patterson, *Copyright in Historical Perspective,* 235–42. For a more cautious estimation of the force of the decree, see Sheila Lambert, "State Control of the Press before 1640," *Censorship and the Control of Print in England and France, 1600–1910,* ed. Robin Myers and Michael Harris (Winchester: St. Paul's Bibliographies, 1992), 12–14.

45. The power to police the trade spelled out in the company charter of 1557 (see Arber, *Transcript* 1:xxxi) is reconfirmed; in 1586, the wardens are given the right not only to destroy unlawfully produced books and arrest offenders, but also to destroy presses and other instruments of book production.

46. His character was unchanged, of course, and his reputation was, in a sense, stable: the scourge of Marprelate publication, he is described in the epistle to *Oh Read Over D. John Bridges* as "John Woolfe alias Machivill, Beadle of the Stacioners" (Martin Marprelate, *The Epistle,* ed. Edward Arber [London: Arber, 1880], 22).

47. See Hoppe's account of Wolfe's later career in "John Wolfe, Printer and Publisher," 263–67. Hoppe notes that after 1593, the year in which Wolfe was appointed official printer to the City of London, he ceased printing altogether and became solely a publisher.

48. On the trend toward specialization in the book trade and the shift in power toward the booksellers, see Blagden, *The Stationers' Company,* 74 and 89–90; as well as Plant, *The English Book Trade,* 59–66; and George Unwin, *Industrial Organization in the Sixteenth and Seventeenth Centuries* (Oxford: Clarendon Press, 1904), 103.

49. On this large-scale shift, see *The Cambridge Economic History of Europe,* eds. M. M. Postan, E. E. Rich, and Edward Miller (Cambridge: Cambridge University Press, 1963), 3:195–221, and particularly 205; see also Douglass C. North and Robert Paul Thomas, *The Rise of the Western World: A New Economic History* (Cambridge: Cambridge University Press, 1973), 53–58 and 93–94.

50. It may be worth recalling here that most "new men" in the late medieval period

invested a third to a half of their new fortunes in land; Wolfe recapitalizes his industrial practices.

51. C. J. Sisson, "The Laws of Elizabethan Copyright: The Stationers' View," *The Library*, 5th ser., 15 (1960): 8–20.

52. For a similar instance in which the self-regulatory rights and expertise of the company was ratified, one which bears on later stages of the argument of this chapter, see the handling of Ponsonby's suit against infringers of his rights in Sidney's *Arcadia*, recorded in *Records of the Court of the Stationers' Company, 1576 to 1602—From Register B*, eds. W. W. Greg and E. Boswell (London: The Bibliographical Society, 1930), 20 November 1600 (p. 80). Ponsonby had begun his complaint as a suit before Star Chamber, which turned it back to the Master of Requests and Recorder of London, who in turn returned it to the Stationers' Company. Their jurisdiction was secure.

53. Greg gives an average, for the years 1557–71, of 114 entrances a year, with minimal fluctuation from year to year; in the years from 1576 to 1640, he figures 147 a year, but here the fluctuations are telling. He notes a sharp fall in registration during the early 1580s followed by a flurry of entrance in the immediate aftermath of the 1586 decrees. He also discerns a striking rise in the proportion of entered texts that were also licensed; see "Entrance, License, and Publication," 1–22 (particularly 1–4). And see Kirschbaum's useful discussion of the shifts in conventions of entrance in *Shakespeare and the Stationers*, 56–74.

54. This includes a furious registration of ballads during August 1586. Arber, *Transcript*, 2:208–10.

55. See George Unwin, *The Gilds and Companies of London*, 3rd ed. (London: G. Allen and Unwin, 1938), 169–71 and 235–42.

56. For a richly theorized discussion of Wolfe's place in the history of the commodification of discourse, see Alexandra Halasz, *The Marketplace of Print*, 28–33. Halasz's work is especially salutary in its recognition of the founding commercial substrate of the public sphere and of the proprietary individual who participates in it, a stratum misconstrued in Habermasian theory as a belated force that compromises the discursive freedoms of that sphere (163–66).

57. See W. A. Copinger and F. E. Skone James, *Copinger and Skone James On Copyright*, 11th ed. (London: Sweet and Maxwell, 1971), pars. 24–26. For the specific innovations of the Licensing Act of 1643, see Patterson, *Copyright in Historical Perspective*, 130—34.

58. C. H. Firth and R. S. Rait, *Acts and Ordinances of the Interregnum, 1642–1660*, 3 vols. (London: H. M. Stationery Office, 1911), 1:185. Patterson construes the act as protecting only stationers, with "owners" *not* entailing authors; his interpretation is almost certainly correct. The context addresses various forms of infringement on the prerogatives of individual stationers and on the stationers as a corporation; the ordinance seems here to designate license and entry as a sign of stationers' ownership of copy. Copinger insists (*On Copyright*, 25–26) that the protections of the act—as well as those modeled on it, the ordinances of 1647, 1649, and 1652—were not limited to stationers, though it is implicit in his discussion that the assertion of common law authorial property is even more firmly asserted in the Licensing Act of 1662 (13 & 14 Car. 2, c. 33).

59. Ong summarizes the tradition of scholarship that he, Lord, Parry, and Havelock instigated in his *Orality and Literacy,* which can be recommended for its useful bibliography; still, his earlier *Presence of the Word: Some Prolegomena for Cultural and Religious History* (New Haven, 1967) sustains a more finely nuanced argument. Eisenstein brings more historiographic rigor to her treatment of *The Printing Press as an Agent of Change.*

60. For a critique of the technologism that hovers over Ong's and Eisenstein's analyses—and that frequently mars McLuhan's—see Michael Warner, *The Letters of the Republic: Publication and the Public Sphere in Eighteenth-century America* (Cambridge: Harvard University Press, 1990), 1–19.

61. For an introduction to the history of Elizabethan book piracy, consult, in addition to Woodfield, *Surreptitious Printing;* and Judge, *Elizabethan Book Pirates;* William A. Jackson, "Counterfeit Printing in Jacobean Times," *The Library,* 4th ser., 15 (1934): 364–76; Francis R. Johnson, "Printers' 'Copy Books' and the Black Market in the Elizabethan Book Trade," *The Library,* 5th ser., 1 (1947): 97–105; and C. J. Sisson, "The Laws of Elizabethan Copyright: The Stationers' View."

62. The original registrant could expect to receive some consideration in such reprintings; it was up to the company master and ardens to determine the level of compensation. See Kirschbaum, *Shakespeare and the Stationers,* 365.

63. *Elizabethan and Jacobean Quartos,* ed. G. B. Harrison (New York: Barnes and Noble, 1966), 6–7.

64. For more on this dispute, see Cyprian Blagden, "The English Stock of the Stationers' Company," 163–85. The article has more general interest, as it narrates a crucial moment in the economic history of the Stationers' Company, involving the erosion of traditional social and economic structures within the guild. Blagden does not note that this dispute may have been a *direct* result of the decrees of the investigating commissioners enacted in the aftermath of the rebellion: among the "helpes" granted in the settlement arranged by the Norton-Hammond commission to "those that have presses and complaine against the patenties" was that "they may have from the companie suche copies they will requier which upon Deathe of any or occurence of yeres fall voyde" (Arber *Transcript,* 2:784). The emphasis on the terminability of privilege and the absence of provision for the inheritance of privilege may have provoked the sudden scramble for books from Day's privilege.

65. Ponsonby offered such defense, however fishy the claim may seem. In his response to Richard Day's bill of complaint, Ponsonby admits to having sold an unspecified number of *A.B.C.'s,* "which bokes of whose pryntynge they were he then knewe not, nor sithence but by report" (Judge, *Elizabethan Book-Pirates,* 152).

66. *Records of the Court of the Stationers' Company,* 20.

67. Arber, *Transcript,* 2:458.

68. The earnest of consumer protection and the maintenance of trade secrecy secured to guilds extremely valuable privileges: industrial monopolies and rights to extensive exploitation of apprentices. As traditions of secrecy, the status of industry as "mystery," were eroded in the early modern period—notably under the influence of print dissemination—the rights of guilds came to rest more and more on the (increasingly

dubious) claim of consumer protection. See T. H. Marshall, "Capitalism and the Decline of the English Gilds," *Cambridge Historical Journal* 3 (1929–31): 23–33; and George Unwin, *Industrial Organization in the Sixteenth and Seventeenth Centuries.*

69. Coldock was himself a somewhat mobile participant in the conflicts of these years. He had been one of the complainants against privilege in the late seventies before becoming company warden in July 1580. An entry in the Stationers' Register for the 1583–84 fiscal year suggests that Coldock had purchased confiscated books pirated by Wolfe from the company, so that he is in many ways one of the most direct beneficiaries of the unrest. Arber, *Transcript,* 1:503.

70. Cited in Sir Philip Sidney, *The Countess of Pembroke's Arcadia,* ed. J. Robertson (Oxford: Clarendon Press, 1973), xl; see the account of these negotiations in H. R. Woudhuysen, *Sir Philip Sidney and the Circulation of Manuscripts, 1558–1640* (Oxford: Oxford University Press, 1996), 224–27.

71. Michael Brennan, "William Ponsonby: Elizabethan Stationer," *AEB* 7 (1983): 91–92.

72. During the 1590s Ponsonby registered Sidney's translations from du Bartas as well as *Astrophil and Stella;* he published translations by the Countess of Pembroke, the *Countess of Pembroke's Ivychurch* by Abraham Fraunce, Fraunce's *Emmanuel,* three editions of the *Arcadia* (one as part of a particularly expensive collected edition of Sidney's works), and, with the exception of the *Shepheardes Calender,* every shred of Spenser's verse. I discuss Ponsonby's relation to Spenser and the Sidney circle and his place in the history of stationer's copyright at greater length in "Spenser's Retrography: Two Episodes in Post-Petrarchan Bibliography," in *Spenser's Life and the Subject of Biography,* ed. Judith H. Anderson, Donald Cheney, and David Richardson (Amherst: University of Massachusetts Press, 1996), 100–102.

73. *Miscellaneous Prose of Sir Philip Sidney,* ed. Katherine Duncan-Jones and J. A. van Dorsten (Oxford: Clarendon Press, 1973), 73.

74. P.R.O. 12/195/33.

75. On Greville and the Herberts, see Brennan, "William Ponsonby," 94.

76. Greg, *Aspects and Problems,* 71–72.

77. That individual works differently authorized also resemble one another is, of course, one of the countervailing effects of print. For further meditations on the various cultural tides produced by typographic leveling, see Eisenstein, *The Printing Press as an Agent of Change,* 82–88, 227–36.

78. "The Meaning of Imprint in Early Printed Books," 137–38.

79. Shaaber actually accumulated a list of fifteen such texts, but, as Leo Kirschbaum has demonstrated, most of the entries on Shaaber's list do not belong there (Kirschbaum, "Author's Copyright in England Before 1640," 53–55).

80. Kirschbaum, "Author's Copyright," 54.

81. See Hirsch, *Printing, Selling, and Reading,* 61.

82. In an entry from 1576, Abraham Veale is referred to as a member of the Drapers' Company and a brother of the Stationers' (Arber, *Transcript,* 2:65), so there is some history of blurred edges round company membership.

CHAPTER THREE

1. "From Censorship to Copyright: Aspects of the Government's Role in the English Book Trade, 1695–1775," in *Books and Society in History: Papers of the Association of College and Research Libraries Rare Books and Manuscripts Preconference,* ed. Kenneth E. Carpenter (New York: Bowker, 1983), 175.

2. Thus, by means of the rise of the press and the punctuating Statute of Anne, the old legal fiction of the *Bishop of Chichester* case (1386) came closer to fact: "for as soon as Parliament has concluded anything the law understands that each person has cognizance of it, for the Parliament represents the body of all the Kingdom" (cited in Steele, *Proclamations,* ix). Because the press had made possible a serious drive toward near-immediate dissemination, the Statute of Anne could project a sphere of public debate sustained in large measure by the press into a forum of extensive parliamentary argument.

3. *Parliamentary History,* vol. 17, col. 958.

4. "Quod nulla persona infra hoc regnum nostrum Angliae vel dominia eiusdem practizabit vel exercet per se vel per ministros suos, servientes suos, seu per aliquam aliam personam, artem sive misteram imprimendi vel excudendi aliquem librum vel aliquam rem vendendum seu barganizandum infra hoc regnum nostrum Angliae vel dominia eiusdem, nisi eadem persona tempore impressionis sive excussionis suae praedictae sit vel erit una de communitate praedictae misterae sive artis Stacionarii civitatis praedictae" (Arber, *Transcript,* 1:xxx—xxxi). Though I have adjusted his translation, I have followed him in rendering *imprimere vel excudere* simply as "to print"; it is possible that *excudere* refers to xylography, or to the casting of type, though in the latter case one might expect a slightly more elaborate locution.

5. *Parliamentary History,* vol. 17, col. 959.

6. See Winger, "Regulations Relating to the Book Trade," 168. On Henrician licensing before 1530, see chapter 2, n. 5.

7. The 1529 proclamation may be found in Hughes and Larkin, *Proclamations,* no. 122. Note that Henry's list of proscribed books substantially antedate the promulgation of most of the continental "Indices." Even Mary's proclamation of 13 June 1555 banning Protestant books (*Proclamations,* no. 422) antedates the famous Tridentine Index by two years.

Note, too, that Henry did continue to make proscriptions. The 1530 proclamation (*Proclamations,* no. 129) contains a list of proscribed texts. By proclamation of 1 January 1536, Henry commanded the surrender of all copies of a sermon by John Fisher and of "any other writing or book wherein shall be contained any error or slander to the King's majesty, or to the derogation or diminution of his imperial crown" (*Proclamations,* no. 161).

8. Hughes and Larkin, *Proclamations,* no. 186. The proclamation indicates (and consolidates) the power of the newly reorganized Privy Council. (On that reorganization, see John Guy, *Tudor England* [Oxford: Oxford University Press, 1988], 156–64.) The regulation of the word instituted in the licensing statutes is the logical administrative prologue to the Act of Proclamations of 1539 (31 Hen. VIII, c. 8), which confers on the published royal word the force of parliamentary acts. And see also the specificatons of that independent royal power in 32 Hen. VIII, c. 26; and 37 Hen. VIII, c. 17.

9. See D. M. Loades, "The Press Under the Early Tudors: A Study in Censorship and Sedition," 29.

10. And it was *indeed* traced to Henry IV: Mary invokes 2 Hen. IV, c. 15, in her 1555 proclamation banning Protestant books (Hughes and Larkin, *Proclamations*, no. 422). The ecclesiastical licensing system of the 1520s is provided for by the statute "Ex officio" (1410), also promulgated as part of the original anti-Lollard campaign. (The statute was anticipated by the constitutions agreed upon during the Canterbury convocation of January 1408/9, which provided for a provincial licensing system.) The other relevant elements of the statutory background are 5 Richard II, st. 2, c. 5, 1382; and 2 Henry V, st. 1, c. 7, 1414. Winger notes ("Regulations Relating to the Book Trade," 165) that Holinshed records the execution of three men charged with distributing seditious books in 1494/5 (*Chronicles of England, Scotland, and Ireland* [London: Johnson, 1807–8] 3:508).

11. Even the 1534 treasons act throws considerable emphasis on the specific crime of publishing books against Henry's ecclesiastical authority; see 26 Henry VIII, c. 13.

12. David Wilkins, *Concilia Magnae Britanniae et Hiberniae*, 4 vols. (London: Gosling, 1737), 3:706–707 and 717–24; and see Patterson, *Copyright*, 23.

13. Hughes and Larkin, *Proclamations*, no. 186.

14. On the threat of the gloss see Stephen Greenblatt, *Renaissance Self-Fashioning* (Chicago: University of Chicago Press, 1980), 94. The suppression of marginalia is one of the constants of attempts to regulate the dissemination of the Bible. In the rules set down to guide the translators in 1611, James I stipulated "No Marginal Notes at all to be affixed, but only for the Explanation of the *Hebrew* or *Greek* Words, which cannot without some circumlocution, so briefly and fitly be express'd in the Text" (cited in A. W. Pollard, *Records of the English Bible: The Documents Relating to the Translation and Publication of the Bible in English, 1525–1611* [London: Oxford University Press, 1911], 54). On the threat of the English New Testament *itself*, see Henry VIII's own reasoning in the 1530 proclamation (Hughes and Larkin, *Proclamations*, no. 129).

15. This is part of Cromwell's remarkable experiment: although the 1530 licensing proclamation had banned the English New Testament, the Canterbury Convocation called for an authorized English Bible in 1534 and in 1536 Cromwell enjoined all parishes to keep copies of both the Latin and the English Bible on display. So for a few years much of Tyndale's Bible, spliced into John Roger's composite translation (the so-called Matthew Bible), served as the *official* English Bible. The 1538 licensing proclamation withdraws royal authority from that most seditious work; in 1539, it was replaced by Coverdale's "Great" Bible. In 1542, the experiment was suddenly abandoned and the ban on the English Bible was reimposed.

16. Hughes and Larkin, *Proclamations*, no. 186.

17. Loades points out ("The Press Under the Early Tudors," 33) that the designation of the Privy Council as the official licensing board in the 1538 proclamation suggests that Henry wished to control political as well as theological dissent.

18. Hughes and Larkin, *Proclamations*, no. 272. The shift of responsibility from the Privy Council to local mayors suggests that the licensing system of 1538 had not taken hold.

19. I am by no means suggesting that Somerset, acting through Edward, was

entirely flexible. (In "Freedom of the Press, Protestant Propaganda, and Protector Somerset," *Huntington Library Quarterly* 40 (1976): 1–9, John N. King, I think, slightly overestimates that flexibility.) In a proclamation of 31 July 1547 (Hughes and Larkin, *Proclamations*, no. 287), he attempted to control preaching by license; a little over a year later, he forbade the preaching of sermons altogether, requiring the reading of officially sanctioned homilies in their stead (no. 313); by a proclamation of 6 August 1549 (no. 344) he forbade all performances of plays and interludes in English. A week later we find him casting about to construct an appropriate and efficient licensing system out of the resources of the Privy Council; see *Acts of the Privy Council of England, 1542–1628*, J. R. Dasent, ed., n.s., 43 vols. (London: H. M. Stationery Office, 1890–1949), 1:107 and 117, and 2:312. These efforts were elaborated by a proclamation of 1551 (Hughes and Larkin, *Proclamations*, no. 371) which requires the written approval of a quorum (six members) of the Privy Council for the import, printing, or sale of any books as well as for the performance, in English, of "any manner interlude, play, or matter."

20. Hughes and Larkin, *Proclamations*, no. 390.

21. Ibid., 422 and 443 (Arber gives old-spelling transcriptions of the proclamations in *Transcript*, 1:52 and 1:92). The 1555 proclamation twins licensing requirements with a simple ban on the printing or sale of works by Luther, Zwingli, Calvin, Melanchthon, Erasmus, Tyndale, Cranmer, and eighteen others.

22. Greg, *Aspects and Problems*, 4.

23. "Rex et Regina omnibus ad quos etc. salutem. Sciatis quod nos considerantes et manifeste percipientes quod nonnulli sediciosi et haeretici libri rythmi et tractatus indies sunt editi, excussi et impressi per diversas scandalosas maliciosas scismaticas et haereticas personas, non solum moventes subditos et ligeos nostros ad sediciones et inobediencias contra maximas et detestabiles haereses contra fidem ac sanam Catholicam doctrinam sanctae Matris Ecclesiae renovandas et movendas, et remedium congruum in hac parte providere volentes, de gratia nostra speciali ac ex certa sciencia et mero motu nostris volumus damus et concedimus . . . quod ipsi de caetero sint in re facto et nomine unum corpus de se imperpetuum, et una communitas perpetua corporata." I give the text as cited and translated in Arber, *Transcript*, 1:xxviii.

24. Arber, *Transcript*, xxxi. The passage providing for the London monopoly, cited above (n. 5), goes on to make a key exception in the case of those who have "therefore licence of us, or the heirs or successors of us the foresaid Queen by the letters patent of us or the heirs or successors of us the foresaid Queen" ("inde habeat licenciam nostram vel haeredum seu successorum nostrae praefatae Reginae per literas patentes nostras vel haeredum seu successorum nostrae praefatae Reginae").

25. Greg and Boswell, *Records of the Court of the Stationers' Company, 1576–1602*, cited in Graham Pollard, "The Company of Stationers before 1557," *The Library*, 4th ser., 18 (1937): 29; A. W. Pollard cited from *Shakespeare's Fight*, 12–13.

26. *Parliamentary History*, vol. 17, col. 958.

27. Arber, *Transcript*, 1:114.

28. G. Pollard, "The Company of Stationers," 29.

29. D. C. Coleman, *The Economy of England, 1450–1750* (Oxford: Oxford University Press, 1977), 74–75; and George Unwin, *The Gilds and Companies of London*, 158–63; see also Loades, "The Press Under the Early Tudors," 45–50.

30. A. B. Hibbert, "The Economic Policies of Towns," chapter 4 of *The Cambridge Economic History of Europe,* 3:185, 194–95; North and Thomas, *The Rise of the Western World: A New Economic History,* 57; and Eli F. Heckscher, *Mercantilism,* trans. Mendel Shapiro, 2nd ed. edited by E. F. Söderlund, 2 vols. (New York: Macmillan, 1955), 1:225.

31. R. H. Britnell, "The Proliferation of Markets in England, 1200–1349," *Economic History Review,* 2nd ser., 34 (1981): 209–21; see also John Merrington on the function of early merchant capital in "Town and Country in the Transition to Capitalism," in *The Transition from Feudalism to Capitalism,* ed. and intro. by Rodney Hilton (London: Verso, 1978), 178.

32. On the relation between municipal and royal policy, see Edward Miller, "The Economic Policies of Governments: France and England" *CEHE,* 3:301.

33. Heckscher, *Mercantilism,* 1:52 and 225; and see also 1:46–47; Robert Brenner, "The Agrarian Roots of European Capitalism," in *The Brenner Debate: Agraraian Class Structure and Economic Development in Pre-Industrial Europe,* eds. T. H. Aston and C. H. E. Philpin (Cambridge: Cambridge University Press, 1985), 255–56; and Miller, "The Economic Policies of Governments: France and England," 3:309–10.

34. Hibbert, *CEHE,* 3:211. The effect of the old *gilda mercatoria* on urban economies became more oppressive during this period, for as markets expanded, the exclusion of nonmembers and aliens from trade became more invidous; see Hibbert, *CEHE,* 3:191–94. This is also the period in which the *Bannmeilenrecht,* restricting imports that could compete with locally produced commodities, was developed in German urban centers.

35. North and Thomas, *Rise,* 71–75.

36. Miller, "The Economic Policies of Governments: France and England," *CEHE,* 3:316; and Harry A. Miskimin, *The Economy of Early Renaissance Europe, 1300–1460* (Cambridge: Cambridge University Press, 1975), 34–35. Such *local* monopoly rights as had been implicit in the *gilda mercatoria* of the pre-Conquest period, exclusive rights to regulate local trading (rights that, by the late thirteenth century, had come to be associated with local government), were finally subordinated to national monopoly rights that had been implicit—again, since before the Conquest—in the power of the Crown. From the fourteenth century on, the power of the Crown is clearly recognized as the ground of English commercial regulation. Here the English economy differs from the continental economy in ways that will provide the basis for the remarkable English achievements of the fifteenth and sixteenth centuries; see Merrington, "Town and Country," 183; and Alessandro Pizzorno, "Three Types of Urban Social Structure and the Development of Industrial Society," from G. Germani, ed., *Modernization, Urbanization and the Urban Crisis* (Boston: Little, Brown, 1973) 125.

37. Fox, *Monopolies and Patents,* 40; Miller, "The Economic Policies of Governments," 3:326.

38. George Unwin, *Industrial Organization,* 88–89. The tendency toward a nationalized industrial economy was encouraged by the erosion of Crown revenues derived from land—which, though continuous since the 1370s, became critical at the end of the fifteenth century. The dissolution of the monasteries is, after all, a desperate economic raid by a monarchy no longer able to meet the demands of military finance by relying on customary land revenues.

39. Fox, *Monopolies and Patents*, 35. Fox's account can be a bit confusing, since he distinguishes imperfectly between the old *gilda mercatoria* and the trading guilds of the thirteenth and fourteenth centuries. The classic treatment of the transition to the craft gild is in C. Gross, *The Gild Merchant*, 2 vols. (Oxford: Clarendon Press, 1890), 1:116–26; and see also Unwin, *Industrial Organization*, 79–80.

40. The statute (37 Ed. III, cc. 5–6) is cited in Stella Kramer, "The English Craft Gilds and the Government," *Studies in History, Economics and Public Law* 23 (1905): 37. Kramer notes that in the late fourteenth century some towns attempted to restrain the Crown-sanctioned independence of some of the craft guilds (43): note the preeminent alliance of local craft with the monarchy. See also May McKisack, *The Fourteenth Century, 1307–1399* (Oxford: Clarendon, 1959), 373–75.

41. Willam Hyde Price, *The English Patents of Monopoly, Harvard Economic Studies*, 1 (Boston: Houghton Mifflin, 1906), 6; and see also Heckscher, *Mercantilism*, 1:242–43. Many of the major London guilds—the Goldsmiths, Girdlers, Skinners, Drapers, Tailors, Fishmongers, and Vintners—secured royal charters by the 1360s.

42. Heckscher, *Mercantilism*, 1:242; and see Unwin, *Gilds and Companies*, 79–81; and Sylvia Thrupp, *The Merchant Class of Medieval London, 1300–1500* (Ann Arbor: University of Michigan Press, 1962), 3. For a telling fifteenth-century example of the extension of London-based industrial power, see T. F. Reddaway, *The Early History of the Goldsmiths' Company, 1327–1509,* ed. Lorna E. M. Walker (London: Arnold, 1975), 140–41.

43. This tendency may be said to culminate in the complaint of the merchants of Hull (c. 1575) that "by meanes of the sayde Companies (the Government whereof is rewlled onely in the Citie of london) all the whole trade of merchandize is in a maner brought to the Citie of london." *Tudor Economic Documents,* ed. R. H. Tawney and Eileen Power, 3 vols. (London: Longmans, 1924), 2:49. And see also *London, 1500–1700: The Making of the Metropolis,* ed. A. L. Beier and Roger Finlay (London: Longman, 1986), 14–15.

44. One can speak of the slow transformation of economic tendencies and administrative norms into royal economic *policy* under the Tudors: the response to the crisis of midcentury, the Statute of Artificers of 1563, is a landmark in the nationalization of England's economy. See Lawrence Stone (arguing against Tawney's economic determinism), "State Control in Sixteenth-Century England," *Economic History Review* 17 (1947): 103–20; Peter Ramsey, *Tudor Economic Problems, Men and Ideas,* ed. R. W. Harris (London: Gollancz, 1972), 98–99; Fox, *Monopolies and Patents,* 40–41; Unwin, *Industrial Organization,* 56, and *Gilds and Companies,* 244; and Penry Williams, *The Tudor Regime* (Oxford: Clarendon, 1979), 155–57 and 168–69. On royal regulation in particular, see M. W. Beresford, "The Common Informer, the Penal Statutes, and Economic Regulation," *Economic History Review,* n.s. 10 (1957–58): 221–38; and Unwin, *Industrial Organization,* 56.

45. G. Pollard, "The Company of Stationers," 18. The city regulations provided that citizens had the right to manufacture and to engage in wholesale trade within the city in any goods, regardless of their company membership, though one was to confine retail sales to the goods proper to one's official craft: a leatherer, that is, was not to retail cloth. The Stationers' Charter abridged this municipal right.

D. M. Loades asserts that production for stock was "normal" by 1520. "The Press Under the Early Tudors," 31.

46. Arber *Transcript*, 1:56, cited in G. Pollard, "The Company of the Stationers," 35. The procedures necessary for guaranteeing the legality of a guild charter are laid out in 19 Henry VII, cap. 7.

47. G. Pollard, "The Company of Stationers," 5–12.

48. Ibid., 16–17. The shift toward wholesaling, standardization, and "Taylorization" of production was already underway before the invention of printing. Paul Saenger has pointed out that, at least in France, "increasing division of labor was introduced into fifteenth-century scriptoria, particularly those serving the aristocracy. . . . The result was a new speed in the preparation of deluxe illustrated manuscripts." "Colard Mansion and the Evolution of the Printed Book," *Library Quarterly* 45 (1975): 407.

49. The fullest account of the internal economics of English printing may be found in Marjorie Plant, *The English Book Trade;* but for a prudent and very useful summary, see Rudolf Hirsch, *Printing, Selling and Reading*, 32–40.

50. In *A Century of the English Book Trade* (London: Bibliographical Society, 1905), E. Gordon Duff points out (xv) that with the exception of Caxton and Thomas Hunte at Oxford no Englishman brought out any printed books until about 1516. Indeed, a great number of early book importers were foreigners, and none were free of the Stationers' Company.

51. By the *Carta Mercatoria* of 1303, foreign traders enjoyed royal protection and special commercial privileges, including freedom from local charges and the right of wholesale trading throughout England. In the course of the fourteenth and fifteenth centuries, however, such privileging of aliens met with steady opposition, particularly in London.

52. 14 & 15 Hen. VIII, cc. 1–2; 21 Hen. VIII, c.16. For an earlier attempt to control alien economic activity, see 3 Hen. VIII, c. 10.

53. Unwin, *Gilds and Companies*, 245–46.

54. 1 Rich. III, c.9.

55. Blagden, *The Stationers' Company*, 28.

56. For the 1523 and 1529 acts, see above, n. 52; the 1534 act is 25 Henry VIII, c. 15.

57. By this act, the Crown took over responsibility for the effort to control the importation of heretical books, which had been originally undertaken by Bishop Tunstall in 1524; in 1525 Wolsey bound over the members of the book trade to refrain from such importing. These ecclesiastical interventions recurred regularly, on into the thirties.

58. *Statutes of the Realm*, 3:456.

59. In 1536, the French printer Regnault claimed that the 1534 act was proposed by the London booksellers to put him out of business, for he had been shipping bound service books to England for years.

60. A. W. Pollard, *Records*, 17–18.

61. Graham Pollard points out that printing for stock must initially have put a strain on the productive capacity of English binders and then asserts that "there can be no doubt that ready bound books were soon being 'dumped' on the English market. The bookbinders and printers in the Stationers' Company were rescued from this menace by an Act of Parliament in 1534" ("The Company of Stationers Before 1557," 27).

62. Blagden, *The Stationers' Company*, 28–29.

63. *Letters and Papers of Henry VIII*, vol. 17, 177; cited by Blagden (*The Stationers' Company*, 29), who treats the draft proclamation as if it had in fact been promulgated.

64. When the office passed to William Faques in 1501, a Norman, it *may* have carried with it a responsibility to print designated royal proclamations (he printed at least two); we do not know whether Faques took over Actor's unrestricted import license or was otherwise compensated for his services. Machlinia and de Worde had both printed proclamations prior to Faques.

65. *Rot. Pat. 21 Henry VIII*, 2, m. 17.

66. He styles himself "Prynter unto the Kingis noble Grace" (*Peregrinatio humani generis*) and "regis impressorem expertissimum" (*Liber presens directorium*) in December 1508.

67. *Rot. Pat. 1 Edward VI*, 7, m 1. The salary is augmented by a twelve-pence fee in payment for the printing of statutes, acts, etc.; the list of official publications exclusive to the working of this patent excepts the Latin grammar, a monopoly in which is part of a grant issued three days earlier conferring the office of king's typographer and bookseller on Reynold Wolfe.

68. Henry R. Plomer, *Wynkyn de Worde and His Contemporaries From the Death of Caxton to 1535* (London: Grafton, 1925), 47–58.

69. An identical grant protects Pynson's edition of a sermon by Cuthbert Tunstall, published simultaneously with Pace's sermon.

70. On the date of this publication see A. W. Reed, *Early Tudor Drama* (London: Methuen, 1926), 11–12, 177, 187–88.

71. Ibid., 112 and 177.

72. Lucien Febvre and H.-J. Martin point out that surviving Venetian imprints from the eighties number about 156, as compared to 82 editions issuing from Milan and 67 from Augsburg, while nearly a quarter of the 1821 European editions issued between 1495 and 1497 were printed in Venice (*L'apparition du livre* [Paris: Michel, 1958], 190–91). For more on Venetian protection of the press, see my "*Idem:* Italics and the Genetics of Authorship," *Journal of Medieval and Renaissance Studies* 20 (fall 1990): 205–24, from which the following discussion is distilled.

73. Hekscher, *Mercantilism*, 2:140–41.

74. Rinaldo Fulin, "Documenti per servire alla storia della Tipografia Veneziana," *Archivio veneto* 23 (1882): 99; for more on John of Speyer, see Victor Scholderer, "Printing at Venice to the End of 1481," *The Library*, 4th ser., 25 (1924): 130–31.

75. The privilege not only provides an incentive for large outlay of capital necessary to *apply* such technical innovations as printing with moveable type, it is also in a sense a governmental guarantee of support, useful as security on potential loans.

76. I count at least ten Venetian editions of the *Historia Naturalis* between 1469 and the end of the century, two of them Italian translations, and at least sixteen editions of the *ad Familiares* during the same period.

77. In England, the shift to what might be called "literacy production"—the printing of grammars, primers, and psalters—is a major breakthrough, since these titles are aimed at a new market, and one which printing is particularly well-equipped to

enlarge and satisfy. A further evidence of the creativity of London printing was the turn to the printing of law books *not* specifically associated with the legal curriculum, but nonetheless of considerable use to the practicing lawyer—a productive practice that transformed the growing London legal corps into a major sector of the English print audience.

78. "Domini Consiliarii deliberarunt et terminarunt, quod opus prefatum per Marcum Antonium [Sabellicum] prefatum dari possit alicui diligenti impressori, qui opus illud imprimat suis sumptibus et edat, sicuti convenit elegantiae historiae, dignae ut immortalis fiat, et nemini praeter eum liceat opus illud imprimi facere sub pena indignationis Serenissimi Dominii et ducatorum quingentorum tam in Venetiis quam in quacumque civitate et loco Serenissimi Dominii." Cited in Carlo Castellani, *La stampa in Venezia dalla sua origine alla morte di Aldo Manuzio seniore* (Venice: Ongania, 1889), 70–71.

79. The grant has been described as an author's copyright by Martin Lowry, *The World of Aldus Manutius: Business and Scholarship in Renaissance Venice* (Oxford: Blackwell, 1979), 28; and Ruth Chavasse, "The First Known Author's Copyright, September 1486, in the Context of a Humanist Career," *Bulletin of the John Rylands University Library* 69 (1986): 11–38; see also Carlo Castellani, *I privilegi di stampa e la proprieté letteraria in Venezia dalla introduzione della stampa nella citta fin verso la del secolo XVIII* (Venice: Visentini, 1888), 6–7.

80. Such regulatory practices were in the air: in 1474, the Senate had passed a law requiring the registration of "any new and ingenious artifice," securing ultimate rights in such new inventions to the state, and providing for ten years' exclusive industrial rights in the invention to the registrant. Cited in Frumkin, "Early History of Patents," from Giulio Mandich, "Le privative industriali Veneziane (1450–1550)," *Rivista del diritto commerciale* (1936): 515. And see Samuele Romanin, *Storia documentata di Venezia,* 2nd ed., 10 vols. (Venice: Fuga, 1912–20), 4:485.

81. My sense that this is a *shift* puts me in slight disagreement with both Fulin (*Documenti per servire alla storia della Tipografia Veneziana,* 88) and Carlo Castellani, who follows him. In his *I privilegi di stampa,* 7, Castellani argues that the decree on Sabellicus's behalf is *essentially* identical with the grant to Tommai.

82. Cited in Castellani, *La stampa in Venezia,* 71.

83. Fulin, *Documenti,* no. 5. This grant to Nigro offers evidence that the non-printing capitalist *publisher* had become a familiar figure within the Venetian book trade of the 1490s (but see Lowry's strictures on the use of the term, *The World of Aldus Manutius,* 17).

84. "During the last decade of the fifteenth century, printing privileges were awarded so frequently that one can hardly find a single book printed in Venice at this time that does not carry the phrase *cum gratia et privilegio*" (Castellani, *I privilegi di stampa,* 8, my translation). Although the Collegio primarily rewarded printers and capitalist publishers thereby, they also extended privileges to scholarly editors and, sometimes, to authors; see Vittore Branca, "Ermolao Barbaro and Late Quattrocento Venetian Humanism," in *Renaissance Venice,* ed. J.R. Hale (London, Faber, 1973), 218–43; and Horatio F. Brown, *The Venetian Printing Press: An Historical Study Based Upon Documents for the Most Part Hitherto Unpublished* (London: Nimmo, 1891), chapters

4 and 7. In these grants the Venetian patriciate had devised a new form of patronage, a new means of rewarding a cultural expertise that was distinctly Venetian.

85. Fulin, "Documenti," 121–22. These applications, from Bernardino Rasma and Benedetto Fontana, nicely exemplify the academic nature of the privileged books: protection is sought for texts by Galen, Scotus, and Aristotle, and for Ancarano's commentary on the Decretals.

86. Even A.-A. Renouard, the great nineteenth-century bibliographer and a specialist in the work of Aldus and his heirs, was himself briefly taken in by the counterfeits: in 1807 he paid a very large sum for an Aldine Virgil which he later discovered to be inauthentic. It is not surprising that modern bibliographers look to Renouard for the fullest account of the history and range of the Lyonnaise counterfeiting industry.

87. I quote here not from the senatorial decree of 17 October but from the ducal letter of the next month, ratifying that decree (itself a ratification of the 1501 grant from the Collegio); the decree is reproduced in Ambroise Firmin-Didot, *Alde Manuce et L'Hellénisme a Venise* (Paris, 1875; repr. Brussels: Culture et Civilisation, 1966), 479–81. For the causes of this compounding of legislation, see the discussion below, p. 73.

88. Idem., 479–80: "*Suppliciter petiit, ne alius quisquam in dominio nostro queat Gracas litteras facere contrafacereve aut Graece imprimere nec Latinarum quidem characteres, quos vulgo cursivos et cancellarios dicunt, facere contrafacereve.*"

89. Others besides Aldus had received typographic grants: in 1498 Ottaviano de Petrucci received a monopoly in the printing of *canto figurato,* and Democrito Terracina received a monopoly in the printing of Arabic.

90. Braccio saw fit to have his privilege reaffirmed a couple of months after the initial grant. On the somewhat intense competition in the printing of Greek during the last few years of the quattrocento, see Robert Proctor, *The Printing of Greek in the Fifteenth Century* (Oxford: The Bibliographical Society, 1900), 99, 111–13; and Lowry, *The World of Aldus Manutius,* 127. In *The Venetian Printing Press,* Brown points out how frequently the Collegio hedged its privileges by granting them with the proviso that they are not to infringe preexisting privileges; see his 57–58.

91. Aldus was perhaps acting out of justified pique: Proctor notes (*The Printing of Greek,* 111) that the preface to Braccio's Phalaris contains a studied insult to Aldus.

92. Harry Carter gives a useful and temperate summary of the manuscript antecedents and typographical virtues of italics in his *A View of Early Typography, Up to About 1600* (Oxford: Clarendon, 1969), 73–74; and see also Lowry, *The World of Aldus Manutius,* 130–41. Lowry is appropriately impatient with much of the almost hagiographic writing that has been done on the Aldine types, though he may be too quick to dismiss the somewhat hard-boiled argument, traditional since first advanced by Firmin-Didot in his *Alde Manuce et l'Hellénisme à Venise* (Paris, 1875), that part of the attraction of the italic lay in the fact that the typeface made it possible to squeeze a good deal more text onto a page than was possible with, say, a roman type (see Lowry, 141–42). Lowry properly argues that Aldus did not exploit italics as a means of cutting either his own costs or those of his consumers; on the other hand, the haste with which Aldus's Lyonnaise and Florentine imitators took up the italic may have a good deal to do with such economic concerns.

93. It is perhaps worth noting that that grant vested responsibility for the enforcement of Aldus's privilege in the Council of Ten, a remarkable assignment. Printing privileges were still relatively new, and the problem of enforcement does not leave many traces on the documentary record. There do seem to have been infringements (for which see Brown, *The Venetian Printing Press,* 58–59), yet those grants that do charge a particular body with enforcement tend not to designate so powerful and prestigious a body: the Council of Ten was charged, after all, with maintaining the security of the state. See Lowry, *The World of Aldus Manutius,* 155.

94. The Senate was trimming the duration of his Greek privilege from twenty years, awarded in 1496, to ten years, yet the 1496 privilege had entailed a monopoly in the Aldine Greek printing technique and in whatever texts Aldus chose to print in Greek, whereas the 1502 privilege forbade anyone but Aldus to engage in *any* Greek printing for ten years.

The appeal to senatorial authority for the grant is itself remarkable. Fulin lists only two precedents: a ten-year privilege granted in 1492 for the printing of the Bible with the *Glossa ordinaria* (Fulin, no. 9) and a 1493 grant, also for ten years, for the printing of Domenico da San Gimignano's commentary on the Decretals (no. 14). Several years after the grant to Aldus we find two instances of direct grants of privilege from the Council of Ten itself (nos. 166 and 178).

95. The "mature" Aldine Greek fonts are cut in such a way as to allow the insertion of compact, separately cast accents and breathings, thus obviating the problems of earlier, less economical Greek types, which required either the casting of letters with accents (which meant casting a huge variety of sorts of type) or the casting of full-sized accent and breathing types to be set on the line above their letters (which meant wasted paper due to a sparsely printed page). For Soncino's charges against Aldus, see G. Manzoni, *Annali tipografici dei Soncino,* 3 vols. (Bologna: Romagnoli, 1886), pt. 2, 3:26–8a.

96. The text of the papal decree is given in A. A. Renouard, *Annales de l'imprimerie des Alde,* 2nd edition, 3 vols. (Paris: Renouard, 1825), 3:226–27, together with texts of the fifteen-year extension of that papal privilege ordained in 1513 by Julius II and Leon X (pp. 228–33).

97. His types and editions were also being copied in Brescia and in Florence, though he probably remained unaware of these activities until at least the end of 1503. For the Florentine forgeries, see pp. 76 f. below.

98. The text of the *Monitum* is reproduced in Renouard, *Annales,* 2:325–30. What Aldus was identifying as the *gallicitatem quandam* is unclear: it may be the sloping capitals—the most striking innovation in the Lyons editions—that have come down to us as *the* italic capital letterform. Aldus had used roman capitals in his otherwise italic texts.

99. Giorgio Vasari, *Le vite de'piu eccellenti pittori, scultori e architettori nelle redazioni del 1550 e 1568,* eds. Rosanna Bettarini and Paola Barocchi, 6 vols. (Florence: Sansoni, 1966–87), 5:6–7. I am grateful to Lisa Pon for bringing the episode to my attention.

100. Cited, in the author's translation, from Joseph Koerner, *The Moment of Self-Portraiture in German Renaissance Art* (Chicago: University of Chicago Press, 1993), 213.

101. General printing privileges appeared outside of Venice after the Aldine forgeries, but *typographic* monopolies did not become common. The next attempt to protect a particular typeface comes over half a century later, in 1557, when Henry II conferred a typographic privilege on Robert Granjon. For a fuller discussion of early modern typographic monopolies, see Herman de la Fontaine Verwey, "Les debuts de la protection des caractères typographiques au XVIe siecle," *Gutenberg-Jahrbuch 1965*, 24–34.

102. "*Guliel. Lilii in p[ro]gymnasmata gramatic. Linacri a plagiaro vindicata:* Pagina que falso latuit sub nomine nuper / Que fuit et multo co[m]maculata luto / Nunc tandem authoris p[er]scribens nomina veri / Linacri dulces pura recepit aquas."

103. Peter Trevers began printing the grammatical texts of Robert Whittinton in about 1530, books that de Worde had been printing and reprinting since the mid-1510s. De Worde retaliated by publishing the following "*hexastichon ad lectorem*" in the 1533 edition of Whittinton's *De octo partibus:*

Quod spersit Trivers odiosa incuria mendis
Inmineris tersum suscipe lector opus
Si tibi vel nostrae sit gratia incuria limae
Winandi ve mei proela operosa satis
Mendosa explodas foedi exemplaria Petri
Trivers, pro meritis nostra polita fovens.
(A_1^v)

104. At first, English printers used both italics and roman (the latter introduced by Pynson c. 1509) as differential types, but, curiously, roman soon lost its emphatic quality; when black letter lost its dominance of the English printed page, roman took its place. Italics, however, retained their alien aura. (In England, italics were first employed in Wynkyn de Worde's 1524 edition of Wakefield's *Oratio de laudibus trium linguarum*, a text that also prints [from block, not type] Arabic and Hebrew: the context thus insists on the obtrusive novelty of the italic letterform.) On the differential use of italics, see Harry Carter, *A View of Early Typography Up to About 1600* (Oxford: Clarendon, 1969), 125–26.

105. See Lowry, *The World of Aldus Manutius*, 156–58.

106. *The Venetian Printing Press*, 57; he goes on to remark that "this proviso is constantly repeated in various forms, for example, *quod non comprehendantur illi quo forte jam initiassent similia opera* (in 1494), and *dummodo prius dicta volumina non fuerint impressa* (in 1502)."

107. See Brown, *The Venetian Printing Press*, 73–75. Brown provides a transcript of the 1517 law on p. 207. The law was framed very badly and served largely to stimulate the market in imported books; revisions were undertaken in 1534 and 1537. The 1534 law limits the number of a printer's copyrights to what he can print in a year; all books so privileged were to be printed in Venice and their prices regulated by a state agency.

108. "The Regulation of the Book Trade Before the Proclamation of 1538," *Transactions of the Bibliographical Society*, 15 (1918), 174–75. Presumably Pynson's privilege was offered as an adjunct to, or a new articulation of, his position as king's printer; Rastell was perhaps being rewarded for the enormous labors involved in the publication of the

three great guides to the English legal Year Books—the *Liber Assisarum* (1513), the *Grand Abridgment* (1516), and the *Table of the Grand Abridgment* (1519).

109. "The Regulation of the Book Trade," 175. He observes that de Worde never seems to have sought a privilege. This may or may not be true; certainly he was never *granted* a privilege. Yet he did have recourse to something resembling Aldus's *Monitum,* for which see n. 103 above.

110. Cited by Reed ("The Regulation of the Book Trade," 177) from R. O., Misc. Bks., T.R., 120, 59.

111. Cited in Pollard, *Records,* 228–29.

112. The third of the injunctions issued by Cromwell on 6 September 1538 on the king's authority stipulates that each parish must provide itself with "one boke of the whole Bible of the largest volume in Englyshe," a reference to the forthcoming Great Bible, according to Pollard, and a vigorous market intervention. See Pollard, *Records,* 261–62; and Greenslade, "English Versions of the Bible, 1525–1611," 150–51.

113. Pollard, *Records,* 243–44. The opening of the letter attempts to dissociate Coverdale from the 1535 and 1537 Bibles that, quite properly, are known as the Coverdale Bible. Grafton is already responding to the particular terms of the November proclamation: Henry had required that no one "shall henceforth print any book of translations in the English tongue unless the plain name of the translator thereof be contained in the said book; or else that the printer will answer for the same as for his own privy deed and act, and otherwise to make the translator, the printer, and the setter forth of the same, to suffer punishment, and make fine at the King's will and pleasure." Grafton counters by insisting "that James Nycolson that dwelleth in Southwark put in prynt the newe testament both in latyn and englyshe. . . . And when Master Coverdale had advysed and consydered thesame. he founde his name added therunto as the translator, with thewhich he never had to do, nether sawe he it before it was full prynted and ended. And also founde the booke so folyshly done, ye and so corrupt, that yt did . . . greve him that the prynter had so defamed him and his learnyng by addynge his name to so fonde a thinge . . ." (243).

Interchapter

1. Kirschbaum believes that Baylie had sold his rights to the printer of the first edition, Simon Stafford, and that Stafford sold his rights to Thomas Creede, who printed the second edition (*Shakespeare and the Stationers,* 138), but no such sale is recorded, and it makes more sense to suppose that Baylie retained the copyright. Neither hypothesis reduces the strangeness of the inclusion of Dallington's letter in the second edition, which, after all, de-authorizes both issues. By including Dallington's letter, Baylie was presumably trying to placate Dallington, who really was powerless to inhibit the reissue, and perhaps thought that this testament to unauthorized publication might add the gloss of surreptitiousness to a book whose first print run was not selling.

2. *The Dramatic Works of Thomas Heywood,* 6 vols. (London : G. Pearson, 1874), 5:163.

3. Crucial as they are to Jonson's professional experience, these proportions must be understood *as proportional,* relative. In "The Jonsonian Corpulence; or, The Poet as

Mouthpiece," *ELH* 53 (fall 1986): 491–519, I offer a sustained discussion of a poem in which print is distinctly a sphere of inhibiting publicity.

4. In the course of a very useful discussion of the peculiar character of parody in the late Elizabethan theaters, James Shapiro refers to this rhythm as "the collapsing of literary generations." See his *Rival Playwrights: Marlowe, Jonson, Shakespeare* (New York: Columbia University Press, 1991), 9.

5. However early the playwright's gifts began to manifest themselves as *his*, the Chamberlain's Men were no doubt crucial to his growing prestige. The names of acting companies continue to appear on title pages: authors join, and do not displace them.

6. Because such matters are of special interest to the literary historian I offer, in chapters 3 and 4 of *Jonson and Possessive Authorship,* a psychological account of Jonson's special sensitivity to the proprieties of attribution and an intellectual history of the forms in which he conceptualized those proprieties.

7. See the final chapter of *Jonson and Possessive Authorship.*

8. At this point Richard Bishop controlled most of the material that Stansby had printed in the 1616 folio.

Chapter Four

1. *Drama and Society in the Age of Jonson* (London: Chatto and Windus, 1937).

2. "Commerce and Coinage, *Shakespeare's England,* eds. Sir Walter A. Raleigh, Sidney Lee, C. T. Onions, 2 vols. (Oxford: Clarendon, 1916), 1:339.

3. Sir William Cockayne's patent (S.P.D. Jac. I, lxxx, 112) gave him an astounding monopoly in the fulling and dying of all woolen cloth. Ostensibly granted to curtail exports to foreign cloth-finishers and to curb the associated currency outflows, it sustains Cecil's crude plan for national economic self-sufficiency.

4. *Drama and Society in the Age of Jonson,* 212; the slackening generalization of Knights's reading takes place on pp. 217–18.

5. Jonson is not the only playwright to have responded to the struggle over monopolies in the late nineties. The author of *1 Edward IV,* almost certainly Heywood, seems to have been equally roused by this struggle. The play was written between 1594 and 1599, but its disparaging references to suits for patents suggest a dating toward the latter part of this range. Jane Shore refuses to intercede on behalf of a petitioner for a patent in transporting grain; John Hobs, the good tanner of Tamworth, refuses the king's offer of exclusive rights "to transport hides or sell leather only in a certain circuit, or about bark, or such like." Heywood, *Dramatic Works,* 1:83 and 46.

6. Lines 4–9, cited from *Lusoria: Or Occasional Pieces,* H&S,11:340.

7. Harrison, A_1 and K_1. It was quite fitting that John Windet should have printed the volume since he was the official city printer.

8. The author in question is Richard Robinson, whose MS, *Eupolemia,* includes detailed records of these transactions. In 1577 he received 26 copies in return for providing Charlewood with the manuscript of *Robinson's Ruby.* One copy went to the dedicatee, for which he received two crowns; the others were probably sold, though his annotation, "I made benefit of 25 bookes mo," is not as revealing as one might like. But his record of the takings for another book of the same year, his *Gesta Romanorum,*

includes the dedicatee's payment "besydes sale of 25 books." Richardson was quite prolific, and his fee was almost invariant—*a* dedication copy, plus "benefit of 25 other books." Robinson's MS is printed by G. M. Vogt, *Studies in Philology* 21 (1924): 631–48.

9. H&S, 8:378 ("Ungathered Verse," xi, ll. 82–85).

10. Cited, from *The Compleat Angler,* in the catalogue of *The Carl H. Pforzheimer Library: English Literature, 1475–1700,* eds. W. A. Jackson and E. V. Unger, 3 vols. (New York: Morrill Press, 1940), 1, no. 218; and see the discussion of *Coryat's Crudities* in Kirschbaum, "Author's Copyright," 60–62.

11. Besides Jonson's lines, the only comparable allusion is in "Mr. Laurence Whitakers Elogie of the Booke . . . to the end that . . . M. Seward [a Preacher] might include it in a Letter that he wrote to one Doctor Mocket, Chaplaine to the Bishop of London that then was, for obtaining his approbation that my Booke might be printed," *Coryat's Crudities,* 2 vols. (New York: Macmillan, 1905), 1:149.

12. H&S, 8:376 ("Ungathered Verse," xi, ll. 8–13). In their own contributions to the sheaf of "Panegyrick Verses" prefixed to *Coryat's Crudities,* John Donne, Christopher Brooke, and George Sydenham also remark on Coryat's prodigal expenditure on the book; see 1:37, 57, and 65.

13. *Coryat's Crudities,* 44 and 34.

14. Greg and Boswell, *Court Book B,* 59.

15. *The Complete Works in Verse and Prose of Samuel Daniel,* A. B. Grosart, ed., 5 vols. (1885, repr. New York: Russell and Russell, 1963), 4:81–82.

16. Moreover, it had closely analogous precedents. Compare East's copyright in a collection of Dowland's songs, printed in 1600 for the musician George Eastland; this publication is discussed in Margaret Dowling, "The Printing of John Dowland's *Second Booke of Songs or Ayres,*" *The Library,* 4th ser., 12 (1931–32): 365–80, particularly 367–68.

17. Arber, *Transcript,* 3:489. I am indebted here to Kirschbaum's discussion of the episode ("Author's Copyright," 63–65).

18. William A. Jackson, *Records of the Court of the Stationers' Company, 1602–1640* (London: The Bibliographical Society, 1957), 57.

19. Jackson and Unger nicely register the irony: "This is a paginary reprint of the first edition, 1612, even to the extent that the note at the end stating that that edition was but a few copies for private distribution is repeated" (*Pforzheimer Catalogue,* no. 242).

20. My account here corresponds most closely with Greg's in "*The Spanish Tragedy*—A Leading Case?" an article written in 1925 and reprinted in his *Collected Papers,* 149–55. He reiterated his argument as part of his 1957 essay, "The Printing of Shakespeare's *Troilus and Cressida* in the First Folio" (*Collected Papers,* 395–96), despite the strenuous challenge of Leo Kirschbaum; see "Is *The Spanish Tragedy* a Leading Case?" *JEGP* 37 (1938): 501–12.

21. *Shakespeare and the Stationers,* 89. Pollard once proposed that Nashe's *Pierce Penniless* provided an instance of copyright relocated from a "piratical" publisher to one favored by the author (*Shakespeare Folios and Quartos,* 3). Richard Jones entered and published the book in 1592, and his prefatory epistle apologizes for his boldness in publishing the work in Nashe's absence. Two more editions appeared before the year

was out, both printed by Jeffes for John Busby, and both containing "a private Epistle of the Author to the Printer," in which Nashe denigrates the first edition—"uncorrected and unfinished it hath offred it selfe to the open scorne of the world" (*The Works of Thomas Nashe*, ed. R. B. McKerrow, with corrections and supplementary notes by F. P. Wilson, 5 vols. [Oxford : B. Blackwell, 1958], 1:153). But whereas Pollard takes the letter to have been written to Busby, to whom he supposes Nashe to have entrusted the second edition, Greg believes it to have been written to Jones, whom he supposes to have unofficially transferred the work to Busby for subsequent publication ("Was the First Edition of *Pierce Penniless* a Piracy?" *Collected Works*, 404).

22. It used to be thought that Beale was counterfeiting Jaggard's edition, but Beale's editions are easy to distinguish from Jaggard's. Indeed, he soon stopped reprinting Jaggard's patched-up edition and began using his own far better 1612 version. See W. A. Jackson, *The Library*, 4th ser., 15 (1934–35): 367–72.

23. Another conspicuous absence from the list of Blount and Jaggard's entrances is *King John. The Troublesome Reign of King John* almost certainly *was* one of Shakespeare's sources for his *Life and Death of King John;* it had never been entered, but it had been thrice printed. Greg supposes that the copyright in *The Troublesome Reign* was "derelict" in 1623 (*The Shakespeare First Folio*, 61)—though Thomas Dewe, who had published *The Troublesome Reign* in 1622, or Anne Helme, whose husband had published the play in 1611, might be supposed to have held the rights. Derelict or not, entered or not, *The Troublesome Reign* had long been in print and Jaggard and Blount did not presume to enter *King John* under these circumstances. They may have made a private accommodation with Dewe or Helme; they are more likely to have decided to risk being charged with infringement after the fact. But to attempt an entrance would have been to excite formal company scrutiny, and they apparently though the easiest way to secure copyright in Shakespeare's play was to avoid raising the question of who might own the copyright in *The Troublesome Reign*.

24. See above, p. 45–47.

25. It is tempting to treat Daniel's *Delia* as a watershed in authorial rights, yet we cannot speak of it as having fundamentally changed the way stationers went about their business. Three years later, another aggrieved author, Sir Lewis Lewkenor, complained that "the coppies of my letters (contrarie to my intention) were . . . by some of them [i.e., his correspondents] given abrode, and lastly not long since, a discourse printed in Paules Church-yarde, conteining some parte of the substance thereof, but manye things that I had written left out, and manye thinges inserted that I never ment, and finally in the whole so falsified and chaunged, aswell in matter as wordes, & ignorantly entermixed with fictions of the publisher, that howsoever the vulgar sorte bee therewith pleased, those that are of farther reach and insight, cannot but condemne it as a thing fabulous, grossely handled and full of absurdities" (*The Estate of English Fugitives Under the King of Spaine*). The "falsified" first edition to which Lewkenor refers, *The Usage of the English Fugitives,* was entered and published by John Drawater early in 1595, but the revised and so "authorized" version in which Lewkenor makes his complaint was also published by Drawater. It is true that William Ponsonby challenged Drawater by entering the same book himself in August, and it may well be that Lewkenor wrote this epistle to the reader as a preface for Ponsonby's ostensibly forthcoming edition. But if so, that edition was evidently forestalled by Drawater, the "proper" owner of copyright.

Although I think it unlikely, Ponsoby may in fact have entered the book after Drawater published the revised edition—but whatever the sequence, Ponsonby's entrance was ineffectual, for Drawater published yet another edition of the revised version in 1596. In 1597, Ponsonby entered the book a second time, as "a booke heretofore printed by John Drawater," and the entry is confirmed by the specification that "the said Drawater hathe yeilded his consente to this entrance." This is not the usual language for a regular transfer of copy; it smacks instead of adjudication and resolution.

26. Appeal to authority outside the company became a reflex for Ponsonby. Thus, in 1598, when several stationers infringed Ponsonby's rights in the *Arcadia,* he began an action in Star Chamber rather than an appeal to the stationers' internal Court of Assistants, this at a time when Ponsonby was a junior warden of the Stationers' Company. See the account in C. B. Judge, *Elizabethan Book-Pirates* (Cambridge: Harvard, 1934), 100–111. It bears noting that the dispute *ended up* before the Court of Assistants.

27. Sir Francis Bacon, *The Essayes or Counsells, Civill and Morall,* ed. Michael Kiernan (Cambridge, Mass.: 1985), 316. The letter is dated 30 January 1597.

28. *The Essayes,* lxviii.

29. *"Cancellatur ista intratio per curiam tentam 7 februarii"* (3:79).

30. But see the discussion below of the dispute that erupted between Jaggard and Augustine Vincent, on the one hand, and Ralph Brooke, on the other.

31. *Shakespeare and the Stationers,* 139–40.

32. *Works,* 3:187 (ll. 1–15).

33. Though continuity of copyright continued to be the rule, the possibility of new kinds of exception, exceptions that did not entail appeal to supervenient authority, seems to have opened. One such exception involves Ralph Brooke's substantial catalogue of the peerage, which issued from Jaggard's press, full of errors, in 1619. Brooke showed no particular eagerness to improve the text until he learned that Jaggard was about to publish Augustine Vincent's *A discoverie of Errours in the First Edition of the Catalogue of Nobility, Published By Ralphe Brooke.* (Jaggard's decision to publish Vincent's *Discoverie of Errours,* and so to advertise the flaws in Brooke's volume, will seem odd only at first glance: the first edition and Vincent's *Discovery* would have complemented each other, rather like a modern boxed set.)

Furious at Jaggard, Brooke hastily prepared a corrected edition, which Stansby published in 1622, before the Vincent-Jaggard volume was completed. In the Stansby edition, Brooke blames the errors in the first edition on Jaggard. By way of response, Jaggard appended a petulant letter to the Vincent volume, attesting to Brooke's vigilance as a proofreader, his attendance at the press during the early stages of printing, and his apparent care over the revises even when illness enforced his absence from the press. Jaggard also insisted that the errors in the original edition could be blamed neither on shoddy presswork nor on inattentive proofreading, but that they derived from Brooke's manuscript($\P_6{}^v$). Vincent is particularly devastating on the subject in the body of his text: "As if untruths in the Historie, or falsifications in the Chronologie . . . or the like materiall errors, which I (his *Envious Detractor*) onely stoope at, were the Printers negligences, and not his owne grosse ignorances"($\P_4$—$\P_4{}^v$). Technically speaking, the Stansby edition would seem either to violate Jaggard's copyright, or to offer evidence that authorial revision could in fact occasionally effect a relocation of copyright. That there is no record of Jaggard's having made formal protest against Stansby's edition of Brooke's *Catalogue* seems to argue for the latter conclusion, that we have here an instance of editorial repossession. An unusual case, to be sure, but like Daniel's it bespeaks a competition between author and stationer the outcome of which is no longer rigged.

34. Examples other than those discussed below include Torrentinus's patent in the *Pandects* (1551); Cooper's for his *Dictionary* (1563); R. Wright, for a translation of *Tacitus;* Stringer, for schoolbooks (1597); Stallenge, for a book on silk production (1607); Woodhouse, for a law report (1608); Jordan and Hooker, by nomination of Lord Morley, for *God and the King* (1615); Hilliard, for engraved portraits of the king (1617); F. Morrison's *Itinerary* (1617); Rathburne and Burgess, for town maps (1618); Mariott, for *Pharmacopoeia* (1618); Fulke, for a book on Bible translations (1618); Alley, for Middleton's *The Peace-maker* (1618), by nomination of the author—this last a complicated case since the book was attributed to King James, the only source of the attribution to Middleton being the assignment to Alley in *S.P.D.*, 19 July 1618. Scrutton, *The Laws of Copyright: An Examination of the Principles Which Should Regulate Literary and Artistic Property in England and Other Countries*, Yorke Prize essay (London: J. Murray, 1883), 93–300.

35. Arber, *Transcript,* 1:111. Arber dates the complaint as c. August 1577.

36. See Fox, *Monopolies and Patents,* 68–70 and 72–73.

37. But cf. F. C. Dietz, *English Public Finance, 1558–1642* (New York, 1932), where the fiscal difficulties are traced specifically to the pressure of military expenditure and of Elizabeth's belief in her need for a war chest.

38. Pollard, *Records of the English Bible,* 21–22.

39. Ibid., 257.

40. Ibid., 259.

41. Rymer, *Foedera* (Hague edition), 6, pt. 3, p. 85. In January 1549 the valuable patent in the printing of service books was slivered: John Oswen received the rights for such printing and publishing in Wales and the Marches; in the next year Thomas Gaultier received a patent in the printing of French service books.

42. Rymer, *Foedera* (Hague edition), 6, pt. 3, p. 85.

43. Ibid., 157; *Calendar of Patent Rolls,* Edw. VI, pt. 7, m. 1.

44. See, for example, Norton's account of the privileges extant in the early eighties in Arber, *Transcript,* 2:775.

45. Blagden speaks of a memorandum of the stationers' "governing body" (presumably the Court of Assistants) in December 1565 that equates the functioning of stationer's copyright and royal privilege (*The Stationers' Company,* 31–32); unfortunately he does not provide full documentation for the assertion. Certainly the 1583 report of the commission investigating Wolfe's insurrection equates the two forms of protection: "where her Majestie graunteth not privilege, they are enforced to have a kind of previleges among them selves by ordinances of the companie whereby everie first printer of any lawefull booke, presenting it in the hall, hath the sane as severall to him self as any man hath any boke by her Majesties previlege." *S.P.D.,* Eliz., 161:1 (article 37), cited in Blagden, *The Stationers' Company,* 42.

46. William Dugdale, *Origines Juridicales,* 4th ed. (London: 1680), 59.

47. Tottel seems to have convinced his colleagues that he was only appealing to them for *confirmation,* and not renewal, of the charter: the entry in the register recording his appeal that the patent be "confirmed and allowed" describes the patent as "dated *anno ii° et iii° philippi et marie*" (Arber, *Transcript,* 1:95), which puts the date a few years later than the actual date of the grant.

48. Greg dryly remarks on the breadth of this privilege by noting that "to define it Totell made an entry in 1583 of what appears to have been his entire stock" (*Aspects and Problems,* 99).

49. Presumably, the inclusion of the catechism among the "other" works was the most valuable aspect of the grant (see Oastler, *John Day,* 70). Recall from chapter 2 that Daye already held the extremely lucrative privilege, for life, in the English catechism together with the works of Becon and Ponet (7 Ed. VI, part 3, m. 23). Note also that the several patents awarded to Jugge, Cawood, and Seres effectively distribute the patents vested in Whitchurch and Grafton.

50. These "Considerations delivered to the Parliament, 1559" (Hatfield MS. 152/96–99b) are summarized in Tawney and Power, *Tudor Economic Documents,* 1:325–30.

51. S. T. Bindoff, "The Making of the Statute of Artificers," *Elizabethan Government and Society: Essays Presented to Sir John Neale,* eds. S. T. Bindoff, J. Hurstfield, and C. H. Williams (London: Athlone, 1961), 56–94, particularly 80–91.

52. "In the letters of protection to John Kempe and his Company dated 1331 (Pat. 5 Ed. iii p. 1, m.25), will be found the earliest authenticated instance of a Royal grant made with the avowed motive of instructing the English in a new industry. Here we have, not a solitary instance of protection, but the declaration of a distinct and comprehensive policy in favor of the textile industry" (Hulme, "The Early History of the English Patent System," 118–119). Hulme records grants of industrial monopolies to foreigners in 1368, for clockmaking; in 1440, for novel forms of salt manufacture; and in 1452 for new mining techniques (119–20); Arthur Allan Gomme (*Patents of Invention* [London: Longmans, 1946], 396) adds a patent granted in 1449 to a Flemish glassmaker who had devised a new method for the fabrication of colored glass.

53. This distinction between monopolies of manufacture and monopolies of sale is Holdsworth's (*History of English Law,*4:346). Though Holdsworth's assertion is true of late medieval grants, it is also the case that significant import, export, and trading monopolies were already being granted under Henry VIII, for which see Hughes and Larkin, *Tudor Royal Proclamations,* 1:xxxi–xxxii. On grants to attract foreign manufacturing methods, see Fox, *Monopolies and Patents,* 46 and 80–81n.

In "Early History of Patents for Invention," (*Transactions of the Newcome Society,* 26 [1947–49]), Maximilian Frumkin points out a crucial way in which the goal of fostering new domestic industries left its traces on the modern patent system: "It is well known that the tradition [sic] term for English patents has been 14 (occasionally 7 or 21 years) and is a period we seldom see on continental grants. That term was linked by Sir Edward Coke [*Third Institutes,* cap. 85] with another traditional English term of seven years—namely, the duration of apprenticeship" (51). For more on the durational quantum, see p. 306, n. 24 below.

54. Thirsk, *Economic Policy and Projects,* 24.

55. Gomme, *Patents of Invention*, p. 8. Such regulatory devices, originating in Italy, were flourishing throughout Europe at this time, becoming characteristic instruments of sixteenth-century rule; see Frank D. Prager, "A History of Intellectual Property from 1545 to 1787," *Journal of the Patent Office Society* 26 (1944): 712–30; and Edith T. Penrose, *The Economics of the International Patent System* (Baltimore: Johns Hopkins University Press, 1951), 2–3. For evidence of the new interest in development entailed by the new policies, see *A Discourse of the Common Weal of this Realm of England*, ed. Elizabeth Lamond (Cambridge: Cambridge University Press, 1893), particularly 89. Although the date of this essay is disputed, Thirsk asserts firmly that the work dates from 1549 (*Economic Policy and Projects*, 13); certainly such protectionism was well under way by the time of Elizabeth, and there was nothing unfamiliar about the recruitment of foreign expertise proposed in the essay: "I have hearde saie in venis, that most flourishing citie at these dayes of all Europe, if they maye heare of anye conninge craftes man in anie facultie, they will find the meanes to alure him to dwell in theire Citie; for it is a wounder to se what a deale of money one good occupier dothe bring into a towne, thoughe he him selfe doe not gayne to his owne commoditie but a poore livinge" (128). The Venetian connection may be as important in this regulatory context as in the book trade. Frumkin, "Early History of Patents for Invention," 52.

56. "Once it was recognized that the alien immigrant was entitled to such protection in order to encourage the establishment of a new trade or industry, it was a logical extension of that policy to accord the same encouragement to the domestic worker" (Fox, *Monopolies and Patents*, 55; see also pp. 80–81). The consequences of this are particularly striking: "The impress of this development, as has before been noted, has been left on the British patent system by the acceptance of the doctrine that a valid patent may be granted on a communication from abroad of a new manufacture, although the patentee himself may not have invented anything" (ibid.). On the shift of intitiative from Crown to "projector," see Holdsworth, *History of English Law*, 4:346; and Thirsk, *Economic Policy and Projects*, 58.

57. The count is Fox's (*Monopolies and Patents*, 61–62), based on the list of monopoly grants compiled by Hulme in "The Early History of the English Patent System." See the saltpeter monopoly to Philip Cockeram and John Barnes in 1561, a particularly telling illustration of this shift (Hulme, "Early History," 122).

58. D. Seaborne Davies ("Acontius, Champion of Toleration, and the Patent System," *Economic History Review* 7 [1936]: 65) argues that monopolies of invention are direct descendants of the printing patent; and see also Fox, *Monopolies and Patents*, 53–54; and Price, *The English Patents of Monopoly*, 8–9 and 14–16.

Charles Webster observes that "75 per cent of the patents granted between 1561 and 1688 were directly (43 per cent) or indirectly (32 per cent) concerned with mining" in *The Great Instauration: Science, Medicine and Reform, 1626–60* (London: Duckworth, 1975), 345. Moreover, so much was mining associated with industrial innovation that, in *The New Atlantis*, Bacon describes those in Salomon's House whose responsibility it is to "try new experiments" as "Pioners or Miners," distinguishing them from those who "collect the experiments of all mechanical arts," called "Mystery-men," (Spedding, 3:164). For Bacon, the new lore associated with mining is significantly different from the old knowledge guarded by the guilds.

59. If one lumps together patents for mining and various smelting techniques,

for water pumps and special furnaces, a very large proportion of the Tudor and Stuart patents of monopoly may be accounted for: in effect, the special provenance of the patent of invention was metal production. For more on the mining patents, see Hulme, "The Early History of the English Patent System," 123–26; W. H. Price, *The English Patents of Monopoly,* 62–63; and M. B. Donald, *Elizabethan Monopolies: The History of the Company of Mineral and Battery Works from 1565 to 1604* (London: Oliver and Boyd, 1961), 1–21.

60. *Cal. S. P. Dom. Eliz.,* 1601–3, addenda, 1547–65, 495. The petition first showed up among the papers for 1559, but it may have been mistakenly filed there; certainly the patent was not granted until 1565.

61. Yet, as Thirsk explains, claims urged on the grounds of innovation were inevitably compromised: "Nearly all new projects settled themselves in a district having some existing connection with the new enterprise. . . . This explains why disputes so often broke out later concerning the novelty of projects" (*Economic Policy and Projects,* 25–26). This increased the pressure on the petitioning projector, who was obliged to inflate the rhetoric of innovation.

62. 1 Hen. IV, c. 6, cited in D. Seaborne Davies, "Early History of the Patent Specification," *Law Quarterly Review* 50 (1934): 260. Providing an exhaustive description of value—or even one inaccessible to challenge—was an impossible prerequisite, so it soon became customary for petitioners to append a disclaimer to their application by means of which they sought to absolutize their monopoly, "any acte statute ordinaunce permission order proclamac[i]on restraynt comaundement custome or whatsoever other thing . . . to the contrary herof notwithstondyng." Davies cites this (p. 262) from the glass patent awarded to Henry Smith in 1552 (P.R. 6 Edw. VI, p. 5), alleging that the terms of the grant were probably copied from the petition. On the historical development of this *non obstantibus* clause, see G. G. Crump, *"Eo Quod Expressa Mentio, etc,"* in *Essays in History Presented to R. Lane Poole,* ed. H. W. C. Davis (Oxford: Oxford University Press, 1927), 30–45.

63. Davies, "Early History," 263–74.

64. Hulme, "The Early History of the English Patent System," 122–23.

65. Hulme's discussion of this semantic development is useful; see ibid., 139–41. That the sense of invention or discovery as the work of practical imagination is new and fragile is evidenced by the fact "that when used in . . . [this] modern sense they are generally preceded or supported by another less equivocal term or phrase, e.g. 'invented and devised' 'devise and invention'" (140). See also Price's observation that, at this pivotal moment, "the popular and even the legal meaning of the word 'inventor' covered not only the originating but also the importing of technical ideas and processes." *English Patents of Monopoly,* 64.

66. D'Ewes, *Journal,* 644.

67. The vocabulary of practical imagination and of motion have long been interrelated and, of course, "invention" itself is etymologically spatial. But when Bacon begins his defense of prerogative from this linguistic register, his purposes are more than etymological: he thereby recalls the insular mercantilism with which the monopoly grant originated.

68. *Poetic Authority,* 5–8.

69. "Gesture and Signature," in *For a Critique of the Political Economy of the Sign*, 104.

70. Thirsk, *Economic Policy and Projects*, 59. It should also be remarked, finally, that the patent became an administrative instrument under Elizabeth, who began conferring regulatory monopolies by patent. On Elizabethan industrial regulation, see Heckscher, *Mercantilism*, 1:246–63.

71. Thirsk, *Economic Policy and Projects*, 59–65.

72. Ibid., 51–53.

73. The earliest precedent for a legal attack on the principle of monopoly may be found in the *Case of Gloucester School* (1410). On the burgeoning protest movement, see chapters 3 and 4 of Thirsk, *Economic Policy and Projects*, pp. 51–105; for the parliamentary history, see J. E. Neale, *Elizabeth and Her Parliaments, 1584–1601* (New York, St. Martin's: 1958), pp. 352–56 and 376–93; David Harris Sacks, "Parliament, Liberty, and the Commonweal," *Parliament and Liberty*, ed. J. H. Hexter (Stanford: Stanford University Press, 1992), 85–121; and Elizabeth Read Foster, "The Procedure of the House of Commons against Patents and Monopolies, 1621–24," *Conflict in Stuart England* (London: Jonathan Cape, 1960).

74. D'Ewes, *Journal*, 649.

75. Heckscher, *Mercantilism*, 245.

76. On the structural transformations marked by the statute, see Heckscher, *Mercantilism*, 1:233–34.

77. The statute also severely curtailed the traditional commercial freedoms of English guildsmen, forbidding members of one guild to trade in goods traditionally the province of another guild. The restriction of commercial mobility might seem a victory for guild power, but it again asserted the royal origins of that power: Cecil was engineering the transformation of local guilds into objects of national economic administration.

78. Arber, *Transcript*, 2:771.

79. Within the book trade the privilege had long been entrenched, and under the sway of its changing functions, the Stationers' Company was polarized. Wolfe and his fellows responded by violating privileges whose propriety was no longer self-evident. Richard Tottel, on the other hand, exemplifies the response of those more richly endowed with power and capital. Having been granted what would be the very valuable patent in law books in 1553, we find him petitioning the Crown in 1585—after the assault on patents—for a monopoly in the collection of linen rags for the manufacture of paper: Tottel was pursuing cartelization, by means of the patent. R. H. Clapperton, *Paper: An Historical Account of Its Making by Hand from the Earliest Times Down to the Present Day* (Oxford: Shakespeare Head, 1934).

80. "Printing and the People," 222–23.

81. See Fox, *Monopolies and Patents*, 54.

82. The fact that the press was potentially a practical weapon against technological monopolies made it the logical *site* of protection. In 1589, therefore, when Timothy Bright sought to monopolize his new shorthand, he secured a fifteen-year patent for the printing of works in this character, a late descendant of the Aldine italics privilege.

Compare also the 1607 patent to William Stallenge for *a book on* silk production (S. P. Dom. 1603–10, 344), as well as Marriott's 1618 patent in the *Pharmacoepia* (12. R. 17,77; S. P. Dom. 1611–18, 536) and Morley's 1627 *ars memorandi* for language acquisition (19. R. 18, 857; S. P. Dom. 1623–25, 364).

83. Fox compiles, and cites other compilations, of the accumulated objects of patent protection in *Monopolies and Patents, 71.*

84. On the growing hostility to monopolies in the nineties, see Price, *The English Patents of Monopoly*, 9–11; on the attacks from the gentry, see John U. Nef, *Industry and Government in France and England, 1540–1640* (Ithaca: Cornell, 1964), 106–107. No less a political theorist than Jean Bodin fixed on monopolies as one of the principle causes of price inflation and dearth in the sixteenth century, second only to the influx of precious metals from the New World; see *La Reponse de Maistre Jean Bodin, Advocat en la Cour au Paradoxe de Monsieur de Malestroit*, in *Écrits Notables Sur la Monnaie*, 4 vols., ed. Jean-Yves Le Branchu (Paris: Alcan, 1934), 1:94–95.

85. Both Unwin (*Industrial Organization*, passim) and Christopher Hill (*The Century of Revolution, 1603–1714: A History of England*, eds. Christopher Brooke and Denis Mack Smith [Edinburgh: Nelson, 1961], 30) identify monopoly practices as focusing the unrest experienced within the urban guilds.

86. Heckscher has useful general reflections on the effect of monopolies on the early weakening of the guilds in England; see *Mercantilism*, 1:245.

87. Cyprian Blagden points out that the Stationers' Register includes the minutes of a partners' meeting in late 1591, though almanacs and prognostications had not yet been included in the associated stock. "The English Stock of the Stationers' Company," *The Library*, 5th ser., 10 (1955): 174.

88. D'Ewes, *Journal*, 648. Hill takes his cue from the anecdote, and must be quoted: "It is difficult for us to picture to ourselves the life of a man living in a house built with monopoly bricks, with windows (if any) of monopoly glass; heated by monopoly coal (in Ireland monopoly timber), burning in a grate made of monopoly iron. His walls were lined with monopoly tapestries. He slept on monopoly feathers, did his hair with monopoly brushes and monopoly combs. He washed himself with monopoly soap, his clothes in monopoly starch. He dressed in monopoly lace, monopoly linen, monopoly leather, monopoly gold thread. His hat was of monopoly beaver, with a monopoly band. His clothes were held up by monopoly belts, monopoly buttons, monopoly pins. They were dyed with monopoly dyes. He ate monopoly butter, monopoly currant, monopoly red herrings, monopoly salmon and monopoly lobsters. His food was seasoned with monopoly salt, monopoly pepper, monopoly vinegar. Out of monopoly glasses he drank monopoly wines and monopoly spirits; out of pewter mugs made from monopoly tin he drank monopoly beer made from monopoly hops, kept in monopoly barrels or monopoly bottles, sold in monopoly-licensed ale-houses. He smoked monopoly tobacco in monopoly pipes, played with monopoly dice or monopoly cards, or on monopoly lute-strings. He wrote with monopoly pens, on monopoly writing-paper; read (through monopoly spectacles, by the light of monopoly candles) monopoly printed books, including monopoly Bibles and monopoly Latin grammars, printed on paper made from monopoly-collected rags, bound in sheepskin dressed with monopoly alum. . . . [the passage continues in this vein] . . . Not all these patents existed at once, but all come from the first four decades of the seventeenth century. In 1621 there were

alleged to be 700 of them" (*The Century of Revolution*, 32–33). The campaign against monopolies in the last Elizabethan parliament was facilitated by the work of the previous parliament, which had done much to curtail monopolistic competition in the commodity markets. The vigorous attack on forestallers and regraters had a kind of rhetorical momentum that was sustained in the subsequent assault on industrial monopolies.

89. The last Elizabethan parliament was convened on 27 October 1601; the debate on patents commenced in mid-November. On the personalities behind early Elizabethan industrial policy, see Bindoff, "The Making of the Statute of Artificers," 80–91.

90. Egerton's communication is slightly variously reported; this is the version cited in Neale, *Elizabeth and Her Parliaments, 1584–1601*, 355.

After the debate of 1601, Elizabeth issued a proclamation revoking a great variety of patents and placing all her subjects at liberty "to take their ordinary remedy" *at common law* against abuses by the holders of the remaining patents (Hughes and Larkin, no. 812). Coke seizes on this jurisdictional principle as the fundamental issue in Elizabethan and Jacobean disputes on monopoly grants; see chapter 85 of his *Third Part of the Institutes of the Laws of England*. This paves the way for subsequent maneuvers. A parliamentary petition of 1624 for relief of monopolies and remedy of grievances against patents was, dangerously, couched as a petition based on common law. This in turn anticipates a similar petition issued in 1628—a petition not of grace, but of right (Elizabeth Read Foster, "The Procedure of the House of Commons," 76). Foster judges these petitions to be even more important than the Statute of Monopolies (1624), which has been called "the first statutory invasion of the prerogative" (Charles Howard McIlwain, *Constitutionalism, Ancient and Modern* [Oxford, 1940], 138).

91. Cited in J. P. Sommerville, *Politics and Ideology in England, 1603–1640* (London: Longman, 1986), 148. For a general introduction to the terms of debate on property, see Clive Holmes, "Parliament, Liberty, Taxation, and Property," *Parliament and Liberty*, ed. J. H. Hexter (Stanford: Stanford University Press, 1992), 122–54, and particularly 138–39; for the relation between the rhetoric of property and the conceptualization of polity, see chapter 1 of Margaret Atwood Judson, *The Crisis of the Constitution: An Essay in Constitutional and Political Thought in England, 1603–1645*, 2nd ed. (New Brunswick: Rutgers, 1988).

92. Noy's Reports, King's Bench, 181. Fuller will continue as the champion of the concept of absolute property and of properties, beyond the reach of the prerogative, not only in goods but in artisanal activity; see his 1610 remarks quoted in *Proceedings in Parliament 1610*, ed. E. R. Foster, 2 vols. (New Haven: Yale University Press, 1966), 2:157.

93. Heckscher, *Mercantilism*, 1:283–84.

94. However, in an important case from 1599, *Davenant v. Hurdis* (otherwise known as the *Merchant Taylors' Case*), even a charter confirmed by act of Parliament was held void on the grounds that it had created a monopoly.

95. "*In huiusmodi casibus fortior et potentior est vulgaris consuetudo quam regalis concessio*," cited in Heckscher, *Mercantilism*, 1:284. I rely heavily on Heckscher's discussion in this paragraph.

96. To some extent, the opposition is a jurisdictional protest. Despite Egerton's undertakings on the queen's behalf, the Privy Council, highest of the royal courts,

remained the central authority in patent disputes; indeed, the common law courts did not fully establish their authority in commercial law until well into the eighteenth century.

97. Useful accounts of the case may be found in Price, *The English Patents of Monopoly*, 318–26; and D. Seaborne Davies, "Further Light on the Case of Monopolies," *Law Quarterly Review* 191 (1932): 394–414.

98. 3 Edw. IV, c. 4.

99. There is good reason to suppose that Allin had been encouraged in his infringement by the aldermen of the city of London. The playing-card monopoly was as unpopular as any, and there had been a history of infringements against the former holder of the patent, so the city officials might well have counted on a good deal of popular support for an action that would make this grant the occasion of a general test of the city's economic rights. For an account of earlier infringements, see Davies, "Further Light on the Case of Monopolies," 400–402. Davies also discusses (406–11) *Allin v. Garrard* (1605), in which Allin charges that the lord mayor and aldermen of London, having promised to indemnify Allin if he would challenge the monopoly, left him to bear his own legal expenses after the infringement.

100. Cited from Price, *The English Patents of Monopoly*, 323.

101. The first of the three, Hastings's patent for the manufacture of a napped woolen fabric known as frizado, had been annulled on the grounds that Hastings had not been the first to introduce this manufacture from abroad and that, moreover, Hastings's methods had long been known in England; the second, Matthew's patent for the production of a certain kind of bone-handled knife, was successfully challenged by the Cutlers' Company on the grounds that they had made similar knives (so that Matthew's patent infringed the customary rights of the company).

102. See Price, *English Patents of Monopoly*, 60, with full references to the case.

103. Fuller's use of the *Humphrey* case (Noy's Reports, K.B. 183) is revealing. The grant was more than a little unusual, since it protected all metallurgic devices contrived by the patentees subsequent to the date of the grant. Though the permissibility of this sort of grant was made an issue, Fuller treats the case as if it were simply a stringent test of the concept of invention.

In *The Third Part of the Institutes*, Coke makes much of Fuller's line of argument, again insisting on the importance of the criterion of novelty. He denies that a refinement of technique merits such protection, for "that was to put but a new button on an old coat." The novelty is the fourth of seven criteria that Coke articulates, and he is building to an explicitly political climax: fifth, a monopoly "must not be injurious to the State by raising of prices of commodities at home"; sixth, "nor to the hurt of trade"; seventh, "nor generally inconvenient." There was a new invention found out heretofore, that Bonnets and Caps might be thickened in a Fulling mill, by which means more might be thickened and fulled in one day than by the labours of Fourscore men, who got their livings by it. It was ordained that Bonnets and Caps should be thickened and fulled by the strength of men, and not in a Fullng mill, for it was holden inconvenient to turn so many labouring men to idleness" (6th ed. [London, 1680], Bb₁ᵛ).

104. Price, *English Patents of Monopoly*, chapter 3.

105. *England's Helicon: 1600, 1614*, ed. Hyder Edward Rollins, 2 vols. (Cambridge:

Harvard University Press, 1935), 1:6. I follow Hebel, Bullen, and Rollins in attributing
the letter, signed L.N., to Ling (see Rollins's ed., 2:41–63).

106. Jonson uses the key term for the first title page of the 1608 masque
collection—*The Characters of Two royall Masques . . . invented by Ben: Jonson*—
and the stationers' recording secretary transcribed the same term for the registration to
Thorpe—"*The Characters of Twoo Royall Maskes, invented by Ben. Johnson.*"

CHAPTER FIVE

1. "Parliament, Liberty, and the Commonweal," 86.

2. *Institutes*, 2:46–47. Fox observes that "the important point of the case is that
an ordinance which created a monopoly was held to be void even though done under
the authority conferred by charter, the terms of which charter had been confirmed by
Parliament. It remained only to hold void a monopoly expressly created by royal charter
and such a case followed close on the heels of the Merchant Tailors' Case" (*Monopolies
and Patents*, 215).

3. Sacks, "Parliament, Liberty, and the Commonweal," 94–96. It may seem odd,
in retrospect, that the legal protest against privatization should have led, as Sacks
shows, to popular defense of the franchise. His complex argument shows how "the
facts of monopoly and of electoral politics converged" (106–109; quotation from
108) and so exposes how much political momentum developed out of the attack
on monopolies. Note the revolutionary force of *Davenant v. Hurdis*, in which the
traditional claims of guilds on monopolistic protections are forced to yield to the
liberty of the subject. That the pursuit of economic justice should adumbrate political
renegotiations might have been predicted from *Darcy v. Allin*, for the arguments in that
case had already established the connection: pleading against monopoly for the defense,
Fuller had adduced Parliament, with its ostensible freedom of political exchange and
diversity of opinion, as an institutional model for the ideal economic market; see Sacks,
"Parliament," 117–18. On the metaphoric extension of "monopoly" in Tudor and Stuart
social and political theory, see A. C. Houston, "The Levellers, Monopolies, and the
Public Interest," *History of Political Thought* 14:3 (1993), particularly 385–87.

4. Foster, "The Procedure of the House of Commons," 67–68, and 75.

5. Ibid., 72–73.

6. Harington clearly took great pleasure in this particular figurative node. Cf. the
beginning of the *Apologie* that follows Coombe's illustrative *Anatomie* in the second issue
of the *Metamorphoses*: "When I had finished the precedent pamphlet, & in mine owne
fantasie very sufficiently evacuated my head of such homely stuffe, of which it might
seeme it was verie full charged, etc."

7. The passages in question (pp. 157–60) bridge the second and third sections of
the *Metamorphosis*. The *dictum*, "And when to natures needs provokt thou art / Do
not forbeare the same in any wise / So shalt thou live long time with little smart," is
translated from the *Regimen Sanitatis Salernitanum;* Harington made a full translation of
the *Regimen* for James in 1607.

8. And cf. p. 121, where Harington, always interested in the promotion of flows,
argues that rivers need governmental attention to maintain inland commerce and urban
sanitation.

9. *Metamorphosis,* 165.

10. *A Brief Apologie of certen Newe Invencions* (this may be the particular book that provoked Harington); *The Jewell House* in 1594–95, printed by P. Short for Ponsonby—this is the first coal-balls treatise (the third coal-balls treatise was also printed by Short in 1603); *A Discoverie of certaine English Wants* (1595), for Ponsonby; *Delights for Ladies,* cosmetic formulae, recipes, etc., in 1600, for Short.

11. Plat admits that his method was derived from a Belgian process.

12. He also asks that his readers "not [be] regarding the censures of those ignorant, or malicious spirits of our age, who presuming to know the simples of my fire, may happily range into base and offensive matter, and thereby labor to discredite that secret" (D4v). He then ends by promising a new cheap kind of compost: which secret he is prepared to sell.

13. In the midst of this passage, Harington observes that "it is a common obloquie, that the Turks (who still keepe the order of Deuteronomie for their ordure) do object to Christians, that they are poisoned with their owne doung, which objection cannot be answered" (170).

14. Persius, *Satires,* 1.27; *Metamorphosis,* 192.

15. Harington's engagement with the press is manifest. He read proof for the *Metamorphosis* fairly carefully, making substantive changes as he read. He seems to have helped prepare printer's copy, writing his own marginal glosses and concerning himself with the details of page layout. There is nothing surprising in this: publication is itself quite continuous with the cultural work that his *Discourse* advocates.

It might be added that a certain amount of snobbery infuses Harington's response to Plat, in this case a disdain for improper forms of gain and perhaps some condescension to the use of the press for specifically commercial purposes. He advocates the vulgarization of invention (in both senses), placing emphasis on the noble freedom, the gratuity of "trew discourse." Owing to what might be called generic ethics, however, Harington's epigrams introduce inconsistencies. Some of these poems attack plagiarisms—e.g., epigram 149, "How *Sextus* laid claim to an Epigram"—while a poem addressed to Daniel defends imitation as "honest Theft" (epigram 126; and cf. 388, addressed to Davies, in *Letters and Epigrams,* ed. Norman Egbert McClure [Philadelphia: University of Pennsylvania Press, 1930]). This epigrammatic ethics (for which see chapter 4 of my *Jonson and Possessive Authorship*) entails greater possessiveness—albeit a possessiveness of light and witty posture—than the *Metamorphosis* records.

16. *Nugae Antiquae,* ed. Thomas Park, 2 vols. (London: Vernor and Hood, 1804), 1:245.

17. That others took this as one of the central issues of the *Metamorphosis* can be gauged from the anonymous *Ulysses Upon Ajax,* cited in the epigraph above, where Harington's mock-proposal that he and Plat form a cartel provokes the following: "In discoursing your Monapole, wherein you angle for nothing but *Carps* to feede other men with, you not onelie wax tooe bitter a curser of your betters (a fault worse then *Burdets* and it were pittie it should be expiated with his destiny). But you prively gird likewise at patents, . . . which beeing priveledges graunted by a prince, fruits of her royall prerogative . . . are not groslie to bee jested at, careleslie to be disgraced, or fondly

to be delt withal" (E$_7$—E$_7$^{v}). The pamphlet indicates how sharp was the topical edge of this dispute.

It is quite conceivable that the prolific Plat is the unnamed author of *Ulysses,* for he is the recipient of unusually generous praise: "Now for mayster *Plat* mine old and honest friende, why what of him? His life inlal [*sic*] mens eies so upright, his birth not to be contmened, his studie for the commoditie of hys countrie, you have ledely Iybed against him beeing a gentleman of your owne societie; and so jested at his coles, that you deserve to be burnt with them for your labor" (E$_5$).

18. Margaret James, *Social Problems and Policy During the Puritan Revolution, 1640–1669* (London: G. Routledge, 1930), 131; Webster, *The Great Instauration,* 250–53 and 256–59.

19. This is not Bacon's only motive: animating his royal apologetics are genuine anxieties about the failure of Elizabethan culture to encourage practical imagination. As early as 1592, he had sketched out the need for a great instauration in an unpublished manuscript, in which he asked, "Are we the richer by one poor invention by reason of all the learning that hath been these many hundred years?" "Mr. Bacon in Praise of Learning," *The Letters and the Life of Francis Bacon,* ed. James Spedding, 17 vols. (London: Longmans, Green, and Co., 1868–90), 1:123.

20. In *A New, Cheape, and Delicate Fire of Cole-Balles* (1603), Plat offers his invention as a way of thwarting the engrossing monopolist.

21. Webster, *The Great Instauration,* 344–45.

22. Price, *English Patents of Monopoly,* 25.

23. Ibid., 28; and Menna Presswich, *Cranfield: Politics and Profits Under the Early Stuarts,* 32–33. The *Book of Bounty* was written in response to a parliamentary petition of grievances dated 7 July 1610, near the beginning of Parliament's third session.

24. Cited in Fox, *Monopolies and Patents,* p. 90. Fritz Machlup traces the establishment of a fourteen-year norm for the duration of patents to this case, which norm, he claims, was chosen because it would provide enough time to train two "generations" of apprentices in the intricacies of a protected technique (*An Economic Review of the Patent System,* Study no. 15, Senate Judiciary Committee, Subcommittee on Patents, Trademarks, and Copyrights [Washington, D.C.: U.S. Government Printing Office, 1958], 9). Such a norm does not in fact govern all early patents, the durations of which vary widely: from four years to fifty-one, for the life of the patentee or for that of his children.

25. The statute is 21 Jac. I, cap. 3. A.D. 1623–24. Fox points out (*Monopolies and Patents,* 115–16) that James had himself revoked a number of monopolies; the point of contention became one of prerogative in economic regulation, with Parliament claiming the primacy of its own authority and that of the common law courts.

26. Fox, *Monopolies and Patents,* 340.

27. The principle was given more emphatic articulation in 1610 in the *Wagoner* case, in which the City of London brought a complaint against a tallow-chandler, on the grounds that he was practicing his craft without being a freeman of the city—the court judged the claims of the city good "by way of custom but not by grant" (cited in Heckscher, *Mercantilism,* 1:284). Heckscher observes that "this formulation recurs in many other cases, and the principle of this ruling was never abandoned."

Later, in 1615, the landmark *Clothworkers of Ipswich* case would tighten screws: the Ipswich clothworkers had brought suit for violation of their apprenticeship require- ment, but the court found that the requirement was unlawful, even though the plaintiff was a royally chartered company. The court held "that the King might make corporations and grant to them that they might make ordinances for the ordering and government of any trade, but thereby they could not make a monopoly" (Fox, *Patents and Monopolies,* 217–18). The strictures on individual monopolies asserted in *The Case of Monopolies* are here extended to corporate monopolies.

28. In the *Case of Monopolies* Fuller had argued the crucial difference between guild rights and those granted by what he deemed illegal patents. *Davenant v. Hurdis,* the *Wagoner* case, and *The Clothworkers of Ipswich* case are bolder; see Heckscher, *Mercantilism,* 1:285–87. For a useful summary of the somewhat confusing record of case law during these years, see Heckscher, 1:290ff.

29. There were a few other such specific exemptions: article 10 also exempted the patent for gunpowder manufacture, after which alum mining (11), trade in sea-coal and licensing of taverns (12), Mansell's patent for glass manufacture (13), and certain smelting privileges (14) were also exempted.

30. See the case of Philip Rosseter, discussed in chapter 2 above.

31. Gerald D. Johnson discusses some Elizabethan uses of this device in "The Stationers Versus the Drapers: Control of the Press in the Late Sixteenth Century," *The Library,* 6th ser., 10 (1988): 8.

32. Minsheu reports on his efforts to secure publication in the second epistle to the reader in the second edition of 1625 (A_4^v). He eventually resorted to a sort of subscription arrangement, reporting in the second edition of his catalogue of subscribers that "Stationers and Printers . . . may not print it"—"may" suggests deliberate, organized refusal—"but for their owne profit, not allowing the Author the benefit" (quoted from a Folger copy of the catalogue by Franklin B. Williams in "Scholarly Publication in Shakespeare's Day: A Leading Case," *Joseph Quincy Adams Memorial Studies,* eds. James G. McManaway, Giles E. Dawson, and Edward E. Willoughby [Washington: Folger Shakespeare Library, 1948], 771).

33. The publishing arrangements may have entailed some special payment to the company as a whole for their assistance in publication—at least this is one way of con- struing the unusual note in *Court Book C* of the Stationers' Records (Jackson, *Records,* 165). For an extremely provocative analysis of the economic relations projected in such publication, see Alexandra Halasz, "Pamphlet Surplus: John Taylor and Subscription Publication," *Print, Manuscript, Performance,* eds. Arthur F. Marrotti and Michael D. Bristol (Columbus: Ohio State University Press, 2000), 90–102.

34. One of the most unsettling of these patents was the grant to Thomas Sym- cock and Roger Wood in 1618 of exclusive right to print broadsides, a grant variously protested by the company during the ensuing decade. But it was renewed by Charles I in 1628, to Symcock alone, and eventually annulled in Chancery after a parliamentary committee determined that the patent must have been awarded on the basis of a misrepresentation.

35. George Sandys's *Metamorphosis* offers another instance in which patent provides a lever for dislodging copyright, an instance more clearly affiliated with Daniel's

device. The book was entered to Barrett and Lownes in 1621, but in 1626 Sandys secured a patent for the exclusive right to print the work for twenty-one years; on this basis, Stansby reentered the work, and printed it *cum privilegio*. See Kirschbaum, "Author's Copyright," 46–48.

36. The stationers involved submitted an official complaint (*S.P. Dom., James I*, vol. 109, art. 106), but the documentary record is silent on the final disposition of the matter. See Arber, *Transcript*, 3:40.

37. The following discussion of Wither's struggle with the stationers appeared in an earlier version as part of my "Wither and Professional Work," in *Print, Manuscript, Performance: The Changing Relations of the Media in Early Modern England*, ed. Arthur F. Marotti and Michael D. Briston (Columbus: Ohio State University Press, 2000), 103–23.

38. "The fourth Eglogue." I cite from the version reprinted from Wither's *Juvenilia* in *Publications of the Spenser Society* no. 10, 3 parts (1871), 2:540.

39. He may have been imprisoned for a 1611 first edition of *Abuses Stript and Whipt;* he was certainly imprisoned for the fourth edition in 1613. According to Allan Pritchard ("*Abuses Stript and Whipt* and Wither's Imprisonment" *RES* 14 [1963]: 337–45), it was widely thought that several passages were aimed at Northampton; the antiparliamentary Northampton seems to have been instrumental in the imprisonment, which endured from the time of the parliamentary elections (March), past Northampton's death in June, and through to the end of the parliamentary session at the end of July. Pembroke helped get him out, although Wither claimed that his satire written in prison and addressed to the king had contributed to his release.

40. Browne published *The Shepherd's Pipe* during Wither's imprisonment, the first eclogue of which was addressed to "Roget" (Wither).

41. *The Works of Charles and Mary Lamb*, ed. E.V. Lucas, 7 vols. (London: Methuen, 1903), 1:181.

42. He appeals to other authorities as well, commending judgment of his grievance to Parliament—which, as we have seen, had taken the problem of regulating monopolies as its proper jurisdiction (G_1).

His argument in *The Schollers Purgatory* may have been motivated by the knowledge that *Abuses Stript and Whipt* had been a valuable enough stationer's property to have been pirated, probably within two years of its initial publication in 1613. See William A. Jackson, "Counterfeit Printing in Jacobean Times," *The Library*, 4th ser., 15 (1935): 365–67.

43. In *Fragmenta Prophetica* (1669) he claimed that the book sold 30,000 copies in the course of its early printings; however exaggerated this may be, Jonson's attack in *Time Vindicated* entails scorn for Wither's broad lower-class appeal.

44. He cleverly cites verses by King James that argue the suasive power of verse (p. 9 in the Spenser Society reprint). It is worth noting here that Okes printed the *Preparation* without license and was fined a pound for the offense.

In *The Schollers Purgatory* Wither claims that he applied for his patent in *Hymns & Songs of the Church* after the first imprisonment, though no documentary evidence supports this.

45. This had been followed in 1620 by the publication of Wither's *Exercises upon the First Psalm*.

46. A few years later Sandys received a patent for his *Metamorphoses* (1626); in 1628 William Alexander was awarded a patent in his translation of the *Psalms of King David*. Sandys' Ovid was pirated in 1628.

47. Cited in Greg, *Companion to Arber*, 213; compare the 1610 patent to John Speed, which stipulated that his *Genealogies recorded in the sacred scriptures* be bound in with all copies of the 1611 English Bible, an arrangement with which the stationers seem to have happily complied. *Companion to Arber*, 301.

48. The psalter was carefully priced for a mass audience; but Wither's grant stipulated that the psalter now be sold with a text that would yield a volume enlarged by 70 percent—perhaps too large now for a small-format book, and now, inevitably, more expensive to produce. Unfortunately for the stationers, James's grant pegged both wholesale and retail prices for Wither's book to prevailing rates for the psalter. Arber, *Transcript*, 4:13–14 and see *Schollers Purgatory*, 30.

49. Cited in Blagden, *The Stationers' Company*, 75.

50. B_2—$B_2{}^v$ [should be B_4—$B_4{}^v$: the book is badly signed and paginated—these two consecutive pages are numbered pp. 25 and 30]. Wither continues, "But having composed a new Booke, which no man could claime a share in, while it remayned myne owne, and in mine owne power to make public or no, & prposing the same to his Majestie . . . I obtayned a free and gratious graunt . . . such as the Stationers would have made of it without a priviledge if so be I had left it in their power."

51. It is hardly surprising that there may have been bad faith on both sides. Wither protests "how willfully they have misenformed the Kings Majestie & diverse honorable personages concerning my Grant (& my procedings) to procure my damage: How unjustly they gave out among their Customers, that my Grant was a Monopoly, & an exaction to the oppression of the people: How impudently & faulsly, they have verefied, that I had procured that no man might buy a Bible, Testament, or Communion-Booke which [*sic*] out my Hymnes" (95). But whether or not he had formulated the plan in 1624, that's exactly where he was headed: he finished his long-projected translation of a singing psalter in 1633 (though continuing hostilities with the stationers obliged him to have it printed in Holland), and he secured a new patent from Charles I stipulating that this psalter be bound with all Bibles. This naturally led to a reprise of the original quarrel with the stationers, who won support for their position from the House of Lords.

52. Jackson, *Records*, 156, only a memorandum; unfortunately no further record survives of the meeting in March 1633 at which they decided how to hadle the challenge from Wither.

53. On Wither's moderate achievements in exploiting the patent during the late twenties, see Norman E. Carlson, "Wither and the Stationers," *Studies in Bibliography* 19 (1966): 210–15.
More could be made of the jurisdictional issues. As was quite necessary, the patent granted Wither the right to enforce compliance: to search for and seize psalters being sold without the *Hymns*. By the early thirties, Wither was plainly frustrated in his efforts to enforce his patent. It is easy to see why he decided to farm the patent to Robert Crosse and Toby Knowles, who, as Messengers of His Majesty in Ordinary, stood a far better chance of success in dealing with noncompliant stationers. As it turned out, they too failed and, in March 1634, petitioned the Privy Council "either to free them from their Contract, or for the better enabling them being so engaged, to confirm unto them, the enjoying of the aforesd royal Patent." *Companion to Arber*, 217.

54. Wither claims that the stationers secured a hearing by detailing "three or four of their Instruments, to clamor against me at the Parliament house dore."

55. Because the book naturally had to be printed surreptitiously, without entrance or license, Wither entrusted it to the hapless Wood: early in September, officials of the Stationers' Company duly raided Wood's shop and destroyed his equipment before the print run was complete. Both Wither and Wood were brought in for interrogation by the Court of High Commission, whereupon, to his discredit, Wither blamed Wood for the failure to secure license. The court seems to have approved the book for printing: by December *The Schollers Purgatory* had appeared, its latter sheets printed in a different font and probably at a different press.

56. See p. 120: "If an Author out of meere necessity, do but procure meanes to make sale of his owne booke, or to pervent the combinations of such as he, by some Royall & lawfull priveledge: He presently cryes it downe for a Monopoly."

57. See, in particular, pp. 108–9.

58. His instincts were not deeply flawed: had it been enforced, Wither's patent might have benefited the bookbinders, at least in the short run. But apparently one of the publishing stationers' principal means of evading its structures was to ship the psalter to the provinces in quires where they could be bound, more or less beyond the reach of official scrutiny, without Wither's *Hymns* included.

59. Robert Lemon, *Catalogue of a Collection of Printed Broadsides in the Posses-sion of the Society of Antiquaries* (London: Society of Antiquaries, 1866), no. 225.

60. To cite this at greater length: "For, by an unjust custome (as most of your Reverences well knowe) the Stationers have so usurped upon the labours of all writers, that when they have consumed their youth and fortunes in perfiting some laborious worke those cruell Bee-masters burne the poore Athenian bees for their hony, or else drive them from the best part therof" (A$_3$ and cf. the georgic figure of H$_4$^{v}). To elaborate the idea of the author as worker, Wither has recourse to a durable rhetoric of capital as the effluvium of personal labor: "Many of our moderne booke-sellers, are but needelesse excrements, or rather vermine, who beeing ingendred by the sweat of schollers, Printers, and book-binders, doe (as wormes in timber, or like the generation of vipers) devour those that bred them. While they did like fleas, but sucke now and then a dropp of the writers blood from him, and skipp off when he found himselfe diseased, it was somwhat tollerable: but since they began to feed on him, like the third plague of AEGIPT without remooving, and to laye clayme to each Authors labours, as if they had beene purposely brought upp to studye for their mayntenance" (10).

61. For an intensification of the rhetoric of work, see C$_5$: "If like an honest harted Gibeonit I have but a little extraordinarily laboured, to hewe wood and drawe water, for the spirituall Sacrifizes . . . what blame worthy have I done?"; see also C$_6$.

62. B$_6$; and see also A$_3$.

63. Intriguingly, Wither himself insisted on the continuity of *The Schollers Purgatory* with his prophetic-satiric writings. He imagines that one of the responses of the "mere Stationer" to the charges of *The Schollers Purgatory* will be to deny the authenticity of the work—to deny, that is, that Wither had written it by claiming that "it is nothing suitable to that Mynd which I have expresse in my Motto" (125). "But, let him examine them together, & he shall fynde they disagree not in a word."

64. Wither's introduction of the language of heritable property calls for more sustained attention. Having urged the "collateral" claims of binder and printer, he entertains, albeit satirically, the idea that the book trade may be subject to eccentric laws of inheritance. If these other tradesmen are not accepted as elder claimants, "at least wise [they] may in Gavile-kind be coheires with him" (B₆)—i.e., heirs by a system, thought to be of Celtic origin, that divided property equally among the children of the deceased. Wither goes on to suppose that the bookseller's counsel alleges that the bookseller's claim preempts the authors' according to a Kentish custom in which the youngest child inherits the entire estate (Idem). The hold of models of filial inheritance on Wither's imagination of authorial rights is hardly surprising; for a discussion of the strains of making the model fit nascent formulations of authorial property, see chapter 6 below.

65. Document 76, *Companion to Arber.*

66. 3 Keble 792, 1 Mod. 256, 84 Eng. Rep. 1015 (emphasis mine); and see E. F. Bosanquet, "English 17th Century Almanacs," *The Library,* 4th ser., 10 (1929–30): 361–97.

67. The prerogative was further delimited in 1775, in *Stationers' Company v. Carnan,* when even almanacs were placed outside the circle of royal property. It was determined in Chancery that the Crown might still control the right to print statutes and proclamations, Bibles and prayerbooks, on the grounds that "codes of religion and of law ought to be under the inspection of the executive power, to stamp an authenticity upon them. Therefore Bibles, Common Prayer Books, and statutes are proper objects of exclusive patents. But almanacs are not of this kind" (96 Eng. Rep. 592). The patent here begins to merge with license.

68. Closely related to this project is Wither's attack on the practice, customary almost continuously since 1586, whereby the wardens of the Stationers' Company functioned as proxy licensers, referring only the hardest cases to the official licensers (p. 34). For another instance in which Wither hedges the claim to absolute authorial property, see the interesting qualification of his assertion of copyright in his *Hymns and Songs of the Church:* "But having composed a new Booke, which no man could claime a share in, while it remayned myne owne, and in mine owne power to make public or no, etc." (B₅ᵛ). Wither here seems to concede the old stationers' principle that publication confers *some* share of copyright on the publisher.

Chapter Six

1. *Moore's Reports,* 671.

2. Fox, *Monopolies and Patents,* 320; *Moore's Reports,* 671; and *Noy's Reports,* 179–81.

3. H&S,9:98.

4. Ibid.

5. Ponsonby had advised Greville or Walsingham that to forestall publication of this *Arcadia* by another stationer they needed to intervene directly with "the archebishope or doctor Cosen, who have . . . a copy of it to peruse to that end" (quoted in Sidney, *The Countess of Pembroke's Arcadia,* ed. Robertson, xl). Like Walkley after him, Ponsonby knew that the relocation of copyright protections vested in accordance with

the norms internal to the Stationers' Company would require appeal to supervenient authority.

6. C. J. Sisson has observed that suits between stationers brought before the Court of Chancery were usually referred back to the arbitrament of the Stationers' Company, though this was not the case with Walkley ("The Laws of Elizabethan Copyright," 11.) Indeed, grievances originating within the book trade seem to have begun a drift to the various prerogative courts. Complaints of infringements against printing patents were occasionally appealed to the Court of High Commission, probably because most of the early infringements concerned devotional texts

7. Wither takes great pleasure in recording this sort of hypocrisy: see, in particular, sigs. H_5—H_6, but also H_2. He reports that the company wardens frequently collude in the printing of works that they know could not secure official license, and that on occasion they have confiscated certain books as "unlawful" and then sold them for their own profit (G_8).

8. Arber, *Transcript*, 2:807. A decree of 1566 had set penalties against stationers who refused to comply with the licensing system erected by the injunctions of 1559; the Star Chamber decree of 1586 increased those penalties. See Blagden, "Book Trade Control in 1566," *The Library*, 5th ser., 13 (1958): 287–92.

9. The right to make adjustments in the number of printers to be allowed in the future is also conferred on these authorities; nominations of new master printers are to be forwarded from the Stationers' Court of Assistants to the ecclesiastical Court of High Commission, either the archbishop of Canterbury or the bishop of London being present, for their approval. In 1604, the company lobbied unsuccessfully for a statute to limit the number of master printers to fourteen. Again, their declared motive was to arrest the publication of "seditious, popish, vain, and lascivious books" (cited in Lambert, "State Control," 14). In 1622, Archbishop Abbott approved George Wood as a master printer over the expressed protests of the company: both the company and the archbishop had adduced the 1586 decree of Star Chamber when the case against Wood was presented before the Court of High Commission (Jackson, *Records,* 376–79). Wither could have learned a good deal about the internal politics of the book trade from Wood during the following year, when his *Hymns and Songs of the Church* went into production at Wood's press.

10. James F. Larkin and Paul L. Hughes, *Stuart Royal Proclamations*, 2 vols., *Volume 1: Royal Proclamations of King James I, 1603–1625* (Oxford: Clarendon, 1973), no. 110. The specific irritant at this juncture was the publication of John Cowell's *Interpreter,* which had stirred up resentment in Commons because of its extravagant claims for the royal prerogative. James's special attention to the proclamation was designed to calm parliamentary outrage: he excoriates "the itching in the tongues and pennes of most men" and promises a new commission of licensers.

11. For a useful general treatment of censorship, clandestine publication, and the import trade, see Leona Rostenberg, *The Minority Press and the English Crown: A Study in Repression, 1558–1625* (Nieuwkoop: De Graaf, 1971).

12. This seems generally to have been an auspicious occasion for increased regulation. In September 1622, the Stationers' Court promulgated new orders designed to strengthen the requirement that all books be registered before printing.

13. S.P. Dom. James I, vol. 187, 118.

14. Blagden, *The Stationers' Company,* 118 (and see Lambert, "State Control," 22). Blagden bases his argument for company intervention on the fact that S.P. Dom. Car. I, vol. 376, 15, preserves a draft version of the decree, and its eighteen clauses contain very few of the provisions most advantageous to the stationers. Blagden does not note corroborating evidence from *Court Book C*, which records a gift of twenty pounds to the attorney general "for his Love & kindnes to the Company" (300) and a payment of fifteen pounds to the clerk of the company, for his pains in procuring the decree (298).

15. A step toward greater inclusiveness in the ban on imports had already been made in 1636, in a proclamation banning imports that compete with English editions of works in the learned languages; Hughes and Larkin, *Proclamations,* 219. The Star Chamber decree of 1637 banned the importation of all books in English. Had both edicts been enforced in 1637, only works in the modern foreign languages not under English patent or copyright protection could have been imported.

16. *Copyright in Historical Perspective,* 125.

17. C. H. Firth and R. S. Rait, *Acts and Ordinances of the Interregnum, 1642–1660,* 3 vols. (London: Stationery Office, 1911), 2:696–99. The Restoration saw the royal appointment of a single surveyor of the press: Sir John Birkenhead held the office from 1660 to 1663; Sir Roger L'Estrange, from 1663 to 1688.

18. Christopher Hill, *The Century of Revolution, 1603–1714* (London: Thomas Nelson and Sons, 1961; new ed. London: Sphere Books, 1974), 100.

19. D'Ewes' *Journal,* xxvii—xxviii.

20. *The Stationers' Company,* 147; *Macaria,* 89.

21. *Freedom of the Press,* 180–81.

22. On the publication of M.P.'s speeches, see also Siebert, *Freedom of the Press,* 174.

23. *Lords Journal,* 4:180, 182; *Freedom of the Press,* 184–85.

24. *Freedom of the Press,* 166–67. See also p. 171, where Siebert observes how, when the office of king's printer fell vacant in the forties, Commons and Lords each appointed official printers.

25. B.M.E. 207 (2).

26. *Freedom of the Press,* 171. Nor would it be prudent to accept Francis Barker's assessment of the order, that it "provided . . . for the protection of copyright vested, for the first time in English law, in the author." *The Tremulous Private Body: Essays on Subjection,* 2nd edition (Ann Arbor: University of Michigan Press, 1995), 45.

27. See N. Frederick Nash, "English Licenses to Print and Grants of Copyright in the 1640s," *The Library,* 6th ser., 4 (1982): 177–79.

28. It was also most likely intended as stopgap legislation until a fully articulated system of parliamentary regulation could be devised; see Milton, *CPW,* 2:160–61.

29. *The Imprint of Gender: Authorship and Publication in the English Renaissance* (Ithaca: Cornell University Press, 1993), 1–3. She cites the introduction to Scolocker's *Daiphantus:* "He is A man in Print, and tis enough he hath under-gone a Pressing (yet not like a Ladie) though for your sakes and for Ladyes, protesting for this poore Infant of his Brayne, as it was the price of his Virginitie borne into the world in teares" (A_2^v).

30. Siebert, *Freedom of the Press,* 167, 173–74; Blagden, *The Stationers' Company,* 130–31, 138–40.

31. It also undermined the position of several patentees outside the company, and in these cases cunning members of the company itself benefited, contriving, in the course of the Interregnum, to exploit their industrial position and persistent antimonopolist sentiment in order to work the now loosely protected patents; see Blagden, *The Stationers' Company,* 131–45.

32. Christopher Hill, *Writing and Revolution in Seventeenth-Century England,* vol. 1 of *Collected Essays,* 3 vols. (Amherst: University of Massachusetts Press, 1985–86), 44–45, 50.

33. Blagden, "The Stationers' Company in the Civil War Period," *The Library,* 5th ser., 13 (1958): 16.

34. Siebert, *Freedom of the Press,* 170–74; David Masson, *The Life of John Milton Narrated in Connection with the Political, Ecclesiastical, and Literary History of His Time,* 7 vols. (2nd ed., London: Macmillan, 1896), 3:268; Blagden, *The Stationers' Company,* 147–48. Elsewhere Blagden emphasizes the cautious response of the powers that be within the Stationers' Company to this disorder—"The Company took action between the summer of 1637 and the meeting of the Long Parliament in the autumn of 1640 to put its house in order: on two separate occasions three Livery men were elected to the Court; twenty-four Yeoman were admitted to the Livery and a committee was set up to take advice on revising the ordinances; agreements were made with rival patentees—the universities and John Speed" ("The Stationers' Company in the Civil War Period," 7–8).

35. Siebert, *Freedom,* 170–71, citing B.M. 669 f. 4 (79).

36. Wallwyn's tract is reproduced in William Haller, *Tracts on Liberty in the Puritan Revolution, 1638–1647, Records of Civilization: Sources and Studies,* gen. ed. Austin P. Evans, 18, 3 vols. (New York: Columbia University Press, 1934), 3, pt. 2, 62 (A_4^v–A_5), and see also 89 (pp. 49–50 [unsigned]).

37. F_4–F_4^v, reproduced in Haller, 3, pt. 2, 155–56.

38. Siebert, *Freedom of the Press,* 180–91.

39. In a maneuver devised to counter antimonopolistic pressure both from outside the book trade and from discontented groups inside it, he lobbied for vesting several important patents, including the law and Bible patents, in the Stationers' Company as a whole, a reorganization of monopoly protections made necessary by the loss of the royal foundation; B.M. Harl. MSS, 5909. (And see the related attempt in January 1643, when the company again petitioned for the assignment of the Bible patent to the company at large; B.M.E. 669 f. 6 [107], reprinted in Arber, *Transcript,* 1:583–84.) The immediate provocation for Prynne's intervention in 1641 seems to have been a petition brought to the Lower House on 21 March by a group led by Thomas Cowper for reversion of the Bible patent (Siebert, *Freedom,* 170). Cowper had long sought ways to circumvent the monopoly in the Bible (see Greg, *Companion,* 91–92) and had recently suffered the confiscation of a large stock of pirated Bibles. Like the more vociferous Sparke, Cowper argued that the monopoly Bible was being sold at prices disproportionate to production costs (*Cal. St. Pap. Dom., 1640/41,* 508).

40. On the other hand, Prynne's allegiance to the goals of the stationers' lead-

ership may be an important force in the development, during the 1640s, of that anti-Tolerationism that earned him Lilburne's profound animosity.

41. In *Scintilla,* Sparke exposes a variety of dirty tricks in the way the Bible was published, rails against printing patents, and calls for the enforcement of price controls, an increase in the size of the Court of Assistants, term limits for mastership of the company, and an end to blocking registrations (A₄ᵛ). The reactions of at least some members of the company can be gauged from complaints presented to the court on 4 October 1641, which allege that in *Scintilla* "all the secretts & misteries of this profession were laid open tending much to the Ruine of the English Stock & Corporacion" (Blagden, "Stationers' Company in the Civil War Period," 8).

42. B.M.E. 669 f. 6 (107), quoted in Arber, *Transcript,* 1:583.

43. Blagden, *Stationers' Company,* 138, and see pp. 138–45 for the narrative of this impressive campaign of engrossing.

44. Haller, 1:46ff.

45. B.M.E. 247, cited in Arber, *Transcript,* 1:585.

46. Ibid. This seems specifically addressed to the parliamentary attempt to cobble together its own licensing system, and particularly the effort to suppress published misrepresentations of parliamentary proceedings, by means of the special order of 24 August 1642 (Steele, no. 2255).

47. Ibid. They were careful to moderate their claims, but in such a way as to consolidate the differential power embedded in company hierarchy: " 'tis not the desire of the Stationers to be solely or confusedly entrusted with the Government of the Presse: They desire no authority in order to judgement or punishment, but onely in order to prosecution of Delinquents; and that power also they desire not to have it committed to the whole Company . . . but to some choice Committee, nominated by the Company, and further approved and allowed by the Parliament." They expected that the authority of this committee was to be limited, although "some abuses there are likely to arise emergently, which without extraordinary provisions *pro re natâ,* can scarcely be suppressed; and therefore that favor which they desire, is That they not be abridged of all power in this kind" (1:585–86). The humility of this remonstrance is dubious; the stationers could also threaten: "As the case now stands, Stationers are so farre from having any encouragement to make them active and alacrious in the service of the state, that they cannot serve it without discouragement" (1:586).

48. 1:587, and cf. 588: "he that is sure of his Copy, though the same cost *3* or *400l* if he cannot raise his money disbursed at the first Impression, yet being assured of benefit by after Editions, he may sell cheaper at first then he buyes, to the great ease of other men."

49. I am not the first to observe Milton's "debt" to this petition: see Elisabeth M. Magnus, "Originality and Plagiarism in *Areopagitica* and *Eikonoklastes," English Literary Renaissance* 21 (1991): 89, 90.

50. Siebert, *Freedom,* 187–88; Masson notes that ten times as many books were registered in the second half of 1643 as were registered in the first half of the year (*The Life of Milton,* 3:268 and 271).

51. *Stationers' Company,* 137.

52. Ibid., 147–51.

53. A version of this scandal had emerged from its industrial enclave, of course, during the parliamentary debate on monopolies in 1601 (see D'Ewes, *Journal*, p. 650, cited as appendix G in Price, *Patents*, pp. 152–53, and cf. appendix C, pp. 145–47), but the contest for monopolies in God's Word was somewhat more disruptive.

54. *Life of Milton*, 4:324.

55. "The Author's Authority: *Areopagitica* and Licensing," in *Re-membering Milton*, eds. Mary Nyquist and Margaret W. Ferguson (New York: Methuen, 1987), 92; and see also Stephen B. Dobranski's discussion of "The Mystery of Milton as Licenser," in *Milton, Authorship and the Book Trade* (Cambridge: Cambridge University Press, 1999), 125–32.

56. Cited in Masson, *Life of Milton*, 3:263. Milton had dedicated the *Doctrine and Discipline of Divorce* not only to Parliament but to the Westminster Assembly, a double provocation. See also Dobranski, *Milton, Authorship, and the Book Trade*, 106–8.

57. J. A. Wittreich Jr., "Milton's *Areopagitica*: Its Isocratic and Ironic Contexts," *Milton Studies* 4 (1972): 101–15.

58. Indeed, later in *Areopagitica*, press licencing is described as a tax on "free spok'n truth" (2:545). This is not to say that Milton is unrelievedly logocentric: on p. 548, he observes that "writing is more publick then preaching" as a way of approving of the written.

59. A portion of that history is taken up in chapter 3 of *Jonson and Possessive Authorship*, where I discuss figures of publication as manumission and of unacknowledged imitation or appropriation as kidnapping.

60. The logocentrism of the foregoing sentence may seem to fly in the face of decades of deconstructive critique, but my assertion is merely anthropological, a description of how writing is used and described in a culture saturated with logocentrism.

61. *Works*, 2:492–93.

62. The figure of genetic or vital potency is compounded later by figurations of the book as meat; the persistent substrate of the genetic can be felt in the formulations like "Bad meats will scarce breed good nourishment in the healthiest concoction; but herein the difference is of bad books, that they to a discreet and judicious Reader serve in many respects to discover, to confute, to forewarn, and to illustrate" (2:512). For useful discussions of networks of imagery in the treatise, see Alan F. Price, "Incidental Imagery in *Areopagitica*," *Modern Philology* 49 (1952): 217–22; and John X. Evans. "Imagery as Argument in Milton's *Areopagitica*," *Texas Studies in Language and Literature* 8 (1966): 189–205. My most important debt in this discussion is to the chapter on *Areopagitica* in Christopher Kendrick, *Milton: A Study in Ideology and Form* (London: Methuen, 1986), 19–51 and particularly 28–29; but see also the excellent analyses of corporeal figures in Milton's treatise by Sandra Sherman, "Printing the Mind: The Economics of Authorship in *Areopagitica*," *ELH* 60 (1993): 323–47; as well as Dobranski's observations in *Milton, Authorship, and the Book Trade*, 120–21.

63. Here again, Bacon's inspiration was felt, and this time acknowledged. Milton imagines the "acute reader" at the bookstall who, scorning the mark of the licenser, challenges, "Who shall warrant me his judgement? The State Sir, replies the Stationer,

but has a quick return, The State shall be my governours, but not my criticks, they may be mistak'n in the choice of a licencer, as easily as thus licencer may be mistak'n in an author: This is some common stuffe; and he might adde from Sir *Francis Bacon,* That *such authoriz'd books are but the language of the times*" (2:534, quoting Bacon's *Advertisement Touching the Controversies of the Church of England*).

64. The more specific, more traditional paternal figure will also recur. The licenser who bans books by deceased authors commits "a treacherous fraud against the orphaned remainders of worthiest men after death" (2:534–35).

65. *Prose Works,* 2:502–503, and see the conclusion (2:505) of the history of licensing begun here: "And thus ye have the Inventors and the originall of Book-licencing ript up, and drawn as lineally as any pedigree."

66. Milton persists in representing licensing as itself a book, even when he is not referring to the Index itself. Thus, on the penultimate page of *Areopagitica,* he offers a summary prediction: "For this *authentic* Spanish policy of licencing books, if I have said ought, will prove the most unlicenc't book itself within short while" (2:569).

67. 2:505–506; once again licensing disrupts natural genetics: either Juno bars its entrance from the womb of thought into the world or, more unnaturally, Radamanthus bars it from a birth that is to be understood as a return from the dead.

68. The idea of writing as recuperation is picked up later in the myth of dismembered Truth (2:549), who is reassembled by the unfettered labor of scholarship.

69. To this might be added the figure of Parliament as inseminator of an active liberty, a figure that establishes, late in *Areopagitica,* an analogy between Parliament and a seeking nation and authors and their potent books: "That our hearts are more capacious, our thoughts more erected to the search and expectation of greatest and exactest things, is the issue of your owne vertu propagated in us: ye cannot suppresse that unlesse ye reinforce an abrogated and percilesse law, that fathers may dispatch at will their own children" (2:559).

70. 2:535–36, and see also 2:558, where the licensers are described as "an *Oligarchy* of twenty ingrossers over it, to bring a famin upon our minds."

71. Here is Kendrick's structural account of the cultural development that I have been describing in rhetorical terms: "Under capitalism the marketplace takes on an unwonted importance in the life of the individual: the individual's relation to society comes to be obscurely mediated by the market—governed, that is, by the reified market categories which now take on a dynamic of their own. It is one effect of this reification that the market itself acquires a natural metaphorical power; thus the market apparatus comes to secrete a corresponding ideological apparatus, what will later be called 'the marketplace of ideas' " (*Milton,* 40).

Elsewhere, Kendrick construes this historical development as having manifested itself in very particular private ways in Milton's thought, particularly on his "organicism of the soul." Generally, however, he argues that "it was by identifying the soul's powers with those of the free commodity, by likening its creative movement to the movement of the integral market formally instated by capitalism, that Milton felt himself free" (*Milton,* 13). I think we are in a position to give an even more particularized formulation—that it was by identifying the soul's powers with those of the book that Milton experienced his freedoms and unfreedom, that, for Milton, the book models both social being and embodiment; that, moreover, the book was, for Milton, the leading instance of commodification.

72. Kendrick makes a small adjustment toward caution: "in being depicted as monopolizable, they have *been seen under the aspect of* the commodity" (my emphasis). The highlighted phrase maintains a blur in which analogy and identity are indistinguishable. Nonetheless, the sentences that follow, which describe how "the commodity places its shadowy imprint on much of the imagery in the tract" (*Milton,* 41) are extremely suggestive for my own argument.

73. In an interesting foreshadowing of tensions in *Paradise Lost,* the figuration of labor and production competes steadily and unsuccessfully with the imagery of military engagement that dominates the last pages of the treatise. Sometimes Milton's language will find a middle ground between the two pools articulated here, of laborious scholarship and cunning "soldiership," as when scholarship is said "to polish and brighten the armoury of Truth" (2:567).

74. The 1642 order was an interim arrangement; Milton misrepresents it as a full-blown institution for press regulation, betrayed when Parliament, misled by the fraud of monopolists in the book trade, replaced it with the act of 1643.

75. I am aware that this central argument is shadowed by enough qualifiers—heresies, errors, affiliations, and dispositions that are not to be tolerated—as to compromise, and perhaps vitiate it. Kendrick takes this sort of political compromise as symptomatic of a radical but very particular instability in the subject (*Milton,* 45–49).

76. Milton has made a good deal of the "signature" provision of the 1642 order. Stimulated by the transitivity of the author function in the 1642 order (which function is, in this instance, to be a punishable, responsible party), he has given us a cluster of images in which the *book*, and not the printer, takes on the corporeal-punishable pathos of the regulated author.

77. Nigel Smith, "*Areopagitica:* Voicing Contexts, 1643–5," *Politics, Poetics and Hermeneutics in Milton's Prose,* eds. David Loewenstein and James Grantham Turner (Cambridge: Cambridge University Press, 1990), 106—a small lapse in an otherwise superb essay.

78. Milton's phrasing here supports what the historical context confirms. The force of "several" is subtle but should be unambiguous: "each his own as distinct from others'." Milton is describing a distinctive rather than an absolute right to copy; were he describing authorial property we might expect to read "each man his own copy"—and then expect to read a good deal of explanation.

79. A letter from several prominent divines supplementing the stationers' petition in 1643 indicates the continued incoherence of authorial property, even at the brink of the reification of that property: "considerable sums of money had been paid by stationers and printers to many authors for the 'copies' of such useful books as had been imprinted, in regard whereof we conceive it to be both just and necessary that they should enjoy a property for the sole imprinting of their copies; and we further declare that unless they do so enjoy a property, all scholars will be utterly deprived of any recompense from the stationers and printers for their studies or labour in writing and preparing books for the press" (cited from Thomas Cartes, *Letters* [London, 1735] in Thomas Edward Scrutton, *The Law of Copyright* [London: Clowes, 1903], 19). The claims of scholarship advanced

here are still matters of gratuitous patronage; property emerges into the argument only when it turns to consider the stationers' industrial sphere.

Dobranski makes a similar case against the misconception that Milton proposes a foundational authorial property in *Areopagitica* (*Milton, Authorship, and the Book Trade*, 115–16); his effort to rehabilitate the members of the book trade as authorial collaborators perhaps scants the degree to which the authorial property *derives* from stationers' property.

80. Not to overstate the case: the tide was turning. Though there is little evidence to suggest that Milton is defending authorial property, he writes at a moment at which such property was receiving occasional reification. The requirement in the Commons' 1642 printing order that stationers secure an author's consent prior to printing was scrupulously honored in the publication of sermons preached before that house on fast-days and was observed sporadically during the 1640s in the publication of many other sermons preached before either or both houses. See N. Frederick Nash, "English Licenses to Print," 174–84 and particularly his account of the publication, one month after the order was promulgated, of Edmund Calamy's sermon *God's Free Mercy to England*, with its confusing imprimatur, which seems to split the right to control publication between Calamy and the House of Commons. The Commons *Journal* records many grants of copyright to the authors of sermons, but such arrangements were plainly felt to represent a special case; not surprisingly, the stationers seem to have been put off by the arrangement. It is clear from the record that these authorial copyrights are to be understood as extraordinary grants, parliamentary analogues to royal patents.

81. Lest it be supposed that the Licensing Act of 1643 had introduced authorial property, the act should perhaps be quoted at some length. It stipulates "that no person or persons shall hereafter print, or cause to be reprinted any Book or Books, or part of Book, or Books heretofore allowed of and granted to the said Company of *Stationers* for their relief and maintenance of their poore, without the licence or consent of the Master, Wardens and Assistants of the said Company; Nor any Book or Books lawfully licensed and entred in the Register of the said Company for any particular member thereof, without the license and consent of the Owner or Owners therof." This is *conceivably* ambiguous, but it is a simple parallel construction: "no one may print books already owned by the Company as a whole without the permission of its officers, nor may anyone print anything already registered to some particular member, without his permission or the permission of his partners." (And not: "no one may print Company property without permission nor may any book be registered to a particular stationer without permission of the Owner or Owners of that book" [as distinguished from the potential registrant].) That "Owner or Owners" designates a member of the book trade is very strongly indicated by the next sentence: "Nor yet import any such Book or Books, or part of Book or Books formerly printed here, from beyond the Seas, upon paine of forfeiting the same to the Owner, or Owners of the Copies of the said Books, and such further punishment as shall be thought fit." Each of the three clauses inhibits infringement of publishing rights settled by the Stationers' Company.

82. On the suturing of printed works to *stationers* during the Civil War and Restoration, see my "Legal Proofs and Corrected Readings: Press-Agency and the New Bibliography," *"Wisemen's Threasure" The Production of English Renaissance Culture,*

ed. D. L. Miller, S. O'Dair, and H. Weber (Ithaca: Cornell University Press, 1994), 93–122.

83. Kevin Dunn, "Milton among the Monopolists: *Areopagitica,* Intellectual Property, and the Harlib Circle," *Samuel Hartlib and Universal Reformation,* eds. Mark Grenngrass, Michael Leslie, and Timothy Raylor (Cambridge: Cambridge University Press, 1994), 181–87.

84. It is thus to be distinguished from *Eikonoklastes* (1649), for which see the following chapter.

CHAPTER SEVEN

1. The parable may leave its traces on Milton's seventh sonnet, written at least two decades earlier, but engaged with the same predicament as "When I consider . . ." The uncanny use of "use" in the earlier poem—"All is, if I have grace to use it so, / As ever in my great task-Master's eye"—anticipates the tonalities of "talent" in the later one.

2. See examples cited in the *OED* for III.6.a—c.

3. Thomas Blount, *Glossographia* (1656) cited in the *OED,* III.6.b; for *talent* as "characteristic disposition or aptitude," see OED, III.7.a.

4. See above, pp. 160–61.

5. The same may be said of the theater at the Restoration when, in 1660, ideological regulation from the quasi independent Revels office of Henry Herbert was effectively undermined by grants to D'Avenant and Killigrew that gave them monopolies of theatrical entertainment in London as well as the responsibility for self-censorship. Herbert struggled to maintain his authority and to recover licensing fees and Killigrew acquiesced, whereas D'Avenant successfully fended off his jurisdiction by litigation. By complying, Killigrew managed to succeed Herbert; and his son succeeded him. External intervention in theatrical business was relatively light until 1695, when antitheatrical agitation erupted in the tense atmosphere that attended on the lapse of press regulation (for which, see below).

6. According to the Printing Act of 1662, the number of allowable printers was to be rolled back to twenty, with the then current roster of fifty-nine to be reduced by attrition.

7. The printers published similar complaints again in 1669 and 1673.

8. See L'Estrange, *Considerations and Proposals in Order to the Regulation of the Press* (1663); and Blagden, *Stationers' Company,* 148–52.

9. See Blagden, *The Stationers' Company,* chapter 8.

10. Kitchin, *Sir Roger L'Estrange,* 103.

11. Atkyns is certainly indebted here to L'Estrange's *Considerations and Proposals* (1663), in which the press is described effectively as a Crown property. In *Atkyns' Case* (1666), counsel seems to have found an even earlier royal precedent, apparently alleging that Alexander the Great had founded intellectual property in a grant to Aristotle of special rights to control the circulation of the *Physics* (Carter, *Common Pleas,* 90).

12. For the refutation, see Conyers Middleton, *Dissertation Concerning the Origin of Printing* (London, 1735).

13. "That *Printing* belongs to your Majesty, in your publique and private Capacity, as Supream Magistrate, and as Proprieter, I do with all boldness affirm. . . . That this Powere which is intire in Your Majesties Person, and inseperable from Your Crown, should be divided, and divolve upon your Officers (though never so great and good) may be of dangerous Consequence" (B₁ᵛ). Seibert gives a concise summary of Atkyn's struggle with the stationers in *Freedom of the Press,* 246.

14. Here Atkyns anticipates the concerns of *Roper v. Streater* (1672), which pitted authorial rights against those of the royal prerogative. Roper had purchased the copy of Crook's law reports from his executors, but Streater claimed a patent to print law reports. The Court of King's Bench found for Roper (Skinner, *King's Bench,* 234), but Parliament reversed the decision (2 Chancery Cases, 67); unfortunately, the record of the grounds for reversal are sketchy. The case law that unfolds from Roper may be traced through *Stationers v. Seymour* (1677), *Stationers v. Wright* (1681), *Stationers v. Parker* (1681), *Stationers v. Edwards* (1696), *Stationers v. Wiellington* (1704), and *Stationers v. Gwillim* (1707)—all of which confirm the claims of the prerogative.

15. *The Original and Growth,* D₁ᵛ-D₂.

16. To Patterson's assessment of the Licensing Act ("simply the Star Chamber Decree of 1637 modified in a few minor respects") we should prefer Kitchin's "the Government's object in a word was not to secure the punishment clauses—that could always be effected by Common Law, or merely by ignoring *Habeas Corpus*—but to secure the right of universal search, which could be extended almost indefinitely" (*Sir Roger L'Estrange,* 128–29).

17. In "Early Copyright Litigation and Its Bibliographical Interest" (*Papers of the Bibliographical Society of America* 36 [1942]: 81–96), R. C. Bald records a count of at least sixteen lawsuits over printing rights brought before English courts between 1660 and 1709, "and nearly all of them were based on privileges conferred by royal patent" (85). Prerogative rights were regularly upheld during these years: see *Stationers' Company v. Seymour* (1677), *Stationers' Company v. Wright* (1681), *Stationers' Company v. Parker* (1681), *Stationers' Company v. Edwards* (1696), *Stationers' Company v. Wellington* (1704), and *Stationers' Company v. Gwillim* (1707).

18. H. Egerton Chesney, "The Transference of Lands in England 1640–1660," *Transactions of the Royal Historical Society,* 4th ser., 15 (1932): 207–10; Joan Thirsk, "The Restoration Land Settlement," *Journal of Modern History* 27 (1954): 315–28; and Christopher Clay, "Landlords and Estate Management in England," in *The Agrarian History of England and Wales,* gen. ed. Joan Thirsk, 8 vols. (Cambridge: Cambridge University Press, 1967—), 5 (part 2): 135–56.

19. His title page flaunts its indebtedness to the language of the Jacobean defenses of monopoly: "*The Original and Growth of printing . . . wherein is also demonstrated, that printing appertaineth to the prerogative royal; and is a flower of the crown of England.*"

20. "Parliament, Liberty, Taxation, and Property," 140.

21. A parliamentary committee declared the law patent a monopoly in 1666, but later in that year Atkyns's claim was confirmed and the patent cleared.

The treatment of literary property as real property must have received practical support in transactions among stationers. Lindenbaum has noted that one of the earliest surviving contracts for the transfer of literary property, a bill of sale from 1688 in which Edward Vize transfers all of his property in Milton's *Judgement of Martin Bucer* to Joseph Watts, "seems to be a standard form (originally designed for leasing or mortgaging a piece of real estate)." "Authors and Publishers in the Late Seventeenth Century: New Evidence on their Relations," *The Library*, 6th ser., 17 (1995): 251–52.

22. Of course, it is Atkyns's anonymous opponent, with his or her resistant, possessive individualism, who most clearly anticipates Locke.

As to the dating of Locke's engagement with the theory of property, I here implicitly accept the arguments concerning the composition history of the *Two Treatises of Government* in Peter Laslett's edition (Cambridge: Cambridge University Press, 1960). Laslett shows that the crucial historical context of Locke's book is not the Glorious Revolution of the year prior to the print publication of the *Two Treatises*, but the Exclusion Crisis of a decade earlier. By suggesting a link between Locke and either Atkyns or Atkyns's opponents, I do not mean to imply, however, that Locke argues that all property must be understood as a version of cultivated real property, any more than it was so understood by those Puritans of the 1640s for whom it was a key term. Locke's use of the word *property* is supple and inclusive; his classic definition of property as the mixture of a person's labor with "whatsoever . . . he removes out of the State that Nature hath provided and left it in" is plainly contrived to include much more than real property. On the semantic range of *property* in the *Two Treatises*, see Laslett, 101 and 104; and Alan Ryan, *Property and Political Theory* (Oxford: Blackwell, 1984), 21. For the prehistory of Locke's approach, see J. G. A. Pocock, "Authority and Property: The Question of Liberal Origins," in *Virtue, Commerce, and History* (Cambridge: Cambridge University Press, 1985), particularly 56–59.

23. In its own way Harrington's thought harks back even further, to the Putney debates on property as a qualification for the franchise, but *Oceana* makes a decisive shift in emphasis, by placing a theory of property at the center of a political theory.

24. Macpherson argued that the struggle between land and market, real and moveable property, subtends the great transformation of the late seventeenth century. Although Pocock and others have subjected Macpherson's analysis to severe criticism, the polarity retains its explanatory power. See Pocock, "Authority and Property," pp. 59–70.

25. *Court Book D*, fol. 63a.

26. In 1679, indeed, when the Licensing Act was allowed to lapse, Chief Justice Scroggs attempted to arrogate press regulation to the courts. George Sensabaugh, *That Grand Whig Milton* (Stanford: Stanford University Press, 1952), 56–57.

27. In the *Seymour* case (1677) and again in *Stationers Company v. Lee*, for example, Charles's grant of a patent in the almanac from 1669 was voided on behalf of an earlier grant by then held by the English Stock. Privileges in the hands of the stationers, it seems, could not be regarded as revocable at the pleasure of the Crown. The stationers were no doubt pleased by the decision, though it eroded their distinctive status: in *Seymour*, the stationers become mere patentees.

28. Bald, "Early Copyright Litigation," 86. He cites the late *Company of Stationers v. Partridge* (1712), in which the stationers came so close to losing the almanac patent

that they withdrew the action. But there were a series of cases in which the claims of the prerogative were confirmed in defense of the patent; see note 14 above.

29. The new charter was surrendered and replaced in 1684, when Charles II undertook the wholesale renovation of all borough charters and all charters of London companies. The stationers were among the first, perhaps the very first, of the London companies to secure a new charter.

30. In point of fact, the new ordinances were not promulgated until 1678. It has long been assumed that these were based on the original bylaws prepared in 1562 and modified over the years, but this cannot be proved, since the original Book of Ordinances, like the original charter, was lost. (Thus, the details of the organization of the Stationers' Company during the Elizabethan period are irrecoverable and are, at best, doubtfully inferred from the 1678 bylaws; see Blagden, *The Stationers' Company,* 154–55.)

31. New bylaws were added in 1681, during the lapse of the Licensing Act; they introduce no new regulatory strategies.

32. Arber, *Transcript,* 1:4.

33. Cited in Lindenbaum, "Authors and Publishers," 252.

34. Lindenbaum prefers the hypothesis of collaboration; ibid., 253–55.

35. Ibid., 268; other works listed on the contract had been registered as well (256).

36. Simmons had sold his rights two months before making that final payment, so the quit claim document was no doubt sought by Aylmer, the new owner of *Paradise Lost;* Lindenbaum, "Authors and Publishers," 256–58.

37. McKenzie, *The London Book Trade,* 29.

38. Ibid., 28. The new charter that the company secured in 1684 includes especially stringent prohibitions on bookbinding and bookselling, in London or Westminster, by nonstationers.

39. Thomas Marshe might also be included in this list, given his sustained interest in such early Elizabethan projects as *The Mirror for Magistrates* and *Seneca His Tenne Tragedies.*

40. McKenzie long urged the almost unmediated continuities between Jonson and Congreve, and particularly between the Jonson folio of 1616 and the Congreve folios of 1710 and 1719, though he conceded that the Congreve folios may show the typographical influence not only of the Jonson folio and its direct descendants but also of midcentury French printing. *The London Book Trade,* 46–48.

41. Such author-effects were anticipated in important ways, if not in durable ones, by the intimate alliance of authors, editors, typefounders, and press correctors centered on such great incunabular and early sixteenth-century enterprises as those of Amerbach, Bade, the Aluses, Froben, or the Estiennes, though this took place at a stage when the industry was distinguished by outputs that were, by later standards, relatively specialized. Sometimes the specialization came about because a printer was catering to a distinctive local audience—a university, for example—and, in the case of humanist press production the synergy of an established local book trade, the proximity of important libraries and human resources, and the availability of capital conduced to the cultivation of what turned out to be a niche market of important cultural consequence. On specialization,

see Hirsch, *Printing, Selling, and Reading,* 50–55; for important studies of humanist specialization, see Martin Lowry, *World of Aldus Manutius: Business and Scholarship in Renaissance Venice* (Oxford: Blackwell, 1979); and Lisa Jardine, *Erasmus, Man of Letters: The Construction of Charisma in Print* (Princeton: Princeton University Press, 1993).

42. This account of the vicissitudes of censorship, and of the historical consequence of those vicissitudes, puts me at odds with Nancy Armstrong and Leonard Tennenhouse, whose remarkable essay into the history of bourgeois privacy, *The Imaginary Puritan* (Berkeley: University of California Press, 1992), glances at press regulation at a crucial juncture, 114–17. See note 47 below.

43. Blount, *A Just Vindication of Learning* (1679), 3.

44. Scroggs tried to fill the vacuum created by this lapse in what Kitchin refers to as "the most flagrant attempt at Judge-made law since the decision on Shipmoney" (*Roger L'Estrange,* 271). As Jeffries reports it in *State Trials,* 7:226, the decision does seem remarkable, for the judges had determined that "no person whatsoever could expose to the public knowledge anything that concerned the affairs of the Public without license from the King or from some such persons as he thought fit to entrust with that affair."

The act was not to be renewed under Charles II—neither the Parliament of 1680 nor that of 1681 was disposed to concede that degree of Crown control over the press provided for in the act, so licensing was not renewed until 1685. Those stationers most disadvantaged by its lapse, the sharers in the various stocks and large holders of copyrights, sought other props for their regulatory traditions. They appealed to the lord mayor to put down the hawkers, on whom the viability of the new "clandestine" book market rested; they reiterated the old rules stipulating registration in their new bylaws, and stiffened the penalties for noncompliance; and in 1684, when Charles sought to consolidate his own recovered authority by calling for the surrender and replacement of all London corporate charters, the stationers eagerly rushed to the head of the queue of loyal guildsmen. This enabled a brief period of renewed self-regulation, and a predictably increased recourse to registration; see A. F. Pollard, "Some Notes on the History of Copyright in England," *The Library,* 4th ser., 4 (1922): 105–6. But Parliament soon reasserted its authority over press matters; indeed, hindsight suggests that even the Whig refusal to renew the Licensing Acts, the temporary freeing of the press, foretold a deeper unfreedom descending on the stationers. See Kitchen, *Sir Roger L'Estrange,* 213–16.

45. In *That Grand Whig Milton,* 58–61, Sensabaugh makes a sustained comparison of Blount's treatise to its source. In his *History of England,* Macauley refers to Blount as "one of the most unscrupulous plagiaries that ever lived." *The History of England from the Accession of James the Second,* ed. Charles Harding Firth, 6 vols. (London: Macmillan, 1914), 5:2303.

46. The *Apology* is appended to Denton's long Shaftesburyan *Jus Caesaris et Ecclesiæ* for which several of Milton's other tracts were mined; again, see Sensabaugh, *That Grand Whig, Milton,* 61–65. Milton's inspiration may be felt in many of the Exclusionist arguments of this moment.

47. Milton was also frequently invoked in the debate on Exclusion, as Sensabaugh has richly documented in *That Grand Whig, Milton,* 76–91. As Blount had ransacked *Areopagitica,* Thomas Hunt and Samuel Johnson would borrow heavily from *Pro Populo Anglicano Defensio.* Indeed, Milton was so firmly allied with the Whig program of the

1680s that Matthew Rider would cite him *against* Exclusion with an air of quiet and insinuating triumph; on the Tory uses of Milton in this period, see Sensabaugh, *That Grand Whig*, 104–10.

Milton's availability to rival camps in the eighties goes some way toward substantiating the caveat delivered in passing by Armstrong and Tennenhouse: "One must deal with the fact that censorship returned with new vigor in 1662. This is what killed off the political Milton, leaving us with the poet—or so a tradition of criticism has claimed" (*The Imaginary Puritan*, 115). But their caveat points in a different historical direction than does my argument: Armstrong and Tennenhouse argue that the political Milton effectively goes underground, as Milton comes to function as a great apologist for privacy (which apologetics are intensely political in a larger sense), whereas I must insist on the continued interest in Milton's practical political engagement.

48. *The Free-born Subject* (1679), C$_1$.

49. Ibid.

50. This was not the last time that L'Estrange would have such a clash with the stationers. When L'Estrange set about to publish a translation of Josephus, several booksellers who held the copyright in an earlier translation claimed copyright, "they and their Predecessors having been in just and quiet Possession of the same for near One Hundred Years." Cited in A. W. Pollard, "Copyright in Josephus," *The Library*, 3rd ser., 7 (1917): 134–45.

51. I cite Locke's *Memorandum* (Locke MSS, b. 4, f. 75) from Peter King, *Life and Letters of John Locke*, 2nd ed. (1829; repr. New York: Burt Franklin, 1972), 203.

52. "What Is an Author?" 153–56.

53. *Journal of the House of Lords*, 15:280 (8 March 1693).

54. Ibid., 15:545.

55. M. A. Thompson is careful to insist that opposition in Commons to the attempt to revive licensing in 1695 is not a defense of liberty of the press; see his *Constitutional History of England, 1642–1801* (London: Methuen, 1938), 298 and note below.

56. Raymond Astbury makes a case for Locke's deep involvement in the legislative machinations that, earlier, secured nonrenewal ("The Renewal of the Licensing Act in 1693 and Its Lapse in 1695," *The Library*, 5th ser., 33 [1978]: 304–15). See also Maurice Cranston, *John Locke: A Biography* (London: Longmans, 1957), 368–69 and 386–87. The formal list of the Commons' objections is a temperate selection from the larger array of objections in his *Memorandum* of late 1694, which reviews the Licensing Bill then up for consideration. Locke had worked through Clarke earlier, in 1693, when he had lobbied for a transformation of the Licensing Act as it came up for renewal (Astbury, 304).

57. Cranston follows Macauley: "Unlike Milton, who called for liberty in the name of liberty, Locke was content to ask for liberty in the name of trade; and unlike Milton, he achieved his end." Astbury, "The Renewal of the Licensing Act," 387.

58. Ibid., 304 and 307.

59. Sensabaugh, *The Grand Whig, Milton*, 155–62; and Astbury, "The Renewal of the Licensing Act," 296–322. Astbury usefully lists the pamphlet literature from 1692–93 that argues for and against renewal on p. 300, n. 19.

60. Milton's exemplary status in the period has been variously asserted—in Arm-

strong and Tennenhouse, *The Imaginary Puritan;* in Kevin Pask, "Milton's Daughters," chapter 5 of *The Emergence of the English Author: Scripting the Life of the Poet in Early Modern England* (Cambridge: Cambridge University Press, 1996), 141–70; and in Leslie E. Moore, *Beautiful Sublime: The Making of Paradise Lost, 1701–1734* (Stanford: Stanford University Press, 1990).

61. See Macauley, *History of England,* 5:2481–82. On trade and legislative developments between the lapse of the Licensing Act and passage of the Statute of Anne, see Ransom, *The First Copyright Statute,* 89–107; and John Feather, "The Book Trade in Politics: The Making of the Copyright Act of 1710," *Publishing History* 8 (1980): 19–44.

62. Various groups of printers continued to lobby for revival of the Licensing Act or for parliamentary grant of at least some of the trade protections that had been part of the act. In each of three sessions, the House of Lords passed the act or versions of it only to have it rejected in the Lower House. Siebert concludes that the reason the press "remained temporarily free was due, not to political or philosophical conviction, but to the quarrel between the two houses of Parliament in the early years of the eighteenth century and to the failure to agree upon a suitable system of regulation." *Freedom of the Press,* 306, and see 307.

63. A small group of printers petitioned on its own, warning that a lapse in the act would open the book trade "to all Persons"—and then comes the predictable yoking of interests—"which may not only prove of dangerous Consequence to the Government, but will be ruinous to the said Trade" (*Journal of the House of Commons,* 11:289).

64. The sense of urgency would increase in the ensuing months. *Reasons humby offer'd to the Consideration of the Honourable House of Commons,* a petition to the parliamentary session of 1696, recurs the need for censorship, but this gives way to pleas for the protection of monopolies. On the dating of this petition, see Feather, "The Book Trade in Politics," 41 n. 25.

65. Astbury, "The Renewal of the Licensing Act," 311–12.

66. *Journal of the House of Lords,* 16:358–59; *House of Lords Manuscripts,* n.s. (London: H.M. Stationery Office, 1900—)3:271–76.

67. Ransom notes that in the half-century preceding the Statute of Anne, almost half of all entrances are assignments of rights in books already published. *The First Copyright Statute,* 85.

68. See Graham Pollard's Sandars Lectures for 1959, "The English Market for Printed Books," *Publishing History* 4 (1978): 21.

69. *Journal of the House of Commons,* 11:305–6. Commons omitted the act from a bill for continuing several acts; the bill was amended in the House of Lords to continue the Licensing Act, but Commons rejected the amendment. They were very clear-sighted about the contradictions in the provisions of the act: "there is no Penalty appointed for Offenders therein, they being left to be punished at Common Law (as they may be) without that Act," this from the list of their reasons for blocking renewal. *Journal of the House of Lords,* 15:545 (18 April 1695).

On the demystifying spirit of the moment see the anonymous petition to Parliament (B.L. 816.m.12.[37.]) quoted in Feather, "The Book Trade in Politics": "Were it not for their Mammon-Monopoly, the Master, Wardens, &c of the Stationers' Company, would cry out against the Slavery and Charge of Licensing as much as any of their Brethren" (24).

70. Still, crude ideological control was not completely disentangled from economic regulation, nor did the courts assume the full responsibility for ideological control. Freedom of speech was taxed, as it were, after 1712, when the Stamp Act was instituted, Parliament having been exhorted by the queen herself "to find a Remedy equal to the Mischief" represented by the "false and scandalous Libels" published in contemporary newspapers. It had been calculated that the tax would cut the circulation of newspapers by at least a third, and whether or not this expectation was realistic, the persistent will of many politicians to constrain the publication of news proved a convenient device for securing a new source of revenue. Siebert, *Freedom of the Press,* 308–10 and 312–16.

71. Holdsworth, *History of English Law,*8:311–17 and 340–45. And see also Seibert, *Freedom of the Press,* 271–73.

72. In the *Algernon Sidney* case, manuscript derogation of the royal prerogative became treasonable, the treasonability of unpublished manuscript expression having already been tentatively established in *Peacham* (1613). Before the Restoration some distinction had been preserved between spoken and written words in the law of treason, the latter being more vulnerable to prosecution, but the distinction was eroded after 1660: spoken words were as treasonable as written, though they were recognizably more difficult to bring in as evidence. The general drift across the seventeenth century was to transform writing or speaking from a status supplementary to overt acts, proof of treasonable intent, into the overt acts themselves; see the *Lord Preston* case (1691). Seditious libel—which preserved the distinction between crimes of speech and crimes of writing—became an equally inclusive category, reaching its greatest capaciousness in *Rex v. Tutchin* (1704): like Holdsworth, Seibert cites Justice Holt's appalling judgment that "If people should not be called to account for possessing the people with an ill opinion of the government, no government can subsist. For it is very necessary for all governments that the people should have a good opinion of it" (*Freedom of the Press,* 271).

73. On retrenchment: in 1696, the royal powers of prosecution for treason were significantly weakened (7, 8 William III, c. 3.), but even here the effect was to elaborate the judicial apparatus for dealing with ideological challenge. Similarly, convictions for seditious libel became more difficult to secure by the very end of the century—partly owing to the lapse of the Licensing Acts; see Holdsworth,*History of English Law,* 8:338 and 345. We therefore cannot speak of a steady and uninterrupted accumulation of jurisdictional authority by the courts.

Despite the moment of retrenchment, Parliament maintained its interest in ideological policing: in 1698, legislation was proposed to provide for censorship but without supplementary provisions for securing copyright. Annabel Patterson reminds us that prosecutions for seditious libel were occasionally instigated by Parliament; *Censorship and Interpretation,* 118. On the new regime of censorship from the 1690s forward, see Laurence Hanson, *Government and the Press, 1695–1763* (Oxford: Clarendon Press, 1936), 36–83.

By adverting here to the quiet terror of post-Restoration ideological control, I have no intention of depreciating earlier mechanisms for producing self-censorship, mechanisms powerfully investigated in Patterson, *Censorship and Interpretation;* Burt, *"Licensed by Authority": Ben Jonson and the Discourses of Censorship* (Ithaca: Cornell

Univesity Press, 1993); and Barker, *The Tremulous Private Body,* 42–44. But causal links bind the legal elaboration of treason in the late seventeenth century to the efflorescence of dark caution and brilliant innuendo, both effects of discursive *self*-regulation.

74. J. R. Moore, ed. (Oxford: Blackwell, 1948), 19.

75. Ibid., 28. A bit later the idea of continuing rights is once more implied: "But if an Author has a Right of Action given him by Law," as Defoe was advocating, "not against him only who shall print his Copy, but against the Publisher of it also; and this Law being made full and express, the Evil will die, for no body will dare sell the Book, when the villainous Pirate has finish'd the Impression" (28).

76. *Journal of the House of Commons,*15:316 and 313.

77. In the final revision of the 1710 Statute of Anne, the House of Lords, which had made adjustments in the bill to benefit the stationers (for which, see n. 81 below), provided for a form of residual authorial copyright. The last clause of the act stipulates "That after the Expiration of the said Term of Fourteen Years [the term limit for copyright in books written after the passage of the Act], the sole Right of Printing or Disposing of Copies shall Return to the Authors thereof, if they are then Living, for another Term of Fourteen Years" (cited from Ransom, *The First Copyright Statute,* 117).

78. *Journal of the House of Commons,* 313*a.*

79. The differentia were being steadily eroded. In an important deposition from 1714, the bookseller John Morphew alleged "that it is a very usual thing for persons to leave books & papers at his house and at the houses of other publishers, and a long time after to call for the value thereof"; *SPD,* 35/1/28(29), 28 August 1714. If this doesn't argue for exclusively *authorial* compensation based on sales, it does imply that such compensation was not unusual by the time of the Statute of Anne. Lindenbaum has come to believe that the sort of contract worked out for Milton may have become quite unexceptional in the latter portion of the seventeenth century (E-mail to author, 5 July 1998).

80. Cited in Feather, "The Book Trade in Politics," 35–36.

81. I cite from Ransom's transcription, *The First Copyright Statute,* 109. The bill was further transformed when it was sent up to the House of Lords. Ransom remarks on a nice adjustment to that portion of the bill securing a copyright of twenty-one-years' duration to authors of books already in print, but "not Transferred to any other"; the original version secured a twenty-one-year copyright in printed books even when not formally "reserved to himself." Ransom construes the revision as designed to stress an author's common law right in manuscripts (96), but the change seems to me to tend in a very different direction. The earlier version guarded authorial property even where the author had made no positive attempt to secure it; the revised version guarded authorial property in the more narrowly defined set of instances in which an author had made no formal transfer of that property. The recalibration seems to have been designed to protect stationers against authors who might claim a (previously unreserved) copyright, despite having transferred it.

82. There were other, minor depredations. A requirement of the 1662 Licensing Act that large-format copies of all new books be deposited at the libraries of Oxford and Cambridge, and at the royal library, was expanded to include six new depositories. Also, the act left imports of foreign-language books unfettered.

83. Ransom, *The First Copyright Statute,* 111–12.

84. The problem of authorial access to registration was probed in *Baller v. Walker* (1737), when Gay's executor brought suit for infringements of the unregistered *Polly.* Ransom lists several features of the act that proved especially difficult to enforce: the pursuit of remedy was more expensive than the penalties that the courts might enforce; the price control system failed to function as planned; the deposit requirements were evaded; because it lay beyond the jurisdiction of the act, Ireland was effectively constituted as a safe haven for piracy; and the authority of the register could not be effectively legislated (*The First Copyright Statute,* 105).

85. Ransom, *The First Copyright Statute,* 112.

86. Patterson's general discussion of the tactics of the act (*Copyright in Historical Perspective,* 144–50) is intriguing here: though he wisely indicates how reserved were its provisions for authors (147), his simple assertion that the bill "was aimed at preventing future monopolies and the monopoly of the company itself" (144) seems curiously unguarded.

87. At the 1991 MLA Convention, Peter Lindenbaum offered a history of the dissevering of Milton's prose from his poetry in the media of what I have been calling the Tonson era. In what follows, I hold that this bibliographical segregation does little to prevent issues foregrounded in the prose, and in debates about the prose, from affecting the cultural history of the poetry.

88. The clash of these two publications was palpable to Thomas Yalden, who wrote a poem "On The Re-Printing Milton's Prose Works with his poems" in his copy of *Paradise Lost.* The full text is given in J. W. Good, *Studies in the Milton Tradition, University of Illinois Studies in Language and Literature* 1 (1915): 59; an exerpt will give the gist:

Whilst here thy bold majestic numbers rise,
And range th' embattled legions of the skies,
With armies fill the azure plains of light,
And paint the lively terrours of the fight,
We owe the poet worthy to rehearse
Heaven's lasting triumphs in immortal verse.
But when thy impious, mercenary pen
Insults the best of princes, best of men,
Our admiration turns to just disdain
And we revoke the fond applause again.
Like the fall'n angels in their state
Thou shar'dst their nature, insolence and fate

. . . .

As they did rebels to the Almighty grow,
So thou profan'st His image here below.
Apostate Bard!

89. He is also quite interested in *Areopagitica,* the discussion of which anticipates Defoe's protest against the uncertainties of the modern censorship by recalling Milton's nostalgia for the Greek and Roman republics, which "never censur'd any but immoral, defamatory, or atheistical Pieces. Nor was it by Inferences and Insinuations they were to judg of Atheism; for they never suppret the Writings of the *Epicureans,* nor such Books

denying even the Doctrins of Providence, and the future State: but it must have bin a formal doubt or denial of the being of a Deity" (127).

90. And cf. Winstanley's observation on Milton in his *Lives of the Most Famous English Poets* (1687): "His fame has gone out like a candle in a snuff, and his memory will always stink, which might have ever lived in honorable repute, had he not been a notorious traitor and villainously bely'd that blessed martyr 'Charles the First' " (cited in Good, *Studies in the Milton Tradition*, 114–15).

91. See Sensebaugh, *That Grand Whig Milton,* chapter 3, 142–55. For more on the king's book during the 1690s, see chapter 5, "King Charles's Head," of J. P. Kenyon's Ford Lectures for 1975–76, *Revolution Principles* (Cambridge: Cambridge University Press, 1977), particularly pp. 61–69.

92. Indispensable to a study of the debate on authorship is Francis F. Madan, *A New Bibliography of the Eikon Basilik, Oxford Bibliographical Society Publications,* n.s. 3 (Oxford: Oxford University Press, 1950). For a leading instance of the attack on Charles's authorship, once thought to have influenced *Eikonoklastes,* see the anonymous *Eikon Alethine,* published in early August 1649, which alleged a specifically clerical forgery.

93. *Eikonoklastes, Works,* 3:362 and 364–65.

94. For more on unoriginality as an ethical failing, see 3:367: "Such a person we may be sure had it not in him to make a prayer of his own, or at least would excuse himself the paines and cost of his invention."

95. Macauley, *History of England,* 5:2299–305; and Astbury, "The Renewal of the Licensing Act," 297.

96. On the earlier history of anonymity, see the excellent work of Marcy North, "Ignoto in the Age of Print: The Manipulation of Anonymity in Early Modern England," *Studies in Philology* 91, 4 (fall 1994): 390–416.

97. William Empson criticizes Madan's evaluation of the evidence in the authorship controversy in an appendix to the revised edition of *Milton's God* (London: Chatto and Windus, 1965); it is the usual breathtaking Empsonian performance, and his conclusion, that Wagstaffe must have been more or less right, must therefore be quoted: "The story does not seem to me to be bad, as propaganda goes. The King was such a liar, to put it another way, that answering him with a lie was only fair. Many critics have refused to believe that Milton could do anything so sordid, and I notice that the same men will usually report the burning of a man alive with respectful deference. . . . The picture we get (fitting the scraps of evidence together) of how Milton tackled his public duty makes him a broader and more adroit kind of man than is usually thought, less pedantic and self-enclosed, more humane, more capable of entering into other people's motives and sentiments." It must be conceded that Milton *had* resorted to such deception in the *Pro Se Defensio,* in which he knowingly misattributed the authorship of the *Regii Sanguinis Clamour* to Alexander More; see *Complete Prose,* 4:1083.

98. *Life,* 144. More waggish than Milton about the plagiarism, Toland identifies the prayer as "plainly stolen and taken without any considerable Variation from the mouth of *Pamela,* an imaginary Lady, to a Heathen Deity" (ibid.).

99. *Amyntor,* in turn, provoked other responses, for which see Good, *Studies in the Milton Tradition,* 117 n. 10.

100. These disputes over authorship, and particularly Thomas Wagstaffe's perfectly counter-balanced argument—that Charles was not a plagiarist; that Milton was a forger—were, I think, determining for the eighteenth-century Milton. To this may be added *The Plagiary Exposed* (1691), which acuses "Ludlow" of being an inauthentic replica of Milton and John Cook.

101. *A Sermon Preached before the Honourable House of Commons,* $C_4{}^v$—D_1. He spoke to no avail: although the House expressed its thanks for the sermon at its next meeting and formally urged that it be printed, they turned to consider a bill for press regulation that had been passed days earlier by the Lords, gave it two readings in immediate succession, and promptly voted it down (*Journal of the House of Commons,* 12:465–66, 468–69). Blackall may have been responding to the immediate provocation of the amendment of the Lords' bill a week earlier, when many of the traditional provisions for controlling seditious and unlicensed printing were removed from the bill; see above, p. 213 and note 66.

102. $C_2{}^v$—$D_7{}^v$. He also took the occasion (B_7) to protest Blackall's misrepresenting "abridgement" of his own words, abridgment being the term of art for the kind of appropriative practice that passed as nonpiratical among turn-of-the-century stationers— the practice that Defoe would protest a few years later.

103. Toland would repeat the device in *Amyntor* (1699), $L_6{}^v$–M_1.

104. For more on this episode, see Sensabaugh, *That Grad Whig, Milton,* 142–55.

105. Blair Worden attributes much of the Ludlow industry to Toland himself, alleging not only that he substantially rewrote the "real" Edmund Ludlow's memoirs for publication in 1698, recasting Ludlow's millenarian account of the Civil War in modern, Whiggish terms, but that he also wrote the Ludlow pamphlets of 1691–93. See Edmund Ludlow, *A Voyce from the Watch Tower, Part Five: 1660–1662,* ed. A. B. Worden, *Camden Fourth Series,* 21 (1978), 34–38.

106. Two ancillary observations may be useful here. First, evasion itself can be ornamental, a means of conjuring an atmosphere of danger and thereby exciting the act of consumption. Second, the evasions of anonymity and pseudonymy are not always necessary. Although they may have been born of terror, anonymity and pseudonymy can survive a regime of palpable threat—survive as an unnecessary atavism, an unintentional discursive habit.

107. Thomson, *Constitutional History,* 333; Peter Fraser, *The Intelligence of the Secretaries of State and Their Monopoly of Licensed News, 1660–1668* (Cambridge: Cambridge University Press, 1956), 39–56; Siebert, *Freedom of the Press,* 102–3 and 202–18.

108. Siebert, *Freedom of the Press,* 100–101 and 115–16.

109. Ibid., 279–88; Astbury, "The Renewal of the Licensing Act," 320; and Hanson, *Government and the Press,* 32–33. On Robert Harley's influential resistance to the reimposition of licensing, a resistance motivated by his experience as a propagandist, see J. A. Downie, *Robert Harley and the Press: Propaganda and Public Opinion in the Age of Swift and Defoe* (Cambridge: Cambridge University Press, 1979), 55. For a fairly sophisticated argument against regulation, an argument indebted to *Areopagitica* but highlighting the specifically political issues entailed, see the *Letter to a Member of Parliament Shewing that a Restraint Press* [sic] *is Inconsistent with the Protes-*

tant Religion and Dangerous to the Liberties of the Nation, printed by J. Darby in 1708.

110. John Tutchin—who, incidentally, had frequently been prosecuted for violating Parliament's privilege by publishing details of their deliberations—took a similar position in the *Observator,* vol. 2, 85 (29 January 1704).

111. *Reasons Against Restraining the Press,* B$_3$^{v}—B$_4$. In *Government and the Press,* 9–10, Hanson alleges that Defoe shares Tindal's estimation of the dangers of compulsory imprint, but this seems to me to be quite at odds with Defoe's argument (*Essay,* pp. 24 and 27). On the practice of anonymity, see David Foxon, *Pope and the Early Eighteenth-Century Book Trade* (Oxford: Oxford University Press, 1991), 4.

112. *The Prose Works of Jonathan Swift,* ed. Herbert Davis, 14 vols. (Oxford: Blackwell, 1951–68), 1:3.

113. Birrell, *Lectures on the History of Copyright,* 21–22.

114. *A Tale of a Tub,* ed. A. C. Guthkelch and D. Nichol Smith (Oxford: Clarendon, 1920), 328.

115. Letter to Tooke, 29 June 1710, *The Correspondence of Jonathan Swift,* 5 vols. (Oxford: Clarendon, 1963), 1:165–66.

116. In fact, the irritation itself is unstable: Swift was himself quite willing to allow or to engage in misattribution throughout the course of his career. The fifth edition of the *Tale* includes notes attributed, surely inaccurately, to "W. Wotton," one of the published critics of the earlier editions.

117. *Correspondence,* 1:165.

118. As has already been observed, this bill was substantially amended on 23 January 1699, but the provision for compulsory imprint and for compulsory report of authors' names survived the amendment; *Journal of the House of Lords,* 16:358–59; *House of Lords Manuscripts,* n.s. (London: H.M. Stationery Office, 1900—), 3:271–76; 4:420.

119. Defoe, *Essay,* 22.

120. 208–9, and cf. 205.

121. This bill was committed after its second reading in Commons on 3 December 1695; see Astbury, "The Renewal of the Licensing Act," 317–18.

122. *House of Lords Manuscripts,* n.s., 3:273–74, and 276.

123. See p. 217–18 and note above. <set slugs>

124. Feather, "The Book Trade in Politics," 34–35.

125. Ransom, *The First Copyright Statute,* 117.

126. In his summary of the early jurisprudence on intellectual property, Augustine Birrell reflects, "All through the 17th and 18th centuries in France, and during the latter half of the 18th century in England, a controversy was carried on between *savants,* booksellers and lawyers as to whether authors were entitled to an exclusive right of multiplying copies of their works as *property* or as *privilege*" (*Seven Lectures on the Law and History of Copyright* [London: Cassell, 1899], 10); the raw material of this dispute was all available within the Statute of Anne.

127. Patterson, *Copyright in Historical Perspective,* 150; and Bald, "Early Copyright Lititgation," 88–89.

128. Foxon, *Pope and the Early Eighteenth-Century Book Trade*, passim, but particularly appendix 1, "Pope and Copyright," 236–51; Mark Rose, *Authors as Owners: The Invention of Copyright* (Cambridge: Harvard, 1993), 58–66; Pat Rogers, "The Case of *Pope v. Curll*," *The Library*, 5th ser., 27 (1972): 326–31, reprinted in *Essays on Pope* (Cambridge: Cambridge University Press, 1993), 184–89, which volume also includes "Pope and His Subscribers," 190–227.

129. "Pope and His Subscribers," 197.

130. See Foxon, chapter 3, "The Problems of Independence," *Pope and the Early Eighteenth-Century Book Trade*, 102–8.

131. Ibid., 107–8, 111–12, 117, 121.

132. *Lives of the Poets*, ed. George Birkbeck Hill, 3 vols. (Oxford: Clarendon, 1905), 3:84.

133. Reproduced in *The Correspondence of Alexander Pope*, ed. George Sherburn, 5 vols. (Oxford, 1956); Foxon offers a sustained commentary on the notes in appendix A of *Pope and the Early Eighteenth-Century Book Trade*.

134. See B. Kaplan, *An Unhurried View of Copyright*, who points out that in the first generation following the promulgation of the Statute of Anne, nonidentical imitations were not held to infringe on statutory copyright. The argument that a new edition should found a new copyright would not be tested in court, however, until *Tonson v. Walker* (1752); see p. 239 below.

135. On Bentley's edition, see Edward Dowden, "Milton in the Eighteenth Century," from the *Proceedings of the British Academy*, vol. 3, but published as a separate pamphlet (London: Oxford University Press, 1908?), 10–15; Ants Oras, *Milton's Editors and Commentators From Patrick Hume to Henry John Todd (1695–1801)* (London: Oxford University Press, 1931), 50–74; and William Empson, "Milton and Bentley: The Pastoral of the Innocence of Man and Nature," from *Some Versions of Pastoral* (London, 1935; 2nd edition, New York: New Directions, 1974), 149–91. The legal grounds for the protection of an edition because of rights in its *notes* are confirmed in Chancellor Hardwicke's injunction in *Tonson v. Walker* (1752), Eng. Rep. 1020.

136. On the early responses to the edition, see Oras, *Milton's Editors*, 75–99.

137. *The Counterfeiters* (Bloomington: Indiana University Press, 1968), 35.

138. 6 February 1731, cited in Good, *Studies in the Milton Tradition*, 177. Fenton is a paragon of caution compared to Bentley.

139. *The Counterfeiters*, 33–34.

140. No. 100, 2 December 1731.

141. James Clifford, "Johnson and Lauder," *Philological Quarterly* 54 (1975): 342–56; Michael J. Marcuse, "The Lauder Controversy and the Jacobite Cause," *Studies in Burke and His Time* 18 (1977): 27–47; and Marcuse, "Miltonoklastes: The Lauder Affair Reconsidered," *Eighteenth-Century Life and Letters* 4 (1978): 86–91.

142. *An Essay on Milton's Use and Imitation of the Moderns in His "Paradise Lost"* (London, 1750), 163. The forced archness of Lauder's manner may be gauged from the following: "it is no difficult task to reply to *Andrew Marvell's judicious query*, addressed to the author of *Paradise Lost*, in his commendatory verses prefixed to that poem; "*Where* could'st thou words of such a compass find? / *Whence* furnish such a vast

expence of mind?" The answer is obvious, namely *from every author who wrote any thing before him, suitable to his purpose, either in prose or verse, sacred or prophane*" (162).

143. See n. 141 above.

144. 36 Eng. Rep. 1017.

145. Patterson, *Copyright in Historical Perspective,* 164.

146. And cf. Isaac Disraeli, *The Calamities and Quarrels of Authors* (London: Routledge, 1859), 21: "The daughter of MILTON need not have craved the alms of the admirers of her father, if the right of authors had been better protected; his own 'Paradise Lost' would then have been her most honourable inheritance."

147. *Journal of the House of Commons,* 11:288.

148. *Gentleman's Magazine* 17 (1747): 322.

149. *The Works of Richard Hurd, D.D.,* 8 vols. (London, 1811), 2:187.

150. *Memoirs of Thomas Hollis,* 2 vols. (1780), 535. Blackburne's attack on the "Life" is sustained, detailed, fervid, and sometimes devastatingly pungent: "Dryden was reprehensible even to infamy for his own vices, and the licentious encouragement he gave in his writings to those of others. But he wrote *Absalom and Achitophel;* and Dr. Johnson, a man of high pretentions to moral character, calls him a wise and an honest man. Milton was a man of the chastest manners, both in his conversation and his writings. But he wrote *Iconoclastes,* and in the same Dr. Johnson's esteem was both a knave and a fool" (575).

151. Even Johnson's description of the *Comus* benefit for Elizabeth Foster is configured thus: "The profits of the night were only one hundred and thirty pounds, though Dr. Newton brought a large contribution; and twenty pounds were given by Tonson, a man who is to be praised as often as he is named. . . . This was the greatest benefaction that Paradise Lost ever procured the author's descendants." Johnson's opposition to Milton has swerved away from Lauder's toward Bentley's, a condescension to a poet incapable of controlling the circulation of his texts, submerged in commercially primitive book culture before the coming of Tonson.

152. The opposition of Johnson's commercial success and Milton's pathetic commercial failure was again played out in the 1843 parliamentary debate on copyright. Talfourd instanced the fate of Elizabeth Foster as part of his argument for a natural property in ideas to be protected by a sixty-year statutory copyright; Macauley instanced the successful Johnson of "a hundred years ago," whom, he urged, could have no psychological interest, and therefore should have no legal interest, in so extensive a term of protections.

153. This latter portion of the decision was reversed five years later in *Donaldson v. Beckett.*

154. 4 Burrow, 2340.

155. Ibid., 2407.

156. Ibid., 2399; and see also Justice Willes's summary of the case, 2303 and 2311. Willes's reflections on the case are especially interesting since they entail much review of the regulatory traditions of the Stationers' Company.

157. 4 Burr. 2399.

158. Letter to William Hayley, 24 February 1793.

CHAPTER EIGHT

1. *Seven Lectures on Copyright,* 19.

2. 7:127a (11th ed.).

3. And see also F. P. Wilson, *Shakespeare and the New Bibliography,* 96–101.

4. *Proceedings of the British Academy* 14 (1928): 152.

5. Citation from p. 1.

6. F. C. Francis, "The Bibliographical Society: A Sketch of the First Fifty Years," *The Bibliographical Society, 1892–1942,* 1–22.

7. See "Our Twenty-First Birthday," 10.

8. *Taste and Technique,* 20.

9. "Just as the stamp album, through the power of irritation exercised by those blank squares, inculcates the desire for completeness, so also does the full-dress author-bibliography." Carter, *Taste and Technique,* 28.

10. Cited from *The Fortnightly Review* in Carter, *Taste and Technique,* 26.

11. Pollard deftly alludes to the society's deliberate but incomplete conversion from aestheticism in a review of one of the New Bibliographers' most important compendia, McKerrow's *English Printers' and Publishers' Devices:* "Few of the devices are beautiful, but the book brings us a long step forward to the time when we shall be able to say with approximate certainty at what date any undated and unsigned fragment of English printing was produced and by whom it was printed and published" ("Our Twenty-First Birthday," 20).

12. "Practical Bibliography," *The Library,* 2nd ser., 4 (1903): 145–46. Brown is particularly infuriated by the bibliographical interest in blank leaves, noting that under the influence of the bibliographer the absence of some key blank leaf ruins a book's market value (147).

13. "Our Twenty-First Birthday," 24; and cf. p. 10 on bibliographic monographs as investments.

14. *The Library,* 2nd ser., 9 (1908): 215–16.

15. "On Certain False Dates in Shakespearian Quartos," *The Library,* 2nd ser., 9 (1908): 396–97.

16. Cited by J. D. Wilson, "Alfred William Pollard," 284.

17. "Our Twenty-First Birthday," 18–19.

18. "Introduction," *Shakespeares Comedies Histories, & Tragedies, Being a Reproduction in Facsimile of the First Folio Edition, 1623* (Oxford: Clarendon), xi; the letter from "A Mere Englishman" to *The Standard* (London) was dated 1 January 1902 and appeared on 3 January, p. 6. Froude, the Oxford publisher, contested these claims in a letter dated 4 January (published 6 January, p. 3), eliciting the slight concession from "AME" that only sixty copies had been reserved for the publisher (7 January, published 9 January, p. 3); in a letter dated 3 January, J & E Bumpus (Ltd) offered to provide "AME" with a copy, boasting of their "refusal of some tempting offers from American traders" (4 January, p. 2).

19. "The Bibliographical History of the First Folio," *The Library,* 2nd ser., 4 (1908): 258.

20. London: Methuen, 1909, v. Assessments of national character continue to

function as the groundwork of historical bibliography and the history of the book trade. Carrying forward the scholarly work of Lee, Pollard, and Greg in his study of "The Laws of Elizabethan Copyright" (*The Library,* 5th ser., 15 [1960]), Sisson feels that he must ground some inferences on the observation that "the Tudor English were an unruly folk, recalcitrant to regulation" (9). Either Pollard or Sisson must have judged Tudor character accurately, or not.

21. Long after Lee's death in 1926, the New Bibliographers mention his name with opprobrium. Although Greg ended up siding with Lee against Pollard on questions of transmission (*The First Folio,* 42–43), he continues to cast aspersions on Lee's learning and scholarly principles. Moreover, character remains an issue for Greg as for Pollard: Greg's defense of the Folio text, in *The Editorial Problem in Shakespeare,* is offered as a vindication of Heminge and Condell (13).

22. *Shakespeare's Hand* (Cambridge: Cambridge University Press, 1923), 16.

23. 2nd ed., Oxford: Clarendon, 1951, liv, n. 2.

24. *The Library,* 4th ser., 13 (1932): 144.

25. For full account of these forgeries see John Carter and Graham Pollard, *An Enquiry Concerning Certain Nineteenth Century Pamphlets* (London: Constable, 1934; 2nd ed., London: Scolar, 1983); and Nicholas Barker and John Collins, *A Sequel to An Enquiry Concerning Certain Nineteenth Century Pamphlets by John Carter and Graham Pollard* (London: Scolar, 1983). The progress of these forgeries is narrated in part two ("Reconstruction") of Pollard and Carter's book, 96–152.

26. Barker's comment in the preface to the *Sequel to an Enquiry* indicates the continuing relation between technical analysis and the historiography of the book trade that was the enduring legacy of the New Bibliography: "It gradually became clear . . . that there were a number of unanswered problems that could only be cleared up by typographic analysis of a new kind: it was also clear that the life of Wise, if better documented than that of Forman, needed a parallel chapter if the joint career of the two were to be properly explained. This led in turn to an attempt to reconstruct the course of the crime, during which we came to realise how much evidence of the traffic in forgeries, piracies and other suspect material, particularly in America, remained (and remains) to be found out." That the research is tied to a sense of scandalized property is indicated by Barker's next sentence: "The distinction between forgery and other forms of fraud became harder to maintain" (12).

27. *The Printing and Proofreading of the First Folio,* 2 vols. (Oxford: Clarendon, 1963), 5.

28. The most interesting particular instance of the combination of caution and daring at this western brink is Paul Werstine's "The Textual Mystery of *Hamlet,*" *Shakespeare Quarterly* 39 (1988): 1–26, but see also the disseminative brilliance variously manifest in the work of Random Cloud.

INDEX

economic (*see* copyright, stationers';
   patents)
ideological (*see* censorship; licensing)
Renuoard, A.-A., 288n. 86
Restitution to the Royal Author, 222
Richardson, Richard, 240
Rider, John, *Latin Dictionary*, 38
Robinson, Henry, *Liberty of Conscience*,
   164–65
Robinson, Richard, 292n. 8
Rogers, Pat, 233
Roper v. Streater, 321n. 14
Rose, Mark, 234
Rosseter, Philip, *Book of Ayres*, 49
Royal Printer, 113
Ryther, Augustin, 50

Sacks, D. H., 132
Saenger, Paul, 285n. 48
Sancino, Gershom, 73–74
Sandys, George, 149
   Metamorphosis, 307n. 35
Sartre, Jean-Paul, *In Search of a Method*,
   266n. 28
Savile's Chrysostom, 95
Scolocker, Anthony, 163
Seres, William, 32, 34, 41, 113, 121
Serger, Richard, 104–5
Shaaber, M. A., 49
Shakespeare, William
   attitude towards theater, 84
   copyright in, after 1700, 235–36
   editing of, 23, 251, 252, 254–57
   First Folio, publication of, 101, 154–55,
      184, 294n. 23
      Lee's facsimile of, 6, 255–57, 259–62
   plagiarism and, 87
   proprietary sentiment in, 82
   publications of quartos, 86
   Henry IV, parts 2 and 3, 101
   King John, 293n. 23
   Richard II, second quarto, 86
   The Taming of the Shrew, 101
   Troilus and Cressida, 85
Sidney, Sir Philip
   aristocracy in, 46–47
   posthumous publications of, 45–48, 279n.
      72

Arcadia, rights to, 45–46, 102–3, 155,
   277n. 52
Astrophil and Stella, 47, 102–3
Defense of Poesie, 46–47
Siebert, F. S., 162–63, 187
Simmons, Samuel, 203–4, 217, 221, 239–40
Sirluck, Ernest, 174, 175, 180, 187
Sisson, C. J., 38
Sparke, Michael, *Scintilla*, 166, 315n. 41
Speed, John, *Geneologies recorded in the
   sacred scriptures*, 309n. 47
Speidell, John, 50
Spenser, Edmund, 127, 185, 279n. 72
Spicer, William, 132
Stamp Act, 327n. 70
Stansby, William, 93, 95, 97, 106, 205, 295n.
   33
Star Chamber Decree of 1586, 37–39, 43, 44,
   45, 156–58, 160
Star Chamber Decree of 1637, 160, 179
Stationers' Company. *See also* copyright,
   stationers'; printers; booksellers
   as authorial surrogate, 229–31
   Charter of, 19, 53–54, 58–63, 66, 122,
      199, 202–3, 273 n. 12–13, 282n.
      24, 323n. 29, 323n. 38
   Court of Assistants, 37, 38, 41, 42, 88, 96,
      98–99, 169, 199, 203
   draft ordinances of (1559), 29
   erosion of regulatory power of
      during Interregnum, 160, 163–64,
         169–70, 196–97, 213, 314nn. 31,
         34
      during Restoration, 202–3, 213
   import trade and, 158–59
   increasing regulatory power of, 37–39, 43,
      275n. 39, 276nn. 41–42, 276n. 45
   licensing and, 14, 38, 58–60, 63–66,
      110–11, 156–60, 166–67, 197,
      312nn. 8–9, 313n. 14, 326n. 62
      (*see also* copyright, stationers',
      licensing and)
   patents, conflicts over within, 31–32, 198,
      300n. 79
   Wolfe's "reformation" and, 33–44
   petition of 1643, 166–68, 171, 177, 188,
      190, 315n. 47, 318n. 79
   playwrights interaction with, 82, 84–88